Educating the "Right" Way

Educating the "Right" Way

MARKETS, STANDARDS, GOD, AND INEQUALITY

SECOND EDITION

MICHAEL W. APPLE

Routledge
Taylor & Francis Group

New York   London

379.73
A648e
2006

24.95

Published in 2006 by
Routledge
Taylor & Francis Group
270 Madison Avenue
New York, NY 10016

Published in Great Britain by
Routledge
Taylor & Francis Group
2 Park Square
Milton Park, Abingdon
Oxon OX14 4RN

Printed in the United States of America on acid-free paper
10 9 8 7 6 5 4 3 2 1

International Standard Book Number-10: 0-415-95272-7 (Softcover)
International Standard Book Number-13: 978-0-415-95272-9 (Softcover)
Library of Congress Card Number 2005021611

Library of Congress Cataloging-in-Publication Data

Apple, Michael W.
    Educating the "right" way : markets, standards, God, and inequality / Michael W. Apple.-- 2nd ed.
        p. cm.
    Includes bibliographical references and index.
    ISBN 0-415-95271-9 (hb : alk. paper) -- ISBN 0-415-95272-7 (pb : alk. paper)
    1. Education--Political aspects--United States. 2. Conservatism--United States. I. Title.

LC89.A8145 2006
379.73--dc22   2005021611

Taylor & Francis Group
is the Academic Division of Informa plc.

Visit the Taylor & Francis Web site at
http://www.taylorandfrancis.com

and the Routledge Web site at
http://www.routledge-ny.com

Contents

Preface to the Second Edition

On Being an "Un-American Creep"

I began thinking about this second edition of *Educating the "Right" Way* soon after my return from giving an address at an international conference in Cuba. An experience I had there brought home to me again the crucial importance of critically examining what is happening to so many people in a time of rightist arrogance.

As many of you will know, it is not easy for U.S. citizens to go to Cuba. Special licenses are required. Permission is only given if the person has a "legitimate" purpose for going. And in the case of academic lectures at conferences, permission is only given if the conference is not sponsored by the Cuban government.

During the time I was in Havana, the United States tightened these regulations even more to make it even harder for Cuban-Americans to send money to, or even to visit, relatives living in Cuba. This was on top of over forty years of economic and cultural/political blockade.

I am decidedly not in favor of these policies, which seem to me and many others—increasingly across the political spectrum—to be deeply flawed. However, my interest here is not in such policies but in my address at the conference itself. I began my address with a statement of political and educational solidarity with the people in the audience—most of whom were educators—and with the large number of countries they represented. I distanced myself from a number of the international economic and cultural policies advocated by the United States. I then critically discussed in much greater detail the problems with two major emphases in education internationally, both of which play a large part in my analysis in this book: (1) neoliberal educational reforms, such as the immense pressure toward marketization and privatization like vouch-

ers and the growth of for-profit schools; and (2) neoconservative policies involving the push for ever-increasing national standards, national
curricula, and (increasingly high-stakes) national testing. Finally,
I stated that these were not only dangerous tendencies but also were
very simplistic. There were alternatives to the policies and practices of
what I called "conservative modernization." I pointed to the schools
represented in *Democratic Schools*,[1] in the work of educators associated
with the progressive educational journal *Rethinking Schools,* and in the
Citizen School and participatory budgeting movements in Porto Alegre,
Brazil.[2] As with any speaker, I was heartened by the fact that the large
international audience greeted my address with applause. I looked forward to some serious discussions with the participants over the course
of the conference. This did occur. But so did something else.

Immediately after my address, a person came up to me. He was vis-
ibly agitated and literally stuck his nose into my face and yelled at me.
"Dr. Apple, you are a creep and a disgrace to the American flag!" He
was an official from a school system in Florida, someone who saw my
arguments and criticisms as unpatriotic. Perhaps he was also personally threatened by my public worries about the move toward vouchers in his own state, about the move toward conservative definitions
of "common culture" in the curriculum and the growing overempha-
sis on reductive forms of testing, and about the concerns I had about
the increasing influence of ultraconservative religious movements on
schooling in the United States organized around people who believe
that God only speaks to them. But whatever his motivations, his attack
says something about the ways in which some "Americans" equate a
lack of substantive criticism as patriotic and define critical sensibilities
in general as outside the boundaries of legitimate expression.[3]

Yet in my mind, when a nation and its government and major institutions do not deliver on their promises and on the sets of values they
officially profess in education and elsewhere, when they even go so far
as to condone torture and subvert international ethical standards, then
substantive criticism is the ultimate act of patriotism. Such criticism
says that "We are not just passing through. This is our country and
our institutions as well, built by the labor of millions of people such as
ourselves. We take the values in our founding documents seriously and
demand that you do so too."

Of course, the arguments I've been making so far are quite political. But that is the point. Over the past three decades, I have argued that
education must be seen as a political act. I've suggested that in order to
do this, we need to think *relationally.* That is, understanding education
requires that we situate it back both into the unequal relations of power

in the larger society and into the relations of dominance and subordination—and the conflicts—that are generated by these relations. Thus, rather than simply asking whether students have mastered a particular subject matter and have done well on our all-too-common tests, we should ask a different set of questions: Whose knowledge is this? How did it become "official"? What is the relationship between this knowledge and who has cultural, social, and economic capital in this society? Who benefits from these definitions of legitimate knowledge and who does not? What can we do as critical educators and activists to change existing educational and social inequalities and to create curricula and teaching that are more socially just?

These are complicated questions and they often require complicated answers. However, there is now a long tradition of asking and answering these kinds of critical challenges to the ways education is currently being carried on, a tradition that has grown considerably since the time when I first raised these issues in *Ideology and Curriculum*.[4] This second edition of *Educating the "Right" Way* stands on the shoulders of this tradition and aims to keep the river of that critical tradition flowing in the direction of a thicker form of democracy in education and elsewhere than that currently being proposed by economic rationalists and conservative ideologues.

It has become increasingly difficult to keep that river flowing toward progressive understandings of democracy because of the constant attacks on "creeps" like so many of us. The media seem to delight in making these attacks public—while at the same time presenting little of the substance that might make people more skeptical of the ideologies and politics that stand behind the rightist barrage. And the Right has become extremely clever itself in publicizing its claims. Let me give one concrete example, one that has recently been circulating electronically and has garnered a good deal of interest.

Dangerous Books

In the preceding section, I argued for the importance of seeing education relationally. The example I use in this section demonstrates why such relational understanding is crucial if we are to be more aware of the interconnectedness of many rightist claims. Some of the conservative positions, although at times bordering on the ludicrous, do reveal the relations among many of the fears that lie behind their public laments and attacks. For example, the strikingly conservative journal *Human Events* recently asked an "expert panel" to compile a list of the "Ten Most Harmful Books" of the nineteenth and twentieth centuries.[5] At the very top was Marx and Engels, *The Communist Manifesto*. The next two are equally political, in the usual sense of that term: *Mein Kampf* by Adolf Hitler and the compilation of Mao Zedong's writings, *Quotations from Chairman Mao*.

After that, the list gets even more interesting. In fourth and fifth place are Alfred Kinsey, *The Kinsey Report*, and even more worthy of note to those of us in education, John Dewey's *Democracy and Education*. Rounding out the list are Karl Marx, *Das Kapital*, Betty Freidan, *The Feminine Mystique*, Auguste Compte, *The Course of Positive Philosophy*, Freidrich Nietzsche, *Beyond Good and Evil*, and finally John Maynard Keynes, *General Theory of Employment, Interest, and Money*.

The list is more than a little fascinating. It combines justifiable horror about genocidal and murderous histories, with a defense of structures that lead to identifiable class and economic inequalities, a belief that private is good and public is bad, clear distaste for particular forms of science (again partly justifiable given the dangers of overly positivist versions of science), fears of relativism, and a very real concern that women's movements are bad things.

All of this becomes clearer when we look at the books on the panel's honorable mention list. The list is long, but bear with me, since it is quite illuminating: Paul Ehrlich, *The Population Bomb*, V. I. Lenin, *What Is To Be Done*, Theodore Adorno, *The Authoritarian Personality*, John Stuart Mills, *On Liberty*, B. F. Skinner, *Beyond Freedom and Dignity*, Georges Sorel, *Reflections on Violence*, Herbert Croley, *The Promise of American Life*, Charles Darwin, *Origin of Species*, Michel Foucault, *Madness and Civilization*, Sydney and Beatrice Webb, *Soviet Communism: A New Civilization*, Margaret Mead, *Coming of Age in Samoa*, Ralph Nader, *Unsafe at Any Speed*, Simone de Beavoir, *Second Sex*, Antonio Gramsci, *Prison Notebooks*, Rachel Carson, *Silent Spring*, Frantz Fanon, *Wretched of the Earth*, Sigmund Freud, *Introduction to Psychoanalysis*, Charles Reich, *The Greening of America*, Club of Rome, *The Limits to Growth*, and, last but certainly not least, Charles Darwin again, his *Descent of Man*.

One is left nearly breathless by this list. And yet, one also wonders what the criteria for inclusion and exclusion were. Critical analysis of and action on class, gender, and race oppressions are "bad," as is seeing the world through the eyes of the oppressed. Culture is a battleground in which secular humanism is winning. Biblical traditions are better explanations than evolutionary science. Science itself is to be mistrusted. The introspective methods of psychoanalysis are to be shunned. Environmental and consumer movements are dangerous.

And once again, social criticism that comes from the left side of the political spectrum (but not the right) is simply illegitimate.

Yet, once again I wonder about the logic behind all this. For example, if we were to be truly concerned about the histories of murderous conduct that took huge numbers of lives as the "experts" at *Human Events* seem to be, wouldn't the Bible (or at least certainly some of its uses) merit some consideration? Wasn't it used to justify the mass expulsion, forced conversion, and murder of Jews in many nations? Wasn't it also used to justify such things as slavery with its murderous consequences not only in the Middle Passage but in the "colonies" themselves, the conquest of peoples throughout the world and the building of an empire, apartheid systems within these conquered regions, and so many other atrocities?

Do not misunderstand me. I am not urging that we see such sacred texts as the Bible as evil. Indeed, all of the horrible practices to which I point were condemned on biblical grounds as well. Nor do I in any way wish to disrespect those whose very grounding lies in the sacredness of such texts. Rather, I want to point to the ideological positions behind the *Human Events* list, to its ultraconservative, authoritarian, and antidemocratic commitments, and how it speaks from a position of historical privilege. In order to understand all this, the key here is not simply the list itself. Rather what counts are the *interconnections* among these issues. It is exactly these interconnections that I focus on in this book. These interconnections among issues and power relations may be complicated and at times may in fact contain elements with which we agree—as in the criticism of the positivism of Compte or the behaviorism of Skinner. But if the world is complicated, so, too, must our understanding reflect this.

Of course, not all rightist positions embody the same things. There will be those who call themselves conservatives who will also be dismayed or at least amused by some of the books on the *Human Events* list. However, there are particular tensions of consciousness, what might be called "structures of feeling," that will cut across most rightist sensibilities and that will create connections among all of them. These structures of feeling, these tensions—and how they play out on the terrain of education and what we might do about them—provide the foci of *Educating the "Right" Way*.

What's New?

There are a number of reasons for engaging in the act of expanding on a book and for refining and revising its arguments. One of the best reasons is a simple one: Times change and events happen that can radically alter the terrain on which education operates. The horrible and murderous events of September 11, 2001 (to be followed by similar tragedies in Madrid, London, and elsewhere), the Patriot Act, the war on Iraq, the growth of the national security state and the fear of terrorism, all have had major effects inside and outside of formal educational institutions.[6] Furthermore, the passage of legislation commonly called No Child Left Behind has profoundly influenced educational policy and practice, often in truly negative ways. The reelection of George W. Bush as president, and the growing power of conservatism in general and the religious right in particular, can radically alter the terrain on which education operates. Any analysis of the limits and possibilities of more progressive educational policies, and of the practices of curricula, teaching, and evaluation that come out of them, must come to grips with all of these movements and transformations.

But it is not only the case that external conditions and politics change. Authors change as well. The radical nature of the current administration in Washington, its national and international arrogance, its instituting of policies that are best thought of as "class warfare" in which the wealthy and the corporate sector seem never to have enough and the poor seem never to have too little—all of this has made it even more important to me and many others to "bear witness to the negativity" of what is happening today. Of course, while such "bearing witness" is absolutely crucial right now, it is not enough. One must also attempt to publicly think about what can be done. And I try to do this in this new expanded edition as well.

Given these changes, I am reminded of the wise statement that "books are bulletins from the progressive states of ignorance a writer passes through over the years."[7] The conservative tendencies that I critically analyzed in the first edition have worsened. The shifts in power have increased. The attacks on the very idea that something that is "public" might actually be valuable have intensified. It's not actually that authors and readers are "ignorant," but that sometimes it's hard to connect all of the dots adequately. Thus, this edition tries to connect the dots in a more complete way than before.

There are significant changes in this new edition. Aside from revising the material that was in the original 2001 book, two new chapters are included. The first places No Child Left Behind (NCLB), a federal act that has radically changed the balance of power over education in the United States, in its larger context. It critically examines the growth of what I call "audit cultures" and how they are consistently linked to an agenda of privatization, marketization, and the centralization of control, tendencies that provide the technical and political underpinnings of NCLB. The new chapter also shows what happened in Texas when policies that were based on the impulses that led to NCLB were put in place. The results were and are not pretty. In the process, I provide a more detailed analysis of the power of the new middle class in education, a group whose influence is noted in the first edition but not discussed in enough detail. I also critically explore the complex and contradictory racial dynamics involved in the acceptance and rejection of the combination of commodification and audit cultures.

The second new chapter goes even further into something I raised serious questions about in the first edition—home schooling. This is one of the fastest growing educational "reforms" in the United States, and increasingly throughout many nations. I considerably extend the arguments I make about home schooling in the first edition and take us inside the home schooling environment to examine even more how it works as a social movement, where it gets its resources from, the role of gender in who is actually doing the work of home schooling, and what the political and educational implications are of all this.

Finally, because a good deal of this book provides a critical reflection on the growing power of conservative religious discourse, identities, and movements inside and outside of education, in the concluding chapter I add new material on the ways in which a number of religious movements and positions may also provide for the possibility of interrupting the growth of certain rightist policies. This is important, because I do not want to be misread about the role of religious convictions in progressive social and cultural movements. Such convictions and the movements that lie behind them continue to provide sustenance in a world in which everything can be bought and sold and where some of our most deeply held ethical and political beliefs are being destroyed as "all that is solid melts in the air and all that is sacred profaned."

The growth of radically conservative and sometimes quite dangerous tendencies within Christianity, Judaism, and Islam, and such things as the rampant Hindu nationalism of the BJP in India, are not things whose importance should be underestimated to say the least. Indeed, conservative religious impulses have historically been used to justify apartheid in places such as the United States and South Africa. And they clearly are having a profound impact on the nature of curricula and teaching in the United States, where under the guise of theories of "intelligent design" that very few reputable scientists support, science education is being radically challenged by those who have never stopped in their attempt to rid the schools of the "ungodly influences" of Darwinian approaches and evolutionary science.[8] Similar tendencies are seen in the attacks on any approach to the teaching of reading not grounded in phonics and in the continual battles over the teaching of mathematics.[9] Furthermore, radically conservative economic groups consistently employ cultural and religious tensions and conflicts to generate support for their economic policies, policies that usually wind up hurting the very people whose cultural and economic issues they have cynically manipulated to ensure electoral victories.[10]

All this needs to be said. But that must not be used as an excuse to marginalize all religious sentiments as unalterably conservative or as having no place in the debates over poverty, globalization, the environment, raising and educating our children, and many other things. Having worked with base community movements throughout Latin America and with antimilitary, pro-democracy, and democratic socialist activists in parts of Asia and the Middle East who were also devoutly Christian, Islamic, or Jewish, I have learned to be more than a little respectful of the grounds on which they base their political struggles.

As you will see later, I am opposed to teaching *for* religion in schools; but that is a very different issue than automatically rejecting—as I believe too many progressives do—the spiritual and religious grounding of many people's actions. Doing so makes it even harder to create the conditions for alternative coalitions that stand in opposition to the current rightist reconstruction of the lives of all too many people in this society. Not only that, but as I show elsewhere, given the fact that conservative discourses circulate so widely in society, such dismissal of some of the core grounding principles of many people can push religious people who otherwise might not find rightist "structures of feeling" that attractive into an alliance with exactly those groups with whom we have the biggest disagreements.[11]

Raymond Williams, one of the wisest cultural critics of his day, reminded us, "It is impossible to discuss communication or culture in our society without in the end coming to discussing power."[12] Focusing on power need not detract from an insistent focus on hope and on building alternatives. Yet, as Williams goes on to say, of course we must speak of hope and possibility, but at the same time we must not "suppress the nature of the danger."[13] This new edition of *Educating the "Right" Way* takes Williams seriously and walks that fine line between danger and hope. Hope is indeed a crucial resource, but it must be grounded in a thoroughly unromantic appraisal of what is happening now and who the winners and losers will be as we move toward a society and an educational system in which collective understandings of the common good wither before our very eyes.

Educating the "Right" Way doesn't stand alone in walking that fine line. Indeed, in my mind it must not stand alone. There are a number of recent books that, when taken together, also help provide a firmer basis for interrupting the right, challenging the left to think more creatively, and giving us practical ideas for action. Among these are Jean Anyon's detailed treatment of the transformative power of progressive social movements inside and outside of education, Eric Gutstein's description of how students can use critical mathematical literacy to both understand and challenge the inequalities they experience everyday, Wolff-Michael Roth and Angela Barton's account that does the same for scientific literacy, and two of my own recent books—one with Petter Aasen and others on successful challenges to state policies and the other with Kristen Buras on the ways in which the subaltern can and do radically challenge dominant groups even on a terrain that favors dominance.[14] There are many more books that could be mentioned. But the point is to stress the fact that interrupting dominance and building alternatives is a collective, not only an individual task. No author gets it all right. And we in essence are all authors of each others' lives. The book you are about to read is my latest attempt to reflect on such authoring. One needn't be a "creep" or a "disgrace to the American flag" to ask, "What can each of us contribute to this process?"

Acknowledgments to the Second Edition

In addition to those whom I thanked in the first edition of this book, there are a few more people who need to be added. First I want to mention my sons Paul and Peter. Both are currently involved in schooling and both know firsthand the classed and raced effects of the current restructuring of economic and educational priorities. Paul has witnessed the effects of the growing economic crisis in the larger economy and in higher education and has suffered through the Right's ability to "make the unsayable sayable" and to thereby make racism seemingly "legitimate" once again. As a mathematics teacher in a small rural high school in an economically depressed region, Peter has provided a running account of the ways such policies as No Child Left Behind have had a truly deleterious impact on schools that are striving to make a real difference in students' lives. Both of them never let me forget what is at stake in our struggles over social justice in schools and society.

Oddly enough, perhaps a word of thanks should go to Diane Ravitch and E. D. Hirsch Jr. They and I engaged in a lively debate at the Brookings Institution that clarified where our disagreements lie. I strongly disagree with much of what they propose concerning common curricula, what counts as good pedagogy and evaluation, what kinds of research are absolutely essential today, and similar things. There are also very real differences among us about the principles and practices of a truly just society and about the nature of full participation in the governance of all of the institutions in that society. However, arguments are best honed by taking one's opponents seriously—and unlike some with whom I have had serious public disagreements, they did provide an opportunity for debate. At the very least, they were more open than both the authors at the Fordham Foundation and the editorial writers at the *Wall Street Journal* whose statements about me have demonstrated a rather interesting combination of arrogance and ignorance.

xix

As with all of my books, the members of the Friday Seminar at the University of Wisconsin, Madison deserve my thanks. They reread the entire book and offered many suggestions for improving its arguments.

A good deal of the work on this edition was done while I was a Visiting Professorial Fellow at the University of London Institute of Education. Colleagues there provided a welcoming environment that was characterized by the serious talk, political interchange, and friendship that always makes me feel as if the Institute is something like a second home. In this regard, special thanks for this must go to Geoff Whitty, David Gillborn, Deborah Youdell, and Stephen Ball.

Others offered criticism and sound advice on the issues raised in this second edition as well: David Apple, Madeleine Arnot, Harry Brighouse, Patricia Burch, Roger Dale, Luis Armando Gandin, Fernando Marhuenda, Mary Metz, Michael Olneck, Mark Olssen, Tom Pedroni, Susan Robertson, Francis Schrag, Kurt Squire, Amy Stambach, Geoffrey Walford, and Lois Weis.

At Routledge, I have been particularly fortunate to have worked with a number of fine editors. But Catherine Bernard stands out as one of the very best. She has been all that any author could hope for.

Various drafts of the two new chapters that have been added to this new edition have been tried out at a number of forums, including the University of Bristol, the University of Melbourne, the University of London Institute of Education, and the University of Wisconsin, Madison. I appreciate the comments made by the faculty and students at these institutions.

Finally, let me say that none of this could have been written without something else. I need to publicly recognize the constant teaching of me by the educational and cultural activists with whom I have been fortunate to work in a considerable number of nations over the years since the first edition of *Educating the "Right" Way* appeared. The list of countries is long. I hope that the effects of your efforts last even longer.

Acknowledgments to the First Edition

Over the past ten years, I have devoted a number of books to the conservative movements that are continuing to reconstruct education in damaging ways. In *Official Knowledge* and *Cultural Politics and Education,* I combined historical, empirical, and conceptual investigations and sought to demonstrate some of the major dangers associated with such "reforms." The hold that such positions now have on society in general and on educational policy and practice in particular has not lessened. If anything, it has deepened and has become even more of a part of the common sense of this and many other societies. This situation requires critical analyses that themselves are even deeper and wider. Hence, this book. *Educating the "Right" Way* stands on the shoulders of the volumes that preceded it, but it extends their critical analysis in what I hope are even more compelling directions.

I need to be honest at the very outset here. My arguments in this book are generated out of a number of things: a considerable amount of national and international evidence of what the effects of current policies in education actually are; my participation in movements against the radically conservative restructuring of education in many nations, experiences that provide evidence of the most compelling nature about the lives and hopes that will be lost if we do not continue the battle against these policies; and last but not least, my own anger at the arrogance of those who are such true believers in market logics that they can't see the damage that this arrogance actually creates in the real world.

Thus, my concerns here are grounded not only in the world of academic debate, but also in a considerable number of personal experiences here and abroad. As I say at greater length in my recent book, *Power, Meaning, and Identity,* the years I spent as a teacher in inner-city and rural schools made it absolutely clear to me that high-sounding words about efficiency and accountability and excellence and higher standards all too often fly above the realities of real schools and real classrooms filled with real teachers and real students and are often hopelessly naive about the economic and social conditions of parents and communities. The fact that I have seen close up what such conservative policies and practices, and the cuts in services that they entail, actually have done to close members of my own family also provides another motivation.

As with any book, this volume is something of a collective accomplishment. There are many individuals inside and outside of education whose wisdom has been important in enabling me to see what I might not have seen. Given the nature of this particular book, however, my debts are even more far ranging and international than usual. The list is long; but my debts are large. Among the people who have helped me think through a number of the arguments in this book are Petter Aasen, Jill Adler, Peter Apple, Shigeru Asanuma, Bernadette Baker, Stephen Ball, Len Barton, Basil Bernstein, Jo Boaler, Barbara Brodhagen, Kristen Buras, Dennis Carlson, Wilfred Carr, Roger Dale, Ann DeVaney, Debbie Epstein, Manuel Fabrega, Stephen Fain, Nilton Fischer, Regina Leite Garcia, David Gillborn, Carl Grant, Beth Graue, Maxine Greene, Richard Hatcher, Diana Hess, Allen Hunter, Michael James, Jonathan Jansen, Knud Jensen, Daniel Kallos, Ki Seok Kim, Herbert Kliebard, Jae-Ho Ko, Julia Koza, Gloria Ladson-Billings, Theodore Lewis, Lisbeth Lindahl, Alan Lockwood, Allan Luke, Eric Margonis, Fernando Marhuenda, James Marshall, Cameron McCarthy, Robert McChesney, Mary Metz, Alex Molnar, Antonio Flavio Moreira, Akio Nagao, Antonio Novoa, Michael Olneck, Jose Pacheco, Stefan Palma, Joao Paraskeva, Bu-Kwon Park, Daniel Pekarsky, Michael Peters, Gary Price, Susan Robertson, Judyth Sachs, Fran Schrag, Simone Schweber, Mi Ock Shim, Tomaz Tadeu da Silva, Parlo Singh, Graham Hingangaroa Smith, Linda Tuhiwai Smith, Richard Smith, Amy Stambach, Gita Steiner-Kamsi, William Tate, Carlos Alberto Torres, Jurjo Santome Torres, Renuka Vital, Amy Stuart Wells, Dylan Wiliam, Anna Zantiotis, and Kenneth Zeichner.

I particularly want to recognize the contributions of Steven Selden, Geoff Whitty, and James Beane. Their friendship and the intense discussions we have had over the years have been significant for this volume.

I have had the opportunity to work with many editors over the years at Routledge and other publishers. No one has been more talented than Heidi Freund. Her friendship and advice are deeply appreciated. Thanks also need to be given to Karita Dos Santos who took over from Heidi at RoutledgeFalmer.

It may be getting monotonous, but in each book I have written I thank the Friday Seminar. For the past three decades, I have met every Friday afternoon both with my graduate students and with the visiting faculty members who have come to work with me. These seminars are truly international and often equally intense. They combine political and cultural criticism; reading each others' work; mobilizing around political and educational issues of local, national, or international significance; and at times working with teachers among the group's members in their schools and classrooms. Of just as much import, these Friday meetings are a nice blend of seriousness and humor, the latter being one of the things that is too often missing in critically oriented groups. Almost everything that is found in this book has been written and rewritten with the help of past and current members of the Friday Seminar. Each and every one of them has my sincere thanks.

Bekisizwe Ndimande worked as a research assistant on portions of this volume. Not only are his efforts appreciated, but his experiences in the struggles over education in South Africa constantly served as a reminder of why the issues I deal with here are crucial.

The arguments in this book have been tried out at many universities, political meetings, and working groups throughout the world. A few specific places need to be given special mention, however. First, the University of Wisconsin, Madison, continues to be the home of serious intellectual, political, and educational debate. It provides a special space where socially and culturally critical positions are located at the center not the periphery. Three other institutions deserve mention. Portions of this book were written when I was in residence at the Department of Education in the Norges Teknisk-Naturvitenskapelige Universitet in Trondheim, Norway, the Institute of Education at the University of London, and at the International Research Institute for Maori and Indigenous Education at the University of Auckland. Each of these institutions was characterized by that rare combination of stimulating discussion and friendship.

Finally, this book is dedicated to Rima D. Apple. Over the years we have lived and worked together; her own dedication to progressive causes and her commitment to excellence in teaching and scholarship have sustained my own commitments in crucial ways.

CHAPTER 1

Markets, Standards, God, and Inequality

Introduction

Open season on education continues. The media, candidates for public office, conservative pundits, corporate leaders, nearly everyone it seems, has an opinion on what's wrong with schools. I have mixed emotions about all this attention. On the one hand, what could be wrong with placing issues of what education does and should do front and center? As someone deeply involved in thinking about and acting upon schools, it's rather pleasing to see that conversations about teaching, curricula, evaluation, funding, and so much more are not seen as the logical equivalent of conversations about the weather. The fact that these discussions often are heated is also something to be welcomed. After all, what our children are to know and the values this should embody is serious business.

On the other hand, all of this attention creates some disquietude. One word in the last sentence of the previous paragraph explains one reason for this—business. For all too many of the pundits, politicians, corporate leaders, and others, education is a business and should be treated no differently than any other business. The fact that this position is now becoming increasingly widespread is evidence of some worrisome tendencies. Of the many voices now talking about education, only the most powerful tend to be heard. Although there is no one unitary position that organizes those with political, economic, and cultural power, the central tendencies around which they are found tend to be more conservative than not.

What are these voices saying? Over the past decades, conservative groups in particular have been pressing for public funding for private and religious schools. Voucher plans have been at the forefront of this movement. In the eyes of voucher proponents, only by forcing schools onto a competitive market will there be any improvement. These pressures are complemented by other kinds of attacks, such as the following argument. "Facts" are missing in the curriculum. Traditional content and methods have been jettisoned as our schools move toward trendy (and overly multicultural) subjects that ignore the knowledge that made us such a great nation. Raise standards. Get more tests in schools, based on "real" knowledge. Raise the stakes for teachers and students who fail them. This will guarantee that our schools return to time-honored content and more traditional methods. If tests are not enough, mandate and legislate traditional methods and content at a state level.

Vouchers are in the air—and in the courts. High stakes testing is also in the air—and in news reports that document the damaging bureaucratic and technical problems that have occurred when such tests were instituted all too quickly in a number of cities and states. Other evidence for some of the latter pressures on traditional content and methods is not hard to find either. In several states, hotly contested bills have been introduced, and in some instances passed, that mandate the use of phonics in literacy instruction. Indeed, the federal government has now put its imprimatur—and its funding—behind such "scientific" models of literacy instruction, and labeled other approaches as basically not worthy of our attention. The stereotype that what are called "whole-language" methods—that is, methods that are grounded in the lived experience of students' actual language and literacy use—have totally replaced phonics is widespread. There is actually little evidence that this is the case, since most teachers seem to use a "bricolage" of multiple approaches depending on the needs that have to be met.[1] However, this has not interrupted the agenda of those who are deeply committed to the politics of conservative restoration in education. The same groups sponsoring legislative mandates of this type also often stand behind the attacks on the teaching of evolution and the supposed loss of God's guiding word in schools.

All these movements are swirling around simultaneously. Every time one begins to understand one set of pressures, another one enters from a different direction. Each has "the" answer, if only we would become true believers and follow them. Each and every one of these pressures is situated within larger dynamics. I want to stop the swirl for a little while in order to make sense of them both in education and in their relation to larger ideological and economic forces in societies like our own. Because these pressures and forces are complicated, let me begin this sense-making process in a straightforward way—with a story about a child, a teacher, and a school in a particular community.

Joseph's Story

Joseph sobbed at my desk. He was a tough kid, a hard case, someone who often made life difficult for his teachers. He was all of nine years old and here he was sobbing, holding on to me in public. He had been in my fourth-grade class all year, a classroom situated in a decaying building in an East Coast city that was among the most impoverished in the nation. At times I wondered, seriously, whether I would make it through that year. There were many Josephs in that classroom, and I was constantly drained by the demands, the bureaucratic rules, the daily lessons that bounced off the kids' armor. Yet somehow that year was satisfying, compelling, and important, even though the prescribed curriculum and the textbooks that were meant to teach it were often beside the point. They were boring to the kids and boring to me.

I should have realized the first day what it would be like when I opened that city's "Getting Started" suggested lessons for the first few days and it began with the suggestion that "as a new teacher" I should circle the students' desks and have them introduce each other and tell something about themselves. It's not that I was against this activity; it's just that I didn't have enough unbroken desks (or even chairs) for all the students. A number of the kids had nowhere to sit. This was my first lesson—but certainly not my last—in understanding that the curriculum and those who planned it lived in an unreal world, a world *fundamentally* disconnected from my life with those children in that inner-city classroom.

But here's Joseph. He's still crying. I've worked extremely hard with him all year long. We've eaten lunch together; we've read stories; we've gotten to know each other. There are times when he drives me to despair and other times when I find him to be among the most sensitive children in my class. I just can't give up on this kid. He's just received his report card and it says that he is to repeat fourth grade. The school system has a policy that states that failure in any two subjects (including the "behavior" side of the report card) requires that the student be left back. Joseph was failing "gym" and arithmetic. Even though he had shown improvement, he had trouble staying awake during arithmetic, had done poorly on the mandatory citywide tests, and hated gym. One of his parents worked a late shift and Joseph would often stay up, hoping to spend some time with her. And the things that students were asked to do in gym were, to him, "lame."

The thing is, he had made real progress during the year. But I was instructed to keep him back. I knew that things would be worse next year. There would still not be enough desks. The poverty in that community would still be horrible, and health care and sufficient funding for job training and other services would be diminished. I knew that the available jobs in this former mill town paid deplorable wages and that even with both of his parents working for pay, Joseph's family income was simply insufficient. I also knew that, given all that I already had to do each day in that classroom and each night at home in preparation for the next day, it would be nearly impossible for me to work any harder than I had already done with Joseph. And there were another five children in that class whom I was supposed to leave back.

So Joseph sobbed. Both he and I understood what this meant. There would be no additional help for me—or for children such as Joseph—next year. The promises would remain simply rhetorical. Words would be thrown at the problems. Teachers and parents and children would be blamed. But the school system would look like it believed in and enforced higher standards. The structuring of economic and political power in that community and that state would again go on as "business as usual."

The next year Joseph basically stopped trying. The last time I heard anything about him was that he was in prison.

This story is not apocryphal. Although the incident took place a while ago, the conditions in that community and that school are much worse today. And the intense pressure that teachers, administrators, and local communities are under is equally worse. It reminds me of why I mistrust our incessant focus on standards, increased testing, marketization and vouchers, and other kinds of educational "reforms" that may sound good in the abstract but often work in exactly the opposite way when they reach the classroom level. It is exactly this sensibility of the contradictions between proposals for reform and the realities and complexities of education on the ground that provides the impetus for this book.

We face what in the next chapter I call *conservative modernization*. This is a powerful, yet odd, combination of forces that is in play in education, a combination that many educators, community activists, critical researchers, and others believe poses substantial threats to the vitality of our nation, our schools, our teachers, and our children. As I noted, we are told to "free" our schools by placing them into the competitive market, restore "our" traditional common culture and stress discipline and character, return God to our classrooms as a guide to all our conduct inside and outside the school, and tighten central control through more rigorous and tough-minded standards and tests. This is all supposed to be done at the same time. It also is all supposed to guarantee an education that benefits everyone. Well, maybe not.

Education is too often thought of as simply the delivery of neutral knowledge to students. In this discourse, the fundamental role of schooling is to fill students with the knowledge that is necessary to compete in today's rapidly changing world. To this is often added an additional caveat: Do it as cost-effectively and as efficiently as possible. The ultimate arbiter of whether we have been successful at this is students' mean gains on achievement tests. A neutral curriculum is linked to a neutral system of accountability, which in turn is linked to a system of school finance. Supposedly, when it works well, these linkages guarantee rewards for merit. "Good" students will learn "good" knowledge and will get "good" jobs.

This construction of good schooling, good management, and good results suffers from more than a few defects. Its foundational claims about neutral knowledge are simply wrong. If we have learned anything from the intense and continuing conflicts over what and whose knowledge should be declared "official" that have raged throughout the history of the curriculum in so many nations, it should have been one lesson. There is an intricate set of connections between knowledge and power.[2] Questions of whose knowledge, who chooses, how this is justified—these are *constitutive* issues, not "add-ons" that have the status of afterthoughts. This construction of good education not only marginalizes the politics of knowledge but also offers little agency to students, teachers, and community members. In some ways, it represents what Stephen Ball has characterized as "the curriculum of the dead."[3]

Furthermore, it is unfortunate but true that most of our existing models of education tend to ratify or at least not actively interrupt many of the inequalities that so deeply characterize this society. Much of this has to do with the relations between schooling and the economy, with gender, class, and race divisions in the larger society, with the intricate politics of popular culture, and with the ways we finance and support (or don't) education.[4] The connections between schooling and good jobs are weakened even more when we closely examine what the paid labor market actually looks like. Rosy statistics of stock market gains and wealth creation obscure the fact that in the real existing economy, all too many jobs require low levels of skills and low levels of formal education. A decided mismatch exists between the promises of schooling and actual job creation in our supposedly glorious free market economy, a mismatch that is distinctly related to the exacerbation of race, gender, and class divisions in this society.[5]

Of course, there are those who see a much different connection between the market and education, one that is much more positive. For them, markets may offer hope for children, but even more so for the entrepreneurs who invest in marketized schooling. In their minds, the $700 billion education sector in the United States is ripe for transformation. It is seen as the "next health care"—that is, as a sphere that can be mined for huge profits. The goal is to transform large portions of publicly controlled nonprofit educational institutions into a "consolidated, professionally managed, money-making set of businesses that include all levels of education."[6] Even though comparatively little money is being made now, for-profit companies are establishing law schools; creating or managing elementary, middle, and secondary schools; and engaging in education on factory floors and in businesses. Billions of dollars from corporations, investment funds, and even your pension funds (if you are lucky enough to have one) are pouring into for-profit educational ventures. In essence, in the words of Arthur Levine, the president of Teachers College at Columbia University, capital has said, "You guys are in trouble and we're going to eat your lunch."[7] The motives of the private companies involved are clear. At the same time as they will eliminate the waste that putatively always comes from public schooling, they will turn education into "an efficiently run and profitable machine—using investors' money instead of tax dollars."[8] I wonder what Joseph would say as he sits in his perhaps soon-to-be for-profit prison, having come from a city whose economic base was destroyed as owners and investors closed the factories there and moved them to nonunionized areas so that they wouldn't have to pay a livable wage, or for decent schooling, health care, or pensions.

Conservative Agendas

From my comments so far, you may have guessed that this book is situated in a specific place on the political/educational spectrum. Although there may occasionally be problems with the traditional categories of "left" and "right" in sorting through the complexities of politics on the ground in all of our nations, I consciously and without apology position myself on the left. In my mind, the United States remains a vast experiment, one in which both right and left argue about what it is an experiment *in*. The debate over this is vital and undoubtedly will continue. Indeed, it is part of the political lifeblood of the nation. However, like Richard Rorty, I also believe that it is the left that keeps it going.

> For the Right never thinks that anything much needs to be changed: it thinks the country is basically in good shape, and may well have been in better shape in the past. It sees the Left's struggle for social justice as mere trouble making, as utopian foolishness. [Yet] the Left, by definition is the party of hope. It insists that our nation remains unachieved.[9]

Rorty is insightful about the role of progressive criticism in keeping this nation moving. After all, almost all of the social programs that many of us now take as "natural"—social security, for example—came about because of progressive mobilizations against the denial of basic human rights. However, Rorty is on less secure grounds when he claims that "the Right never thinks anything much needs to be changed," for a good deal of the right is very much involved in radical transformations. Over the past two to three decades, the right has mounted a concerted attack on what many of us took as natural. The entire public sphere has been brought into question. Although these attacks on public institutions are broader than education, educational institutions have been centrally located in rightist criticisms. For this very reason, I want to devote this book to an analysis of rightist educational beliefs, proposals, and programs—and to their effects in the real world.

My reason for doing this is grounded in a particular political claim. Not only are rightist social movements exceptionally powerful now, but one of the most important elements of learning how to interrupt them is to understand what they did and do. Rightist movements have engaged in a vast social and ideological project. Examining how this has worked and why it has been successful can tell those of us who oppose it how it might best be countered. In my mind, if you want to stop the right, it is absolutely crucial to study what it did. This is what this book is about.

We need to be careful about essentializing here. The right is not a unitary movement. It is a coalition of forces with many different emphases; some overlap and others conflict with each other. Thus, one of the goals of this book is to examine the contradictions within this movement, demonstrating how these tensions are creatively solved so that this society *does* in fact change—but in particular directions. In none of these directions, however, will children such as Joseph be helped in the long run. Yet it is important to realize that although I disagree profoundly with many of the conservative proposals for education, it would be foolish to mindlessly support schools as they exist today. One of the reasons some people listen carefully to rightist criticisms is because there *are* problems in these institutions. Indeed, this is one of the reasons behind the popularity as well of a number of more critical and democratic school reforms.[10] Recognizing problems, however, does not mean that conservative "solutions" are correct.

One of the most important objects of the rightist agendas is changing our common sense, altering the meanings of the most basic categories, the key words, we employ to understand the social and educational world and our place in it. In many ways, a core aspect of these agendas is about what has been called identity politics. The task is to radically alter who we think we are and how our major institutions are to respond to this changed identity. Let me say more about this, especially since who we are and how we think about our institutions are closely connected to who has the power to produce and circulate new ways of understanding our identities. Both the politics of education and of the construction of common sense have played large parts here.

Mapping the Right

The concepts we use to try to understand and act on the world in which we live do not by themselves determine the answers we may find. Answers are not determined by words but by the power relations that impose their interpretations of these concepts.[11] Yet there are key words that continually surface in the debates over education. These key words have complicated histories, histories that are connected to the social movements out of which they arose and in which they are struggled over today.[12] These words have their own histories, but they are increasingly interrelated. The concepts are simple to list. In fact, they form the subtitle for this book: markets, standards, God, and inequality. Behind each of these topics is an assemblage of other words that have an emotional valence and that provide the support for the ways in which differential power works in our daily lives. These concepts include democracy, freedom, choice, morality, family, culture, and a number of other key concepts. And each of these in turn is intertextual. Each and every one of these is connected to an entire set of assumptions about "appropriate" institutions, values, social relationships, and policies.

Think of this situation as something of a road map. Using one key word—*markets*—sends you onto a highway that is going in one direction and that has exits in some places but not others. If you are on a highway labeled market, your general direction is toward a section of the country named *the economy*. You take the exit named *individualism* that goes by way of another road called *consumer choice.* Exits with words such as *unions, collective freedom, the common good, politics,* and similar destinations are to be avoided if they are on the map at all. The first road is a simple route with one goal—deciding where one wants to go without a lot of time-wasting discussion and getting there by the fastest and cheapest method possible. There is a second route, however, and this one involves a good deal of collective deliberation about where we might want to go. It assumes that there may be some continuing deliberation about not only the goal, but even the route itself. Its exits are the ones that were avoided on the first route.

As we shall see, powerful interests have created the road map and the roads. Some want only the road labeled market, because this supposedly leads to individual choice. Others will go down that road, but only if the exits are those that have a long history of "real culture" and "real knowledge." Still others will take the market road because for them God has said that this is "his" road. And finally, another group will sign on to this tour because they have skills in map-making and in determining how far we are from our goal. There's some discussion and some compromise—and perhaps even some lingering tension—among these various groups about which exits will ultimately be stopped at, but by and large they all head off in that direction.

This exercise in storytelling maps on to reality in important ways. Although I develop this in much greater detail in the next chapter, the first group is what I call *neoliberals.* They are deeply committed to markets and to freedom as "individual choice." The second group, *neoconservatives,* has a vision of an Edenic past and wants a return to discipline and traditional knowledge. The third is what I call *authoritarian populists*—religious fundamentalists and conservative evangelicals who want a return to (their) God in all of our institutions. And finally, the mapmakers and experts on whether we got there are members of a particular fraction of the managerial and professional *new middle class.*

In analyzing this complex configuration of interests on the right, I want to act in a way similar to what Eric Hobsbawm described as the historian's and social critic's duty. For Hobsbawm (and for me), the task is to be the "professional remembrancers of what [our] fellow citizens wish to forget."[13] That is, I want to detail the absent presences, the "there that is not there," in most rightist policies in education. How does their language work to highlight certain things as "real" problems while marginalizing others? What are the effects of the policies that they have promoted? How do the seemingly contradictory policies that have emerged from the various fractions of the right—such as the marketization of education through voucher plans, the pressure to "return" to the Western tradition and to a supposedly common culture, the commitment to get God back into the schools and classrooms of America, and the growth of national and state curriculum and national and state (and often "high stakes") testing—actually get put together in creative ways to push many of the aspects of these rightist agendas forward? These are the questions that guide this book.

Contested Freedom

One of the key concepts that is at stake in the discussions over who we are and how our institutions should respond to us is the idea of freedom. Many of the ideological positions that are currently embattled in the arena of education have different presuppositions about this key word. Some of the history of the dominant uses of this concept may be useful here, as these varied uses surface continually in the current debates over education.

Some of our earliest intuitions about the meaning of freedom are religious. For example, Christianity had an ideal of freedom. However, by and large it was not a worldly one but a spiritual one. Ever since "the Fall," "man has been prone to succumb to his lusts and passions."[14] Freedom has a specific meaning here, one involving abandoning this life of sin and in turn embracing the teachings of Christ in all of one's activities. This definition of freedom can seem contradictory since in essence freedom and servitude exist side by side. Yet these are seen as mutually reinforcing. Those who accept the teachings of Christ are at the very same time "free from sin" and "servants of God."[15] This spiritual definition of freedom was planted early on in the history of the United States by the Puritan settlers of Massachusetts. It is clearly in evidence in the distinction between "natural liberty" and "moral liberty" made in 1645 by John Winthrop, the Puritan governor of the Massachusetts Colony. The former was "a liberty to do evil," whereas the latter was "a liberty to do only what is good." The distinction itself has an interesting history of effects.

> This definition of freedom as flowing from self-denial and moral choice was quite compatible with severe restraints on freedom of speech, religion, movement, and personal behavior. Individual desires must give way to the needs of the community, and "Christian liberty" meant submission not only to the will of God but to secular authority as well, to a well-understood set of interconnected responsibilities and duties, a submission

no less complete for being voluntary. The most common civil offense in the courts of colonial New England was "contempt of authority."[16]

Religious definitions of freedom were partly countered and sometimes supplanted by what might be called "republican" visions. Here, the citizen reached his (and it was quite gender specific) highest fulfillment in pursuing the common good rather than private self-interest. This too had contradictory elements. It could be embodied as a form of "thick" democracy by valorizing the common rights of an entire community. Yet such republicanism could embody a distinctly class-based vision when it was applied to the real world. This is visible in its assumption that only those who owned property "possessed the quality known as virtue."[17] Ordinary men were clearly not virtuous.

The religious and republican visions of freedom were not alone. The freedom of living with God and the freedom of living in a state bound by the consent of the governed through a common will were joined by a particular theory of liberty, which was essentially private and individual, enshrined in eighteenth-century liberalism. For classical liberals, only by shielding the realm of private life and personal concerns (the family, religion, and above all economic activity) from the state's interference could freedom be guaranteed. "The public good was less an ideal to be consciously pursued by government than the outcome of free individuals' pursuit of their myriad private ambitions."[18]

There were positive moments here. It needs to be recognized that such classical liberalism did call into question an entire array of hierarchical privileges and arrangements that made individual advancement extremely difficult. It established rights both of chartered corporations independent of the aristocracy and of religious tolerance. Furthermore, there can be no doubt that its grounding in a belief that "mankind" had natural rights that government could not legitimately violate enabled disenfranchised women, paid workers, and slaves to challenge the social and educational barriers they constantly faced. Yet, having said this, it is equally important to note that both republicanism and classical liberalism were also themselves grounded in a belief that only certain kinds of persons were actually capable of exercising the rights of freedom. "Dependents lacked a will of their own and thus were unable to participate in public affairs." Given the central place that self-direction and self-government held in these ideas of freedom, those who were not able to control their own lives should not be given a voice in governance. In this way, economic independence became a defining element in political freedom. Freedom and property became intertwined, and economic independence became the identificatory sign of being worthy.[19]

It is not too difficult to see how this connects with the dynamics of class, gender, and race. Any definition of freedom based on economic independence must by its very nature draw a line between those classes of people who have it (economic independence) and those who do not. The definition is also rooted in gender relations, since this ideal of autonomy has historically been defined as a masculine trait, with woman being seen as dependent.[20] Furthermore, slaves and people of color in general were usually seen as either animalistic or childlike. Freedom cannot be extended to those who by their very nature are dependent, especially since "they are not people, but property."

In opposition to these ways of understanding the meaning of freedom, progressive movements took certain elements of the classical liberal understanding of personal freedom, radicalized them, and mobilized around them. By organizing around issues of free speech, labor rights, economic security, women's rights, birth control and the control of one's body, a socially conscious national and regional state, racial justice, the right to a truly equal education, and many other struggles for social justice, a much more expansive positive definition of freedom has been fought for both inside and outside of education. Because of the long history of sacrifices extending beyond even this extensive list to include the struggles by environmental, gay and lesbian, and disability rights activist groups, major elements of this more expansive definition of freedom have been institutionalized within both the state and civil society. Our very idea of freedom has been deepened and transformed, and extended into realms well beyond the more limited positions I described earlier in this section.[21] However, this more expansive ideal of freedom, and each and every one of the gains associated with it, are now under threat.

For example, as consumer culture has grown, the measure of freedom's success has moved away from issues involving, say, the social relations surrounding paid and unpaid labor and has moved toward the gratification of market desires.[22] Although this does have its roots in the notions of personal freedom associated with classical definitions of liberalism, freedom means, as a number of commentators have reminded us, more than satisfying one's market desires and more than doing what one pleases. It requires real chances to "formulate the available choices," something many of our fellow citizens are effectively denied.[23] Educational questions enter here in powerful ways, as we shall see.

The turn to freedom as the market is registered in the influential writings of Friedrich von Hayek, in many ways the intellectual progenitor of the neoclassical economist Milton Friedman, who delights in voucher plans as the solution to educational problems. For von Hayek, the problem of freedom is related to the fact that conservatives supposedly have let the left both define the concept and mobilize it in debates over what our institutions should do. Instead of apologizing for capitalism, libertarian conservatives influenced by von Hayek and others pressed forward the case that "real" freedom can only come from a combination of decentralized political power, extremely limited government, and unregulated markets. Only in this way can conservatives reclaim the idea of freedom and win the consent of the public. To win this kind of freedom, this meant instilling a belief in what are truly radical policies. The public had to be convinced that the unregulated marketplace of the neoliberals was not only the truest expression of individual freedom, but the marketplace must be expanded into every sphere of life. Only through market competition can "people [get] what they want."[24] Why should a marketized society keep schools out of such a market? They must be "freed" as well.

Yet the idea of freedom as a market was too libertarian for some conservatives. It placed individual choice as the arbiter of freedom. This ignored the need for "transcendental" values, for absolute truths. Only in reasserting a definition of freedom grounded in "tradition" and in the primacy of a return to Christian moral values and the values and traditions of the "West" could "virtue" be restored. For without virtue, there could be no freedom. For them, von Hayek's and Friedman's vision of freedom did not lay the foundation for a moral community whose members shared a common heritage. Naked self-interest, in Marx's apposite phrase, was hardly an appropriate starting point for the defense of "timeless" values. The bottom-line individualism of neoliberals conflicts with the organic society united by the strong moral authority of tradition envisioned by neoconservatives such as William Bennett, who decries the loss of virtues, character, and "real" knowledge in schools.[25] This is one of the defining tensions of conservative movements today, a tension that must be resolved if conservative movements are to move society in the directions they ardently desire to go.[26] How this tension is resolved in practice in education is a focal point of this book.

Part of the problem of moving a society in conservative directions has been the association of neoconservative arguments with elitism. How could people be won to a position that seemed so committed to abstract ideas of truth and virtue? Some of this was accomplished through the development of an antigovernment populism, a stress on law and order, on the evils of welfare and on the breakdown of morality and the family, and on the sanctity of property. Virtue was being lost because of government interference not only into the market, but also into one's home and schools. Morality was lost when government entered, especially liberal government. As Thomas Frank has shown, rightist groups often cynically manipulated such cultural issues to win support for neoliberal economic policies; but cynical or not, they were—and continue to be—very effective strategies.[27]

Part of this dilemma was also solved through the growth, and then integration within the larger conservative cause, of conservative evangelical movements. Estranged from a culture "that seemed to trivialize religion and exalt immorality," conservative Christians embraced not only the free market but also the need for strong moral authority. Freedom here was the combination of capitalism and what they perceived as the moral life as ordained by God.[28] Authoritarian populist religious conservatives had found a home under the conservative umbrella.

As we shall see later on, much of this movement was and is organized around both conscious and unconscious racial dynamics.[29] It has at its basis as well specific histories and dynamics surrounding gender relations. It also occurred at exactly the same time as the transfer of wealth upward in the United States and from the "Third World" to the "First World" reached almost obscene levels. And it was successful in part because the concept of freedom that became dominant, and that looked forward both to a modernized economy of stimulating desire and giving individual choice, was itself combined with a set of backward-looking visions that brought us closer to supposedly traditional Western values and to the God that established them. Let me preview many of my arguments in this book by saying somewhat more about each of these visions.

Marketizing the World

If we were to point to one specific defining political/economic paradigm of the age in which we live, it would be neoliberalism. This term may be less visible in the United States, but it is definitely known throughout the rest of the world. Although we here in the United States may be less familiar with the term itself, we are not unfamiliar with its tendencies and effects. Robert McChesney defines it in the following way:

> Neoliberal initiatives are characterized as free market policies that encourage private enterprise and consumer choice, reward personal responsibility and entrepreneurial initiative, and undermine the dead hand of the incompetent, bureaucratic

and parasitic government, that can never do good even if well intended, which it rarely is.[30]

Such policies almost never require justification any more. They have become the common sense of an emerging international consensus. Indeed, even with the recent powerful and one would hope lasting protests in Seattle, in Washington, D.C., in Prague, in Genoa and elsewhere against the arrogant policies of the World Trade Organization, neoliberal policies still have something of a sacred aura now, especially since we are repeatedly told that there are *no* alternatives worth considering. It may be imperfect, but it is the only system that is even feasible in a world governed by global markets and intense competition. Although we are constantly told that nothing else is possible, it is important to realize that neoliberalism is in essence "capitalism with the gloves off."[31]

As I have argued elsewhere and as I demonstrate in the chapters that follow, neoliberalism transforms our very idea of democracy, making it only an economic concept, not a political one.[32] One of its effects is the destruction of what might best be seen as "thick democracy," substituting a much "thinner" version of possessive individualism. Once again, McChesney puts it well in his usual biting way:

> To be effective, democracy requires that people feel a connection to their fellow citizens, and that this connection manifests itself through a variety of nonmarket organizations and institutions. A vibrant political culture needs community groups, libraries, public schools, neighborhood organizations, cooperatives, public meeting places, voluntary associations, and trade unions to provide ways for citizens to meet, communicate, and interact with their fellow citizens. Neoliberal democracy, with its notion of the market *uber alles*, takes dead aim at this sector. Instead of communities, it produces shopping malls. The net result is an atomized society of disengaged individuals who feel demoralized and socially powerless.[33]

Even with these effects, it is still possible to argue on the grounds of efficiency that corporate models should dominate our societies. After all, they do allow for choice. Yet to valorize this vision of democracy as the correct one is to neglect one simple but crucial point. Most major corporations are anything but democratic. In many ways, they are more totalitarian than is admitted openly. Thus, jobs are cut ruthlessly. Profits are much more important than the lives, hopes, and well-being of employees who have given their working lives to these organizations.

In general, no level of profit ever makes these jobs secure; profit must be constantly increased, no matter what the cost to families and employees. One must question if this is the ethic we should be introducing as *the* model for our public institutions and our children.

Although the marketizers and privatizers feel free to hearken back to Adam Smith for justification of their policies, they are being more than a little selective. Yes, Smith sang the praises of the division of labor. But he also was more than a little clear in his denunciation of many of its inhuman effects. Government action was to be constantly promoted to overcome the destructive effects of the "invisible hand." For Smith, government "regulation in favour of the workmen is always just and equitable," but not "when in favour of the masters." Indeed, underpinning much of his argument was a call for equality of outcome, a position that was at the heart of his argument for markets.[34] It is easy to forget that it was not Karl Marx but Adam Smith who recognized that for every one rich person there must be five hundred poor ones.[35]

Of course, there are multiple ways of understanding this. Grasping what this means is made harder in daily life for all of us because of the dominant forms of interpretation that are now made available or *not* made easily available in education and in the media. As I noted earlier, the very concepts we employ to make sense out of the social relations that organize our lives not only reflect these relations but produce them. For example, our system of economic production and exchange can be understood within very different ideological frameworks using very different systems of representation. The discourse of the "market" brings distinctly different visions front and center than, say, the discourse of production. The language of "consumer" creates a reality that is not the same as the language of worker, capitalist, owner, or producer. Each term posits one of those road maps I discussed earlier; each term situates us as social actors in particular relations in economic and social processes. Each has attached to it an identity that positions us in relation to the account of the process as depicted in the discourse itself. In the words of Stuart Hall:

> The worker who relates to his or her condition of existence in the capitalist process as "consumer" ... participates in the process by way of a different practice from those who are inscribed in the system as "skilled laborer"—or not inscribed in it at all as "housewife." All of these inscriptions have effects which are real. They make a material difference, since how we act in certain situations depends on what our definitions of the situation are.[36]

For these very reasons, in this book I displace our usual understanding of concepts such as the "consumer" and the "market" in which we see these things as good. I place them in a different and much more socially critical framework, one that interrogates their actual functioning in the real world of education. Unless this is done, the use of market categories and concepts prevents us from seeing the process as a whole.[37] Looking at education as part of a mechanism of market exchange makes crucial aspects literally invisible, thereby preventing critique before it even starts.[38] There are no exits to such a critique on its map.

Restoring Cultural Order

As I demonstrate in the chapters that follow, the economic focus on flexible accumulation, economic insecurity, and the marketization of social life does not stand alone. An ideology of market freedom and equality based on "choice" is not sufficient to deal with the contradictions and conditions that emerge from such economic, social, and educational policies. Impoverishment, the loss of job security and benefits, racial and gender disparities in the ways "fast capitalism" trickles down to those on the bottom, and so much more—all of these also require a much stronger state to complement the weak state supposedly favored by neoliberals. This smaller strong state, however, is often a repressive one. It is involved in rigorously policing the population of those left out by the economy. Thus, in state after state, a huge amount of money is being spent on prison construction and maintenance. In many states, this is even more than similar expenditures on higher education. As I have argued in *Cultural Politics and Education,* the United States has found a way to deal with many of the effects of poverty; we jail poor people, and especially poor persons of color.[39]

However, as I hinted at before, these things are also accompanied by other ideological movements that are connected, but not reducible, to neoliberal economic policies and their associated small but strong state. It should come as no surprise that in times of insecurity and fragmentation, there is a concomitant rise in longings for social and cultural stability and an increased emphasis on the authority of basic institutions. Against the fears of moral decay and social and cultural disintegration, there is a sense of a need for a "return." In conditions such as these, a romantic past is often constructed, a past that glorifies (particular versions of) family and tradition, patriotism, Victorian values, hard work, and the maintenance of cultural order.[40] Barbarians are at the gates. And unless we restore "our" knowledge, values, and traditions to the central place they once had, civilization will be lost. It should not be surprising that here, too, schools and the curricula, teaching, and testing that are found or not found in them become prime areas of attack. That the United States did suffer a murderous attack in September 11, 2001, adds more steam to this ideological project and makes it seem as if "civilization" is indeed under attack—even when the understandings of Islam that may underpin some people's fear may be more than a little ahistorical and incorrect.[41]

Again, we should not be too surprised by the rather checkered history these concerns have had both inside and outside of education. Let me give an example.

The manufacturing baron Abram Hewitt said it best when, in the latter part of the nineteenth century, he claimed that the task of social science and education was to find ways of making "men who are equal in liberty [content with the] inequality in distribution inevitable in modern society."[42] Not only the rich, but the middle class in general as well, believed that one's inability to advance in society was simply evidence of a lack of "character." A failure to advance bespoke a moral incapacity, the absence of those characteristics that guaranteed mobility—self-reliance and perseverance. Unions were not the answer, nor was government help. The only way to advance was to demonstrate the force of character to do it oneself, "to practice personal economy, keep out of debt, and educate their children in the principles of the marketplace."[43]

Thus, the suturing together of the needs and norms of the market and conservative views of appropriate character has a long history. Fears of economic decline, of the loss of "genteel" culture, of the loss of a common language and culture have constantly surfaced, often in times of market crisis and surges in immigration. Hybrid cultures are in essence bad cultures. They exacerbate our fears of cultural decline and economic uncertainty. The nature of this is indicated in the invention of (compulsory) common rituals. As Foner writes:

> Wracked by fears that the economic and ethnic unity of American society were in danger of disintegrating, government and private organizations in the 1890s promoted a unifying, coercive patriotism. These were the years when rituals like the Pledge of Allegiance and the practice of standing for the playing of "The Star-Spangled Banner" came into existence, Americans had long honored the Stars and Stripes, but the "cult of the flag," including an official Flag Day, dates to the 1890s.[44]

The current emphasis on "character education," on patriotism, and on restoring "our" culture must be understood in relation to this history. It is not an accident that it has occurred at this time. Nor is it a mere coincidence that those who promote these educational and social answers are also less than critical about both this history and the ways in which dominant economic dynamics may produce the ideological conditions they so lament—although we should remember that the truly tragic events of September 11 also brought out feelings of patriotism in a very wide swath of our population.[45] The fact that widespread sympathy for the United States internationally in the wake of the murders of so many people unfortunately has been squandered by the current administration is too often forgotten.

Church and State

Markets and the restoration of character and "real" knowledge in education do not stand alone today. For a rapidly growing segment of the conservative population, God's message to all of us is to turn to both capitalism and tradition. Hence, in a tense but still complementary way, much of this emphasis on a "return" is supported by major elements of the Christian right currently. They believe that only by turning one's entire life over to *their* particular religious beliefs will this society and its schools be saved. Because of this, I shall need to pay a good deal of attention to them in this volume.

As odd as it seems, given my own political and educational beliefs, let me state that the Christian right is correct to the extent that in much of the colonial United States there was no firm separation between church and state. Although they would see this positively, as ratification of the status of the United States as a Christian nation, the reality was often rather less positive. In Pennsylvania, while offering "Christian Liberty" to all of those who acknowledged "one Almighty God," all officeholders had to swear to an oath affirming their belief in Jesus Christ. Discrimination against Catholics, Jews, and even dissenting Protestants was rife.[46] Indeed, up until the Revolutionary War, those Baptists who refused to pay taxes to support Congregational ministers were jailed in Massachusetts.[47]

The drive to separate church and state, to build a "wall of separation" as the deist Thomas Jefferson would say, was based on an attempt both by people such as Jefferson and others to free politics and "reason" from theological control and by a number of evangelical movements that wanted to protect religion from the "corrupting embrace of government." Only through such toleration would people be able to lead "truly Christian lives." In the process, many powerful churches lost their supply of public revenue and their special privileges. Yet, in many states, church and state were still closely wedded. Non-Christians were barred from public office; blasphemy and breaches of the Sabbath were rigorously prosecuted.[48] Any current reminder that the United States is and was a Christian nation also needs itself to be reminded that this is what it meant to be a Christian nation as well.

In saying this and in pursuing my arguments throughout this book, I do not wish to imply that religion has no place in schools. I have some sympathy with Warren Nord's position when he argues on secular and liberal grounds that "all students should receive a liberal education that takes seriously a variety of ways of making sense of the world, religious ways included, if they are to be informed, reasonable, and responsible individuals."[49] For Nord, America's public schools are illiberal in their refusal to take religion seriously enough. In the world of elite academic and educational life, religious sensibilities play little or no role. In the process, educational institutions have "disenfranchised large segments of the American people."[50] Nord may be overstating his case a bit here, but clearly religion plays a central role in the lives of a considerable number of people—and they do feel disenfranchised by the absence of religion in schools. Of course, for many of them it is not the study of religion as one of the aforementioned multiple perspectives that they wish to promote. Rather, it is a particular vision of religious truth, of biblical authority in all realms of life, that guides them.[51] And there is a world of difference here.

Economics and Religion

There is nothing new about movements that try to put all of these elements—capitalist markets, a romantic cultural past, and God— together. Take Christianity and its historical connection to capitalism as an example.

The great economist John Maynard Keynes, the author of one of the "dangerous" books on the *Human Events* list, once wrote that modern capitalism is "absolutely irreligious." The love of money, and the accumulation of capital, had led to the steady decay of religion. Religion had lost its moral significance because it did not touch on matters economic, except in the most tangential ways. The "creative destructiveness" of capitalism and the marketization of all aspects of our lives disrupted families, communities, traditions, paid and unpaid work, the "natural rhythms" of daily life, indeed all of our life.[52] In what is perhaps one of the most famous quotes about this process of creative destruction, Marx and Engels wrote that all "ancient and venerable prejudices and opinions are swept away, all new-formed ones become antiquated before they can ossify. All that is solid melts into air, all that is sacred is profaned."[53]

Yet there has been a powerful sociological and historical tradition that, although admitting the profaning of the sacred under capitalism, argues that capitalism and, say, particular forms of Protestantism have formed a symbiotic relation, each informing and shaping the other. The emphasis in Calvinism on hard work, saving, and asceticism, for example, closely paralleled the needs of an emerging capitalist economy.[54]

This set of tensions—capitalism destroys traditional religions and uproots any sense of tradition, on the one hand, and capitalism and particular religions form a couplet that support each other, on the other—is creatively solved in the conservative evangelical movement. Capitalism is "God's economy." "Economic freedom" and market economies in education and the larger society are given biblical warrant. As we shall see, this is done quite creatively in schools and the larger society in such a way that the individual choice to be "born again" is mirrored in a market that allows for personal accumulation of wealth and choice.

Yet choice has its limits. For conservative evangelicals, one cannot choose without firm and foundational knowledge of what is right. And there is but one way, one place, to find this out. That is the Bible—and the Bible says what it means and means what it says. This inerrantist position is best exemplified and codified in the Chicago Statement on Biblical Inerrancy. "Holy Scripture, being God's own Word, written by men prepared and superintended by His Spirit, is of infallible divine authority in all matters upon which it touches. ... Being wholly and verbally God-given, Scripture is without error or fault in its teaching."[55] The Bible, then, is not "man's truth" but God's truth. Its truth does not change; it was given *fully* in biblical times.[56]

Such "truth" is not new to education, by any means. Even a brief examination would show the ways in which biblical forms were powerfully influential in early schooling in the United States. Take as one example the ways in which children were to be instructed in literacy in the New England colonies. The most commonly used schoolbook in the later part of the seventeenth century, the *New England Primer*, instructed children in the alphabet in the following way:

A wise son makes a glad Father, but a foolish son is the heaviness of his mother.

B etter is little with the fear of the Lord, than great treasure and trouble therewith.

C ome unto Christ all ye that labour and are heavy laden, and He will give you rest.[57]

The *Primer* did not stop there. Lessons followed on "The Dutiful Child's Promises" in which one vowed that "I will fear GOD, and honour the KING." It included the Lord's Prayer, the Apostle's Creed, and a listing of the books of the Bible. Numbers were to be learned in order to "serve for the ready finding of any Chapter, Psalm, and Verse in the Bible." It ended with the Westminster Assembly's Shorter Catechism, including questions such as "What is the chief end of Man?" The answer is "Man's chief end is to glorify God, and to enjoy him forever." Another question asks, "What rule hath God given to direct us how we may glorify and enjoy him?" This is answered by, "The word of God which is contained in the Scriptures of the Old and New Testament, is the only rule to direct us how we may glorify and enjoy him."[58] Thus, there is no doubt that religion was central to the founding of schooling in America.

Later texts showed this continued influence. The McGuffey Readers, of which over 120 million were printed and used in the nineteenth and early twentieth centuries, read as much like a text in theology as in literacy. God was omnipresent within it, just but stern. The truths of the Bible were unquestioned; nor did one question their relevance to everyday life. Life was "God-conscious and God-centered." Students are to "live for salvation." All elements of the natural world can only be understood as "the expression of God's order." Indeed, as Nord reminds us, there are more references to God in the *Annotated McGuffey* than any other subject. Interestingly, the subject of death has the second largest number.[59]

These are not the only possibilities of understanding religion and its relations to the larger society, of course. The ways we think socially about religion have been varied. For some commentators, religion symbolizes the "felt whole" of a society and involves the deployment of symbols of social identity. Thus, religious meanings and institutions provide integrative forms that keep societies together and promote harmony. For others, such as Emile Durkheim, religion's very action in dividing the sacred from the profane is a positive response that celebrates sociality. It "sacralizes the fact and manner of human bonding as a prerequisite of any particular form of society."[60] For still others, such as some versions of Marx and Engels, religion played a less positive symbolic and material role. Beliefs in the supernatural and in divine powers represented ways in which social relations and inequalities were masked. Their social function was to obscure or distort the prevailing distribution of power and wealth and the social relations that supported them.[61] For those such as Weber and Simmel, religion is a vast symbolic resource in which meanings are able to be produced, transmitted, and contested. It is separated from other symbolic resources by the fact that it provides a warrant for claims to ultimate significance, but it could be adapted to suit the interests of particular sections of the society.[62] Thus, for Weber, there were close connections between particular kinds of Protestantism and the rationalization of the modern world.

Closer in time to us, those observers such as Peter Berger argue that religion plays another crucial role in "modern" societies. It keeps the existential nightmare away. For him, culture today is unstable, as are people's identities. Religious beliefs enable one to better withstand the corrosive effects of bureaucratic rationality and the development of *homo economicus*, the person who is defined only by her or his place as an economic being.[63] Finally, Michel Foucault traces out the ways in which the "pastoral power" that had been fostered by the major Christian churches spread out throughout society. It was assimilated into the state and used as an "individualizing tactic which character- ized a series of powers: those of the family, medicine, psychiatry, edu- cation, and employers."[64] Yet, no matter what the differences in each of these perspectives on religion, each sees religion fundamentally *socially*, not as apart from society in some otherworldly realm but as integral to society. It has power—individually and collectively, positively and neg- atively. This is exactly what I wish to explore in the latter parts of this book when I discuss the growing influence of authoritarian populist religious conservatism on education as well.

However, I want to do this in a particular way. Following the lead- ership of Antonio Gramsci, I believe that the social meaning of religion has to be decoded in terms of the real-life experiences of people at par- ticular times and places. He urged us to examine the ways in which churches worked to prevent a gap from forming between its formal- ized institutions and rituals and "the people"—that is, how at specific times and places religion connected to popular culture and the mean- ings of daily life. Gramsci's interest was in making organic connections between working-class and poor people and progressive movements for social justice.[65] My own interest is grounded in a similar politics; but I want to explore how organic connections are now made between people's daily lives and *conservative* religious movements, as these are the one's increasingly dominant today and these are the ones that seem to be exceptionally powerful in polarizing our beliefs about school- ing currently. At the same time, I want to show connections that have been made between such religious tendencies and the growing belief that only through markets and a return to an Edenic past can schools, our children, and our nation itself be "saved." In doing this, I again want to be absolutely clear that I am not taking a position that religious meanings and institutions must by their very nature be conservative. Popular religious meanings, movements, and institutions are not a priori radical or conservative. Much depends on the uses to which they are put and on the balance of social and ideological forces at a given time.[66] (Actually, from my own personal experiences working outside the United States, I tend to believe that in many nations it would be impossible to develop larger liberatory movements without religious mediations as one of the major dynamics. I take this position not only for empirical reasons—that is, because of the power of religion in these nations—but because I believe that utopian hopes are important for envisioning a better future. And religious yearnings often embody such dreams and must be treated with the respect they deserve.)

Managerialism

The three previous elements of the radical restructuring of education and other institutions that I've just described—neoliberalism, neoconservatism, and authoritarian populism—do not cover all of the tendencies currently in motion on the conservative side of the spectrum. A final one concerns the impulses driving the restructuring of the role of government and the ways in which a relatively autonomous fraction of the managerial and professional middle class has taken on even more power in directing social and educational policies in directions that actually give this particular group of people more power and new identities as well. I pointed out earlier that the role of the state has been altered along the lines of a radical redefinition of the boundaries between public and private. We can think of this as involving three strategic transformations. First, many public assets have been privatized. Public utilities are sold off to the highest bidder; schools are given to corporations to run. Second, rigorous competition between institutions is sponsored so that public institutions are constantly compared with supposedly more efficient private ones. Hence, even if schools and other institutions are still state funded, their internal procedures increasingly mirror those of the corporate sector. Third, public responsibilities have been shifted onto the informal sector, under the argument that the government can no longer afford the expense of such services. In practice this has meant that a good deal of child care, caring for the elderly and the infirm, and so much more has been "dumped" onto the local community and the family. This is one of the reasons that it is crucial to realize that behind a good deal of the new managerialism and the importation of business models into the state is a specifically patriarchal set of assumptions and effects, as it is largely the unpaid labor of women in the family and in local communities that will be exploited to deal with the state's shedding of its previous responsibilities.[67] At the same time, although some aspects of the state are indeed dumped onto local communities, other aspects of state control are enhanced and made even stronger, especially its control over knowledge and values in schools and over the mechanisms of evaluating institutional success or failure in such cultural reproduction. One of the most powerful examples of this process in the United States is the legislation commonly called "No Child Left Behind." Underneath its rhetoric of helping those children who have not been well-served by existing schooling (and this clearly *cannot* be denied), its characteristics include a massive centralization of control, a loss of local autonomy, and a redefinition of what counts as good or bad education that is simply reduced to scores on problematic tests of achievement. As we shall see, it can actually create even more inequalities than before.

However, managerialism is not only about altering what the state does and how much power it has. It also offers new and powerful roles for the individuals and groups who occupy positions within the state. In technical terms, we might say that managerial discourse provides "subject positions" through which people can imagine themselves and their institutions in different ways. Thus, one of the key characteristics of managerial discourse is in the positions it offers to managers. They are not passive, but active agents—mobilizers of change, dynamic entrepreneurs, shapers of their own destinies.[68] No longer are the organizations they inhabit ploddingly bureaucratic and subjected to old-fashioned statism. Instead, they and the people who run them are dynamic, efficient, productive, "lean and mean."[69]

By importing business models and tighter systems of accountability into education and other forms of public services, managerialism doesn't just offer state managers new ways of thinking about their lives and their organizations. Aside from giving new meaning to the lives of managers within the new middle class, it promises—in the words of new managerialism—transparency, at the same time as it supposedly empowers the individual consumer. It is an ideal project, merging the language of empowerment, rational choice, efficient organization, and new roles for managers all at the same time. Although the "spartan language" of efficiency does have its attractiveness to certain business groups, it has only limited appeal to many others. By reappropriating the discourse of antipaternalism and user-centeredness, it offers metaphors for a range of people to see their place in the new more responsive future. One can modernize the machinery of schools and of the government in general, be an efficient and business-like manager, and help people by ensuring "quality" at the same time.[70] What could be wrong with that? As I show later, however, this is not the rolling back of state power, nor is it really "empowering" for either the least-advantaged members of our communities or people who work in those institutions now subject to managerialism's demands. Furthermore, its vision of managers organized around an efficient and revitalized professionalism in the service of consumers is partly a fiction. Active professionals are free to follow their entrepreneurial urges—as long as they "do the right thing."[71] As we shall see, Foucault's panopticon is everywhere.

Analyzing Conservative Modernization

In the chapters that follow, I provide a picture of how the odd combination of markets, return to lost traditions and values, a godly education, and the managerialism of tightened standards and guaranteeing "quality" are pulled together. In the process, I want to demonstrate which groups of people will wind up winning and losing as this constellation of "reforms" goes forward. In pursuit of this, I must bring to the attention of people in the United States not only research and arguments about what is happening here, but also evidence of similar reforms that have appeared in other nations. There are several reasons for approaching these issues with an international perspective. All too many discussions of education in the United States are characterized by a particular form of arrogance. "We" have nothing to learn from other nations. Or such discussions are unaware that many of the things in which we are engaged here have a history elsewhere, a history whose effects should make us rather cautious about engaging in the same policies. Or, finally, there is an assumption that our motives are pure and our traditions democratic. Hence, whatever has occurred in educational reforms in other nations (say, an increase in social inequalities in education when a particular change is instituted) simply couldn't happen here. It can and it is.

Chapter 2 goes into more detail about the assumptions that underpin the forces of conservative modernization specifically in education today and gives a clearer sense of the tensions and contradictions in the conservative movements. Chapter 3 deals with the actual effects that "reforms" such as establishing a competitive market in schooling, national and state curricula, ever-rising standards, and the increasing mandates of testing have had in schools in a number of countries. Its focus is on the neoliberal and neoconservative proposals that are having such a profound effect on educational policy and practice. This chapter also critically examines the ways in which the supposed alternative to these proposals—that is, ones that center around the literature on "critical pedagogy"—are weak in crucial ways, and thus will have a hard time interrupting rightist transformations. (This is a difficult issue for me, since I have long been associated with this tradition.) Chapter 4 is new to this edition and specifically focuses on the processes and effects of such reforms as No Child Left Behind and their attempts at recasting education along the logics of what I call "audit cultures." In the process, the complicated roles that class and race dynamics play in this logic and in various groups' reactions to it are highlighted.

Chapters 5 and 6 deal directly with the growing power of conservative religious groups in debates over the ends and means of schooling. Chapter 5 discusses some of their recent effects and traces out the history of such movements, whereas Chapter 6 critically illuminates the ways in which their beliefs about curricula and pedagogy cohere with their larger positions on the economy, government, the family, gender relations, and the politics of class and race. Chapter 7 examines the ways in which the home schooling movement provides a mechanism for many of these emphases to come together. Chapter 8 goes further into the home schooling movement, both into its status as a social movement and into the ways in which it is carried out. As will be evident here as in other chapters, understanding the ways in which gender politics works is absolutely crucial if we are to also understand the actual practices of teaching and learning in home schooling. In Chapter 9, I assess the possibilities of interrupting the movement toward the right and suggest some strategies for doing so.

As you will see, a good deal of time is spent on conservative religious critics of schooling in the later sections of this book. I do this for a number of reasons. First, although it is crucial to pay close attention to the criticism of markets, standards, and testing (and I do), too often the creative ways in which many other groups have been brought under the umbrella of neoliberal leadership have been largely ignored. Second, such religious groups have been very powerful in putting pressure on schools in states and municipalities throughout the country, often making educators think twice (or three or four times) about what they will and will not teach and how they will and will not teach it. These groups have also been growing rapidly in influence so that many more people now consider themselves to be conservative evangelicals and are willing to take a public position on education based on this identification than ever before in recent history. Third, perhaps unlike many other people on the left, as I've noted I believe that there are elements of insight in the position of the populist religious critics and that they have been stereotyped and ignored. Not only do I think that this is intellectually suspect, but it is also dangerous strategically if we do wish to counter the rightist turn in education in serious ways.

Because of this, although I am deeply concerned about what their implications are, throughout the chapters on conservative religious impulses I also want to be fair to the concerns they express—many of which cannot be easily dismissed. Thus, I will be at pains to show the elements of "good sense" as well as "bad sense" in their criticisms of some aspects of formal education.

These are the complicated tendencies I focus on in this new edition of *Educating the "Right" Way*. I wish that it could be simpler. That certainly would make the story I need to tell much easier. However, when reality itself is complex and contradictory, so too must be our critical analyses. Throughout this book I combine the theoretical and the empirical. I must admit to being deeply worried that we have played the theoretical card so often at such a level of abstraction that we have vacated the empirical space and left it open for neoliberals and neoconservatives to occupy—which they predictably have done. Yet at times we positively *need* the distance that theory gives us in order to think through difficult issues.

Because of this, I fully recognize that there are tensions in what I do here. I criticize the kinds of theories and assumptions that underpin many of the current educational reforms; and sometimes I do this theoretically as well as empirically. However, having done this I tend to take the position that "the only theory worth having is that which you fight off, not that which you speak with profound fluency."[72] This is a bit of an overstatement of course, since we do need to be "fluent" in any theory we propose to use. But it does point out that one's theoretical success should not be measured by whether there is an exact "fit." Rather, the efficacy of our theories needs to be measured by our ability to work productively with theories that are almost always inadequate in some ways but push us "further down the road" and enable us to see things that were hidden before.[73] The road I want us to travel on has exits that are not visible on the maps about education, culture, government, and the economy provided to us by dominant groups. Let us now look at these maps in more detail.

CHAPTER 2

Whose Markets, Whose Knowledge?

Introduction

In the first chapter, I described the general directions this society has taken. I employed key concepts such as freedom to analyze the ideological dynamics that underpin these directions. In this and the next two chapters, our attention will be more specifically on education—on the educational positions of each of the elements within the groups I identified and on a number of their largely negative effects on schooling here and elsewhere.

As I noted, we have entered a period of reaction in education. Our educational institutions are seen as total failures. High dropout rates, a decline in "functional literacy," a loss of standards and discipline, the failure to teach "real knowledge" and economically useful skills, poor scores on standardized tests, and more—all these are charges leveled at schools. And all of these, we are told, have led to declining economic productivity, unemployment, poverty, a loss of international competitiveness, and so on. Return to a "common culture," make schools more efficient, more responsive to the private sector. Do this and our problems will be solved.

Behind all of these charges is an attack on egalitarian norms and values. Although hidden in the rhetorical flourishes of the critics, in essence "too much democracy"—culturally and politically—is seen as one of the major causes of "our" declining economy and culture. Similar tendencies are quite visible in other countries as well. The extent of the reaction is captured in the words of Kenneth Baker, former British Secretary of Education and Science in the Thatcher government, who evaluated nearly a decade of rightist efforts in education by saying, "The age of egalitarianism is over."[1] He was speaking decidedly positively, not negatively.

The threat to egalitarian ideals that these attacks represent is not usually made quite this explicitly, as they are often couched in the discourse of "improving" competitiveness, jobs, standards, and quality in an educational system that is seen as in total crisis. This discourse is clearly present today in "New Labour" in the United Kingdom and in similar policies in the United States. In all too many ways, both nations' educational policies continue trends established under earlier conservative (and sometimes supposedly "liberal") governments.

It would be simplistic, however, to interpret what is happening as only the result of efforts by dominant economic elites to impose their will on education. Many of these attacks do represent attempts to reintegrate education into an economic agenda. Yet they cannot be fully reduced to that, nor can they be reduced to being only about the economy. Cultural struggles and struggles over race, gender, and sexuality coincide with class alliances and class power.

Education is a site of struggle and compromise. It serves as a proxy as well for larger battles over what our institutions should do, whom they should serve, and who should make these decisions. And, yet, by itself it is one of the major arenas in which resources, power, and ideology specific to policy, finance, curriculum, pedagogy, and evaluation in education are worked through. Thus, education is both cause and effect, determining and determined. Because of this, no one chapter could hope to give a complete picture of this complexity. What I hope to do instead is to provide an outline of some of the major tensions surrounding education in the United States as it moves in conservative directions. A key word here is directions. The plural is crucial to my arguments, because, as I showed, there are multiple and at times contradictory tendencies within the rightist turn.

Although my focus in this chapter is largely internal, it is impossible to understand current educational policy in the United States without placing it in its international context. Thus, behind the stress on higher standards, more rigorous testing, education for employment and a much closer relationship between education and the economy in general, and so on was the fear of losing in international competition and the loss of jobs and money to Japan, Mexico, and increasingly now the "Asian Tiger" economies such as China and elsewhere (although this has been mediated by the economic upheavals still being experienced in parts of Asia).[2] In the same way, the equally evident pressure in the United States to reinstall a (selective) vision of a common culture, to place more emphasis on the "Western tradition," on religion, on the English language, and similar emphases are deeply connected to cultural fears about Latin America, Africa, and Asia. This context provides a backdrop for my discussion.

The rightward turn has been the result of the successful struggle by the right to form a broad-based alliance. This new alliance has been so successful in part because it has been able to win the battle over common sense.[3] That is, it has creatively stitched together different social tendencies and commitments and has organized them under its own general leadership in issues dealing with social welfare, culture, the economy, and as we shall see in this chapter, education. Its aim in educational and social policy is what I called "conservative modernization."[4]

As I noted in my introductory chapter, this alliance contains four major elements. Each has its own relatively autonomous history and dynamics, but each has also been sutured into the more general conservative movement. These elements include neoliberals, neoconservatives, authoritarian populists, and a particular fraction of the upwardly mobile professional and managerial new middle class. I pay particular attention to the first two of these groups here since they—especially neoliberals—are currently in leadership in this alliance to "reform" education. However, in no way do I want to dismiss the power of the latter two groups, and I return to them in later chapters.

Neoliberalism: Schooling, Choice, and Democracy

I made the point in Chapter 1 that neoliberals are the most powerful element within the alliance supporting conservative modernization. They are guided by a vision of the weak state. Thus, what is private is necessarily good and what is public is necessarily bad. Public institutions such as schools are "black holes" into which money is poured—and then seemingly disappears—but which do not provide anywhere near adequate results. For neoliberals, one form of rationality is more powerful than any other—economic rationality. Efficiency and an "ethic" of cost-benefit analysis are the dominant norms. All people are to act in ways that maximize their own personal benefits. Indeed, behind this position is an empirical claim that this is how *all* rational actors act. Yet, rather than being a neutral description of the world of social motivation, this is actually a construction of the world around the valuative characteristics of an efficiently acquisitive class type.[5]

Underpinning this position is a vision of students as human capital. The world is intensely competitive economically, and students—as future workers—must be given the requisite skills and dispositions to compete efficiently and effectively.[6] Furthermore, any money spent on schools that is not directly related to these economic goals is suspect. In fact, as "black holes," schools and other public services as they are currently organized and controlled waste economic resources that should go into private enterprise. Thus, for neoliberals, not only are public schools failing our children as future workers, but like nearly all public institutions they are sucking the financial life out of this society. Partly this is the result of "producer capture." Schools are built for teachers and state bureaucrats, not "consumers." They respond to the demands of professionals and other selfish state workers, not the consumers who rely on them. The increasingly virulent attacks on teachers unions and professional associations by the right is but the tip of the iceberg here.

The idea of the "consumer" is crucial here. For neoliberals, the world in essence is a vast supermarket. "Consumer choice" is the guarantor of democracy. In effect, education is seen as simply one more product like bread, cars, and television.[7] By turning it over to the market through voucher and choice plans, education will be largely self-regulating. Thus, democracy is turned into consumption practices. In these plans, the ideal of the citizen is that of the purchaser. The ideological effects of this position are momentous. Rather than democracy being a *political* concept, it is transformed into a wholly *economic* concept. The message of such policies is what might best be called "arithmetical particularism," in which the unattached individual—as a consumer—is deraced, declassed, and degendered.[8]

The metaphors of the consumer and the supermarket are actually quite apposite here. For just as in real life, there are individuals who indeed can go into supermarkets and choose among a vast array of similar or diverse products. And there are those who can only engage in what can best be called "postmodern" consumption. They stand outside the supermarket and can only consume the image.

The entire project of neoliberalism is connected to a larger process of exporting the blame from the decisions of dominant groups onto the state and onto poor people. After all, it was not the government that made the decisions to engage in capital flight and to move factories to those nations that have weak or no unions, fewer environmental regulations, and repressive governments. And it was not working-class and poor communities (such as those in which Joseph and his parents lived) that chose to lose those jobs and factories, with the loss of hope and schools and communities in crisis that were among the results of these decisions. And it was neither of them who chose to lay off millions of workers—many of whom had done rather well in school—because of mergers and leveraged buyouts, trends that have again become more pronounced.

With their emphasis on the consumer rather than the producer, neoliberal policies need also to be seen as part of a more extensive attack on government employees. In education in particular, they constitute an offensive against teacher unions that are seen to be much too powerful and much too costly. Neoliberal policies, although they may not have been created as a conscious attack on women, need to be interpreted as part of a longer history of attacks on women's labor, as the vast majority of teachers in the United States—as in so many other nations—are women.[9]

Varied policy initiatives have emerged from the neoliberal segments of the new hegemonic alliance. Most have centered on either creating closer linkages between education and the economy or placing schools themselves into the market. The former is represented by widespread proposals for "school to work" and "education for employment" programs, and by vigorous cost-cutting attacks on the "bloated state." The latter initiative is no less widespread and is becoming increasingly powerful. It is represented by both national and state-by-state proposals for voucher and choice programs.[10] These include providing public money for private and religious schools (although these are highly contested proposals). Behind this is a plan to subject schools to the discipline of market competition.[11] Such "quasi-market solutions" are among the most divisive and hotly debated policy issues in the entire nation, with important court cases concerning funding for private or religious schools through voucher mechanisms having been decided or now being closely watched.[12]

Some proponents of "choice" argue that only enhanced parental "voice" and choice will provide a chance for "educational salvation" for minority parents and children.[13] Moe, for instance, claims that the best hope for the poor to gain the right "to leave bad schools and seek out good ones" is through an "unorthodox alliance."[14] Only by allying themselves with Republicans and business—the most powerful groups supposedly willing to transform the system—can the poor succeed, a set of arguments I shall take up and critically analyze later.

As I show in more detail in Chapter 3, growing empirical evidence indicates that the development of "quasi-markets" in education has led to the exacerbation of existing social divisions surrounding class and race.[15] There are now increasingly convincing arguments that while the supposed overt goal of voucher and choice plans is to give poor people the right to exit public schools, among the ultimate long-term effects may be the increase of "white flight" from public schools into private and religious schools and the creation of the conditions where affluent white parents may refuse to pay taxes to support public schools that are more and more suffering from the debilitating effects of the fiscal crisis of the state. The result is even more educational apartheid, not less.[16]

In his own review of evidence from the U.S. experience, Whitty argues that although advocates of choice assume that competition will enhance the efficiency and responsiveness of schools, as well as give disadvantaged children opportunities that they currently do not have, this may be a false hope. These hopes are not now being realized and are unlikely to be realized in the future "in the context of broader policies that do nothing to challenge deeper social and cultural inequalities." As he goes on to say, "Atomized decision-making in a highly stratified society may appear to give everyone equal opportunities but transforming responsibility for decision-making from the public to the private sphere can actually reduce the scope for collective action to improve the quality of education for all."[17]

This position is ratified by Henig, who states that "the sad irony of the current education-reform movement is that, through overidentification with school choice proposals, the healthy impulse to consider radical reforms to address social problems may be channeled into initiatives that further erode the potential for collective deliberation and collective response."[18] When this effect is coupled with the fact that such neoliberal policies in practice may reproduce traditional hierarchies of class, race, and gender, these proposals should give us serious pause.[19]

There is a second variant of neoliberalism. This one *is* willing to spend more state and/or private money on schools, if and only if schools meet the needs expressed by capital. Thus, resources are made available for "reforms" and policies that further connect the education system to the project of making our economy more competitive. Two examples can provide a glimpse of this position. In a number of states, legislation has been passed that directs schools and universities to make closer links between education and the business community. In the state of Wisconsin, for instance, all teacher education programs had to include identifiable experiences on "education for employment" for all of its future teachers; and all teaching in the public elementary, middle, and secondary schools of the state had to include elements of education for employment in its formal curricula.[20]

The second example is seemingly less consequential, but in reality it is a powerful statement of the reintegration of educational policy and practice into the ideological agenda of neoliberalism. I am referring here to Channel One, a for-profit television network that is now being broadcast into schools enrolling over 40 percent of all middle and secondary school students in the nation (many of these schools are financially hard-pressed given the fiscal crisis, even though some states are currently experiencing slightly better budgets). In this "reform," schools are offered a "free" satellite dish, two VCRs, and television monitors for each of their classrooms by a private media corporation. They are also offered a free news broadcast for these students. In return for the equipment and the news, all participating schools must sign a three- to five-year contract guaranteeing that their students will watch Channel One every day.

This agreement sounds relatively benign. However, not only is the technology "hardwired" so that *only* Channel One can be received but also *mandatory advertisements* for major fast food, athletic wear, and other corporations are broadcast along with the news, which students—by contract—also must watch. Students, in essence, are sold as a captive audience to corporations. Because, by law, these students must be in schools, the United States is one of the first nations in the world to consciously allow its youth to be sold as commodities to those many corporations willing to pay the high price of advertising on Channel One to get a guaranteed (captive) audience.[21] Thus, under a number of variants of neoliberalism not only are schools transformed into market commodities, but so too now are our children.[22]

As I noted, the attractiveness of conservative policies in education rests in large part on major shifts in our common sense—about what democracy is, about whether we see ourselves as possessive individuals ("consumers"), and ultimately about how we see the market working. Underlying neoliberal policies in education and their social policies in general is a faith in the essential fairness and justice of markets. Markets ultimately will distribute resources efficiently and fairly according to effort. They ultimately will create jobs for all who want them. They are the best possible mechanism to ensure a better future for all citizens (consumers).

Because of this, we of course must ask what the economy that reigns supreme in neoliberal positions actually looks like. Far from the positive picture painted by neoliberals in which technologically advanced jobs will replace the drudgery and the under- and unemployment so many people now experience if we were to only set the market loose on our schools and children, the reality is something else again. Unfortunately, markets clearly are as powerfully destructive as they are productive in people's lives.[23]

Let us take as a case in point the paid labor market to which neoliberals want us to attach so much of the education system. Even with the growth in proportion in high-tech-related jobs, the kinds of work that are and will be increasingly available to a large portion of the American population will not be highly skilled, technically elegant positions. Just the opposite will be the case. The paid labor market will increasingly be dominated by low-paying, repetitive work in the retail, trade, and service sectors. This is made strikingly clear by one fact. More cashier jobs will be created by the year 2005 than jobs for computer scientists, systems analysts, physical therapists, operations analysts, and radiologic technicians *combined*. In fact, it is projected that 95 percent of all new positions will be found in the service sector. This sector broadly includes personal care, home health aides; social workers (many of whom are now losing or have lost their jobs because of cutbacks in social spending); hotel and lodging workers; restaurant employees; transportation workers; and business and clerical personnel. Furthermore, eight of the top ten individual occupations that will account for the most job growth in the next ten years include the following: retail salespersons, cashiers, office clerks, truck drivers, waitresses/waiters, nursing aides/orderlies, food preparation workers, and janitors. The majority of these positions obviously do not require high levels of education. Many of them are low-paid, nonunionized, temporary, and part-time, with low or no benefits. And many are dramatically linked to, and often exacerbate, the existing race, gender, and class divisions of labor. These trends are predicted to continue.[24] This is the emerging economy we face, not the overly romantic picture painted by neoliberals who urge us to trust the market.

Neoliberals argue that making the market the ultimate arbiter of social worthiness will eliminate politics and its accompanying irrationality from our educational and social decisions. Efficiency and cost-benefit analysis will be the engines of social and educational transformation. Yet among the ultimate effects of such "economizing" and "depoliticizing" strategies is actually to make it ever harder to interrupt the growing inequalities in resources and power that so deeply characterize this society. Nancy Fraser illuminates the process in the following way:

> In male dominated capitalist societies, what is "political" is normally defined contrastively against what is "economic" and what is "domestic" or "personal." Here, then, we can identify

two principal sets of institutions that depoliticize social discourses: they are, first, domestic institutions, especially the normative domestic form, namely the modern restricted male-headed nuclear family; and, second, official economic capitalist system institutions, especially paid workplaces, markets, credit mechanisms, and "private" enterprises and corporations. Domestic institutions depoliticize certain matters by personalizing and/or familializing them; they cast these as private-domestic or personal-familial matters in contradistinction to public, political matters. Official economic capitalist system institutions, on the other hand, depoliticize certain matters by economizing them; the issues in question here are cast as impersonal market imperatives, or as "private" ownership prerogatives, or as technical problems for managers and planners, all in contradistinction to political matters. In both cases, the result is a foreshortening of chains of in-order-to relations for interpreting people's needs; interpretive chains are truncated and prevented from spilling across the boundaries separating the "domestic" and the "economic" from the political.[25]

This very process of depoliticization makes it very difficult for the needs of those with less economic, political, and cultural power to be accurately heard and acted on in ways that deal with the true depth of the problem. For Fraser, this outcome occurs because of what happens when "needs discourses" get retranslated into both market talk and "privately" driven policies.

For our purposes here, we can talk about two major kinds of needs discourses: oppositional and reprivatization discourses. *Oppositional* forms of needs talk arise when needs are politicized from below and are part of the crystallization of new oppositional identities on the part of subordinated social groups. What was once seen as largely a "private" matter is now placed into the larger political arena. Sexual harassment, race and sex segregation in paid labor, and affirmative action policies in educational and economic institutions provide examples of "private" issues that have now spilled over and can no longer be confined to the "domestic" sphere.[26]

Reprivatization discourses emerge as a response to the newly emergent oppositional forms and try to press these forms back into the "private" or the "domestic" arena. They are often aimed at dismantling or cutting back social services, deregulating "private" enterprise, or stopping what are seen as "runaway needs." Thus, reprivatizers may attempt to keep issues such as, say, domestic battery from spilling over into overt political discourse and will seek to define it as purely a family matter. Or they will argue that the closing of a factory is not a political question but instead is an "unimpeachable prerogative of private ownership or an unassailable imperative of an impersonal market mechanism."[27] In each of these cases, the task is to contest both the possible breakout of runaway needs and to depoliticize the issues.

In educational policy in the United States, there are a number of clear examples of these processes. The state of California provides a well-known instance. A binding referendum that prohibited the use of affirmative action policies in state government, in university admission policies, and so on was passed overwhelmingly as reprivatizers spent an exceptional amount of money on an advertising campaign that labeled such policies as "out of control" and as improper government intervention into decisions involving "individual merit." The California referendum has spawned similar, and quite controversial, initiatives in other states. Voucher plans in education—where contentious issues surrounding whose knowledge should be taught, who should control school policy and practice, and how schools should be financed are left to the market to decide—offer another prime example of such attempts at "depoliticizing" educational needs. Finally, giving primary responsibility over the definition of important "work skills" to the private sector—an act that evacuates the possibility of criticism of the ways work is actually constructed, controlled, and paid—enables a definition of work both as a "private" matter and as purely a technical choice to go unchallenged. All these examples show the emerging power of reprivatizing discourses.

A distinction that is useful here in understanding what is happening in these cases is that between "value" and "sense" legitimation.[28] Each signifies a different strategy by which powerful groups or states legitimate their authority. In the first (value) strategy, legitimation is accomplished by actually giving people what may have been promised. Thus, the social democratic state may provide social services for the population in return for continued support. That the state will do this is often the result of oppositional discourses gaining more power in the social arena and having more power to redefine the border between public and private.

In the second (sense) strategy, rather than providing people with policies that meet the needs they have expressed, states and/or dominant groups attempt to *change the very meaning* of the sense of social need into something that is very different. Thus, if less powerful people call for "more democracy" and for a more responsive state, the task is not to give "value" that meets this demand, especially when it may lead to runaway needs. Rather, the task is to change what actually *counts* as democracy. In the case of neoliberal policies, democracy is now redefined as guaranteeing choice in an unfettered market. In essence, the state withdraws. The extent of acceptance of such transformations of needs and needs discourses shows the success of the reprivatizers in redefining the borders between public and private again and demonstrates how a people's common sense can be shifted in conservative directions during a time of economic and ideological crisis.

Neoconservatism: Teaching "Real" Knowledge

Although neoliberals largely are in leadership in the conservative alliance, I noted that the second major element within the new alliance is neoconservatism. Unlike the neoliberal emphasis on the weak state, neoconservatives are usually guided by a vision of the strong state. This is especially true surrounding issues of knowledge, values, and the body. Whereas neoliberalism may be seen as being based in what Raymond Williams would call an "emergent" ideological assemblage, neoconservatism is grounded in "residual" forms.[29] It is largely, though not totally, based in a romantic appraisal of the past, a past in which "real knowledge" and morality reigned supreme, in which people "knew their place," and where stable communities guided by a natural order protected us from the ravages of society.[30]

Among the policies being proposed under this ideological position are mandatory national and statewide curricula, national and statewide testing, a "return" to higher standards, a revivification of the "Western tradition," patriotism, and conservative variants of character education. Yet underlying some of the neoconservative thrust in education and in social policy in general is not only a call for "return." Behind it as well—and this is essential—is a fear of the "Other," fears that have been exacerbated and often cynically employed for political purposes and used to drive wedges between religious traditions since the tragedy of September 11. This is expressed in its support for a standardized national curriculum, its attacks on bilingualism and multiculturalism, and its insistent call for raising standards.[31]

That the neoconservative emphasis on a return to traditional values and "morality" has struck a responsive chord can be seen in the fact that among the best-selling books in the nation during the past decade was William Bennett's *The Book of Virtues*.[32] Bennett, a former Secretary of Education in a conservative Republican administration, has argued that for too long a period of time, "We have stopped doing the right things [and] allowed an assault on intellectual and moral standards." In opposition to this, we need "a renewed commitment to excellence, character, and fundamentals."[33] Bennett's book aims at providing "moral tales" for children to "restore" a commitment to "traditional virtues" such as patriotism, honesty, moral character, and entrepreneurial spirit. Such positions not only have entered the common sense of society in quite influential ways but also have provided part of the driving force behind the movement toward charter schools. These schools have individual charters that allow them to opt out of most state requirements and develop curricula based on the wishes of their clientele. Although in theory there is much to commend in such policies, as I demonstrate later all too many charter schools have become ways through which conservative religious activists and others gain public funding for schools—and home schooling—that would otherwise be prohibited such support.[34]

Behind much of the neoconservative position is a clear sense of loss—a loss of faith, of imagined communities, of a nearly pastoral vision of like-minded people who shared norms and values and in which the "Western tradition" reigned supreme. It is more than a little similar to Mary Douglas's discussion of purity and danger, in which what was imagined to exist is sacred and "pollution" is feared above all else.[35] We/they binary oppositions dominate this discourse and the culture of the "Other" is to be feared.

This sense of cultural pollution can be seen in the increasingly virulent attacks on multiculturalism (which is itself a very broad category that combines multiple political and cultural positions),[36] on the offering of schooling or any other social benefits to the children of "illegal" immigrants and even in some cases to the children of legal immigrants, in the conservative English-only movement, and in the equally conservative attempts to reorient curricula and textbooks toward a particular construction of the Western tradition.

In this regard, neoconservatives lament the "decline" of the traditional curriculum and of the history, literature, and values it is said to have represented.[37] Behind this worry is a set of historical assumptions about "tradition," about the existence of a social consensus over what should count as legitimate knowledge, and about cultural superiority.[38] Yet it is crucial to remember that the "traditional" curriculum whose decline is lamented so fervently by neoconservative critics "ignored most of the groups that compose the American population whether they were from Africa, Europe, Asia, Central and South America, or from indigenous North American peoples."[39] Its primary and often exclusive focus was typically only on quite a narrow spectrum of those people who came from a small number of northern and Western European nations, in spite of the fact that the cultures and histories represented in the United States were "forged out of a much larger and more diverse complex of peoples and societies." The mores and cultures of this narrow spectrum were seen as archetypes of "tradition" for everyone. They were not simply taught, but taught as superior to every other set of mores and culture.[40]

As Lawrence Levine reminds us, a selective and faulty sense of history fuels the nostalgic yearnings of neoconservatives. The canon and the curriculum have never been static. They have always been in a constant process of revision, "with irate defenders insisting, as they still do, that change would bring with it instant decline."[41] Indeed, even the inclusion of such "classics" as Shakespeare within the curriculum of schools in the United States came about only after prolonged and intense battles, ones that were the equal of the divisive debates over whose knowledge should be taught today. Thus, Levine notes that when neoconservative cultural critics ask for a "return" to a "common culture" and "tradition," they are oversimplifying to the point of distortion. What is happening in terms of the expansion and alteration of official knowledge in schools and universities today "is by no means out of the ordinary; certainly it is not a radical departure from the patterns that have marked the history of [education]—constant and often controversial expansion and alteration of curricula and canons and incessant struggle over the nature of that expansion and alteration."[42]

Of course, such conservative positions have been forced into a kind of compromise in order to maintain their cultural and ideological leadership as a movement to "reform" educational policy and practice. A prime example is the emerging discourse over the history curriculum—in particular the construction of the United States as a "nation of immigrants."[43] In this hegemonic discourse, everyone in the history of the nation was an immigrant, from the first Native American population who supposedly trekked across the Bering Strait and ultimately populated North, Central, and South America, to the later waves of populations who came from Africa, Mexico, Ireland, Germany, Scandinavia, Italy, Russia, Poland, and elsewhere, to finally the recent populations from Asia, Latin America, Africa, and other regions. Although it is true that the United States is constituted by people from all over the world—and that is one of the things that makes it so culturally rich and vital—such a perspective constitutes an erasure of historical memory. For some groups came *in chains,* with massive numbers of death in the Middle Passage, and were subjected to state-sanctioned slavery and apartheid for hundreds of years. Others suffered what can only be called bodily, linguistic, and cultural destruction.[44]

This said, however, it does point to the fact that although the neo-conservative goals of national curricula and national testing are pressed for, they are strongly mediated by the necessity of compromise. Because of this, even the strongest supporters of neoconservative educational programs and policies have had to also support the creation of curricula that at least partly recognize "the contributions of the Other."[45] This is partly because there is an absence of an overt and strong national department of education and a tradition of state and local control of schooling. The "solution" has been to have national standards developed "voluntarily" in each subject area.[46] Indeed, the example I gave earlier about history is one of the results of such voluntary standards.

Because it is the national professional organizations in these subject areas—such as the National Council of Teachers of Mathematics (NCTM)—that are developing such national standards, the standards themselves are compromises and thus are often more flexible than those wished for by neoconservatives. This very process does act to provide a check on conservative policies over knowledge. However, this should not lead to an overly romantic picture of the overall tendencies emerging in educational policy. Leadership in school "reform" is increasingly dominated by conservative discourses surrounding "standards," "excellence," "accountability," and so on. Because the more flexible parts of the standards have proven to be too expensive to actually implement and have generated considerable conservative backlash,[47] standards talk ultimately functions to give more rhetorical weight to the neoconservative movement to enhance central control over "official knowledge" and to "raise the bar" for achievement. The social implications of this in terms of creating even more differential school results are increasingly worrisome.[48]

Yet it is not only in such things as the control over legitimate knowledge where neoconservative impulses are seen. The idea of a strong state is also visible in the growth of the regulatory state as it concerns teachers. There has been a steadily growing change from "licensed autonomy" to "regulated autonomy" as teachers' work is more highly standardized, rationalized, and "policed."[49] Under conditions of licensed autonomy, once teachers are given the appropriate professional certification they are basically free—within limits—to act in their classrooms according to their judgment. Such a regime is based on trust in "professional discretion." Under the growing conditions of regulated autonomy, teachers' actions are now subject to much greater scrutiny in terms of process and outcomes.[50] Indeed, some states in the United States not only have specified the content that teachers are to teach but also have regulated the only appropriate methods of teaching. Not following these specified "appropriate" methods puts the teacher at risk of administrative sanctions. Such a regime of control is based not on trust, but on a deep suspicion of the motives and competence of teachers. For neoconservatives it is the equivalent of the notion of "producer capture" that is so powerful among neoliberals. For the former, however, it is not the market that will solve this problem, but a strong and interventionist state that will see to it that only "legitimate" content and methods are taught. And this will be policed by statewide and national tests of both students and teachers. The imprint of these kinds of commitments are thoroughly visible in such policies as No Child Left Behind, something I will document at much greater length in Chapter 4.

I have claimed elsewhere that such policies lead to the "deskilling" of teachers, the "intensification" of their work, and the loss of autonomy and respect. This is not surprising, as behind much of this conservative impulse is a clear distrust of teachers and an attack both on teachers' claims to competence and especially on teachers' unions.[51]

The mistrust of teachers, the concern over a supposed loss of cultural control, and the sense of dangerous "pollution" are among the many cultural and social fears that drive neoconservative policies. However, as I noted earlier, underpinning these positions as well is often an ethnocentric, and even racialized, understanding of the world. Perhaps this can be best illuminated through the example of Herrnstein and Murray's volume, *The Bell Curve*.[52] In a book that sold hundreds of thousands of copies, the authors argue for a genetic determinism based on race (and to some extent gender). For them, it is romantic to assume that educational and social policies can ultimately lead to more equal results, since differences in intelligence and achievement are basically genetically driven. The wisest thing policy makers can do would be to accept this and plan for a society that recognizes these biological differences and does not provide "false hopes" to the poor and the less intelligent, most of whom will be black. Obviously, this book has reinforced racist stereotypes that have long played a considerable part in educational and social policies in the United States.[53]

Rather than seeing race as it is—as a fully *social* category that is mobilized and used in different ways by different groups at different times[54]—positions such as those argued by Herrnstein and Murray provide a veneer of seeming scientific legitimacy for policy discourses that have been discredited intellectually many times before. The sponsored mobility given to this book, in which it is reported that the authors received large sums of money from neoconservative foundations to write and publicize the volume, speaks clearly not only to the racial underpinnings of important parts of the neoconservative agenda but also to the power of conservative groups to bring their case before the public. (As we shall see in Chapter 4, the same foundations that supported such racializing discourses are behind attempts to bring some African-American and Latino/a groups under the umbrella of conservative leadership, with voucher plans being the wedge issue in this case.)

The consequences of such positions are not only found in educational policies, but in the intersection of such policies with broader social and economic policies, where they have been quite influential. Here too we can find claims that what the poor lack is not money, but both an "appropriate" biological inheritance and a decided lack of values regarding discipline, hard work, and morality.[55] Prime examples here include programs such as "Learnfare" and "Workfare" in which parents lose a portion of their welfare benefits if their children miss a significant number of school days or in which no benefits are paid if a person does not accept low-paid work, no matter how demeaning or even if child care or health care are not provided by the state. Such policies reinstall earlier "workhouse" policies that were so popular—and so utterly damaging—in the United States, Britain, and elsewhere.[56]

I have spent much of my time in this section documenting the growing power of neoconservative positions in educational and social policy in the United States. Neoconservatives have forged a creative coalition with neoliberals, a coalition that—in concert with other groups—is effectively changing the landscape on which policies are argued out. Yet, even given the growing influence of neoliberal and neoconservative policies, they would be considerably less successful if they had not also brought authoritarian populist religious fundamentalists and conservative evangelicals under the umbrella of the conservative alliance. It is to this group that we now turn.

Authoritarian Populism: Schooling as God Wanted It

Perhaps more than in any other major industrialized nation, it is not possible to fully understand educational politics in the United States without paying a good deal of attention to the "Christian Right." It is exceptionally powerful and influential, beyond its numbers, in debates over public policy in the media, education, social welfare, the politics of sexuality and the body, religion, and so on. Its influence comes from the immense commitment by activists within it, its large financial base, its populist rhetorical positions, and its aggressiveness in pursuing its agenda. As I showed in Chapter 1, "New Right" authoritarian populists ground their positions on education and social policy in general in particular visions of biblical authority, "Christian morality," gender roles, and the family.

The New Right sees gender and the family, for instance, as an organic and divine unity that resolves "male egoism and female selflessness."

As Hunter puts it:

> Since gender is divine and natural ... there is [no] room for legitimate political conflict. ... Within the family women and men—stability and dynamism—are harmoniously fused when undisturbed by modernism, liberalism, feminism, and humanism which not only threaten masculinity and femininity directly, but also [do so] through their effects on children and youth. ... "Real women," i.e., women who know themselves as wives *and* mothers, will not threaten the sanctity of the home by striving for self. When men or women challenge these gender roles they break with God and nature; when liberals, feminists, and secular humanists prevent them from fulfilling these roles they undermine the divine and natural supports upon which society rests.[57]

In the minds of such groups, public schooling thus is *itself* a site of immense danger, a point I develop in considerably more detail in Chapters 5, 6, 7, and 8. In the words of the conservative activist Tim LaHaye, "Modern public education is the most dangerous force in a child's life: religiously, sexually, economically, patriotically, and physically."[58] This is connected to the New Right's sense of loss surrounding schooling and the family.

> Until recently, as the New Right sees it, schools were extensions of home and traditional morality. Parents could entrust their children to public schools because they were locally controlled and reflected Biblical and parental values. However, taken over by alien, elitist forces, schools now interpose themselves between parents and children. Many people experience fragmentation of the unity between family, church, and school as a loss of control of daily life, one's children, and America. Indeed, [the New Right] argues that parental control of education is Biblical, for in God's plan, the primary responsibility for educating the young lies in the home and directly in the father.[59]

It is exactly this sense of "alien and elite control," the loss of biblical connections, and the destruction of "God-given" family and moral structures that drives the authoritarian populist agenda. It is an agenda that is increasingly powerful, not only rhetorically, but in terms of funding and in conflicts over what schools should do, how they should be financed, and who should control them. This agenda includes, but goes beyond, issues of gender, sexuality, and the family. It extends as well to a much larger array of questions about what is to count as "legitimate" knowledge in schools. And in this larger arena of concern about the entire corpus of school knowledge, conservative activists have had no small measure of success in pressuring textbook publishers to change what they include and in altering important aspects of state educational policy on teaching, curriculum, and evaluation. This is crucial, as in the absence of an overt national curriculum, the commercially produced *textbook*—regulated by individual state's purchases and authority—remains the dominant definition of the curriculum in the United States,[60] a point to which I return in Chapter 5.

The power of these groups is visible, for example, in the "self-censorship" in which publishers engage. For instance, under conservative pressure a number of publishers of high school literature anthologies have chosen to include Martin Luther King's "I Have a Dream" speech, but *only* after all references to the intense racism of the United States have been removed.[61] At the level of state curriculum policy, this is very visible in the textbook legislation in, say, Texas, which mandates texts that stress patriotism, obedience to authority, and the discouragement of "deviance."[62] Because most textbook publishers aim the content and organization of their textbooks at what will be approved by a small number of populous states that in essence approve and purchase their textbooks *statewide,* this gives states such as Texas (and California) immense power in determining what will count as "official knowledge" throughout the entire country.[63]

Thus, in concert with neoconservative elements within the conservative alliance, authoritarian populist religious activists have had a substantial influence on curriculum policy and practice. For them, only by recentering issues of authority, morality, family, church, and "decency" can schools overcome the "moral decay" so evident all around us.[64] Only by returning to inerrantist understandings of biblical teachings and fostering (or mandating) a climate in schools where such teachings are given renewed emphasis can our culture be saved.[65]

As I showed in *Cultural Politics and Education,* although a number of states and school systems have been able to create mechanisms that deflect some of these pressures, the bureaucratic nature of many school systems and of the local and regional state in general has actually produced the conditions where parents and other community members who might otherwise disagree with the New Right ideologically are convinced to join them in their attacks on the content and organization of schooling.[66]

Although authoritarian populist struggles over curriculum and texts have been growing rapidly, this mistrust of public schools has also fueled considerable and intense support among them for neoliberal policies such as voucher and choice plans. The New Right, as a largely populist assemblage, has some very real mistrust of the motives and economic plans of capital. After all, such rightist populists have themselves experienced the effects of downsizing, layoffs, and economic restructuring. However, even given their partial insights into the differential effects of global competition and economic restructuring, they see in proposals for educational marketization and privatization a way in which they can use such "reforms" for their own purposes. Either through reduced school taxes, through tax credits, or through the allocation of public money to private and religious schools, they can create a set of schools organized around the more moral "imagined communities" they believe have been lost.[67] I take this up in more detail later on.

This search for the reconstitution of imagined communities points to one of the effects of reprivatization talk on the politics surrounding educational policy. In the process of denying the legitimacy of oppositional claims, reprivatization discourses may actually tend to politicize the issues even more. These issues become even more a part of public, not "domestic," contestation. This paradox—reprivatization talk may actually lead to further public discussion of breakaway needs—does not always lead to victories by oppositional groups such as feminists, racially subjected peoples, or other disempowered groups, however. Rather, such politicization can in fact lead to the growth of new social movements and new social identities whose fundamental aim is to push breakaway needs back into the economic, domestic, and private spheres. New, and quite conservative, coalitions can be formed.

This is exactly what has happened in the United States, where a set of reprivatizing discourses "in the accents of authoritarian populism" has made creative connections with the hopes and especially the fears of a range of disaffected constituencies and has united them into a tense but very effective alliance supporting positions behind reprivatization.[68] And this could not have been done if rightist groups had not succeeded in changing the very meaning of key concepts of democracy in such a way that the Christian Right could comfortably find a place under the larger umbrella of the conservative alliance.

The Professional and Managerial New Middle Class:
More Testing, More Often

Although I speak somewhat more briefly about them here because of their relatively limited—but rapidly growing—power, as I argued in Chapter 1 and as I will argue in more detail in Chapter 4 there is a final group that provides some of the support for the policies of conservative modernization. This is a fraction of the professional new middle class that gains its own mobility within the state and within the economy based on the use of technical expertise. These are people with backgrounds in management and efficiency techniques who provide the technical and "professional" support for accountability, measurement, "product control," and assessment that is required by the proponents of neoliberal policies of marketization and neoconservative policies of tighter central control in education.

Members of this fraction of the upwardly mobile professional and managerial new middle class do not necessarily believe in the ideological positions that underpin the conservative alliance. In fact, in other aspects of their lives they may be considerably more moderate and even "liberal" politically. However, as experts in efficiency, management, testing, and accountability, they provide the technical expertise to put in place the policies of conservative modernization. Their own mobility *depends* on the expansion of both such expertise and the professional ideologies of control, measurement, and efficiency that accompany it. Thus, they often support such policies as "neutral instrumentalities," even when these policies may be used for purposes other than the supposedly neutral ends to which this class fraction is committed.[69]

Because of this situation, it is important to realize that a good deal of the current emphasis in schools on high-stakes testing, on more rigorous forms of accountability, and on tighter control is not totally reducible to the needs of neoliberals and neoconservatives. Rather, part of the pressure for these policies comes from educational managers and bureaucratic offices who fully believe that such control is warranted and "good." Not only do these forms of control have an extremely long history in education, but tighter control, high-stakes testing, and (reductive) accountability methods provide more dynamic roles for such managers, a point I noted earlier. These policies enable such actors to engage in a moral crusade and enhance the status of their own expertise.

Yet, in a time when competition for credentials and cultural capital is intense, the increasing power of mechanisms of restratification such as the return of high levels of mandatory standardization also provides mechanisms that enhance the chances that the children of the professional and managerial new middle class will have *less competition* from other children. Thus, the introduction of devices to restratify a population enhances the value of the credentials that the new middle class is more likely to accumulate, given the stock of cultural capital it already possesses.[70] I am not claiming that this is necessarily intentional, but creating such devices does *function* to increase the chances for mobility by middle-class children who depend not on economic capital but on cultural capital for advancement.

In such a situation, I believe that this group is not immune to ideological shifts to the right. Given the fear generated by the attacks on the state and on the public sphere by both neoliberals and neoconservatives, this class fraction is decidedly worried about the future mobility of its children in an uncertain economic world. Thus, they may be drawn more overtly to parts of the conservative alliance's positions, especially those coming from the neoconservative elements that stress greater attention to traditional "high-status" content, greater attention to testing, and a greater emphasis on schooling as a stratifying mechanism. This can be seen in a number of states where parents of this class fraction are supporting charter schools that will stress academic achievement in traditional subjects and traditional teaching practices. Where the majority of members of this class grouping will align in the future in the debates over policy remains to be seen. Given their contradictory ideological tendencies, it is possible that the right will be able to mobilize them under conditions of fear for the future of their jobs and children.[71] I shall also discuss this in greater detail in Chapter 4.

Conclusion

Because of the complexity of educational politics in the United States, I have devoted most of this chapter to an analysis of the conservative social movements that are having a powerful impact on debates over policy and practice in education and in the larger social arena. I have suggested that conservative modernization in education is guided by a tense coalition of forces, some of whose aims partly contradict others.

The very nature of this coalition is crucial. It is more than a little possible that the alliance underpinning conservative modernization can overcome its own internal contradictions and can succeed in radically transforming educational policy and practice. Thus, although neoliberals call for a weak state and neoconservatives demand a strong state, these very evident contradictory impulses can come together in creative ways. The emerging focus on centralized standards, content, and tighter control paradoxically can be the first and most essential step on the path to marketization through voucher and choice plans.

Once statewide or national curricula and tests are put in place, comparative school-by-school data will be available and will be published in a manner similar to the "league tables" on school achievement published in England. Only when there is standardized content and assessment can the market be set free, since the "consumer" can then have "objective" data on which schools are "succeeding" and which schools are not. Market rationality, based on "consumer choice," will ensure that the supposedly good schools will gain students and the bad schools will disappear. This assemblage is embodied in many of the impulses behind No Child Left Behind, for example.

In my next two chapters, I focus on the effects of this and similar kinds of policies on real schools. But let me say here that one of these effects is that when the poor "choose" to keep their children in underfunded and decaying schools in the inner cities or in rural areas (given the decline and expense of urban mass transportation, poor information, the absence of time, and their decaying economic conditions, to name but a few of the realities), *they* (the poor) will be blamed individually and collectively for making bad "consumer choices." Reprivatizing discourses and arithmetical particularism will justify the structural inequalities that will be (re)produced here. In this way, as odd as it may seem, neoliberal and neoconservative policies, ones ultimately supported by authoritarian populists and even by many members of the professional middle class, that are seemingly contradictory may mutually reinforce each other in the long run,[72] a point I also take up in the next chapter.

Yet, although I have argued that the overall leadership in educational policy is exercised by this alliance, I do not want to give the impression that these four elements under the hegemonic umbrella of this coalition are uncontested or are always victorious. This is simply not the case. As a number of people have demonstrated, scores of counterhegemonic programs and possibilities exist at the local level throughout the United States. Many institutions of higher education, schools, and even entire school districts have shown remarkable resiliency in the face of the concerted ideological attacks and pressures from conservative restorational groups. And many teachers, academics, community activists, and others have created and defended educational programs that are both pedagogically and politically emancipatory.[73]

Indeed, we are beginning to see cracks in the alliance's power in unanticipated ways. For example, a growing number of students in elementary, middle, and secondary schools are actively refusing to take the mandatory tests that many states have introduced. This action has been supported by groups of teachers, administrators, parents, and activists.[74] Clearly, things are bubbling up from below the surface whose effects will be "interesting" to say the least.

Having said this, however, it is important to note the obstacles in creating the conditions for large-scale movements to defend and build progressive policies. We need to remember that there is no powerful central ministry of education in the United States. Teachers' unions are relatively weak at a national level (nor is there any guarantee that teachers' unions always act progressively). There is no consensus about an "appropriate" progressive agenda in educational policy here, as there is a vast multiplicity of compelling (and unfortunately at times competing) agendas involving race/ethnicity, gender, sexuality, class, religion, "ability," and so on. Thus, it is structurally difficult to sustain long-term national movements for more progressive policies and practices.

Because of this, most counterhegemonic work is organized locally or regionally. However, there currently are growing attempts at building national coalitions around what might best be called a "decentered unity." Organizations such as the National Coalition of Educational Activists and those centered around "Rethinking Schools" are becoming more visible nationally.[75] None of these movements have the financial and organizational backing that stands behind the neoliberal, neoconservative, and authoritarian populist groups. None have the ability to bring their case before the "public" through the media and through foundations in the ways that conservative groups have been able to do. And none have the capacity or the resources to quickly mobilize a large base of nationally directed membership to challenge or promote specific policies in the ways that the members of the alliance can.

Yet, in the face of all of these structural, financial, and political dilemmas, the fact that so many groups of people have not been integrated under the alliance's hegemonic umbrella and have created scores of local examples of the very possibility of difference shows us in the most eloquent and lived ways that educational policies and practices do not go in any one unidimensional direction. Even more important, these multiple examples demonstrate that the success of conservative policies is never guaranteed. This is crucial in a time when it is easy to lose sight of what is necessary for an education worthy of its name.

Why taking a position that might be called "optimism, but without illusions" is important will become clearer in the next chapter, in which I discuss in much greater depth not only the effects of the forces of conservative modernization on the policies and practices of schools but also weaknesses of many of the ways the supposed alternative—"critical pedagogy"—deals with them.

CHAPTER 3

Producing Inequalities
Conservative Modernization
in Policy and Practice

Gritty Materialities

For the past two or more decades, even before the new hegemonic bloc I have been describing assumed power, a body of literature in education has grown that has sought to help us think politically about curriculum, teaching, and evaluation. I myself have participated in the building of these critical perspectives. Much of the literature on "critical pedagogies" has been politically and theoretically important and has helped us make a number of gains. However, given what I said in the past two chapters, this literature has some characteristics that limit its effectiveness in mounting serious challenges to what is happening all around us. It too often has not been sufficiently connected to the ways in which the current movement toward conservative modernization both has altered common sense and has transformed the material and ideological conditions surrounding schooling. It, thereby, sometimes becomes a form of what can best be called "romantic possibilitarian" rhetoric, in which the language of possibility substitutes for a consistent tactical analysis of what the balance of forces actually is and what is necessary to change it.[1]

In this chapter, I examine in even more detail the ways in which the social and cultural terrain of educational policy and discourse has been altered "on the ground" so to speak. I argue that we need to make closer connections between our theoretical and critical discourses on the one hand and the real transformations that are currently shifting educational policies and practices in fundamentally rightist directions on the other. Thus, part of my discussion is conceptual, but part of it appropriately is more empirical than in Chapter 2 in order for me to pull together what is known about the real and material effects of the shift to the right in education.

My focus on the "gritty materialities" of these effects is not meant to dismiss the importance of theoretical interventions. Nor is it meant to suggest that dominant discourses should not be constantly interrupted by the creative gains that have emerged from various neo-Marxist, feminist, postmodern, poststructural, postcolonial, queer, disability, environmental, and other communities. Indeed, critical pedagogies *require* the fundamental interruption of common sense. However, although the construction of new theories and utopian visions is important, it is equally crucial to base these theories and visions in an unromantic appraisal of the material and discursive terrain that now exists. Common sense is already being radically altered but not in directions that any of us on the left would find comforting. Without an analysis of such transformations and of the balance of forces that have created such discomforting alterations, without an analysis of the tensions, differential relations of power, and contradictions within it, we are left with increasingly elegant new theoretical formulations, but with a less than elegant understanding of the field of social power on which they operate.[2]

Right Turn

In his influential history of curriculum debates, Herbert Kliebard has documented that educational issues have consistently involved major conflicts and compromises among groups with competing visions of "legitimate" knowledge, what counts as "good" teaching and learning, and what is a "just" society.[3] That such conflicts have deep roots in conflicting views of racial, class, and gender justice in education and the larger society is ratified in even more critical recent work as well.[4] These competing visions have never had equal holds on the imagination of educators or the general citizenry nor have they ever had equal power to effect their visions. Because of this, no analysis of education can be fully serious without placing at its very core a sensitivity to the ongoing struggles that constantly shape the terrain on which education operates.

Today is no different from the past. As I argued in Chapter 2, a "new" set of compromises, a new alliance, and new power bloc have been formed that have increasing influence in education and all things social. This power bloc combines multiple fractions of capital who are committed to neoliberal marketized solutions to educational problems, neoconservative intellectuals who want a "return" to higher standards and a "common culture," authoritarian populist religious fundamentalists who are deeply worried about secularity and the preservation of their own traditions, and particular fractions of the professionally oriented new middle class who are committed to the ideology and techniques of accountability, measurement, and "management." Although clear tensions and conflicts exist within this alliance, in general its overall aims are to provide the educational conditions believed necessary both for increasing international competitiveness, profit, and discipline and for returning us to a romanticized past of the "ideal" home, family, and school.[5]

In essence, the new alliance has integrated education into a wider set of ideological commitments. The objectives in education are the same as those that guide its economic and social welfare goals. They include the dramatic expansion of that eloquent fiction, the free market; the drastic reduction of government responsibility for social needs; the reinforcement of intensely competitive structures of mobility both inside and outside the school; the lowering of people's expectations for economic security; the "disciplining" of culture and the body; and the popularization of what is clearly a form of Social Darwinist thinking, as the recent popularity of *The Bell Curve* so obviously and distressingly indicates.[6]

The seemingly contradictory discourse of competition, markets, and choice, on the one hand, and accountability, performance objectives, standards, national and state testing, and national and statewide curriculum, on the other, has created such a din that it is hard to hear anything else. Even though these seem to embody different tendencies, they actually oddly reinforce each other and help cement conservative educational positions into our daily lives.[7]

Although lamentable, the changes that are occurring present an exceptional opportunity for serious critical reflection. In a time of radical social and educational change, it is crucial to document the processes and effects of the various and sometimes contradictory elements of the conservative restoration and of the ways in which they are mediated, compromised with, accepted, used in different ways by different groups for their own purposes, and/or struggled over in the policies and practices of people's daily educational lives.[8] I give a more detailed sense of how this might be happening in current "reforms" such as marketization and national curricula and national testing in this chapter and then extend it in the following one. For those interested in critical educational policies and practices, not to do this means that we act without understanding the shifting relations of power that are constructing and reconstructing the social field of power. Although Gramsci's saying "Pessimism of the intellect, optimism of the will" has a powerful resonance to it and is useful for mobilization and for not losing hope, it would be foolish to substitute rhetorical slogans for the fuller analysis that is undoubtedly required if we are to be successful.

New Markets, Old Traditions

Historically, behind a good deal of the New Right's emerging discursive ensemble was a position that emphasized "a culturalist construction of the nation as a (threatened) haven for white (Christian) traditions and values."[9] This involved the construction of an imagined national past that is at least partly mythologized, and then employing it to castigate the present. Gary McCulloch argues that the nature of the historical images of schooling has changed. Dominant imagery of education as being "safe, domesticated, and progressive" (that is, as leading toward progress and social/personal improvement) has shifted to become "threatening, estranged, and regressive."[10] The past is no longer the source of stability but a mark of failure, disappointment, and loss. This is seen most vividly in the attacks on the "progressive orthodoxy" that supposedly now reigns supreme in classrooms in many nations.[11]

For example, in England—although much the same is echoed in the United States, Australia, and elsewhere—Michael Jones, the political editor of *The Sunday Times,* recalls the primary school of his day:

> Primary school was a happy time for me. About 40 of us sat at fixed wooden desks with ink wells and moved from them only with grudging permission. Teacher sat in a higher desk in front of us and moved only to the blackboard. She smelled of scent and inspired awe.[12]

The mix of metaphors invoking discipline, scent (visceral and almost "natural"), and awe is fascinating. But he goes on, lamenting the past thirty years of "reform" that transformed primary schools. Speaking of his own children's experience, Jones says:

My children spent their primary years in a showplace school where they were allowed to wander around at will, develop their real individuality and dodge the 3Rs. It was all for the best, we were assured. But it was not.[13]

For Jones, the "dogmatic orthodoxy" of progressive education "had led directly to educational and social decline." Only the rightist reforms instituted in the 1980s and 1990s could halt and then reverse this decline.[14] Only then could the imagined past return.

Much the same is being said on this side of the Atlantic. These sentiments are echoed in the public pronouncements of such figures as William Bennett, E. D. Hirsch Jr., Diane Ravitch, and others, all of whom seem to believe that progressivism is now in the dominant position in educational policy and practice and has destroyed a valued past. All of them believe that only by tightening control over curriculum and teaching (and students, of course), restoring "our" lost traditions, making education more disciplined and competitive as they are certain it was in the past—only then can we have effective schools. These figures are joined by others who have similar criticisms, but who instead turn to a different past for a different future. Their past is less that of scent and awe and authority, but one of market "freedom." For them, nothing can be accomplished—even the restoration of awe and authority—without setting the market loose on schools so as to ensure that only "good" ones survive.

We should understand that these policies are radical transformations. If they had come from the other side of the political spectrum, they would have been ridiculed in many ways, given the ideological tendencies in our nations. Furthermore, not only are these policies based on a romanticized pastoral past, these reforms have not been notable for their grounding in research findings. Indeed, when research has been used, it has often either served as a rhetoric of justification for preconceived beliefs about the supposed efficacy of markets or regimes of tight accountability or they have been based—as in the case of Chubb and Moe's much publicized work on marketization—on quite flawed research.[15]

Yet, no matter how radical some of these proposed "reforms" are and no matter how weak the empirical basis of their support, they have now redefined the terrain of debate of all things educational. After years of conservative attacks and mobilizations, it has become clear that "ideas that were once deemed fanciful, unworkable—or just plain extreme" are now increasingly being seen as common sense.[16]

Tactically, the reconstruction of common sense that has been accomplished has proven to be extremely effective. For example, clear discursive strategies are being employed here, ones that are characterized by "plain speaking" and speaking in a language that "everyone can understand." (I do not wish to be wholly negative about this. The importance of these things is something many "progressive" educators, including many writers on critical pedagogy, have yet to understand.)[17] These strategies also involve not only presenting one's own position as "common sense," but also usually tacitly implying that there is something of a conspiracy among one's opponents to deny the truth or to say only that which is "fashionable."[18] As Gillborn notes,

> This is a powerful technique. First, it assumes that there are no genuine arguments against the chosen position; any opposing views are thereby positioned as false, insincere or self-serving. Second, the technique presents the speaker as someone brave or honest enough to speak the (previously) unspeakable. Hence, the moral high ground is assumed and opponents are further denigrated.[19]

It is hard to miss these characteristics in some of the conservative literature such as Herrnstein and Murray's publicizing of the unthinkable "truth" about genetics and intelligence or E. D. Hirsch's latest "tough" discussion of the destruction of "serious" schooling by progressive educators.[20]

Markets and Performance

Let us take as an example of the ways in which all of these arguments operate one element of conservative modernization—the neoliberal claim that the invisible hand of the market will inexorably lead to better schools. As Roger Dale reminds us, "the market" acts as a metaphor rather than an explicit guide for action. It is not denotative, but connotative. Thus, it must itself be "marketed" to those who will exist in it and live with its effects.[21] Markets are marketed, are made legitimate, by a depoliticizing strategy. They are said to be natural and neutral, and governed by effort and merit. And those opposed to them are by definition, hence, also opposed to effort and merit. Markets, as well, are supposedly less subject to political interference and the weight of bureaucratic procedures. Plus, they are grounded in the rational choices of individual actors.[22] Thus, markets and the guarantee of rewards for effort and merit are to be coupled together to produce "neutral," yet positive, results. Mechanisms, hence, must be put into place that give evidence of entrepreneurial efficiency and effectiveness. This coupling of markets and mechanisms for the generation of evidence of performance is exactly what has occurred. Whether it works is open to question. Indeed, as I shall show shortly, in practice neoliberal policies involving market "solutions" may actually serve to reproduce—not subvert—traditional hierarchies of class and race. Perhaps this should give us reason to pause?[23]

Thus, rather than taking neoliberal claims at face value, we should want to ask about their hidden effects that are too often invisible in the rhetoric and metaphors of their proponents. I shall select a number of issues that have been given less attention than they deserve, but on which there is now significant research.

The English experience is apposite here, especially since proponents of the market such as Chubb and Moe rely so heavily on it[24] and because that is where the tendencies I analyze are most advanced. In England, the 1993 Education Act documents the state's commitment to marketization. Governing bodies of local educational authorities (LEAs) were mandated to formally consider "going GM" (that is, opting out of the local school system's control and entering into the competitive market) every year.[25] Thus, the weight of the state stood behind the press toward neoliberal reforms there.[26] Yet, rather than leading to curriculum responsiveness and diversification, the competitive market has not created much that is different from the traditional models so firmly entrenched in schools today.[27] Nor has it radically altered the relations of inequality that characterize schooling.

In their own extensive analyses of the effects of marketized reforms "on the ground," Ball and his colleagues point to some of the reasons why we need to be quite cautious here. As they document, in these situations educational principles and values are often compromised such that commercial issues become more important in curriculum design and resource allocation.[28] For instance, the coupling of markets with the demand for and publication of performance indicators such as "examination league tables" in England has meant that schools are increasingly looking for ways to attract "motivated" parents with "able" children. In this way, schools are able to enhance their relative position in local systems of competition. This represents a subtle but crucial shift in emphasis—one that is not openly discussed as often as it should be—from student needs to student performance and from what the school does for the student to what the student does for the school. This is also accompanied too uncomfortably often by a shift of resources away from students who are labeled as having special needs or learning difficulties, with some of these needed resources now being shifted to marketing and public relations. "Special needs" students not only are expensive but also deflate test scores on those all important league tables.

Not only does this make it difficult to "manage public impressions," but it also makes it difficult to attract the "best" and most academically talented teachers.[29] The entire enterprise does, however, establish a new metric and a new set of goals based on a constant striving to win the market game. What this means is of considerable import, not only in terms of its effects on daily school life but in the ways all of this signifies a transformation of what counts as a good society and a responsible citizen. Let me say something about this generally.

I noted earlier that behind all educational proposals are visions of a just society and a good student. The neoliberal reforms I have been discussing construct this in a particular way. While the defining characteristic of neoliberalism is largely based on the central tenets of classical liberalism, in particular classic economic liberalism, there are crucial differences between classical liberalism and neoliberalism. These differences are absolutely essential in understanding the politics of education and the transformations education is currently undergoing. Mark Olssen clearly details these differences in the following passage. It is worth quoting in its entirety.

> Whereas classical liberalism represents a negative conception of state power in that the individual was to be taken as an object to be freed from the interventions of the state, neo-liberalism has come to represent a positive conception of the state's role in creating the appropriate market by providing the conditions, laws and institutions necessary for its operation. In classical liberalism, the individual is characterized as having an autonomous human nature and can practice freedom. In neo-liberalism the state seeks to create an individual who is an enterprising and competitive entrepreneur. In the classical model the theoretical aim of the state was to limit and minimize its role based on postulates which included universal egoism (the self-interested individual); invisible hand theory which dictated that the interests of the individual were also the interests of the society as a whole; and the political maxim of laissez-faire. In the shift from classical liberalism to neo-liberalism, then, there is a further element added, for such a shift involves a change in subject position from "homo economicus," who naturally behaves out of self-interest and is relatively detached from the state, to "manipulatable man," who is created by the state and who is continually encouraged to be "perpetually responsive." It is not

that the conception of the self-interested subject is replaced or done away with by the new ideals of "neo-liberalism," but that in an age of universal welfare, the perceived possibilities of slothful indolence create necessities for new forms of vigilance, surveillance, "performance appraisal" and of forms of control generally. In this model the state has taken it upon itself to keep us all up to the mark. The state will see to it that each one makes a "continual enterprise of ourselves" ... in what seems to be a process of "governing without governing."[30]

The results of Ball and his colleagues' research document how the state does indeed do this, enhancing that odd combination of marketized individualism and control through constant and comparative public assessment. Widely publicized league tables determine one's relative value in the educational marketplace. Only those schools with rising performance indicators are worthy. And only those students who can "make a continual enterprise of themselves" can keep such schools going in the "correct" direction, a discussion to which I return shortly. Yet, although these issues are important, they fail to fully illuminate some of the other mechanisms through which *differential* effects are produced by neoliberal reforms. Here, class issues come to the fore in ways that Ball, Bowe, and Gewirtz make clear.

Middle-class parents are clearly the most advantaged in this kind of cultural assemblage, and not only as we saw because schools seek them out. Middle-class parents have become quite skilled, in general, in exploiting market mechanisms in education and in bringing their social, economic, and cultural capital to bear on them.[31] "Middle-class parents are more likely to have the knowledge, skills and contacts to decode and manipulate what are increasingly complex and deregulated systems of choice and recruitment. The more deregulation, the more possibility of informal procedures being employed. The middle class also, on the whole, are more able to move their children around the system."[32] As I argue in more detail later on, both because class and race intersect and interact in complex ways and because marketized systems in education often *expressly* have their conscious and unconscious raison d'être in a fear of "the Other" and these often are hidden expressions of a racialization of educational policy, the differential results will "naturally" be decidedly raced as well as classed.[33]

Economic and social capital can be converted into cultural capital in various ways. In marketized plans, more affluent parents often have more flexible hours and can visit multiple schools. They have cars—often more than one—and can *afford* driving their children across town to attend a "better" school. They can as well provide the hidden cultural resources such as camps and after-school programs (dance, music, computer classes, etc.) that give their children an "ease," a "style," that seems "natural" and acts as a set of cultural resources. Their previous stock of social and cultural capital—who they know, their "comfort" in social encounters with educational officials—is an unseen but powerful storehouse of resources. Thus, more affluent parents are more likely to have the informal knowledge and skill—what Bourdieu would call the habitus[34]—to be able to decode and use marketized forms to their own benefit. This sense of what might be called "confidence"—which is itself the result of past choices that tacitly but no less powerfully depend on the economic resources to actually have had the ability to make economic choices—is the unseen capital that underpins their ability to negotiate marketized forms and "work the system" through sets of informal cultural rules.[35]

Of course, it needs to be said that working-class, poor, and/or immigrant parents are not skill-less in this regard, by any means. (After all, it requires an immense amount of skill, courage, and social and cultural resources to survive under exploitative and depressing material conditions. Thus, collective bonds, informal networks and contacts, and an ability to work the system are developed in quite nuanced, intelligent, and often impressive ways here.)[36] However, the match between the historically grounded habitus expected in schools and in its actors and those of more affluent parents, combined with the material resources available to more affluent parents, usually leads to a successful conversion of economic and social capital into cultural capital.[37] And this is exactly what is happening in England and elsewhere.

These claims both about what is happening inside of schools and about larger sets of power relations are supported by even more recent synthetic analyses of the overall results of marketized models. This research on the effects of the tense but still effective combination of neoliberal and neoconservative policies examines the tendencies internationally by comparing what has happened in a number of nations—for example, the United States, England and Wales, Australia, and New Zealand—where this combination has been increasingly powerful. The results confirm the arguments I have made here. Let me rehearse some of the most significant and disturbing findings of such research.

It is unfortunately all too usual that the most widely used measures of the "success" of school reforms are the results of standardized achievement tests. This simply will not do. We need to constantly ask what reforms do to schools as a whole and to each of their participants, including teachers, students, administrators, community members, local activists, and so on. To take one set of examples, as marketized "self-managing" schools grow in many nations, the role of the school principal is radically transformed. More, not less, power is actually consolidated within an administrative structure. More time and energy is spent on maintaining or enhancing a public image of a "good school" and less time and energy is spent on pedagogic and curricular substance. At the same time, teachers seem to be experiencing not increased autonomy and professionalism, but intensification.[38] And, oddly, as noted before, schools themselves become more *similar,* and more committed, to standard, traditional, whole-class methods of teaching and a standard and traditional (and often monocultural) curriculum.[39] Only directing our attention to test scores would cause us to miss some truly profound transformations, many of which we may find disquieting.

One of the reasons these broader effects are so often produced is that in all too many countries, neoliberal visions of quasi markets are usually accompanied by neoconservative pressure to regulate content and behavior through such things as national curricula, national standards, and national systems of assessment. The combination is historically contingent; that is, it is not absolutely necessary that the two emphases are combined. But neoliberalism has characteristics that make it more likely that an emphasis on the weak state and a faith in markets will cohere with an emphasis on the strong state and a commitment to regulating knowledge, values, and the body.

This is partly the case because of the increasing power of the "evaluative state" and the members of the managerial and professional middle class who tend to populate it. This signifies what initially may seem to be contradictory tendencies. At the same time as the state appears to be devolving power to individuals and autonomous institutions that are themselves increasingly competing in a market, the state remains strong in key areas.[40] As I claimed earlier, one of the key differences between classical liberalism and its faith in "enterprising individuals" in a market and current forms of neoliberalism is the latter's commitment to a regulatory state. Neoliberalism does indeed demand the constant production of evidence that one is in fact "making an enterprise of oneself."[41] Thus, under these conditions not only does education become a marketable commodity like bread and cars in which the values, procedures, and metaphors of business dominate, but its results must be reducible to standardized "performance indicators."[42] This is ideally suited to the task of providing a mechanism for the neoconservative attempts to specify what knowledge, values, and behaviors should be standardized and officially defined as "legitimate," a point I expand on in the next section of this chapter.

In essence, we are witnessing a process in which the state shifts the blame for the very evident inequalities in access and outcome it has promised to reduce, from itself onto individual schools, parents, and children. This is, of course, also part of a larger process in which dominant economic groups shift the blame for the massive and unequal effects of their own misguided decisions from themselves onto the state. The state is then faced with a very real crisis in legitimacy. Given this, we should not be at all surprised that the state will then seek to export this crisis outside itself.[43]

Of course, the state is not only classed but inherently *sex/gendered* and *raced* as well.[44] This is evident in Whitty, Power, and Halpin's arguments. They point to the gendered nature of the ways in which the management of schools is thought about, as "masculinist" business models become increasingly dominant.[45] Although there is a danger of these claims degenerating into reductive and essentializing arguments, there is a good deal of insight here. They do cohere with the work of other scholars inside and outside of education who recognize that the ways in which our very definitions of public and private, of what knowledge is of most worth, and of how institutions should be thought about and run are fully implicated in the gendered nature of this society.[46] These broad ideological effects—for example, enabling a coalition between neoliberals and neoconservatives to be formed; expanding the discourses and practices of new middle-class managerialism; the masculinization of theories, policies, and management talk—are of considerable import and make it harder to change common sense in more critical directions.

Other, more proximate, effects inside schools are equally striking. For instance, even though principals seem to have more local power in these supposedly decentralized schools, because of the cementing in of neoconservative policies principals "are increasingly forced into a position in which they have to demonstrate performance along centrally prescribed curricula in a context in which they have diminishing control."[47] Because of the intensification that I mentioned before, both principals and teachers experience considerably heavier workloads and ever-escalating demands for accountability, a never-ending schedule of meetings, and in many cases a growing scarcity of resources both emotional and physical.[48]

Furthermore, as in the research in England, in nearly all of the countries studied the market did not encourage diversity in curriculum, pedagogy, organization, clientele, or even image. It instead consistently devalued alternatives and increased the power of dominant models. Of equal significance, it also consistently exacerbated differences in access and outcome based on race, ethnicity, and class.[49]

The return to "traditionalism" led to a number of things. It *delegitimated* more critical models of teaching and learning, a point that is crucial to recognize in any attempt to think through the possibilities of cultural struggles and critical pedagogies in schools. It both reintroduced restratification within the school and lessened the possibility that de-tracking would occur. More emphasis was given to "gifted" children and "fast track" classes, whereas students who were seen as less academically able were therefore "less attractive." In England, the extent of this was nowhere more visible than in the alarming rate of students being excluded from schools. Much of this was caused by the intense pressure to constantly demonstrate higher achievement rates. This was especially powerful in marketized contexts in which the "main driving force appeared to be *commercial* rather than *educational*."[50]

In their own analysis of these worrisome and more hidden results, Whitty, Power, and Halpin and others demonstrate that among the dangerous effects of quasi markets are the ways in which schools that wish to maintain or enhance their market position engage in "cream-skimming," ensuring that particular kinds of students with particular characteristics are accepted and *particular* kinds of students are found wanting. For some schools, stereotypes were reproduced in that girls were seen as more valuable, as were students from some Asian communities. Afro-Caribbean children were often clear losers in this situation.[51]

So far I have focused largely on England. Yet, as I mentioned in my introductory points, these movements are truly global. Their logics have spread rapidly to many nations, with results that tend to mirror those I have discussed so far. The case of New Zealand is useful here, especially because a large percentage of the population of New Zealand is multi-ethnic, and the nation has a history of racial tensions and inequalities. Furthermore, the move toward New Right policies occurred faster there than elsewhere. In essence, New Zealand became the laboratory for many of the policies I am analyzing. In their exceptional study, based in large part on a conceptual apparatus influenced by Pierre Bourdieu, Lauder and Hughes document that educational markets seem to lead to an overall decline in educational standards. Paradoxically, they have a negative, not a positive, effect on the performance of schools with large working-class and minority populations. In essence, they "trade off the opportunities of less privileged children to those already privileged."[52] The combination of neoliberal policies of marketization and the neoconservative emphasis on "tougher standards," about which I say more in the next section, creates an even more dangerous set of conditions.

Lauder and Hughes's analysis confirms the conceptual and empirical arguments of Ball, Brown, and others that markets in education are not only responses by capital to reduce both the sphere of the state and of public control. They are also part of an attempt by the middle class to alter the rules of competition in education in light of the increased insecurities their children face. "By changing the process of selection to schools, middle class parents can raise the stakes in creating stronger mechanisms of exclusion for blue collar and post-colonial peoples in their struggle for equality of opportunity."[53]

The results from New Zealand not only mirror what was found elsewhere, but also demonstrate that the further one's practices follow the logics of action embodied in marketizing principles, the worse the situation tends to get. Markets *systematically* privilege families with higher socioeconomic status (SES) through their knowledge and material resources. These are the families who are most likely to exercise choice. Rather than giving large numbers of students who are working class, poor, or of color the ability to exit, it is largely higher SES families who exit from public schools and schools with mixed populations. In a situation of increased competition, this in turn produces a spiral of decline in which schools populated by poorer students and students of color are again systematically disadvantaged and schools with higher SES and higher white populations are able to insulate themselves from the effects of market competition.[54] "White flight" then enhances the relative status of those schools already advantaged by larger economic forces; schooling for the "Other" becomes even more polarized and continues a downward spiral.[55]

Having said this, however, we need to be cautious not to ignore historical specificities. Social movements, existing ideological formations, and institutions in civil society and the state may provide some support for countervailing logics. In some cases, in those nations with stronger and more extensive histories of social democratic policies and visions of collective positive freedoms, the neoliberal emphasis on the market has been significantly mediated. Hence, as Petter Aasen has demonstrated in Norway and Sweden, for instance, privatizing initiatives in education have had to cope with a greater collective commitment than in, say, the United States, England, and New Zealand.[56] However, these commitments partly rest on class relations. They are weakened when racial dynamics enter in. Thus, for example, the sense of "everyone being the same" and hence being all subject to similar collective sensibilities is challenged by the growth of immigrant populations from Africa, Asia, and the Middle East. Greater sympathy for marketized forms may arise once the commonly understood assumptions of what it means to be, say, Norwegian or Swedish are interrupted by populations of color who now claim the status of national citizenship. For this reason, it may be the case that the collective sensibilities that provide support for less market oriented policies are based on an unacknowledged *racial contract* that underpins the ideological foundations of a national "imagined community."[57] This, then, may also generate support for neoconservative policies, not because of neoliberalism's commitment to "perpetual responsiveness" but, rather, as a form of cultural restoration, as a way of reestablishing an imagined past when "we were all one." Because of this, it is important that any analysis of the current play of forces surrounding conservative modernization is aware of the fact that not only are such movements in constant motion, but once again we need to remember that they have a multitude of intersecting and contradictory dynamics including not only class but race and gender as well.[58]

Most of the data I have drawn on come from schools outside the United States, although they should make us stop dead in our tracks and give some very serious thought to whether we want to proceed with similar policies here. Yet the United States still sits at the center of much of the discussion in this literature. For example, charter schools and their equivalents in the United States and England are also put under critical scrutiny. In both places, although we need to be careful not to overstate this, they tend to attract parents who live and work in relatively privileged communities. Here, too, "it would appear that any new opportunities are being colonized by the already advantaged, rather than the 'losers' identified by Chubb and Moe."[59]

In the process, this critical research suggests that there are hidden similarities between advocates of school effectiveness research and those committed to neoliberal "reforms." Both tend to ignore the fact that external characteristics of schools such as poverty, political and economic power, and so on consistently account for much more of the variation in school performance than things like organizational features or those characteristics that supposedly guarantee an "effective school."[60]

The overall conclusions are clear. "[In] current circumstances choice is as likely to reinforce hierarchies as to improve educational opportunities and the overall quality of schooling."[61] As Whitty, Power, and Halpin put it in their arguments against those who believe that what we are witnessing in the emergence of "choice" programs is the postmodern celebration of difference:

> There is a growing body of empirical evidence that, rather than benefiting the disadvantaged, the emphasis on parental choice and school autonomy is further disadvantaging those least able

to compete in the market. ... For most disadvantaged groups, as opposed to the few individuals who escape from schools at the bottom of the status hierarchy, the new arrangements seem to be just a more sophisticated way of reproducing traditional distinctions between different types of school and the people who attend them.[62]

All of this critical information gives us ample reason to repeat Henig's insightful argument I quoted in the previous chapter that "the sad irony of the current education-reform movement is that, through over-identification with school-choice proposals rooted in market-based ideas, the healthy impulse to consider radical reforms to address social problems may be channeled into initiatives that further erode the potential for collective deliberation and collective response."[63]

This is not to dismiss either the possibility or necessity of school reform. However, we need to take seriously the probability that only by focusing on the exogenous socioeconomic features, not simply the organizational features, of "successful" schools can all schools succeed. Eliminating poverty through greater income parity, establishing effective and much more equal health and housing programs, and positively refusing to continue the hidden and not-so-hidden politics of racial exclusion and degradation that so clearly still characterize daily life in many nations (and in which marketized plans need to be seen as partly a structure to avoid the body and culture of the Other)—only by tackling these issues together can substantive progress be made.[64] Unless discussions of critical pedagogy are themselves grounded in a recognition of these realities, they too may fall into the trap of assuming that schools can do it alone.

These empirical findings are made more understandable in terms of Pierre Bourdieu's analysis of the relative weight given to cultural capital as part of mobility strategies today.[65] The rise in importance of cultural capital infiltrates all institutions in such a way that there is a relative movement away from the *direct* reproduction of class privilege (where power is transmitted largely within families through economic property) to *school-mediated* forms of class privilege. Here, "the bequeathal of privilege is simultaneously effectuated and transfigured by the intercession of educational institutions."[66] This is *not* a conspiracy; it is not "conscious" in the ways we normally use that concept. Rather, it is the result of a long chain of relatively autonomous connections between differentially accumulated economic, social, and cultural capital operating at the level of daily events as we make our respective ways in the world, including as we saw in the world of school choice.

Thus, although not taking an unyieldingly determinist position, Bourdieu argues that a class habitus tends to reproduce the conditions of its own reproduction "unconsciously." It does this by producing a relatively coherent and systematically *characteristic* set of seemingly natural and unconscious strategies—in essence, ways of understanding and acting on the world that act as forms of cultural capital that can be and are employed to protect and enhance one's status in a social field of power. He aptly compares this similarity of habitus across class actors to handwriting:

> Just as the acquired disposition we call "handwriting," that is a particular way of forming letters, always produces the same "writing"—that is, graphic lines that despite differences in size, matter, and color related to writing surface (sheet of paper or blackboard) and implement (pencil, pen, or chalk), that is despite differences in vehicles for the action, have an immediately recognizable affinity of style or a family resemblance—the practices of a single agent, or, more broadly, the practices of all agents endowed with similar habitus, owe the affinity of style that makes each a metaphor for the others to the fact that they are the products of the implementation in different fields of the same schemata of perception, thought, and action.[67]

This very connection of habitus across fields of power—the ease of bringing one's economic, social, and cultural resources to bear on "markets"—enables a comfort between markets and self that characterizes the middle-class actor here. This constantly *produces* differential effects. These effects are not neutral, no matter what the advocates of neoliberalism suggest. Rather, they are themselves the results of a particular kind of morality. Unlike the conditions of what might best be called "thick morality" where principles of the common good are the ethical basis for adjudicating policies and practices, markets are grounded in aggregative principles. They are constituted out of the sum of individual goods and choices. "Founded on individual and property rights that enable citizens to address problems of interdependence via exchange," they offer a prime example of "thin morality" by generating both hierarchy and division based on competitive individualism.[68] And in this competition, the general outline of the winners and losers *has* been identified empirically.

National Standards, National Curriculum, and National Testing

I showed in the previous section that there are connections between at least two dynamics operating in neoliberal reforms, "free" markets and increased surveillance. This can be seen in the fact that in many contexts, marketization has been accompanied by a set of particular policies for "producers," for those professionals working within education. These policies have been strongly regulatory and have been quite instrumental in reconstituting common sense. As in the case of the linkage between national tests and performance indicators published as league tables, they have been organized around a concern for external supervision, regulation, and external judgment of performance[69] and have increasingly been colonized by parents who possess what is seen as "appropriate" economic, social, and cultural capital. This concern for external supervision and regulation is not only connected with a strong mistrust of "producers" (e.g., teachers) and to the need for ensuring that people continually make enterprises out of themselves. It is also clearly linked both to the neoconservative sense of a need to "return" to a lost past of high standards, discipline, awe, and "real" knowledge and to the professional middle class' own ability to carve out a sphere of authority within the state for its own commitment to management techniques and efficiency. The focus on efficient management plays a prime role here, one that many neoliberals and neoconservatives alike find useful.

A shift has occurred in the relationship between the state and "professionals." In essence, the move toward a small strong state that is increasingly guided by market needs seems inevitably to bring with it reduced professional power and status.[70] Managerialism takes center stage here. Managerialism is largely charged with "bringing about the cultural transformation that shifts professional identities in order to make them more responsive to client demand and external judgement." It aims to justify and to have people internalize fundamental alterations in professional practices. It both harnesses energy and discourages dissent.[71]

There is no necessary contradiction between a general set of marketizing and deregulating interests and processes—such as voucher and choice plans—and a set of enhanced regulatory processes—such as plans for national or state standards, curricula, and testing.[72] "The regulatory form permits the state to maintain 'steerage' over the aims and processes of education from within the market mechanism."[73] Such "steerage at a distance" has often been vested in such things as national standards, national curricula, and national testing. Forms of all of these are being pushed for in the United States both at national and state levels currently and are the subject of considerable controversy, some of which cuts across ideological lines and shows some of the tensions within the different elements contained under the umbrella of conservative modernization.

I have argued that paradoxically a national curriculum and especially a national testing program are the first and most essential steps toward increased marketization. They actually provide the mechanisms for comparative data that "consumers" need to make markets work as markets.[74] Absent these mechanisms, there is no comparative base of information for "choice." Yet we do not have to argue about these regulatory forms in a vacuum. Like the neoliberal markets I discussed in the previous section, they too have been instituted in England; and, once again, important research is available that can and must make us duly cautious in going down this path.

One might want to claim that a set of national or state standards, national or state curricula, and national or state tests would provide the conditions for thick morality. After all, such regulatory reforms are supposedly based on shared values and common sentiments that also create social spaces in which common issues of concern can be debated and made subject to moral interrogation.[75] Yet what counts as the "common," and how and by whom it is actually determined, is rather more thin than thick.

Although the national curriculum now so solidly in place in England and Wales is clearly prescriptive, it has not always proven to be the kind of straitjacket it has often been made out to be. As several researchers have documented, it is not only possible that policies and legislative mandates are interpreted and adapted, but it seems inevitable. Thus, the national curriculum is "not so much being 'implemented' in schools as being 'recreated,' not so much 'reproduced,' as 'produced.'"[76]

In general, it is nearly a truism that there is no simplistic linear model of policy formation, distribution, and implementation. Complex mediations always occur at each level of the process. A complex politics goes on within each group and between these groups and external forces in the formulation of policy, in its being written up as a legislative mandate, in its distribution, and in its reception at the level of practice.[77] Thus, the state may legislate changes in curriculum, evaluation, or policy (which is itself produced through conflict, compromise, and political maneuvering), but policy writers and curriculum writers may be unable to control the meanings and implementations of their texts. All texts are "leaky" documents. They are subject to "recontextualization" at every stage of the process.[78]

However, this general principle may be just a bit too romantic. None of this occurs on a level playing field. As with market plans, there are very real differences in power in one's ability to influence, mediate, transform, or reject a policy or a regulatory process. Granted, it is important to recognize that a "state control model"—with its assumption of top-down linearity—is much too simplistic and that the possibility of human agency and influence is always there. However, having said this, this should not imply that such agency and influence will be powerful.[79]

The case of national curriculum and national testing in England and Wales documents the tensions in these two accounts. The national curriculum that was first legislated and then imposed there was indeed struggled over. It was originally too detailed and too specific and, hence, was subject to major transformations at the national, community, school, and then classroom levels. However, even though the national curriculum was subject to conflict, mediation, and some transformation of its content, organization, and invasive and immensely time consuming forms of evaluation, its utter power is demonstrated in its radical reconfiguration of the very process of knowledge selection, organization, and assessment. It changed the entire terrain of education radically. Its subject divisions "provide more constraint than scope for discretion." The "standard attainment targets" that have been mandated cement these constraints in place. "The imposition of national testing locks the national curriculum in place as the dominant framework of teachers' work whatever opportunities teachers may take to evade or reshape it."[80]

Thus, it is not sufficient to state that the world of education is complex and has multiple influences. The purpose of any serious analysis is to go beyond such overly broad conclusions. Rather, we need to "discriminate degrees of influence in the world," to weigh the relative efficacy of the factors involved. Hence, although it is clear that although the national curriculum and national tests that now exist in England and Wales have come about because of a complex interplay of forces and influences, it is equally clear that "state control has the upper hand."[81]

The national curricula and national tests *did* generate conflict about issues. They did partly lead to the creation of social spaces for moral questions to get asked. (Of course, these moral questions had been asked all along by dispossessed groups.) Thus, it was clear to many people that the creation of mandatory and reductive tests that emphasized memory and decontextualized abstraction pulled the national curriculum in a particular direction—that of encouraging a selective educational market in which elite students and elite schools with a wide range of resources would be well (if narrowly) served.[82] Diverse groups of people argued that such reductive, detailed, and simplistic paper-and-pencil tests "had the potential to do enormous damage," a situation that was made even worse because the tests were so onerous in terms of time and record keeping. Teachers had a good deal of support when as a group they decided to boycott the administration of the test in a remarkable act of public protest. This also led to serious questioning of the arbitrary, inflexible, and overly prescriptive national curriculum. Although the curriculum is still inherently problematic and the assessment system does still contain numerous dangerous and onerous elements within it, organized activity against them did have an impact.[83]

Yet, unfortunately, the story does not end there. By the mid-1990s, even with the government's partial retreat on such regulatory forms as its program of constant and reductive testing, it had become clearer by the year that the development of testing and the specification of content had been "hijacked" by those who were ideologically committed to traditional pedagogies and to the idea of more rigorous selection.[84] The residual effects are both material and ideological. They include a continuing emphasis on trying to provide the "rigor [that is] missing in the practice of most teachers, … judging progress solely by what is testable in tests of this kind" and the development of a "very hostile view of the accountability of teachers" that was seen as "part of a wider thrust of policy to take away professional control of public services and establish so called consumer control through a market structure."[85]

The authors of an extremely thorough review of recent assessment programs instituted in England and Wales provide a summary of what has happened. Gipps and Murphy argue that it has become increasingly obvious that the national assessment program attached to the national curriculum is more and more dominated by traditional models of testing and the assumptions about teaching and learning that lie behind them. At the same time, equity issues are becoming much less visible. In the calculus of values now in place in the regulatory state, efficiency, speed, and cost control replace more substantive concerns about social and educational justice. The pressure to get tests in place rapidly has meant that "the speed of test development is so great, and the curriculum and assessment changes so regular, that [there is] little time to carry out detailed analyses and trialing to ensure that the tests are as fair as possible to all groups."[86] Echoes of these very same effects are seen throughout major cities in the United States as well. The conditions for "thin morality"—in which the competitive individual of the market dominates and social justice will somehow take care of itself—are reproduced here. The combination of the neoliberal market and the regulatory state, then, does indeed "work." However, it works in ways in which the metaphors of free market, merit, and effort hide the differential reality that is produced, a fact that I shall take up again in my discussion of reforms such as No Child Left Behind in the next chapter. Whereas, on the one hand, this makes a socially and culturally critical pedagogy even more essential, on the other hand it also makes it much more difficult to actually accomplish.

Basil Bernstein's discussion of the general principles by which knowledge and policies ("texts") move from one arena to another is useful in understanding this. As Bernstein reminds us, when talking about educational change, we must be concerned with three fields. Each field has its own rules of access, regulation, privilege, and special interests: (1) the field of "production" where new knowledge is constructed; (2) the field of "reproduction" where pedagogy and curriculum are actually enacted in schools; and, between these other two; (3) the "recontextualizing" field where discourses from the field of production are appropriated and then transformed into pedagogic discourse and recommendations.[87] This appropriation and recontextualization of knowledge for educational purposes is itself governed by two sets of principles. The first—delocation—implies that there is always a *selective* appropriation of knowledge and discourse from the field of production. The second—relocation—points to the fact that when knowledge and discourse from the field of production is pulled within the recontextualizing field, it is subject to ideological transformations because of the various specialized and/or political interests whose conflicts structure the recontextualizing field.[88]

A good example of this, one that confirms Gipps and Murphy's analysis of the dynamics of national curricula and national testing during their more recent iterations, is found in the process by which the content and organization of the mandated national curriculum in physical education were struggled over and ultimately formed in England. In this instance, a working group of academics both within and outside the field of physical education, headmasters of private and state-supported schools, well-known athletes, and business leaders (but no teachers) was formed.

The original curriculum policies that arose from the group were relatively mixed educationally and ideologically, taking account of the field of production of knowledge within physical education. That is, they contained both critical and progressive elements and elements of the conservative restoration, as well as academic perspectives within the specialized fields from the university. However, as these policies made their way from report to recommendations and then from recommendations to action, they steadily came closer to restorational principles.

An emphasis on efficiency, basic skills and performance testing, on the social control of the body, and on competitive norms ultimately won out. Like the middle-class capturing of the market discussed earlier, this too was not a conspiracy. Rather, it was the result of a process of "over-determination." That is, it was not due to an imposition of these norms, but to a combination of interests in the recontextualizing field—an economic context in which public spending was under severe scrutiny and cost savings had to be sought everywhere; government officials who were opposed to "frills" and consistently intervened to institute only a selection of the recommendations (conservative ones that did *not* come from "professional academics" preferably); ideological attacks on critical, progressive, or child-centered approaches to physical education; and a predominant discourse of "being pragmatic." These came together in the recontextualizing field and helped ensure in practice that conservative principles would be reinscribed in policies and mandates, and that critical forms were seen as too ideological, too costly, or too impractical.[89] "Standards" were upheld; critical voices were heard, but ultimately to little effect; the norms of competitive performance were made central and employed as regulatory devices. Regulatory devices served to privilege specific groups in much the same way as did markets. If this is the case in physical education, it is not hard to predict what is happening and will happen in those curriculum areas that are socially defined as even higher status, and where the stakes seem higher as well.

But it is important not to leave our discussion at such an abstract level or at the level of curriculum planning. What has happened in schools themselves in the United States and elsewhere when such "pragmatic" standards, curricula, and tests are actually instituted?

Creating Educational Triage

Analyses here in the United States have begun to document similar kinds of effects.[90] However, unfortunately, the predominance of relatively unreflective and at times almost self-congratulatory policies around markets, standards, testing, and reductive forms of accountability is exactly that here—predominant. Even given the exceptional work that is being done, for example, by Jeannie Oakes, Amy Stuart Wells, Pauline Lipman, Mary Lee Smith, and others on the hidden effects of some of these kinds of policies and practices, and even given the fact that there are numerous examples of extremely effective schools in our urban and rural areas that succeed through using much more democratic and critical models of curriculum, teaching, and evaluation,[91] it

still feels as if one has to constantly swim against the tide of conservative modernization.[92]

Given this state of affairs, it is now even more important that we
pay attention to material that demonstrates what can happen in situations where the stress on higher standards and higher test scores hits
both the realities of schools and the different populations they serve.
David Gillborn and Deborah Youdell's volume *Rationing Education* is
just such a book.[93] It goes into even more detail about the powerful,
and often damaging, effects on teachers and students of our seeming
fascination with ever-rising standards, mandated curricula, and over-
emphasis on testing.

The volume is based on in-depth research on the equivalent of middle and secondary schools in England. It details the overt and hidden
effects of policies that are currently being undertaken in the United
States as well. These include such things as creating a situation where
the tail of a high-stakes test "wags the dog" of the teacher, pressuring
schools to constantly show increased achievement scores on such standardized tests no matter what the level of support or the impoverished
conditions in schools and local communities, to publicly display such
results in a process of what might be realistically called shaming, and
to threaten schools that do not show "improvement" on these tests with
severe sanctions or loss of control.

Of course, there are poor schools and there are ineffective practices
in schools. However, the reduction of education to scores on what are
often inadequate measures, often used in technically and educationally
inappropriate ways for comparative purposes, has some serious consequences. What these consequences are provides the context for the
story Gillborn and Youdell tell.

In many ways, *Rationing Education* provides what might be called a
microeconomy of school life. It examines the ways in which certain valued commodities are accumulated by schools in a time of intense competition for scarce resources. In this case, the commodities are higher
test scores and the resources are both numbers of students and public
recognition of being a "good" school. The authors' way of describing
this is what they call the "A–C economy."

In England, as in the United States, schools exist in what is really
a hierarchical ordering, a market, in prestige and reputation. They are
valued by the number of students who get passing scores on particular
national tests. The national tests are made public as a form of "league
tables" in which schools are rank-ordered according to their relative
results. Schools with large numbers of students getting grades A–C are
more highly valued than those with students whose rates of passing are

less—even though everyone tacitly knows that there is a very strong relationship between school results and poverty. (We need again to remember in the United States, for example, that poverty explains *much* more of the variance in school achievement than any school reform.)

This is straightforward and not surprising. However, this situation creates an economy that has certain characteristics. Students with predicted higher test scores are even more valuable. Students with predicted lower test scores are seen as less useful to the school's place in the market. This too is not surprising. The results of such an economy, however, are powerful. Another key group of students is focused upon and on whom considerable resources, energy, and attention are devoted—students who are on the border between passing grades and failing grades. These students—often seen as middle-class "underachievers"—become objects of great value in the school. After all, if this key group can be pulled across the border into the A–C column, the school's results will be that much more positive.

What could be wrong with an increased focus on students on the border? Here is one of the places where Gillborn and Youdell's results are ominous. In such an A–C economy, specific students are seen as movable. Other students' abilities are seen as increasingly fixed and less worthy of attention. The class and race characteristics of these latter students are striking. Poor and working-class students, students of African descent, and other ethnically "different" children are not valued commodities on this kind of market. Even though gender divisions were less pronounced in the schools that Gillborn and Youdell studied, divisions strongly rooted in racializing and class-based structures were not simply mirrored in the schools. They actually were *produced* in these institutions.

Thus, policies that were put in place to raise standards, to increase test scores, to guarantee public accountability, and to make schools more competitive had results that were more than a little damaging to those students who were already the least advantaged in these same schools. Yet it was not only the students who witnessed these negative effects. The voices of teachers and administrators indicate what happens to them as well. They too begin to harden their sense of which students are "able" and which students are not. Tracking returns in both overt and covert ways. And once again, black students and students in government-subsidized lunch programs are the ones most likely to be placed in those tracks or given academic and career advice that nearly guarantees that they will have limited or no mobility and will confirm their status as students who are "less worthy."

Equally worth noting here is the specific way the A–C economy works to choose those students who are deemed to have worthiness. Often, students whose behavior and test results are quite similar have very different careers in the school. Thus, a black student and a white student may be, say, on the border of the A–C/failing divide, but the black student will not be the beneficiary of the added attention. These situations are all too often characterized by tacitly operating visions of ability, ones that have been hardened by years of discourse on the "problem" of black student achievement and especially by the increased visibility once again of supposedly scientific (and ultimately racist and empirically problematic) "research" on genetic differences in mean intelligence between blacks and whites. As I noted, not only would no reputable population geneticist make such a claim, but these theories have been discredited multiple times.[94] The fact that they reenter into our commonsense decision making in schools in times of scarce resources and increased pressure shows how deeply seated such preconceived notions are in the sets of assumptions educators may unconsciously mobilize in their attempt to be pragmatic in dealing with large numbers of students.

As previous research has clearly indicated, students are not passive in the face of these tendencies. Indeed, as Gillborn and Youdell show, students "interpret, question, and on occasion, resist." However, "the scope for resistance is severely constrained, and pupils are clearly positioned as the subject of numerous organizational and disciplinary discourses in which the young people themselves play little active role."[95] In what is perhaps one of the most powerful messages of the book, the authors summarize the effects of this entire process in the following way. "It is a cruel irony that the processes of selection and monitoring that have been adopted with the aim of heightening attainment are so frequently experienced as disempowering and demotivating by the students."[96] These experiences are turned into feelings of being treated unfairly, of teachers and schools being organized in ways that privilege the already privileged in terms of class and race. If this is the case, some of the most powerful messages "reforms" of this type may send is that not only is the world deeply unfair but also that schools themselves are prime examples of institutions that simply respond to those who already possess economic and cultural capital. This is decidedly *not* the message that any society that is serious about what might be called thick democracy wants to teach. But it may be what our children, including many like Joseph, learn in school systems that are so driven by the assumption that putting into place higher standards and higher-stakes testing will somehow magically solve deep-seated educational and social problems. A close reading of *Rationing Education* should make us much more cautious about such unwarranted assumptions.

Unfortunately, recent research on the effects of all the preceding issues in the United States confirms these worries. Although I will go into more detail about this in the next chapter, some of this is still important to note here. For example, Linda McNeil's powerful and detailed investigation of what has actually happened in Texas when state-mandated "reforms" involving imposed standards and curricula, reductive and competitive testing, and attacks on teachers' professionalism were instituted demonstrates in no uncertain terms that the very children and schools that these policies and practices are supposed to help are actually hurt in the process.[97] The same is true in Pauline Lipman's insightful research on Chicago public schools.[98] Similar tendencies toward producing inequalities have been documented in the conservative modernization reforms in tax credits, testing, and curricula in Arizona and elsewhere.[99] Thus goeth democracy in education.

Thinking Strategically

In this chapter, I have raised serious questions about current educational "reform" efforts now under way in a number of nations. I have used research from England, New Zealand, the United States, and elsewhere to document some of the hidden differential effects of two connected strategies—neoliberal-inspired market proposals and neoliberal-, neo-conservative-, and middle-class-managerial-inspired regulatory proposals. Taking a key from Herbert Kliebard's historical analysis, I have described how different interests with different educational and social visions compete for dominion in the social field of power surrounding educational policy and practice. In the process, I have documented some of the complexities and imbalances in this field of power. These complexities and imbalances result in thin rather than thick morality and in the reproduction of both dominant pedagogical and curricular forms and ideologies and the social privileges that accompany them. I have suggested that the rhetorical flourishes of the discourses of critical pedagogy need to come to grips with these changing material and ideological conditions. Critical pedagogy cannot and will not occur in a vacuum. Unless we honestly face these profound rightist transformations and think tactically about them, we will have little effect either on the creation of a counterhegemonic commonsense or on the building of a counterhegemonic alliance. The growth of that odd combination of marketization and regulatory state, the move toward pedagogic similarity and "traditional" academic curricula and teaching, the ability of dominant groups to exert leadership in the struggle over this, and the accompanying shifts in commonsense—all this cannot be wished away. Instead, it needs to be confronted honestly and self-critically.

Having said this, however, I want to point to a hidden paradox in what I have done. Even though much of my own and others' research recently has been on the processes and effects of conservative modernization, we should be aware of the dangers in such a focus. Research on the history, politics, and practices of rightist social and educational movements and "reforms" has enabled us to show the contradictions and unequal effects of such policies and practices. It has enabled the rearticulation of claims to social justice on the basis of solid evidence. This is all to the good. However, in the process, one of the latent effects has been the gradual framing of educational issues largely in terms of the conservative agenda. The very categories themselves—markets, choice, national curricula, national testing, standards—bring the debate onto the terrain established by neoliberals and neoconservatives. The analysis of "what is" has led to a neglect of "what might be." Thus, there has been a withering of substantive large-scale discussions of feasible alternatives to neoliberal and neoconservative visions, policies, and practices, ones that would move well beyond them.[100]

Because of this, at least part of our task may be politically and conceptually complex, but it can be said simply. In the long term, we need to "develop a political project that is both local yet generalizable, systematic without making Eurocentric, masculinist claims to essential and universal truths about human subjects."[101] Another part of our task, though, must be and is more proximate, more appropriately educational. While I say more about this throughout the book and especially in my final chapter, defensible, articulate, and fully fleshed out alternative critical and progressive policies and practices in curriculum, teaching, and evaluation need to be developed and made widely available. But this too must be done with due recognition of the changing nature of the social field of power and the importance of thinking tactically and strategically. Let me be specific here.

For example, in the United States, the increasingly popular journal *Rethinking Schools* has provided an important forum for social and educational criticism and for descriptions of critical educational practices in schools and communities. At times influenced directly by the work of Paulo Freire and by educators who have themselves elaborated and extended it, and at other times coming out of diverse indigenous radical educational traditions specific to the United States, *Rethinking Schools* and emerging national organizations such as the National Coalition of Educational Activists have jointly constructed spaces for critical educators, cultural and political activists, radical scholars, and others to teach each other, to provide supportive criticism of one another's work, and to build a more collective set of responses to the destructive educational and social policies coming from the conservative restoration.[102]

In using the phrase "collective responses," however, I need to stress that this phrase does not signify anything like "democratic centrism" in which a small group or a party cadre speaks for the majority and establishes the "appropriate" position. Given that there are diverse emancipatory movements whose voices are heard in publications like *Rethinking Schools* and in organizations such as the National Coalition of Educational Activists—antiracist and postcolonial positions, radical forms of multiculturalism, gays and lesbians, multiple feminist voices, neo-Marxists and democratic socialists, "greens," and so on—a more appropriate way of looking at what is happening is to call it a *decentered unity*. Multiple progressive projects, multiple "critical pedagogies," are articulated. Like Freire, each of them is related to real struggles in real institutions in real communities. We of course should not be romantic about this. There are very real differences—political, epistemological, and/or educational—in these varied voices. But they are united in their opposition to the forces involved in the new conservative hegemonic alliance. There *are* tensions, but the decentered unity has remained strong enough for each constituent group to support the struggles of the others.

This is not all. At the same time as these critical movements are being built, critical educators are also attempting to occupy the spaces provided by existing "mainstream" publication outlets to publish books that provide *critical* answers to teachers' questions about "What do I do on Monday?" during a conservative era. This space has too long been ignored by many theorists of critical pedagogy. Some of these attempts have been remarkably successful. Let me give one example. One very large "professional" organization in the United States—the Association for Supervision and Curriculum Development (ASCD)—publishes books that are distributed each year to its more than 150,000 members, most of whom are teachers or administrators in elementary, middle, or secondary schools. ASCD has not been a very progressive organization, preferring to publish largely technicist and overtly depoliticized material. Yet it has been concerned that its publications have not sufficiently represented socially and culturally critical educators. It, thus, has been looking for ways to increase its legitimacy to a wider range of educators. Because of this legitimacy problem and because of its large membership, it became clear to a number of people who were part of the critical educational traditions in the United States that it might be possible to convince ASCD to publish and widely circulate material that would demonstrate the actual practical *successes* of critical models of curriculum, teaching, and evaluation in solving real problems in schools and communities, especially with working-class and poor children and children of color.

After intense negotiations that guaranteed an absence of censorship, a colleague of mine and I agreed to publish a book—*Democratic Schools*[103]—with ASCD that provided clear practical examples of the power of Freirean and similar critical approaches at work in classrooms and communities. *Democratic Schools* was not only distributed to all 150,000 members of the organization, but it has gone on to sell an additional 100,000 copies. Thus, nearly 250,000 copies of a volume that tells the practical stories of the largely successful struggles of critically oriented educators in real schools are now in the hands of educators who daily face similar problems.[104] This is an important intervention. Although there is no guarantee that teachers will always be progressive (nor is there any guarantee that those who are progressive around class and union issues will be equally progressive around issues of gender, sexuality, and race), many teachers do have socially and pedagogically critical intuitions. However, they often do not have ways of putting these intuitions into practice because they cannot picture them in action in daily situations. Because of this, critical theoretical and political insights, then, have nowhere to go in terms of their embodiment in concrete pedagogical situations where the politics of curriculum and teaching must be *enacted*. This is a tragic absence and strategically filling it is absolutely essential. Thus, we need to use and expand the spaces in which critical pedagogical "stories" are made available so that these positions do not remain only on the theoretical or rhetorical level. The publication and widespread distribution of *Democratic Schools* provides one instance of using and expanding such spaces in ways that make Freirean and similar critical educational positions seem actually doable in "ordinary" institutions such as schools and local communities.

Although crucial, it is then not enough to deconstruct restorational policies in education. The right has shown how important changes in common sense are in the struggle for education. It is our task to collectively help rebuild it by reestablishing a sense that thick morality, and a thick democracy, are truly possible today.

This cannot be done without paying considerably more attention to two things. The first—the material and ideological transformations that the right has effected—has been a key topic of this chapter. Yet another element needs to be stressed—the building of large-scale counterhegemonic movements that connect educational struggles to those in other sites and also assist both in creating new struggles and defending existing ones within educational institutions themselves. In the current conservative context, some of the material on critical pedagogy has characteristics that make this an even more difficult act, however.

In the past, I have warned that the stylistic politics of some of our most "advanced" work forces the reader to do all of the work.[105] Neologism after neologism reigns supreme. As Dennis Carlson and I have argued elsewhere,[106] the discourse of critical pedagogy in its Freirean and feminist forms has increasingly been influenced by postmodern theories. While this has proven to be very useful in reconceptualizing the field and its politics, it has also opened up the discourse to the criticism that it has become too theoretical, abstract, esoteric, and out of touch with the conflicts and struggles that teachers, students, and activists act on. Henry Giroux and others have defended these discourses as necessary in critical pedagogy, as to reconstruct the world one must first learn to speak a new language and "new ideas require new terms."[107] This is undoubtedly correct. Indeed, such a position is one I consciously took when I first introduced Gramscian and Habermasian theories into education in the early 1970s.

Yet, having said this, given the very real success of the strategy of "plain speaking" by neoliberals and neoconservatives, some of the criticisms of material on critical pedagogy do have power. Even though a good deal of it is rich and provocative, some of it *is* conceptually and politically confused and confusing. Some of it *is* disconnected from the gritty materialities of daily economic, political, and educational/cultural struggles. Some of it *does* romanticize the cultural at the expense of equally powerful traditions of analysis based in political economy and the state. And some of it *does* place so much emphasis on the "post" that it forgets the structural realities that set limits on real people in real institutions in everyday life.

Thus, as many commentators have argued repeatedly, much more effort must be given to ground the discourse of critical pedagogy in the concrete struggles of multiple and identifiable groups.[108] Much of it needs to be considerably less dismissive of previous critical traditions that—rightly—continue to influence educational and cultural activists. Just as important, as I just noted, what critical pedagogies actually look like when put into practice—not only their theoretical elaborations—needs to made much more visible than we have been apt to do. Unfortunately, when rightist mobilizations have had no small measure of success in creating a reactionary common sense about education (and even among many educators), the linguistic styles of all too much critical work gets labeled as "arrogant" (sometimes appropriately) and cuts itself off from many of the radical teachers and activists it wants to support.

It is *hard* work not to be sloppy. It is hard work to write in such a way that theoretical and political nuance are not sacrificed on the altar of common sense, but also in a way that the hard work of reading can actually pay off for the reader her- or himself. And it is hard and time-consuming work to write at multiple levels. But if we don't, neoliberals and neoconservatives will. And we will be much the worse for it. In this time of conservative restoration, the multiple projects of critical education are indeed crucial. A good dose of reality will do no harm, and I believe will actually make them more effective in the long run.

Although populism can and has been a double-edged sword, being effective, then, requires a somewhat more populist set of impulses than those that have dominated critical pedagogy over the past years. However, the terrain out of which such populist forms grow is already being occupied by a very different kind of "popular" consciousness. Nearly all populisms are critical of elitist tendencies. Yet who and what actually counts as elitism is part of a contested terrain. Unfortunately, in part because the left has evacuated that terrain, the kinds of populism that are currently growing most rapidly are authoritarian in nature. Although they do cohere around themes that are based on "plain speaking" and "letting the people decide," they are all too often based on assumptions that God has selected "the people" whose voices are more important than anyone else's. As I noted in Chapters 1 and 2, authoritarian populism is an increasingly powerful and persuasive social movement in many nations throughout the world. Its adherents have been integrated under the umbrella of conservative moderniza-tion also in part because neoliberals and neoconservatives have been able to tap into the strong undercurrents of populist resentment that exist among many segments of the (especially) white population. The right has understood Gramscian strategies—and has used them for ret-rogressive purposes. We shall turn to the structures of the authoritar-ian populist world shortly. No progressive counterhegemonic strategy, no critical pedagogy, can succeed unless it understands the reality con-structed by these groups. I devote Chapters 5, 6, 7, and 8 to their his-tory; to their economic, political, and cultural arguments; and to their claims about educational policy and practice.

But before we examine these issues, we still need to spend a bit more time on what is happening in dominant reforms in the United States and elsewhere, so that the growing power of the new middle class and

the complicated politics of race involved in neoliberal and neoconservative policies are made more visible. This is the task of Chapter 4 and its
critical examination of the assumptions and effects of the logics underpinning No Child Left Behind and similar educational "reforms."

CHAPTER 4

Who "No Child Left Behind" Leaves Behind

The Class and Race Realities of Audit Cultures

Introduction

Much of what I have discussed in the past three chapters now has an official imprimatur. A considerable portion of these kinds of policies has been institutionalized, not only at the state and local levels but also increasingly at a national level in the United States. Most of us living in the United States are now familiar with the key elements of the federal reauthorization of the Elementary and Secondary Education Act, commonly known as No Child Left Behind, passed by Congress in 2001 and signed by President Bush in January 2002. This represents a set of initiatives that can radically transform the federal role in policing and controlling core aspects of education and that bears witness to the power of neoliberal, neoconservative, and especially new managerial discourse in education today.[1] The major components of the legislation center around testing and accountability and also provide inroads toward a larger agenda of privatization and marketization.

The major provisions include the following:[2]

1. There must be regular testing in key subjects. Thus, starting in 2002–2003, states must engage in an annual assessment of English language proficiency for students who are learning the English language. By the year 2005–2006 annual tests in mathematics and reading/language arts must be given to all children in grades 3–8. By the year 2007–2008, science tests are added at specific grade levels. Finally, to check on the accuracy of the tests that each state has developed, states have to administer the NAEP (National Assessment of Educational Progress) tests to a portion of their students in grades 4 and 8.

2. The tests that states develop must be aligned with each state's standards and must have results that are comparable from year to year. The tests are to be used both to determine whether the state is indeed meeting its standards and in theory to assist teachers in diagnosing the academic problems and needs of students.

3. The scores on these tests are to be disaggregated so that the average scores of specific populations (for example, by race/ethnicity, income, disability, limited English proficiency) are visible.

4. With the above disaggregated information, a state is to follow a specific timeline to close any gaps in achievement among racial/ethnic and income groups. Starting with the year 2002–2003, states have twelve years for all students to move to the state benchmark for mathematical and reading proficiency.

5. At least 95 percent of all students in each school must be tested. Every group of students in each school needs to meet or exceed their annual objectives. Failure to meet these objectives leads to formal notification and for those schools receiving Title I money it can lead to various kinds of interventions.

   This involves technical assistance if a Title I—a key source of federal funding—school has not met its performance objectives for two consecutive years. As well, parents have a choice to send their children to another public school within the school district. After three consecutive years of failure, the assistance and choice options continue, but an additional option now comes into play. Students can now use their share of Title I funding to pay for tutoring and other supplemental services. The expenditure of this money is not limited to public institutions but is expanded to cover other state-approved entities such as religious institutions, for-profit companies, or a private nonprofit institution.

If a school continues to fail for a fourth consecutive year, there is a continuation of assistance, public school choice, and the above-noted public or private supplemental services. However, now the school itself is required to make fundamental alterations such as staffing changes. By the fifth year, a school can be required to make changes in its governance. This might include transforming itself into a charter school, having the state itself take over the school, or turning school management over to a private company.

6. Report cards are to be issued annually, publicly documenting a school's achievement levels. Parents also have the right to get information on teacher qualifications at their school.

7. In core academic subjects, a state's teachers must all be highly qualified by 2005–2006. This will be demonstrated usually through the use of a state test of subject matter and pedagogical skill in addition to certification and degree requirements. Newly hired paraprofessionals who engage in instruction and are paid through Title I funds must pass a rigorous test or must document that they have at least two years of postsecondary education. Already employed paraprofessionals have a few more years in order to meet these requirements.

8. More flexibility is given to school systems in the use of federal money. This enables them, for example, to use Title I funding more flexibly in any school that has at least 40 percent of its children as poor, rather than the older criterion of 50 percent. The legislation also allows schools to shift half of the funds they get from four specific federal programs among these programs in ways that they find useful.

9. In addition to making changes in how federal money is distributed so that more money goes to the poorest districts, more money was appropriated for the poorest districts.

10. New initiatives are established. These include such things as the "Teacher Quality" program that helps schools districts in their efforts to recruit, retain, and provide professional development to teachers and administrators, and "Reading First," a program that is aimed at reforming the ways in which reading is taught in schools throughout the country.

There are of course other important elements included in the No Child Left Behind legislation. It should be immediately clear that the proposals incorporate a number of progressive-sounding issues and are couched in seemingly progressive language. This is partly a result of the compromises made in order to get the legislation passed with bipartisan support in Congress. But it also continues an established tradition of the conservative production of discourse that incorporates progressive language, while simultaneously advancing key elements of the neoliberal and neoconservative agendas. It in essence creates what Smith and others have called a "political spectacle," one in which proposals that seemingly lead to reforms that are wanted by the least powerful actors in society are instead largely used to gain legitimacy for very different kinds of agendas and policies.[3]

Because of both the history of such political spectacles and the realities of inequalities in our society, many of the provisions of NCLB, and their hidden effects and connections to other aspects of the conservative agenda, are—and should be—controversial. Controversies continue to swirl and intensify around such things as its redefinition of literacy and reading instruction and its emphasis on only one set of strategies for teaching such things. There are major questions as well about its budget priorities and about whether the supposed increase in funding is "real" or not or whether the legislation is largely an unfunded or inadequately funded mandate as it seems to be.[4] To these, others can be added. Its redefinition of accountability as reducible to scores on standardized achievement tests, and used inappropriately for comparative purposes, is more than a little problematic.[5] The manner in which NCLB defines success and failure, and the shaming practices associated with these processes, has caused numerous complaints and even rebellions in some states and districts. The accompanying loss of local control has also been a consistent worry, with even largely conservative states such as Utah publicly challenging facets of the law.[6]

There has been little thought about the effect as well on the ways in which the constant stress on "failing public schools" can act to make such things as home schooling—one of the fastest growing transformations in education today, with many more children and parents involved than in charter schools or voucher programs—that much more attractive. With little accountability at all in home schooling, the stress on reductive forms of accountability in NCLB can have the paradoxical effect of actually creating a situation in which ever more children are educated in institutions that have minimal if any forms of public oversight, a point I will make in even more detail in Chapters 7 and 8.

Furthermore, the clear implication that what counts as good teaching is to be evaluated only on improvements in students' scores on the tests is less than satisfactory and shows a profound misunderstanding of the complexity of the teaching act.[7] The ways in which it tacitly defines what counts as legitimate knowledge as only that which can be included on such reductive tests flies in the face of decades of struggle over the politics of official knowledge and over the inclusion of the cultures, languages, histories, values, and habitus of a country made of cultures from all over the world.[8] Not least, as Valenzuela and her colleagues have so clearly demonstrated, and as I shall indicate in the next section of this chapter, this assemblage of "reforms" has had truly damaging consequences for a large number of our most dispossessed peoples, with race/ethnicity being a prime marker of these negative consequences.[9] Finally, hidden within the legislation is a requirement that schools provide information on students to, and support contact with, military recruiters. In a time of very real disagreement about the current wars in which the United States is engaged and about whether such wars are wise, this has created another area in which NCLB is more than a little controversial.[10]

All of these issues are crucial, and I have talked about a number of them elsewhere.[11] But of particular concern to me here is point 5 in the description of the legislation given earlier. This is a key element, because it sutures together the requirements of strong accountability measures with an even further opening toward funding for private education. Even though many conservative members of Congress had to back away from their original plan to include federal support for vouchers in the legislation, it would be a grave mistake to not see the connection between privatization and increased federal control and intervention through testing. As Valenzuela has documented in Texas, for example, these connections are often very overt in the political actions of conservative advocates.[12] And as we shall see later in this chapter, the politics of race and the contradictory impulses and effects involved in such politics need to be taken very seriously in thinking about all of this.

Earlier I argued that there is no contradiction between supposedly decentralized market-based models of education and centralization through strong regimes of curricular control, testing, and accountability. As I said, the movement toward marketization and "choice" *requires* the production of standardized data based on standardized processes and "products" so that comparisons can be made and so that "consumers" have relevant information to make choices on a market.

Given the negative effects of such "reforms" that I documented in my previous chapters, I want here to expand my discussion of the connections between the neoliberal vision of markets, neoconservatism's sense of control, and the new middle class's commitment to managerial impulses. I will direct much of my attention to the logics that underpin interventions such as No Child Left Behind and similar initiatives, on the creative ideological/political work that has gone on to make them acceptable, and on the complicated class and race dynamics that both created them and are the effects of them. In order to do this, I need to go even further in laying out the general context and shifting logics in which No Child Left Behind operates, logics that work to place strong state models of accountability in close contact with marketization. NCLB does not stand alone and appears on the same terrain on which the crucial ideological work I critically analyzed in the previous chapters has already been done. I want to pay particular attention to Texas in this chapter, as the roots of NCLB lie directly in the soil of what was built there. It was used as both the model for and testing ground of the policies that are central to the federal legislation. I shall begin my discussion by focusing on the ways in which NCLB and its progenitors in Texas have constructed the issue of *accountability,* as that is the key to the ways in which we can pry loose what the effects have been and are.

Accountability and Inequality

"Accountability" is quite an interesting word. As Padilla reminds us, in both of the dominant languages in the United States—English and Spanish—the word accountability in the former and "contabilidad" in the latter come from the same Latin root, "putare," to think. In Spanish, the verb "contar" has two meanings. It refers both to count and to recount. Thus, it implies numbers and narratives. In English, the word accountability still carries with it a history of giving an account, of a story or narrative.[13] We do damage to the history of giving accounts by reducing it to simply number counting. But this is what has happened—and not only in Texas.

What does this mean for the process of creating a responsive and serious education, especially for our poorest children and for children of color? The authors of a recent book that critically examines what has actually happened to identifiable students, teachers, and schools beneath the rhetoric of No Child Left Behind, *Leaving Children Behind,*[14] are clear in their answers. Their conclusions are many, but the results can be summarized by saying that the system of accountability in Texas, the one that provided a good deal of the underpinnings and the justification for No Child Left Behind, has failed—and it has failed minority children the most. This can perhaps be best stated in the following way.

The dramatic educational improvement attributed to Texas's system of accountability is itself questionable. The state's methods of collecting and reporting educational data, including the critically important high stakes test scores, hide as much as they reveal. When the focus is shifted to Texas students' performance on nationwide tests such as the American College Test (ACT) and the Scholastic Aptitude Test (SAT) 1, or when skyrocketing dropout and projected retention rates are factored in, the state's "miracle" looks more like a mirage.[15]

Few of those who have studied and then raised issues about this system reject the importance of accountability. Rather, they raise questions about the manner in which this specific model works. They show how high stakes testing, the centerpiece of the Texas model, is so deeply flawed as to create more problems than it solves. And it covers these problems with rhetorical artifice that makes the public less likely to recognize the hidden consequences of the policies. The consequences are numerous, but three stand out. The negative results in promotion, retention, and graduation are deeply worrisome and fully raced. Much of this comes from using a standardized test as the only "legitimate" measure of student abilities. As we saw in England, these results are also generated by "attaching high-stakes consequences to schools and districts and thereby encouraging a reductive, test-driven curriculum."[16] Such a system excludes almost everything that is harder to test and establishes a curriculum in which certain subjects are seen as important (mathematics and reading) because they are tested, while other equally important subjects (e.g., science and social studies) are either done in increasingly surface ways or even neglected.[17]

In addition, the accountability system interrupts the ways of knowing that are powerful in the cultures and languages of a diverse student population, making it even more difficult to connect the curriculum to students' lived realities. When added together, all of this creates what might be called a "subtractive approach to the education of racial, cultural, and linguistic minorities," one in which a student's worth—especially to the school system—is reduced to her or his test scores.[18]

We have seen this repeatedly in other contexts where such testing regimes are in effect. As I showed in Chapter 3, those students who are seen to be "moveable," who are seen to be able to produce higher scores, are also seen as much more valuable. Those whose predicted educational futures are seen as less likely to move upward in terms of test scores are either given considerably less attention and/or are subject to a schooling experience that is constantly simply drill and test (sometimes called "drill and kill"). Nor is it unusual for schools to "creatively" find ways of not having these students actually take the tests. This too is exactly what happened all too often in Texas, where schools found ways of excluding thousands of students from taking the tests.[19] That this is exactly what has occurred with NCLB as school systems attempt to position themselves positively in the public eye has become ever more clear as well.

The evaluation community is not unaware of many of the problems associated with high stakes testing and with using tests inappropriately. Indeed, in 2000 the U.S. Department of Education in association with the U.S. Office of Civil Rights and the National Academy of Sciences produced a set of guidelines and a resource guide for school leaders. It is unclear why the current Bush administration withdrew the document, but it is no longer distributing it.[20]

I can think of no better restatement of these arguments than that offered by Linda McNeil. It is worth quoting her at length here. Asserting that the Texas models incorporated into No Child Left Behind function in exactly the opposite way—that is, many identifiable children are indeed left behind—she says that:

> The Texas accountability system succeeds—that is it produces positive indicators—only when it loses a significant number of children. By far the majority of those losses are among poor, Spanish-language-dominant, and other Latino children, with equally significant losses incurred by African-American children as well. That 25% of the White (Anglo) children are also lost from public schools would be a crisis in many states, but in Texas the figure seems less urgent because it is barely half the percentage rates of those lost in the other ethnic categories. The record of losses incurred during the decade of experience under the Texas testing system provides a cautionary tale to those states that are only now beginning to adopt the Texas accountability system or where federal law is imposing the Texas system on their schools. They will find that an accountability system based on standardized testing reduces educational quality, produces unnecessary failures, and fakes its claims to more equitable schooling.[21]

One of the most progressive-sounding elements found in No Child Left Behind is its insistence that test scores be disaggregated by ethnicity. Supposedly, this will enable us to pay closer attention to the differential results of schooling by making public who gains and who loses in current practices. This is something that I, too, approve of in theory.

What could be wrong with focusing attention on those for whom we already know existing curricular and teaching policies and practices are less successful? What is good in theory however may be contradicted in practice.

The data assembled by Valenzuela and her colleagues does not paint a pretty picture. It is possible to show mean gains on specific tests over time, and Texas districts—like so many school districts throughout the entire nation—proudly publicize results such as these. However, the result has more often than not been a strikingly impoverished education, one in which everything is sacrificed to show "improvement" on one standard—and problematic—measure. When the results of students on this measure are compared with their results on other wider measures of ability and achievement, there has actually been a serious decline in broader abilities and competencies.[22]

This is an interesting paradox. The public has been convinced that one quite limited test in Texas tells all. They look at its results and assume that it shows progress. What they are not presented with is the more complicated picture: decreases in completion rates, misused test scores and the manipulation of test results through the exclusion of students, the loss of autonomy, a drastic truncating of the curriculum so that students actually get less in the guise of getting more, schools and entire systems becoming factories that are aimed at producing one thing—increased test scores.[23]

This had lasting effects. Once again, the fact is that by and large such a system ultimately created even more inequalities. The demand that African-American and Latino/a students in what are clearly underresourced schools quickly show higher scores on the Texas test meant that rather than having a varied (and perhaps interesting) curriculum that might prepare them with necessary intellectual and valuative resources, they got hour after hour and day after day of "test prep" and test practice. That became their curriculum. Rather than having "well-stocked classrooms, labs, and libraries, and highly qualified teachers instead of long-term substitute teachers on emergency credentials—impediments that already kept them from achieving at the levels of children in more well-supported schools"[24]—they once again were called upon to "make do." Making do required only that they show mean gains on the only goal that mattered, even if it meant that they consistently spent less and less time studying many of the subjects they were supposed to go to school to get. Given this opportunity structure, in the end the gap between a poor Latino and African-American child, on the one hand, and a student from more affluent families and districts, on the other hand, would and did actually widen.[25] These kinds of effects are an increasing danger in our rush to meet the impositions brought to us by No Child Left Behind. They make even more powerful the arguments I marshaled in Chapter 3 about how particular policies produce inequalities "naturally."

But this was not all. The overriding attention given to that one goal—improving test scores at whatever cost—shifted attention away from the very real inequalities in resources, staff experience, tax base and support, impoverishment, lack of jobs with respect and a living wage, poor housing and health care, and so on between poor and rich districts and areas, thereby making it even harder to deal with some of the most difficult to solve causes of educational inequality.[26] Yet, as Jean Anyon shows, for example, lasting educational reforms that do not attempt to take these kinds of issues seriously are not themselves serious enough.[27] This of course raises a difficult question, one with which we are not totally comfortable. When will we stop our demand for quick fixes and treat education (and educators) with the respect it deserves? Showing respect means that we stop assuming that educational reform can stand alone, that it can do it by itself, and that the answers we need can come from that part of the business community that is so enamored with bottom lines that it has lost its soul in the process. This should not serve as an excuse for not doing our best to provide the financial, institutional, human, legal, and intellectual resources so necessary for an education that makes a real difference. What it does do is ask us to "get real," to deal with education with the complexity it deserves. And simplistic attempts at reducing all of schooling to "bottom-line" measures and to import business models into it are not working.

Changing Common Sense and the Growth of Audit Cultures

We can only understand the causes and effects of these policies more fully if we continue the process of critically interrogating the assumptions that underpin them and the complicated alliance that stands behind them. A significant place to begin is to start with what may seem obvious—the importation of business models as the prime way of understanding and acting on education and the entire public sphere—but it still needs further elaboration.

In many nations there have been attempts, often more than a little successful, to restructure state institutions.[28] Among the major aims of such restructuring were: to ensure that the state served business interests; to have the state's internal operations model those used in business; and to "take politics out of public institutions," that is to reduce the possibility that government institutions would be subject to political pressure from the electorate and from progressive social movements.[29] Chubb and Moe's arguments about voucher plans that place educational institutions on a market mirror this latter point, for example.[30]

This last point, removing politics from government institutions, is based on a less-than-accurate understanding not only of the state but of the market as well. Although most economics textbooks may give the impression that markets are impersonal and impartial, they are instead highly political as well as inherently unstable. To this, other points need to be added. To guarantee their survival, firms must seek ways of breaking out of the boundaries that are set by state regulation. Increasingly, this has meant that the boundaries established to divide nonmarket parts of our lives must be pushed so that these spheres can be opened to commodification and profit-making. As Leys reminds us, this is a crucially important issue. "It threatens the destruction of nonmarket spheres of life on which social solidarity and active democracy have always depended."[31]

It is not an easy process to transform parts of our lives and institutions that were not totally integrated into market relations so that they are part of a market. As I noted in the previous chapter, the market needs to be marketed. To do this, at least four significant things must be worked on.[32]

1. The services or goods that are to be focused upon must be reconfigured so that they can indeed be bought and sold.
2. People who received these things from the state must be convinced to want to buy them.
3. The working conditions and outlook of the employees who work in this sector must be transformed from a model based on collective understandings and providing service to "the public" on the one hand to working to produce profits for owners and investors and subject to market discipline on the other.
4. When business moves into what were previously nonmarket fields, as much as possible their risks must be underwritten by the state.

Under these kinds of pressures, standardized and competitive labor processes begin to dominate the lives of the newly marketized workers. But this is not all. A good deal of labor is shifted to the consumer. She or he now must do much of the work of getting information, sorting through the advertising and claims, and making sense of what is often a thoroughly confusing welter of data and "products."[33] In the process as well, there is a very strong tendency for needs and values that were originally generated out of collective deliberations, struggles, and compromises, and which led to the creation of state services, to be marginalized and ultimately abandoned.[34] Once again, in Leys's words, "The facts suggest that market-driven politics can lead to a remarkably rapid erosion of democratically-determined collective values and institutions."[35]

These arguments may seem abstract, but they speak to significant and concrete changes in our daily lives in and out of education. For more than two decades, we have witnessed coordinated and determined efforts not only to reconstruct a "liberal" market economy, but a "liberal" market society and culture. This distinction is important. In Habermas' words, the attempt is to have "system" totally colonize the "life-world."[36] As many aspects of our lives as possible, including the state and civil society, must be merged into the economy and economic logics. Although there will always be counterhegemonic tendencies,[37] our daily interactions—and even our dreams and desires—must ultimately be governed by market "realities" and relations. In this scenario—and it is increasingly not only a scenario, but also a reality—a society and a culture is not to be based on trust and shared values. Rather, all aspects of that society are to be grounded in and face "the most extreme possible exposure to market forces, with internal markets, profit centers, audits, and 'bottom lines' penetrating the whole of life from hospitals to playgroups" to schools.[38] Again, as Margaret Thatcher once famously put it, "The task is not to just change the economy, but to change the soul."

Interestingly, because of the focus on measurable results and central control over important decisions, the federal government's power has actually been sharply enhanced. (Clearly, No Child Left Behind—in which schools labeled as "failing" on standardized tests are to be subject to market competition and central sanctions—becomes a good example of this at the level of elementary and secondary schools.) This has been accompanied by a loss of local democracy. At the same time, the role of the state in dealing with the destructive rapaciousness produced by "economically rational" decisions has been sharply reduced.[39]

At the risk of redundancy, let me restate Mark Olssen's point about the shift involving a change in subject position from "homo economicus, who naturally behaves out of self-interest and is relatively detached from the state, to manipulatable man, who is created by the state and who is continually encouraged to be perpetually responsive." As he said, "In an age of universal welfare, the perceived possibilities of slothful indolence create necessities for new forms of vigilance, surveillance, 'performance appraisal' and of forms of control generally. In this model the state has taken it upon itself to keep us all up to the mark. The state will see to it that each one makes a 'continual enterprise of ourselves' ... in what seems to be a process of 'governing without governing.'"[40]

The power of Olssen's point is to remind us that neoliberalism requires the constant production of evidence that you are doing things "efficiently" and in the "correct" way. We are witnessing the effects of the suturing together of the seemingly contradictory tendencies of neoliberal and neoconservative discourses and practices on the ground in many nations, for as I showed this is exactly what is happening at all levels of education, from elementary, middle, and secondary schools to higher education. And this is occurring at the same time as the state itself becomes increasingly subject to commercialization. This situation has given rise to what might best be called an audit culture. To get a sense of the widespread nature of such practices, ones that are represented in but also extend well beyond the reach of No Child Left Behind, it is useful here to quote from Leys, one of the most perceptive analysts of this growth:

> [There is a] proliferation of *auditing*, i.e., the use of business derived concepts of independent supervision to measure and evaluate performance by public agencies and public employees, from civil servants and school teachers to university [faculty] and doctors: environmental audit, value for money audit, management audit, forensic audit, data audit, intellectual property audit, medical audit, teaching audit and technology audit emerged and, to varying degrees of institutional stability and acceptance, very few people have been left untouched by these developments.[41]

The widespread nature of these evaluative and measurement pressures, and their ability to become parts of our common sense, crowd out other conceptions of effectiveness and democracy.

> In place of a society of citizens with the democratic power to ensure effectiveness and proper use of collective resources, and relying in large measure on trust in the public sector, there emerged a society of "auditees," anxiously preparing for audits and inspections. A punitive culture of "league tables" developed (purporting to show the relative efficiency and inefficiency of universities or schools or hospitals). Inspection agencies were charged with "naming and shaming" "failing" individual teachers, schools, social work departments, and so on; private firms were invited to take over and run "failing" institutions.[42]

The ultimate result of an auditing culture of this kind is not the promised decentralization that plays such a significant role rhetorically in most neoliberal self-understandings, but what seems to be a massive recentralization and what is best seen as a process of dedemocratization.[43] Making the state more "business friendly" and importing business models directly into the core functions of the state such as hospitals and education—in combination with a rigorous and unforgiving ideology of individual accountability—these are the hallmarks of life today.[44] Once again, the growth of for-profit ventures such as Edison Schools in the United States, the increasing standardization and technicization of content within teacher education programs so that social reflexivity and critical understanding are nearly evacuated from courses,[45] the constant pressure to "perform" according to imposed and often reductive standards in our institutions of education, and similar kinds of things are the footprints that these constantly escalating pressures have left on the terrain of education.

A key to all of this is something to which I pointed in an earlier chapter, the *devaluing* of public goods and services. It takes long-term and creative ideological work, but once again people must be made to see anything that is public as "bad" and anything that is private as "good." And anyone who works in these public institutions must be seen as inefficient and in need of the sobering facts of competition so that they work longer and harder.[46] When the people who work in public institutions fight back and argue for more respectful treatment and for a greater realization that simplistic solutions do not deal with the complexities that they face every day in the real world of schools, universities, and communities, they are labeled as recalcitrant and selfish and as uncaring. Sometimes, as in the case of former U.S. Secretary of Education Page's public comments to what he thought was a sympathetic audience, they are even called "terrorists." And these "recalcitrant, selfish, and uncaring" employees—teachers, academics, administrators, social workers, and almost all other public employees—can then have their labor externally controlled and intensified by people who criticize them mercilessly, often as in the case of major corporations while these same businesses are shedding their own social responsibilities by paying little or no taxes.

I noted earlier that it is not just the labor of state employees that is radically altered; so too is the labor of "consumers." When services such as hospitals and schools are commodified, a good deal of the work that was formerly done by state employees is shifted onto those using the service. Examples of labor being shifted to the "consumer" include online banking, airline ticketing and check-in, supermarket self-checkouts, and similar things. Each of these is advertised as enhancing "choice" and each comes with a system of incentives and disincentives. Thus, one can get airline miles for checking in on one's computer. Or as some banks are now doing, there is an extra charge if you want to see a real live bank teller rather than using an ATM (which itself often now has an extra charge for using it).

The effects of such changes may be hidden but that does not make them any less real. Some of these are clearly economic: the closing of bank branches; the laying off of large numbers of workers, including in elementary, middle, and secondary schools and in higher education; the intensification of the workload of the fewer workers who remain. Some are hidden in their effects on consumers: exporting all of the work and the necessary commitment of time onto those people who are now purchasing the service; searching for information that was once given by the government; doing one's banking and airline work oneself; bagging and checking out at supermarkets.[47] The classed and raced specificities of this are crucial, because the ability to do such electronic searching and education for example is dependent on the availability of computers and especially time to engage in such actions. It requires resources—both temporal and financial, to say nothing of emotional— that are differentially distributed.[48]

This all may seem so trivial. But when each "trivial" instance is added up, the massiveness of the transformation in which labor is transferred to the consumer is striking. For it to be successful, our common sense must be changed so that we see the world only as individual consumers and we see ourselves as surrounded by a world in which everything is potentially a commodity for sale. To speak more theoretically, as I claimed in an earlier chapter the subject position on offer is indeed the deraced, declassed, and degendered "possessive individual," an economically rational actor who is constructed by and constructs a reality in which democracy is no longer a political concept but is reduced to an economic one.[49]

Mark Fowler, Ronald Reagan's chair of the Federal Communications Commission, once publicly stated that television is simply a toaster with pictures. A conservative media mogul in England seemed to agree, when he said that there is no difference between a television program and a cigarette lighter.[50] Both positions are based on an assumption that cultural form and content and the processes of distribution are indeed commodities. There are few more important mechanisms of cultural selection and distribution than schools and universities. And under this kind of logic, one might say that educational institutions are simply toasters with students. There is something deeply disturbing about this position not only in its vision of education, but profoundly in its understanding of the lives of the people who actually work in such institutions and in the often underfunded, understaffed, and difficult conditions now being experienced there. Although it would be too reductive to see educational work merely in labor process terms, the intensification that has resulted from the conditions associated with this assemblage of assumptions has become rather pronounced.[51]

Of course, many of us may be apt to see such things as relatively humorous or innocuous. Aren't market-based proposals for such things as schools, universities, health care and so much more just another, but supposedly more efficient, way of making services available? But not only are these ideologically driven "reforms" *not* all that efficient,[52] the process of privatization is strikingly different than public ownership and control. For example, in order to market something like education, it must first be transformed into a commodity, a "product." The product is then there to serve different ends. Thus, rather than schooling being aimed at creating critically democratic citizenship as its ultimate goal (although we should never romanticize an Edenic past when this was actually the case; schooling has always been a site of struggle over what its functions would actually be, with the working class and many women and people of color being constructed as "not quite citizens"),[53] the entire process can slowly become aimed instead at the generation of profit for shareholders or a site whose hidden purpose is to document the efficiency of newly empowered managerial forms within the reconstituted state.[54]

The fact that such things as the for-profit Edison Schools in the United States have not generated the significant profits that their investors had dreamed of means that the process of commodification is at least partly being rejected. For many people in all walks of life, the idea of "selling" our schools and our children is somehow disturbing, as the continuing controversy over Channel One amply demonstrates.[55] These intuitions demonstrate that in our everyday lives there remains a sense that there is something very wrong with our current and still-too-uncritical fascination with markets and audits.

However, this optimism needs to be immediately balanced by the immense growth of for-profit online universities such as the University of Phoenix, an institution that exemplifies the transformation of education into a saleable commodity. It also needs to be balanced by a recognition of the army of tutoring companies and administrative services companies that have taken advantage of the many opportunities for profit provided by No Child Left Behind. The latter are growing rapidly. As Burch says, these new federal mandates "raised the stakes on standardized test performance and encouraged [school] districts to purchase new services and products in order to comply with the law."[56] Indeed, there are increasingly explicit references to NCLB in the for-profit companies' marketing strategies. Schools throughout the nation are witnessing a rapidly growing demand for such services. Unyielding and cumbersome accountability requirements, then, stimulate even more marketization. "The new educational privatization is being spurred by an expanded federal role in educational policy ... [and the] overriding influence of the State invite[s] new forms of education industry."[57] Entire schools systems are seen as sites not of public service but as sites of profit. This brings to mind the point I made earlier that business will constantly seek to redefine pubic services into things that can bought and sold. It also once again shows how crucial it is for us to see the connections, both overt and covert, between NCLB's supposed focus on efficiency and accountability, on the one hand, and the creation of markets and a commitment to privatization, on the other.

David Marquand summarizes the worrisome tendencies I have been describing in the following way:

> The public domain of citizenship and service should be safeguarded from incursions by the market domain of buying and selling. ... The goods of the public domain—health care, crime prevention, and education—should not be treated as commodities or proxy commodities. The language of buyer and seller, producer and consumer, does not belong in the public domain; nor do the relationships which that language implies. Doctors and nurses do not "sell" medical services; students are not "customers" of their teachers; policemen and policewomen do not "produce" public order. The attempt to force these relationships into a market model undermines the service ethic, degrades the institutions that embody it and robs the notion of common citizenship of part of its meaning.[58]

I agree. In my mind, public institutions are the defining features of a caring and democratic society. The market relations that are sponsored by capitalism should exist to pay for these institutions, *not* the other way around. Thus, markets are to be subordinate to the aim of producing a fuller and thicker participatory democratic polity and daily life.[59] It should be clear by now that a cynical conception of democracy that is "on sale" to voters and manipulated and marketed by political and economic elites does not adequately provide for goods such as general and higher education, objective information, media and new forms of communication that are universally accessible, well-maintained public libraries for all, public health, and universal health care. At best, markets provide these things in radically unequal ways, with class, gender, and especially race being extremely powerful markers of these inequalities.[60] If that is the case—even if the definitions of the "public" were and often still are based on the construction of gendered and raced spaces[61]—the very idea of public institutions is under concerted attack. They need to be provided—and defended—collectively. Such things are anything but secondary. They are the defining characteristics of what it means to be a just society.[62]

Unfortunately, the language of privatization, marketization, and constant evaluation has increasingly saturated public discourse. In many ways, it has become common sense—and the critical intuitions that something may be wrong with all of this may slowly wither. Yet, in many nations where conditions are even worse, this has not necessarily happened, as the growth of participatory budgeting, "Citizen Schools," and close relations between teacher education programs and building more socially responsive and critical curricular and pedagogical initiatives in Porto Alegre, Brazil, and elsewhere documents.[63] We can learn from these nations' experiences and we can relearn what it means to reconstitute the civic in our lives.[64] Education has a fundamental role to play in doing exactly that. But it can only do so if it is protected from those who see it as one more product to be consumed as we measure it and who interpret the intellectual and emotional labor of those who are engaged in educational work though the lenses of standardization, rationalization, and auditing.

Having said this, however, interrupting conservative modernization requires that we have a more adequate understanding of both some of its fundamental dynamics and its social functions and roots. I want to turn to this now.

New Managerialism in Class Terms

Throughout this chapter, I have been broadly describing particular kinds of tendencies that are reconstructing what counts as legitimate knowledge, legitimate education, legitimate evidence, and legitimate labor, as evidenced in policies such as No Child Left Behind. Yet, we need to be cautious about reductive analyses in understanding where these ideological movements come from. It would be too easy to simply say that these are the predictable effects of competitive globalization, of capital in crisis and its accompanying fiscal crisis of the state, or in more Foucauldian terms of the micro-politics of governmentality and normalization, although there is some truth to all of these.[65] These tendencies underpinning conservative modernization are also "solutions" that are generated by particular actors, and here we need to be more specific about class relations inside and outside of higher education.

In the interests of time, and to bring the argument directly into this chapter's critical reading of the specific reforms involved in the United States, here I need to reiterate much of what I said about the new middle class in Chapter 2. This is not the most readerly strategy, and I thank you in advance for your patience. But it does provide for a logical coherence in which the arguments I've made about this class fraction can now sit side by side with the critical analysis of the relationship between audit cultures and markets that I do in this chapter.

As Basil Bernstein has reminded us and as I have argued at much greater depth elsewhere, a good deal of the genesis of and support for the policies of conservative modernization, and especially of the constant need for audits, the production of "evidence," rationalization, and standardization of both labor and knowledge comes not only from capital and its neoliberal allies in government, but from a particular fraction of the professional and managerial new middle class.[66] This fraction of the professional new middle class gains its own mobility within the state and within the economy based on the use of technical expertise. These are people with backgrounds in management and efficiency techniques who provide the technical and "professional" support for accountability, measurement, "product control," and assessment that is required by the proponents of neoliberal policies of marketization and neoconservative policies of tighter central control in education.

Members of this fraction of the upwardly mobile professional and managerial new middle class do not necessarily believe in the ideological positions that underpin all aspects of the conservative alliance. In fact in other aspects of their lives they may be considerably more moderate and even "liberal" politically. However, as experts in efficiency, management, testing, and accountability, they provide the technical expertise to put in place the policies of conservative modernization. As I noted, their own mobility *depends* on the expansion of both such expertise and the professional ideologies of control, measurement, and efficiency that accompany it. Thus, they often support such policies as "neutral instrumentalities" even when these policies may be used for purposes other than the supposedly neutral ends this class fraction is committed to.

Because of this, it is important to realize that a good deal of the current emphasis on audits and more rigorous forms of accountability, on tighter control, and a vision that competition will lead to greater efficiency is not totally reducible to the needs of neoliberals and neoconservatives. Rather, part of the pressure for these policies comes from educational managers and bureaucratic offices who fully believe that such control is warranted and "good." Not only do these forms of control have an extremely long history in education,[67] but tighter control, high-stakes testing, and (reductive) accountability methods provide more dynamic roles for such managers.

Let me briefly say more about this, as this is significant in terms of the self-understanding of class actors within the administrative apparatus of the state. The decades of attacks on state employees have not only had the predictable effects of lost employment and worsening working conditions, although these kinds of things are continuing within education and elsewhere. These attacks also have had profound effects on identities and have produced a crisis among many state employees and managers about doubts to their expertise and their ability to "help" the public.[68] New identities that are centered around enhanced technical proficiency and a set of assumptions that deep-seated problems in education and the entire social sphere can be provided by enhancing efficiency and holding people more rigorously accountable for their actions have developed over time, sponsored in part by neoliberal discourses that have opened spaces within the state for such expertise. This enables those class fractions with technical forms of cultural capital centered on accountability and managerial efficiency to occupy these spaces and to guarantee a place for the uses of their knowledge. This is an ideal situation for the professional and managerial new middle class. They can see themselves as engaging in a moral crusade—seeing themselves as being endlessly responsive to "clients" and "consumers" in such a way that they are participating in the creation of a newly reconstituted and more efficient set of institutions that will "help everyone"—and at the same time enhancing the status of their own expertise. In Bourdieu's terms, this allows for particular kinds of conversion strategies, ones in which their cultural capital (technical and managerial expertise) can be converted into economic capital (positions and mobility within education and the state).[69]

This needs to be situated in the ways in which such cultural markets and conversion strategies operate in the larger set of class relations in which such new middle-class actors participate. My claims here are complicated and I can only outline a wider set of arguments. However, the implications of these arguments are serious if we are to fully understand why all of education, including higher education and who does and does not go there, seems to be experiencing a number of the restructurings I have discussed earlier.

This is a time when competition for credentials and cultural capital is intense. The increasing power of mechanisms of restratification such

as the return of high levels of mandatory standardization, more testing more often, and constant auditing of results also provides mechanisms—and an insistent logic—that enhance the chances that the
children of the professional and managerial new middle class will have
less competition from other students. Thus, the introduction of devices
to restratify a population—for this is what much of it is—enhances the
value of the credentials that the new middle class is more likely to accumulate, given the stock of cultural capital it already possesses.[70] I am
not claiming that this is necessarily intentional, but it does *function* to
increase the chances for mobility by middle-class children who depend
not on economic capital but on cultural capital for advancement.[71]
The effects of such policies and procedures on working-class students
and on students of oppressed minorities is more than a little visible in
an entire series of detailed and insightful studies,[72] and is made even
clearer in the data on Texas and the worsening of inequalities that I
reported earlier in this chapter.

As I did before, I want to stress the importance of this element
within conservative modernization, not only because it already occu-
pies considerable power within the state. It is crucial to focus on this
groups as well because, as I argued in an earlier part of this book, in the
situation I have described this group is not immune to ideological shifts
to the right and thus may not be as able to be self-conscious about the
role they may be playing in the restructuring of educational and social
policies I have been discussing in this chapter. Given the fear generated
by the attacks on the state and on the public sphere by both neoliberals
and neoconservatives, this class fraction is decidedly worried about the
future mobility of its children in an uncertain economic world. Thus,
they may be drawn even more overtly to parts of the conservative alliance's positions, especially those coming from the neoconservative elements that stress greater attention to traditional "high-status" content,
greater attention to testing, and a greater emphasis on schooling (and
the entire university system) as a stratifying mechanism.

Stephen Ball illuminates the tensions that the new middle class may
feel about this, as in many ways its members do have an ethical belief
in supporting equality of educational opportunity. But when it comes
to making decisions that may affect their own children, their choice is
clear. In a competitive system, in general anything that increases their
children's advantages will be the path that will be taken.[73] This can be
seen in a number of states in the United States, for example, where parents of this class fraction are supporting charter schools that will stress
academic achievement in traditional subjects and traditional teaching practices and in their engagement with other policies around, say,

choice programs that historically have been shown to largely benefit the children of the most advantaged.

I suggested in Chapter 2 that it remains to be seen where the majority of members of this class grouping will align in the future in the debates over policy. Given their contradictory ideological tendencies, it is possible that the Right will be able to mobilize them under conditions of fear for the future of their jobs and children, even when they still vote for, say, the Democrats in the United States or New Labour in the United Kingdom in electoral terms. At the very least, it would be romantic to assume that they will be responsive to the claims from those people who are employed in institutions of higher education and in education in general that the conditions under which they are increasingly working are damaging and that they are creating an education that is less and less worthy of its name. Indeed, given the panic over schooling that the Right has created and given the toxic combination both of the fiscal crisis in education and of the ways in which No Child Left Behind helps create the impression that public schooling itself is massively failing (a situation not helped by the fact that NCLB has proven to be largely an unfunded or underfunded mandate), the new middle class may vote its pocketbook and may position itself against increased funding and better working conditions for educators.

The Dispossessed and Support for Audit Cultures and Markets

So far I have asked us to step back from the specifics of policies such as No Child Left Behind so that we can critically assess the general tendencies surrounding the increasing marketization of everyday life and the growth of an audit culture. I have critically examined the logics that stand behind NCLB and have suggested that it is important that we see the linkages between its focus on audit and constant public scrutiny and evaluation on the one hand and its somewhat more hidden commitment to and openings for privatization on the other. I have argued that such tendencies are connected to class logics and that they will have deeply problematic effects on public schools and on the people who attend them and who work in them.

However, we need to be careful not to romanticize a past in which the state was supposedly responsive to all its citizens. As Charles Mills so powerfully argues, underlying our very idea of the modern liberal state and underlying the social commitments for which it supposedly stands is a *racial* contract.[74] Furthermore, as Gloria Ladson-Billings and others have claimed, in education as in so much else, "Race is always already present in every social configuring of our lives."[75] For these very reasons, it is imperative that we take a second look at the ways in which markets and audit cultures function—this time placing race at the center of our analysis, as different social positionings in society may give different meanings to neoliberal, neoconservative, and new managerial policies.

The criticisms of market relations and logics that I and others have made are crucial and must be continued and expanded.[76] But no matter how powerful they may be, we also need to acknowledge that these criticisms may often carry a number of unacknowledged assumptions about race. The market has been much less responsive to particular groups than others. Indeed, the subject position of "consumer" has been much less available to African-Americans and Latino/as than it has been for dominant groups. Thus, being actually *seen* as a "consumer," as someone who is a "rational economic actor" who uses audits and strong forms of accountability to evaluate one's institutions and to make thoughtful choices, does have partly progressive tendencies within it when this position is compared to the histories of the ways people of color have been socially coded in the United States and elsewhere. When people of color actively take on this different coding, they are not simply being incorporated into dominant economic discourses and relations; they are also partly engaged in a form of counterhegemonic action, one employing dominant economic discourses to subvert historically powerful racializing views that have had immense power in society.[77] Let us examine this somewhat more closely. The movement toward choice and the legitimation of private institutions that sit side by side with an unyielding commitment to a process of punitive evaluations in NCLB makes this examination of even greater import.

At the outset of this section, as I argued strongly in a previous chapter and shall develop more in my concluding chapter, race has always been a key presence in the structures of feeling surrounding markets and choice plans in education. Many of the strongest proponents of vouchers and similar plans may claim that their positions are based on a belief in the efficiency of markets, on the fear of a secularization of the sacred, or on the dangers of losing the values and beliefs that give meaning to their lives. (As I showed, these latter two fears are especially pronounced among the authoritarian populist religious conservative who are among the strongest proponents of both vouchers and home schooling.) However, historically, neither the economic nor the moral elements of this critique can be totally set apart from their partial genesis in the struggles over racial segregation, over busing to achieve integration, and in the loss of a federal tax exemption by conservative—and usually white only—religious academies. In short, the fear of the "racial

Other" has played a significant role in this discursive construction of the "problem of the public school."

Having said this, however, there is also increasing support for strong forms of accountability and for voucher and similar choice plans among "minority" groups. Given the fact that so much of the conservative tradition in the United States was explicitly shaped by racist and racializing discourses and practices,[78] and by a strongly anti-immigrant heritage as well, and given the fact that much of the current neoliberal and neoconservative attacks on the public sphere have had disproportionate effects on the gains of poor communities and on communities of color, the existence and growth of support among some members of dispossessed groups is more than a little striking.[79] A complex process of discursive and positional disarticulation and rearticulation is going here, as dominant groups attempt to pull dispossessed collectivities under their own leadership and dispossessed groups themselves attempt to employ the social, economic, and cultural capital usually possessed by dominant groups to gain collective power for themselves. As we shall see, even with what I said in my section on the growth of new managerial forms and who benefits from them, this is not only about new middle class conversion strategies; nor can the label "conservative" be employed easily in understanding the actions of all of the dispossessed groups who do ally themselves with conservative causes without at the same time reducing the complexity of the particular social fields of power on which they operate.

Perhaps the most interesting example of the processes of discursive and social disarticulation and rearticulation that one could find today involves the growing African-American (at least among *some* elements of the African-American community) support for neoliberal policies such as voucher plans[80]—and remember that behind NCLB is a movement not only to create strong forms of reductive accountability but also a larger agenda that includes proposals for vouchers and tax credits, inclusions that were muted for tactical reasons but were very clear in Texas, for instance.[81] A key instance is the Black Alliance for Educational Options (BAEO), a group of African-American parents and activists that is chaired by Howard Fuller, the former superintendent of Milwaukee public schools, one of the most racially segregated school systems in the United States. BAEO provides vocal support for holding schools and educators accountable both for their many failures in educating children from oppressed communities and for voucher plans and similar neoliberal proposals. It has generated considerable support within black communities throughout the nation, particularly within poor inner-city areas.

A sense of the language that underpins BAEO's commitment can be seen in the following quotes from its Web site:

> Our children are our most precious resource. It is our responsibility to love them, nurture them and protect them. It is also our responsibility to ensure that they are properly educated. Without a good education, they will [not] have a real chance to engage in the practice of freedom: the process of engaging in the fight to transform their world.

BAEO's mission is clear.

> The Black Alliance for Educational Options is a national, non-partisan member organization whose mission is to actively support parental choice to empower families and increase educational options for Black children.

The use of language here is striking. The language of neoliberalism (choice, parental empowerment, accountability, individual freedom) is reappropriated and sutured together with ideas of collective black freedom and a deep concern for the community's children. This creates something of a "hybrid" discourse that blends together meanings from multiple political sources and agendas. In some ways, this is similar to the long history of critical cultural analyses that demonstrate that people form bricolages in their daily lives and can employ language and commodities in ways undreamed of by the original producers of the language and products.[82]

Although this process of rearticulation and use is important to note, it is equally essential to recognize something that makes the creative bricolage in which BAEO is engaged somewhat more problematic. A very large portion of the group's funding comes directly from conservative sources such as the Bradley Foundation. The Bradley Foundation, a well-known sponsor of conservative causes, has not only been in the forefront of providing support for vouchers and privatization initiatives but also is one of the groups that provided significant support for Herrnstein and Murray's book, *The Bell Curve*,[83] the volume that argued that African-Americans were on average less intelligent than whites and that this was genetic in nature.

Thus, it would be important to ask about the nature and effects of the connections being made between rightist ideological and financial sources and BAEO itself. It is not inconsequential that neoliberal and neoconservative foundations provide not only funding but media visibility for "minority" groups who support—even critically—their agendas. The genesis of such funding is not inconsequential. Does this mean that groups such as BAEO are simply being manipulated by neo-liberal and neoconservative foundations and movements? An answer to this question is not easy, but even with my cautions stated above it is certainly not a simple "yes."

In public forums and in discussions that Tom Pedroni and I have had with some of leaders of BAEO, they have argued that they will use any funding sources available so that they can follow their own specific program of action. They would accept money from more liberal sources; but Bradley and other conservative foundations have come forward much more readily.[84] In the minds of the leaders of BAEO, the African-American activists are in control, not the conservative foundations. Thus, for BAEO, they see themselves as strategically positioning themselves in order to get funding from conservative sources. What they do with this funding, such as their strong (and well advertised in the media) support for voucher plans (although this support too is contingent and sometimes depends on local power relations), is wholly their decision. For them, the space provided by educational markets can be reoccupied for black cultural or nationalist politics and can be employed to stop what seems to them (more than a little accurately in my opinion) to be a war on black children.

However, although I have a good deal of respect for a number of the leaders of BAEO, it is important to remember that they are not the only ones strategically organizing on this social field of power. Like BAEO, groups affiliated with, say, the Bradley Foundation also know *exactly* what they are doing and know very well how to employ the agendas of BAEO for their own purposes, purposes that in the long term often may run directly counter to the interests of the majority of those with less power at both the national and regional levels. Is it really in the long-term interests of people of color to be affiliated with the same groups who provided funding and support for books such as *The Bell Curve*? I think not, although once again we need to recognize the complexities involved here.

I am certain that this kind of question is constantly raised about the conservative stances taken by the people of color who have made alliances with, say, neoliberals and neoconservatives—and by the activists within BAEO itself. When members of groups who are consistently "Othered" in this society strategically take on identities that support dominant groups, such questioning is natural and I believe essential. However, it is also crucial to remember that members of historically oppressed and marginalized groups have *always* had to act on a terrain that is not of their choosing, have always had to act strategically and creatively to gain some measure of support from dominant groups to advance their causes.[85] It is also the case that more recently national and local leaders of the Democratic Party in the United States have too often assumed that black support is simply *there,* that it doesn't need to be worked for.[86] Because of this, we may see the further development of "unusual alliances" over specific issues such as educational policies. When this is coupled with some of the tacit or overt support within some communities of color not only for voucher plans but also for anti-gay, antiabortion, pro-school prayer, and similar initiatives, the suturing together of some black groups with larger conservative movements on particular issues is not totally surprising.[87]

The existence and growing power of committed movements such as BAEO, however, does point out that we need to be careful about stereotyping groups who may publicly support neoliberal and neoconservative policies and who believe that things such as NCLB hold promise as first steps toward a more responsive and accountable educational process. Their perspectives need to be examined carefully and taken seriously, not simply dismissed as totally misguided, as people who have been duped into unthinking acceptance of a harmful set of ideologies. There are complicated strategic moves being made on an equally complex social field of power. I may—and do—strongly disagree with a number of the positions that groups such as BAEO take. However, to assume that they are simply puppets of conservative forces is not only to be too dismissive of their own attempts at social maneuvering, but I also believe that it may be tacitly racist as well.

Saying this doesn't mean that we need to weaken the arguments against audit cultures and the marketization and privatization of schooling and the larger society that I articulated earlier in this book. Voucher and tax-credit plans (the latter ultimately may actually be more dangerous) will still have some extremely problematic effects in the long term. One of the most important effects could be a *demobilization* of social movements within communities of color. Schools have played central roles in the creation of movements for justice. In essence, rather than being peripheral reflections of larger battles and dynamics, struggles over schooling—over what should be taught, over the relationship between schools and local communities, over the very ends and means of the institution itself—have provided a crucible for the *formation* of larger social movements toward equality.[88] These collective movements have transformed our definitions of rights, of who should have them, and of the role of the government in guaranteeing these rights. Absent organized, community-wide mobilizations, these transformations would not have occurred.

This is under threat currently. As I argued earlier, our more political and collective understandings of democracy are currently under attack, often more than a little successfully. These new definitions of democracy are largely based on possessive individualism, on the citizen as only a "consumer," and are inherently grounded in a process of deracing, declassing, and degendering.[89] These are the very groups that have employed struggles over educational access and outcomes to form themselves as self-conscious actors. If it is the case, as I strongly believe it is, that it is the organized efforts of social movements that ultimately have led to the transformation of our educational system in more democratic directions[90]—and this has been especially the case for mobilizations by people who have been labeled as society's "Others"—the long-term effects of neoliberal definitions of democracy may be truly tragic for communities of color (and working class groups), not only in increasing inequalities in schools[91] but also in leading to a very real loss of the impetus for *collective* solutions to pressing social problems. Once audit cultures discredit the very idea of public schooling (and this is one of the major hidden effects that may come from "reforms" such as No Child Left Behind and similar policies), if all problems are simply "solved" by individual choices on a market, then collective mobilizations tend to wither and perhaps even disappear. Given the crucial role played by organized movements surrounding education in the formation and growth of mobilizations among African-Americans, Latino/as, and many other communities of color against the denial of their rights,[92] this is not something to be welcomed. If history is any guide here, the results will not be pleasant. Thus, although short-term support for neoliberal and neoconservative policies may seem strategically wise to some members of less powerful groups, and may in fact generate short-term mobilizations, I remain deeply worried about what will happen over time.[93] It is the long-term implications of individuating processes and ideologies, and their effects on the necessity of larger and constantly growing social mobilizations that aim toward substantive transformations within the public sphere, that need to be of concern as well.

Other points should be added here about what might be called the political economy of everyday life. I argued earlier that marketization and commodification, when accompanied by the shrinking of state responsibility, intensifies the labor of the "consumer." This process relegates to the individual or the family all of the tasks of information gathering and evaluation. This often entails an extensive amount of work, especially for those communities and families with fewer economic resources, less technical skill, underresourced or closed libraries and social service centers, and the emotional and physical burdens of simply providing for human needs in an unforgiving economy. Because, as VanDunk and Dickman show, the major urban areas where marketizing tendencies such as vouchers are now in place are doing a very poor job of making information on schools, curricula, teaching, and so on easily available to the public and especially to poor persons of color,[94] this puts these "consumers" at a serious disadvantage.

Even with these difficulties, there is something much more complicated ideologically than meets the eye going on here. As I suggested earlier and as Pedroni and I have discussed at greater length,[95] when persons of color take up the position of "rational economic actor," of consumer, this does have counterhegemonic possibilities and does provide for opportunities for different social codings. However, while noting this—and it must be noted—possibilities are just that, possibilities. They require objective material conditions and resources in people's lived environments in order for them to be acted on. Such possibilities may not be easily acted on under the conditions of neoliberal restructuring in the economy, in social and cultural services, health care, and in so much more in urban and rural communities populated by those who are seen as the constitutive outsiders in this society.[96]

On Possibilities

I began this chapter with a critical reading of No Child Left Behind and of the negative effects that the policies and practices embodied in it and in similar "reforms" have had. I placed it within certain larger worrisome tendencies within our societies. I pointed to the steady growth of neoliberal restructurings of institutions and identities, and to the hard and creative ideological work that such transformations require. In the process, I noted that commodification and audit cultures tend to reinforce each other and that these processes are played out on multiple terrains, with education being one of the most significant.

There has been exceptional work done on the ways in which class works in altered contexts such as these. For example, I drew on this research for my arguments in Chapter 3 that middle-class parents often have a store of cultural and social capital that enables them to employ such things as audits and "choice" in education as part of complex conversion strategies that guarantee their own children's advantage.[97] There is also an emerging body of work on how this is related to gendered labor, particularly the work of mothers.[98] However, there has been less attention paid to the ways in which members of historically oppressed "minority" groups, particularly poor persons of color, *strategically* deal with issues of accountability, marketization, privatization, and "choice" in the United States.[99]

Because of this, part of my interest in the latter sections of this chapter has been not only to criticize No Child Left Behind and the ideological tendencies embodied in it, although that is of considerable importance. I also wanted to provide a context for a serious discussion both of the meaning and the effects of the strategic actions on the parts of those who must act on a terrain in which historically grounded power relations and struggles take on even more complicated forms. These actions require a much more nuanced reading than our usual critical appraisals are apt to do. We must continue to engage in the critical work of detailing the ways in which conservative modernization is restructuring our lives and institutions. But this needs to be done with a thorough and historically grounded understanding of the need to broaden the "we" and, hence, to recognize the contradictory and multiple daily realities that govern these effects. Thus, I have focused as well on the growing support for vouchers and strict accountability measures among *some* persons of color to enable us to see the ways in which the right has had some success in its attempt to bring groups who would normally find little to support in its agenda under the ideological leadership of the conservative alliance.[100]

In this chapter I also have discussed some of the ways in which certain elements of conservative modernization have had an impact on education at multiple levels. I have pointed to the growth of commodifying logics and the audit culture that accompanies them. In the process, I have highlighted a number of dangers that we currently face.

However, I have also urged us not to assume that these conditions can be reduced to the automatic working out of simple formulae. We need a much more subtle and complex picture of class relations and class projects to understand what is happening—and a more sensitive and historically grounded analysis of the place of racial dynamics in the vision both of "a world out of control" that needs to be policed and of "cultural pollution" that threatens "real knowledge" in the growth of markets and audit cultures. I also have asked us to listen carefully to the critiques coming from collective voices within oppressed communities and to not assume that one can read off their positions by reducing their agency to simply expressions of rightist ideological formula. Becoming more nuanced about such constitutive dynamics will not guarantee that we can interrupt the tendencies on which I have focused here. But it is one essential step in understanding the genesis of what is at stake in a serious politics of interruption.

If the issue of interruption is not to only be an academic one, however, it requires something else. We need to think more clearly about what needs to be defended and what needs to be changed. Just as Marx reminded us that capitalism might actually be an improvement over feudalism, we may need to take seriously the possibility that some of the intuitions behind new managerial impulses and audits also may constitute an improvement over previous visions of educational policies and practices. Let me say more about this.

There is a complicated and sometimes contradictory politics at work here. Schools and universities have been very real sites of cultural conflict: over collective memory, over what counts as legitimate knowledge, over voice and participation, and over their social and educational aims and effects. Take the university for example. It has also been a site of considerable conflict over who can and cannot go to it. The intense struggles over the university's gendered and raced hiring practices, ones in which it has taken decades to even begin to address the cultural and social imbalances in serious ways, stand as eloquent witness to the continuing nature of the problems that need to be faced. Because of this, some forms of public accountability—to ask universities to provide evidence that they are taking seriously their social responsibilities concerning hiring practices for example—were and continue to be partial victories. And the same needs to be said about the demand for forms of accountability in our public schools. There *are* racist practices in our schools. Class differentials still *count* and they count in powerful ways. And with all of the public attention now being given to the question of "What about the boys?", gender relations and the treatment of girls in schools are still powerful dynamics that generate very real inequalities.

Furthermore, elementary, middle, and secondary schools and institutions of higher education are increasingly complex places financially and organizationally. Because of this as well, (*democratically* inclined) management skills are indeed necessary. By not taking the development and refinement of these skills and dispositions seriously, we may be creating a space that will predictably be filled with those committed to neoliberal and new managerial impulses. The issue is not whether or not we need accountability, but the kinds of logics of accountability, and the question of accountability to whom, that tend to now guide the process of public schools and higher education. An alternative to the external imposition of targets, performance criteria, and quantifiable outcomes—but one that still takes the issue of public accountability seriously—needs to and can be built.[101] Absent our taking these issues more seriously, policies such as No Child Left behind and similar kinds of "reforms" will increasingly occupy that space.

Workable Alternatives

Of course, these issues are complicated. However, complexity doesn't necessarily have to lead to paralysis. There are practical alternatives to a system of accountability that relies on a single score on a single test as so much of the current love affair with audits seems to imply. Valenzuela, for example, points to the proposals developed by the Coalition for Authentic Reform in Education. (Details of this can be found at the following Web site: http://www.fairtest.org/arn/masspage.html.) In this approach, standardized tests in literacy and numeracy are given, but their use is limited and complemented by a wide array of other information—student exhibitions, portfolios, products, and performance tasks. Broadly defined competencies, not only reductive and atomized bits of knowledge, are stressed. By relying on a less regimented and more local curricular focus that is "authentically situated within the values and opportunity structures of communities," this not only enables more democratic involvement on the part of parents and the community, but it also provides space for innovation through the use of "more robust and authentic forms of assessment."[102] This kind of emphasis is already having profound effects in other nations. As I have repeatedly noted, such things as the "citizen school" and "participatory budgeting" in Brazil where accountability is much more participatory and democratic provide impressive examples of what can be done even in times of fiscal hardship.[103]

But although we have much to learn at times from other nations, we need not look only outside our borders. Parts of this alternative model can be found in place in a number of states already. Maine, for example, has instituted a model of assessment that includes the use of standardized instruments, but also relies on tests developed by teachers, and on portfolios, student presentations, district-wide "writing prompts," and a number of other locally developed ways of "giving accounts" of how students are actually doing.[104] Although not perfect, the fact that there are examples of such alternatives is evidence that it is possible to build and use workable approaches to accountability that are not limited to those found in Texas or in No Child Left Behind. Such models can include as constituent parts, not add-ons, locally derived and authentic forms of assessment, can have academic rigor, and can be based on and promote a rich set of educational experiences.[105] And they can have markedly less racializing effects than those approaches now being instituted throughout the United States currently.

Being Honest about Educational Reform

These reforms are beginnings, not an end point. As first steps, they need to be built on. We need to be honest. Unlike current forms, any serious transformation of how we collectively think and act on accountability would need to rest, and to be constantly rebuilt, upon the constitution of "processes of [critical] deliberation that enable understanding and agreement out of differing accounts of public purpose and service."[106] And this cannot be based on a simple assertion that everything we have now needs to be defended against initiatives such as No Child Left Behind or similar things. A key here, of course, is what and who counts as the "public" and whose voices are heard.

As Nancy Fraser and Charles Mills have argued and as I noted earlier, the public sphere has historically been constructed as a gendered and raced space.[107] The prevailing definitions of "public" and "private" were based on a particular assemblage of assumptions about who was a legitimate participant and who was not. Because of this, the simple assertion that public schools and the university play crucial roles based on their importance as part of the public sphere is an insufficient defense. Yes, they need to be defended and the public sphere is certainly under attack. But what kind of public sphere(s) do we have in mind? How should "it" be reconstituted? How would this reconstitution be integrated into what Fraser calls a politics of redistribution and a politics of recognition?[108] In more everyday words, given the criticisms that have been made of the ways in which the public sphere in general and schools and universities in particular have actually operated over time, what needs to change to take account of these criticisms?

What we should not be doing is defending all of the actually existing practices of our public schools and universities, since many of these may be discriminatory, classist, sexist, racist, or have a history that is based in elitism. Instead, we must ask what *specifically* do we wish to defend? In asking this question, as I mentioned earlier we may need to recognize that there are elements of good sense as well as bad sense in the criticisms that are made about schools and universities. The space of criticism has been taken up by neoliberal claims and managerial impulses. But this does not mean that our educational system did not need to change or that a simple return to the previous form and content of education is anywhere near a sufficient set of policies. Here the right is at least partly correct; and the powerful complaints about this by dispossessed parents and activists within poor communities cannot be ignored by simply adopting a defensive posture. Realizing that there are indeed elements of good sense as well as bad sense in those positions that may challenge accepted forms of schooling doesn't mean we must accept rightist interpretations of causes and solutions, but rejecting that fact that there are serious problems simply plays into the hands of those who wish to integrate even more people under the umbrella of the conservative alliance. As the father of a black child myself, I certainly can see why many activists within communities of color would find parts of the rejection of our taken-for-granted practices of schooling compelling, for example.

Again, let us be honest. If a simple return to past practices is neither possible nor wise, it is hard to specify in advance other than in broad strokes the exact character of the kinds of models of structures, practices, and deliberative agency that should guide public life inside and outside of our elementary, middle, and secondary schools and in higher education. As Raymond Williams reminded us, the "common" has to be ongoingly built, since what counts as the common is the never-ending process of critical deliberation over the very question of the common itself.[109] This more critical understanding is evacuated under the aegis of the logics of markets and audits, since we do know that what is currently being built/imposed is often destructive, even in its own terms of assuming that establishing markets and audits will restore responsiveness and even trust.

Stuart Ranson summarizes these arguments in the following way.

> This neo-liberal regime cannot realize its purpose of institutional achievement and public trust. Achievement grows out of the internal goods of motivation to improve (that follows recognition and the mutual deliberation of purpose) rather than the external imposition of quantifiable targets, while public trust follows deliberation of common purpose out of difference and discord, rather than the forces of competition that only create a hierarchy of class advantage and exclusion.[110]

Ranson is not sanguine about the possibility of building a public sphere that both challenges the neoliberal and neoconservative construction of an audit culture and commodification and goes beyond the limits of older versions of what counts as the public sphere. However, he does articulate a sense of what is required to do so. A reconstituted vision of the public and a set of practices and structures that support it are grounded in the following.

> Trust and achievement can only emerge in a framework of public accountability that enables different accounts of public purpose and practice to be deliberated in a democratic public

sphere: constituted to include difference, enable participation, voice and dissent, through to collective judgment and decision, that is in turn accountable to the public.[111]

Such a vision is not simply utopian. Indeed, take the history of higher education. This history—from early mechanics institutes, to "people's universities," to the construction of colleges that were and are organic to historically black communities and struggles, to the many attempts at creating closer cooperative connections between universities and in particular teacher education programs and culturally, politically, and economically dispossessed groups[112]—suggests that there is a rich storehouse of knowledge on possibilities for doing this. But this requires the restoration of memory. Thus, historical work is absolutely essential if we are to go forward. Here I do not mean a nostalgic longing for an imagined past; but an honest appraisal of the limits and possibilities of what has been done before. And here we need to listen to a much broader array of voices, including Paulo Freire, Miles Horton, W.E.B. DuBois, Carter Woodson, and the voices of the thousands of teachers (most of whom were and are women) and community activists within the multiple oppressed communities within this nation who struggled to build an education that was responsive to the lives and hopes of their students.

The task is not only historical, however. There are concrete examples of systemic educational reform in a number of nations—as I've stressed repeatedly, in particular in Porto Alegre, Brazil. Indeed, as I have indicated, the successes surrounding the Citizen School and the process of participatory budgeting provide powerful instances of what can be done to build an education that takes the complexities of class, race, gender, and other social positionings seriously and enhances the present and future lives of the least advantaged people of a community.[113] What is happening in Porto Alegre also demonstrates something else. By reversing the international patterns of who is the teacher and who is the taught—by having the South teach the North about "what works" in powerful models of school reform—we are also challenging the manner in which information flows from the imperial center to the supposedly less advanced periphery.

The responsibilities and opportunities do not end there. Undoubtedly, within each and every institution of education at all levels, within the crevices and cracks so to speak, there are counterhegemonic practices being built and defended. But they are too often isolated from each other and never get organized into coherent movements and strategies. Part of the task is to make public the successes in contesting the control over curricula, pedagogy, and evaluation and in reaching the children that our educational system has in fact "left behind"—over all of our work.[114] Although public "storytelling" may not be sufficient, it performs an important function. It keeps alive and reminds ourselves of the very possibility of difference in an age of audits, commodification, and disrespect.

We have successful models for doing this, such as the crucial discussions of respectful and successful pedagogic work done by my colleague Gloria Ladson-Billings.[115] Important resources also can be found in the critical education journal *Rethinking Schools* and in the book *Democratic Schools*.[116] As I said, in that book, James Beane and I saw our role as researchers very differently. We acted as "secretaries" for socially critical educators and made public their stories of building curricula and pedagogies that expressly embodied Ranson's vision of a reconstituted public sphere based on difference, participation, voice, and dissent. The fact that this book went on to sell hundreds of thousands of copies in multiple languages points to how ready critical educators and community members are to do something that actually makes a difference.

To all of this can be added the work of Gutstein and Peterson on critical mathematics education, Roth and Barton on critical science education, Debbie Meier and her colleagues in demonstrating that there can be and are powerful and successful alternatives to the reductive and alienating policies embodied in No Child Left Behind, and so many others.[117] But can teachers be educated to actually do these alternatives in a time when the pressures on them to perform in accordance with "more testing, more often" are so intense? We have evidence that this is the case. Morva MacDonald's analysis of how a socially responsive and educationally wise teacher education can be built, one that takes account of these things, demonstrates as well that teacher education can successfully engage with such practical and political issues in realistic and workable ways.[118]

Although *Democratic Schools* and these other resources are about elementary, middle, and secondary schools, and can provide important exemplars of how education based on "thick" democracy can actually work in real schools in real communities, they also point to the ways in which such strategic interruptions can proceed in other institutional contexts.

This, then, is another task. Can we, too, act as secretaries for some of our colleagues in education and for the activists in multiple communities, making public their partial, but still successful, resistances to the regime of regulation that we are currently experiencing? The narratives of their (our) political/pedagogic lives can bear witness to the possibility of taking steps toward building a reconstituted public sphere within the spaces in which we live and work. And can we constantly hold our definitions of who the "we" is up to critical scrutiny so that it becomes a more decentered unity that builds multiple movements that challenge the neoliberal, neoconservative, and new managerial impulses that stand behind NCLB?

We cannot answer this question unless we examine why such neoliberal and neoconservative positions make *popular* sense to another group, the rapidly growing and increasingly powerful part of the alliance that I've called authoritarian populists. The next four chapters engage in a detailed analysis of the world as seen through the eyes of these religiously committed groups and explore the contradictory politics and tensions within their positions on education and the larger society.

CHAPTER 5

Endangered Christianity

Darwin, God, and Evil

To understand authoritarian populist religious conservatives, we have to go further than was done in my analysis of neoliberalism, neoconservatism, and the managerialism of the new middle class. We also need to think historically both about particular theological impulses and about the importance of how race, class, gender, and religious and regional relations interact over time. But this needs to be in such a way that the intersections and contradictions of these relations are not ignored. In this chapter, I focus largely on the historical genesis of such movements. In Chapter 6, I examine the ways in which all of the major elements within such conservative religious beliefs can make sense to their proponents, even when they seem repressive to an outsider. Then, in Chapters 7 and 8, I take one of the most powerful results of their anti-school sentiments—home schooling—and critically analyze its social, ideological, and educational impulses and a number of its hidden costs. However, it is important to remember at the outset of this section of the book Gramsci's admonition that there will be elements of good sense as well as bad sense in such conservative positions. Not to realize this makes authoritarian populists into mere puppets. This is decidedly not the case.

One should never underestimate the power of religion in the United States. Although polling data are clearly skewed by the specific construction and wording of questions and by who is doing the asking, the results are often striking in terms of religious leanings. A sense of the nature and extent of religious beliefs in my own state, Wisconsin—historically one of the most progressive states in the nation—is indicative of the situation. When asked by the University of Wisconsin's Survey Research Laboratory about their religious beliefs, 94 percent of respondents said that they believed in God; 67 percent affirmed their belief in the devil; and 80 percent believed in the existence of angels. It is the latter two that may be surprising. That two-thirds of the people asked believe in the existence of the devil is evidence of the power of a sense of evil—real and embodied—in people's psyche. For many people, this very sense of embodied good and evil is rooted in a strict reading of the Bible. This inerrantist (the Bible is without error) position has certainly had an impact on debates over educational policy and practice.

In the 1980s, the Institute for Creation Research created a model piece of legislation, the Balanced Treatment for Creation-Science and Evolution-Science Act. It required that equal time be given in schools for both creationist and evolutionary perspectives. It described creation-science as based on six tenets:

> Creation-science includes the scientific evidences and related inferences that indicate: (1) Sudden creation of the universe, energy, and life from nothing; (2) The insufficiency of mutation and natural selection in bringing about development of all living kinds from a single organism; (3) Changes only within fixed limits of originally created kinds of plants and animals; (4) Separate ancestry for men and apes; (5) Explanation of the earth's geology by catastrophism, including the occurrence of a worldwide flood; and (6) A relatively recent inception of the earth and living kinds.[1]

A decade later, on August 11, 1999, the Kansas Board of Education voted to delete virtually any mention of evolution from the state's science curriculum. Although this did not officially prevent the teaching of evolution, it did make it much less likely as questions on evolution will not be included on the statewide assessment tests. Thus, instead of attempting to push creationism into the curriculum—something that historically has not been successful by itself—creationists have found more success in keeping Darwinism out of the curriculum or in having it presented as merely an unproved theory. Even where it is not prohibited, many teachers have decided that teaching evolution is too risky in the face of outcries from conservative parents, school boards, and churches.[2]

Not only did the state's Board of Education delete most references to biological evolution, but it also expunged any mention of such things as the "big bang theory." For creationists, a position that holds that the universe was born out of a vast primordial explosion contradicts the entire premise of the Bible and Genesis. The curriculum that was approved by the state Board went so far as to include a case study that creationists use to debunk evolution.[3] The creationist sympathizers have again gained significant power in Kansas and elsewhere and are again pushing their agenda on schools and textbooks.

This has become a very difficult situation for many teachers and administrators as you might imagine. A biology teacher in Birmingham, Alabama, explained that "she simply ignored evolution because she knew she'd get in trouble with the principal if word got out that she was teaching it. … Other teachers were doing the same thing."[4] For many principals, "We don't have time to teach everything so let's leave out the things that will cause us problems."[5]

A sense of what is at stake for creationists in their consistent historical attempt to remove Darwinian evolution from the curriculum of the schools of the nation can be seen in the following quote from the leader of a creationist group, Answers in Genesis:

> Students in the public schools are being taught that evolution is a fact, that they're just products of survival of the fittest. There's not meaning in life if we're just animals in a struggle for survival. It creates a sense of purposeless and hopelessness, which I think leads to pain, murder and suicide.[6]

The Kansas decision is likely to embolden other efforts. It gives support to those who insist that the world can be no more than ten thousand years old (what is called "flood geology" with its vision of a cataclysmic event) even more so than the less strict creationists who believe that the world is too complex to be explained without the intervention of God ("intelligent design"). Even more important, the decision will undoubtedly lead to even greater attempts at local school district levels to adopt creationist textbooks, something that is already occurring.[7]

Thus, the repeated protests and lawsuits stimulated by conservative religious activists have had powerful effects. One of the key effects has been less overt than that in the Kansas decision. It involves the self-censorship by publishers who are more than a little conscious of the "bottom line."[8] In one of the best analyses of the influence of such conservative attacks on textbooks, Joan Delfattore quotes a representative of one of the largest textbook publishers: "When you are publishing a book, if there's something that is controversial, it's better to take it out."[9]

The contentious nature of this dispute and how it works at the level of school knowledge can be seen in the decision by the superintendent of schools of a district in Kentucky to have the pages that discussed evolution in an elementary school textbook glued together. In yet another school district, this time in a suburban area outside of Atlanta, school officials asked that a chapter on "The Birth of the Earth" be removed from a fourth-grade textbook. Using electronic publishing, Macmillan/McGraw-Hill excised the seventeen offending pages and customized the text specifically for Cobb County, Georgia. The list goes on. In 1995, the state school board of Alabama demanded that all biology textbooks used in the state have a disclaimer that says that evolution is simply one theory among many. It states, "No one was present when life first appeared on earth. Therefore, any statement about life's origins should be considered as theory, not fact." It goes on, raising questions that have their basis in scientific creationism's rejection of much of evolutionary biology. Among the questions are:

> Why did the major groups of animals suddenly appear in the fossil record? Why have no new major groups of living things appeared in the fossil record for a long time? Why do major groups of plants and animals have no transitional forms in the fossil record? How did you and all living things come to possess such a complete and complex set of "Instructions" for building a living body?[10]

Although the text of this pasted-in statement of "A Message from the Alabama State Board of Education" concludes with the words "Study hard and keep an open mind,"[11] the underlying message clearly is one of supporting the tenets of creation-science. Such stickers have become more widespread. The tactic of challenging evolution by having it declared only one theory among many has proven effective and is being given renewed emphasis throughout the nation, especially in struggles over textbooks. The new key word has become "intelligent design," which for people on both sides of this debate is often a symbol of the larger struggle over creationism.[12]

These are not isolated incidents. Past and present politicians such as Ronald Reagan, Pat Buchanan, and many others have insisted that parents have the "right to insist that Godless evolution not be taught to their children." Throughout the nation, Republican parties have made certain that creationist planks are part of their platforms. Creationists run for school boards at state and local levels and often win. Legislatures in some states have proposed laws that would lead to the firing of any teacher who teaches evolution as fact rather than theory.[13]

Perhaps the most telling fact is that recent polls have indicated that 47 percent of the people in the United States believe that "God created man pretty much in his present form at one time within the last 10,000 years." A further 35 percent believe that there was divine guidance behind the process of evolution. The growth of such beliefs has not stopped at the borders of the United States. The active evangelizing of conservative Christians has led to the growing popularity of scientific creationism in Europe, Asia, and the South Pacific as well.[14]

Oddly enough, although most conservative Christians assume that this is what they have always believed, the roots of creation-science are rather complex. They can be traced directly back to the Seventh-Day Adventist emphasis on both a literal six-day creation and a fossil-forming flood. This moves from George McCready Price's 1906 work, *Illogical Geology,* to Whitcomb and Morris's 1961 book, *The Genesis Flood.*[15] The popularity of this latter book provided a significant impetus to the revival of creationism in the last decades. What is interesting about this history is the fact that Price's "flood geology" was *not* based on traditional biblical accounts of creation that were most accepted by evangelical churches. Price's account was specifically developed to support Adventist theology. Many evangelical Christians who see this as "the tradition" are unaware of its actual history.[16]

Yet, having said this, we need to be careful not to assume that all of the antipathy of conservative religious groups toward evolution means that they equally and totally reject it. Historically, there is no doubt that theological conservatives saw Darwinism as both erroneous and dangerous, especially when it was applied to humans. Seeing Darwin as implying that "might makes right," they felt quite strongly that not only would this undermine Christian morality, but that the very act of drawing a line from apes to modern humans would invalidate their belief that human beings were created in the image of God.[17]

However, this general rejection of Darwin did not always take the same form. Those conservative Christians who defended the recent appearance of life on earth (the world was literally created no more than ten thousand years ago in six twenty-four-hour days) were clear that the description of creation and of Noah's flood in the Bible explained all of the fossil record. These positions generally went by the name of "flood geology." Yet other groups were rather less literal. Holders of "day-age theory" interpreted the seven days in Genesis metaphorically as vast geological ages. Others followed what was called "gap theory," believing that an entire series of catastrophes and recreations or ruins and restorations occurred, which they inserted into an imagined gap between the Bible's first two verses.[18] Although the positions based on flood geology became stronger over the years, especially within fundamentalist circles, it is important not to stereotype the opposition.

There was little organized opposition to evolution before the 1920s. After that, the opposition picked up considerable intensity when fundamentalist Christians began a state-by-state crusade to make the teaching of evolution in public schools illegal. Although they ultimately only succeeded in outlawing such teaching in three states—Tennessee, Mississippi, and Arkansas[19]—by the end of that decade there can be no doubt that the conflict itself made the teaching of evolution in public schools much more difficult in general for decades to come, including as we saw today.

To understand the more current revival, we need to think beyond the sphere of theological disagreements to see the connections between schooling and larger issues surrounding international relations and the state. The creationist controversy was reignited in the aftermath of the Soviet Union's launching of Sputnik into space in 1957 before an embarrassed America. Cold warriors, conservative critics, academics, and policy experts were quick to place the blame on the inferior teaching of science in schools. The federal government established programs to funnel considerable amounts of money into discipline-based curricula, especially in the sciences.[20] A good deal of money went into biology, as well as physics and chemistry. One of the major results was a spate of new curricular materials, including the Biological Sciences Curriculum Study (BSCS) and "Man: A Course of Study." With many leading biologists proclaiming that "one-hundred years without Darwinism is enough," the study of evolution was turned into one of the centerpieces of biological study in schools.

Predictably, the dissemination of such pro-evolution material that was sponsored and funded by the federal government immediately generated protests from conservative Christians. For them, "Man: A Course of Study" and similar material was an "attempt to ram evolution down the throats of our children."[21] Not only was it ungodly, but it signified a federal government out of control. This suturing together of the themes of ungodliness, government intervention and control, and a major distrust of school texts and curricula was of considerable import since it became a trope in which any of these three themes nearly automatically brought the others to the fore in the same way that when you look into one facet of a diamond or crystal all of the other facets are reflected up into it.

The threat that this perceived constellation posed to conservative Christians led many of them to harden their positions. Retreating ever more to a literal reading of the Bible, they became even stronger in their position that the task was *not* to accommodate the Bible into science, but to fit science into inerrant readings of Genesis. The strict creationism of flood geology became even more dominant as a dramatic shift occurred. "Old-earth" theories lost their adherents to "new-earth" advocates.[22] It is clear through all this that the school and struggles over it have played a truly momentous role in the formation of ideological and religious movements that seek to challenge secularity. Thus, as I have stressed elsewhere, seeing the school as a passive reflection of social forces does not do justice to its centrality as an arena of struggle.[23]

The reasons for this robust revival (a term that seems appropriate given the history of revival meetings in parts of the evangelical and fundamentalist traditions) are complex and "overdetermined" and thus undoubtedly have multiple causes: Cold War fears, the threats to traditional beliefs by the growth in the power of science, the centralization of power within federal structures, the decline of local community sensibilities given the suburbanization of populations and increased geographical mobility, struggles over race and gender that seemed to some to threaten both family stability and "acceptable" roles and behaviors, the anger over racial integration, and so much more. Although acknowledging a number of these root causes, however, Ronald Numbers, one of the clearest historical interpreters of the reactions to Darwinism in the United States, asks us not to ignore the theological in our attempts to understand the reasons for such growth. For him, the "prodigious popularity" of scientific creationism in the late twentieth century and now had important roots in theological impulses:

> Many converts were attracted by the creation scientists' insistence on giving the Bible priority over science. As believers who took the Bible as literally as possible, they found the young-earth creationists' non-figurative reading of the days of creation, the genealogies of the Old Testament, and the universal deluge of Noah to be especially appealing. No longer did they have to *assume* (as day-age advocates did) that Moses meant "ages" when he wrote "days" in Genesis 1; nor did they have to *assume* (as gap theorists did) that Moses, without explanation or comment, skipped the longest period of earth's history—between

the creation "in the beginning" and the far later Edenic creation—simply to accommodate Scripture to science.[24]

Although it is absolutely crucial to ask *why* this need to embrace certainty in all things arose at this particular period, to inquire into what social conditions created these feelings, desires, and intellectual/emotional needs, the theological issues cannot be ignored. But one thing is clear, out of this assemblage, a narrative is created in which books mean what they say, the complexity of texts is made satisfyingly clear, and science itself is given a respected place—under biblical authority. In a world in which "all things solid melt in the air" and "all that is sacred is profaned," the acceptance of such narratives and such a politics of reading is partly understandable.

The 1960s and 1970s witnessed a major tactical shift among strict creationists. Rather than denying the power of evolutionary science as so many religious conservatives had done before, scientific creationists argued for granting creation and evolution equal scientific standing. Unlike the 1920s when conservative religious activists sought to ban the teaching of evolution from the classrooms of public schools, these activists demanded that creation-science be accorded equal time. In their public arguments, creation-science was not primarily a religious belief, "but ... an alternative scientific explanation of the world in which we live."[25] Although this was a change in tactics stimulated in part by the formation of the Creation Research Society in the early 1970s, it did not mark a total break. Even though they were successful in gaining a conviction of Thomas Scopes for illegally teaching evolution in Tennessee in the famous Scopes trial in 1925, conservative religious activists suffered a string of legislative defeats in the next years. This convinced many of them that rather than focusing on statehouses, they would have considerable success if they turned their attention to the local level and to schoolhouses in particular.[26]

Indeed, throughout the nation, and especially in the South, heated debates about evolution took place during the early decades of the twentieth century. The three states mentioned earlier—Tennessee, Mississippi, and Arkansas—prohibited its teaching. Two additional states—Oklahoma and Florida—either prohibited the adoption of textbooks with evolutionary content or condemned Darwinism as "improper and subversive." The South's reputation for antiscientific backwardness was not helped by the national and international attention devoted to the Scopes trial.[27] Yet it is important to realize that most legislatures in the South did not outlaw such teaching.[28] However, although there was not an overwhelming surge in legal prohibitions to the teaching of Darwinism, at the level of popular culture and local community sentiments antievolutionary positions were more than a little visible.

Once again, this is a complicated situation, and it is wise to be wary of reductive explanations of antievolutionary declarations of faith. For example, most critical commentators miss the class dynamics that may help to explain the growth of antievolutionary sentiments in the South during the early decades of the twentieth century. The popularity of Darwin among the *educated* classes of the South, a region in which not only race but class dynamics had played such a major role in the development of education,[29] would have generated rejection among those who felt that these educated classes looked with disdain on those with little formal education. A sign of this can be found in the fact that the word *redneck* was not originally a label with negative connotations when applied to the poor and working class of the South. Exactly the opposite was the case. Redneck was a description applied proudly to oneself. It referred to those people who did "real" work, hard work. It was meant to differentiate people who did such labor from the pale and wan elitist and affluent upper classes who lived what were seen as parasitic lives.

The antielitist impulses that have stood behind some of this ferment over God, evolution, and schooling are clear in the ways that the religious right now sees itself as oppressed. It feels that secular humanist "bigots" who do not understand the long struggle by religious people to gain respect in the public arena are not listening to them. Oddly enough, this viewpoint has actually led to a reinterpretation of the Scopes trial.

One of the more interesting current effects of the changes in how the Scopes trial is now seen is the way in which the prosecutors—antievolutionary activists—now use the words of the defense counsel, Clarence Darrow. In defending Thomas Scopes against the charges that he had taught the forbidden subject of evolution, it is claimed that Darrow said that "teaching only one theory of evolution is sheer bigotry." He was, of course, speaking against the insistence on biblical inerrancy by fundamentalists. Scientific creationists have since reappropriated these words, arguing that it is "sheer bigotry" to not give equal weight to creation-science in textbooks and the curriculum.[30] Such strategic reappropriations demonstrate that political language is something of a floating signifier. It can be used for multiple purposes by decidedly different groups. The authoritarian populist right has been successful in part because they have taken the rhetoric of what they see as hegemonic liberalism and recast it around their own core concerns. As I show in considerably more detail in the next chapter, the language of equal access, discrimination, and rights has provided them with both ideological and linguistic resources[31] and has helped in their integration under the umbrella of conservative modernization.

A number of themes have emerged from my discussion so far. The authoritarian populist religious right believes *they* are under attack. Their traditions are disrespected; the very basis of their understanding of the world is threatened. Evolutionary perspectives are not simply one element among many in the curriculum that wrong them. Such perspectives go to the very core of their universe, even though they may not fully understand their own history in regard to the positions they take. Notice that not only were there and are there ideological and religious differences among these groups, but elements of good sense exist as well. Class dynamics did and *do* count in schools and the larger society. Thus, even when many people may not agree with authoritarian populist conservatives on their position on evolution and much else, there may be elements that demand and deserve a more sympathetic reading. This may be difficult, but I believe that it is essential if we are to avoid arrogance ourselves and to understand how they have creatively worked to build a growing movement that is having no small measure of success.

To more fully understand not only what conservative religious advocates stand against but what they stand for and why they take the positions they do, I next look at their history and the complex ideological structuring that organizes their beliefs in more detail. First, I briefly examine some of the current struggles in which they are engaged. Then, in this and the next chapter, I discuss a number of the key moments in the historical development of fundamentalism and conservative evangelicalism. After that, I engage in a considerably more detailed analysis of the larger ideological assemblage that stands behind the conservative religious attacks on schools.

Secular Dangers

In February 1999, the Committee to Restore American Values, a coalition of conservative leaders that includes Paul Weyrich and Phyllis Schlafly, continued their war over cultural politics. They asked prospective presidential candidates a number of questions to check their conservative and religious credentials. Among the questions were the following:

1. Should the words "In God We Trust" remain on the currency of the United States?

2. Would you support a removal of the words "under God" from the Pledge of Allegiance?

3. Should a constitutional amendment guaranteeing the right to life be enacted?

4. What commitments relative to abortion would you require from appointees to the Supreme Court or lower Federal judiciary appointments?

5. Do you believe gun control reduces crime?

6. Would you place a creche on the White House lawn if ordered to refrain from doing so by the Supreme Court?[32]

Clearly, then, for this group and the organizations they represent, religion, the state, gun control, abortion, and patriotism form a seamless web of religious beliefs and issues that should be uppermost in our minds when we ask someone to lead the nation.

Media reports and headlines in national and local newspapers have highlighted the supposed turmoil within groups such as this, especially the Christian Coalition. The seamless web is supposedly cracking. Problems over finances and leadership are said to be endemic; membership lists are reported to have been inflated. The Coalition's infamous voter guides, ones based on candidates' responses to questions similar to those with which I began this section, were not delivered in the numbers they originally reported. State affiliates of organizations such as this are considerably less strong than before.[33] These reports are being seen as evidence of a loss of power of conservative Christian activists. I believe that the case is much less clear, especially as so much of what the Christian right stands for has become accepted as common sense and since they have now made such successful inroads into local and regional politics. The Kansas example I used earlier is but the tip of the iceberg and the ways in which current policies that are emanating from Washington clearly seek to increase the current administration's legitimacy with rightist religious groups provides mounting evidence that the supposed waning in power of these groups was if anything rather temporary.

In *Official Knowledge,* I traced out both how the social democratic accord between capital and labor grew in the years after World War II and how it began to disintegrate under the weight of social protest mobilizations, economic crises, attacks by the corporate sector on labor, and rightist movements.[34] The effects of a new conservative accord are visible all around us in education and the entire social and cultural fabric of this society.

Accords such as this are only temporary. They must be constantly reinforced and rebuilt on the terrain of culture and everyday life if they are not to be seen as outside impositions. For this very reason, "culture wars" are and have been among the most powerful forms of politics. This is the case because "they cut to the heart of how people identify themselves and what they think constitutes acceptable behavior."[35] Education has always found itself caught up in such conflicts. It has been a site of moral crusades throughout its history, some progressive and others decidedly conservative. As I have argued, it is the latter that have attained dominance over the last decades.

While many groups constantly (and often legitimately) raise questions about the content that is taught in schools (e.g., race and gender stereotypes, disability, and homophobia) and the methods used to teach it, the sheer number and range of these protests by religious conservatives exceed those by all other groups.[36] Many members of this particular moral crusade feel as if secular society has in essence declared war on Christians. Hence, for a large number of conservative Christians, "official knowledge" opposes Christianity, lawful authority, the family, the military, and free enterprise while promoting feminism, idolatry, "demon worship," evolution, and secular humanism in general.[37] One conservative protestor who sued his school district defined secular humanism as a "lethal religion," one that denies both moral absolutes and God. "The doctrines of humanism include evolution, self-authority, situation ethics, distorted realism, gun control, sexual permissiveness, anti-Biblical bias, anti-free enterprise, one-world government, and death education."[38] For him, and for a growing segment of the population who feel under cultural and economic threat, any and all of these are evidence of extreme danger to their children's identity and to their own. Some activists go so far as to argue that even such a seemingly benign curricular emphasis in school such as multiculturalism is dangerous. Respect for a wide range of cultures and ideas is suspect, since respecting, say, non-Christian societies and beliefs is often interpreted as an attack on one's foundational belief that an absolute faith in Jesus Christ is the *only* means of salvation.[39] (The horrible events of 9/11, and then those in Madrid and London, have reinforced such sentiments and created a climate where truly disturbing sentiments about Islam and "non-Christians" now circulate, often distressingly unchallenged.)

One of the roots of the "evil" done in schools is John Dewey and his progeny. His emphasis on both personal experience and experimentation is seen as the very embodiment of secular "religion." For these conservative critics, anything that involves moral choice is in fact a religion, whether or not it is grounded in faith in a higher power.[40] Dewey and his followers' faith in experimentation, their rejection of absolutism, their sense of the individual/collective relationship at the core of democracy, and above all the integration of all this in their theories of education have led schools astray.

Although many protests against these "secular dangers" begin at a local level, there are national organizations that both sponsor and support them. Among the groups involved in challenging the "biases" in public schools are the American Family Association, based in Mississippi and led by Donald Wildmon; Citizens for Excellence in Education, based in California and led by Robert Simonds; Concerned Women for America, based in Washington, D.C., and led by Beverly LaHaye; the Eagle Forum, based in the Midwest and led by Phyllis Schlafly; Focus on the Family, based in Colorado and led by James Dobson; and the National Legal Foundation, based in Virginia and led by Pat Robertson.[41] There are a number of others, but all of them are deeply committed to turn the nation and our schools back to God.

For these groups and for many conservative evangelicals and fundamentalists, only through a return to inerrantist readings of the Bible can we save ourselves and especially our children from these dangers. The Bible and it alone provides us with the path toward a truly ethical and correct society in all of our institutions. Thus, according to Pat Robertson, the Bible is "a workable guidebook for politics, government, business, families, and all the affairs of mankind." It provides us with universal spiritual laws that are "as valid for our lives as the laws of thermodynamics."[42] As one conservative minister asked his congregation about a vexing social problem, "Does the Bible have anything to say about that? Or are we going to let the government feed us everything they want?"[43]

As I noted earlier, this turn back to the Bible and the entire feeling of endangered Christianity is related to multiple causes. Its connections to antigovernment sensibilities are also complex, but the situation was clearly exacerbated by the decision of the Internal Revenue Service in 1978 to challenge the tax-exempt status of all-white Christian academies. It was also heightened by the profound disappointment among conservative evangelicals that a presidential administration guided by one of their own, Jimmy Carter, did not live up to their expectations. On the aforementioned tax case, on abortion, school prayer, busing, the Equal Rights Amendment to the Constitution, gay rights—on all of these the Carter administration was not "upholding the faith."[44] The results can be seen in the rigorous questioning that presidential candidates now go through that forms the introduction to this section.

This sense of betrayal as a larger theme needs to be taken quite seriously. It is absolutely crucial to understand that for many evangelicals and fundamentalists who see the New Testament as an inerrant history of the early Christian church, one thing is inescapable. To be a Christian is to be *persecuted*.[45] This very theme, so clear in many biblical texts, underpins (though not always at the level of consciousness) much of the emotional economy present within conservative evangelical movements. It has also been one of the central parts of the narrative of this nation (the pilgrims/religious persecution/freedom). A better sense of the history of evangelical movements may help us realize both how this works and why—even given their disagreements with some aspects of the larger alliance—they can be integrated within it.

From Insiders to Outsiders

The term *evangelicalism* is derived from the Greek "evangelion," meaning good news. It was a dominant social and intellectual current in American society until the late nineteenth century. As we shall see, over time a number of forces undermined the literal authority of the Bible. Science penetrated the logic of daily lives. The growing pluralism of the United States made it much more difficult for evangelicalism to provide such a diverse people with a common set of values. The increasing separation of public and private spheres of life also helped deprive evangelicalism of its public and political role. This emerging secularization served to remove religious institutions, symbols, and values from the central place they had occupied. In the process, a sea change occurred in the role of evangelicals. There was a steady shift from being what might be called cultural insiders to cultural *outsiders*.[46]

We can date the formal beginnings of the modern evangelical movement as April 7, 1942, when approximately two hundred "moderate fundamentalists" met in St. Louis to launch a religious movement. This group believed that they could both transform conservative Protestantism and radically change the course of religious history in the United States.[47] Thus, the movement started out with grand ambitions. These ambitions have been at least partly met, as more than twenty million Americans identify themselves as part of the evangelical movement.[48] How has this waxing and waning occurred?

The movement actually has quite a long historical tradition. As I noted, well before the well-known battles split the Protestant house into modernist and fundamentalist wings, "conservative Protestantism enjoyed a remarkable public respectability, influence, and relevance."[49] Indeed, it could be said that during the Victorian era in particular, broadly evangelical Protestants were in fact the establishment.[50] This was not just the case in the United States. Throughout the world, American evangelicals "mobilized a missionary enterprise of vast proportions."[51] In the words of Lewis French Stearns in 1890, "Today Christianity is the power which is moulding the destinies of the world. The Christian nations are ... ascendant. ... The old promise is being fulfilled; the followers of the true God are inheriting the world."[52]

Overarching all the influence that this set of triumphal perspectives had in the worlds of business, education, culture, and the polity in general was a pervasive belief that the United States was a (the) Christian nation. It was blessed by God; it had a particular destiny to become not only the kingdom of heaven on earth but the place that God would make into a "central spot for the whole earth."[53]

As we shall see shortly, key elements of this position will remain and will resurface with considerable power again later on. However, the dominance of such beliefs began to falter during the end of the nineteenth and the beginning of the twentieth centuries. A more liberal theology, the growth of biblical criticism, and skepticism about the supernatural challenged accepted orthodoxies within the church. The importance of the act of individual conversion was jeopardized in the eyes of a considerable number of evangelicals by the more structural reforms being proposed by the Social Gospel movement. The growth of naturalistic assumptions about reality and the shift within science itself away from the Newtonian paradigm undercut the role of the Bible within the scientific community, a fact that was heightened by the growing influence of Darwinian understandings of evolution. When all this is coupled with rapid industrialization, a radically changing demographics brought about by immigration, and an equally powerful set of religious changes accompanying the increase in Catholic, Jewish, and other populations, the situation made it seem as if conservative Protestantism's hegemony—as the very embodiment of what it meant to be a "civilized and civilizing" nation—was constructed on a foundation of sand. As Christian Smith puts it, "and the rains were pouring down."[54]

For some, the "rains" led to a slow movement away from the old orthodoxy and toward more "modern" and "liberal" positions. For others, much of the orthodox vision was maintained, but perhaps in a somewhat weaker form as they "adjusted to the new reality." But for a significant minority this was a painful process, one that could not and would not be accepted. They chose to fight back against what they deeply believed was an "assault on Christian truth and civilization."[55] From their very beginnings in the first two decades of the twentieth century, the positions of the leaders of this countermovement were clear. They sought to mobilize a conservative coalition whose aim was to combat modernism in churches and schools. Two strategic goals were focused upon: to wrest control of major Protestant denominations from the forces of liberalism and, especially in the South, to make the teaching of Darwinian evolutionism illegal in the public schools. "In time, these fighting conservatives were labeled 'fundamentalist'—a term coined from a booklet series published between 1910 and 1915 called *The Fundamentals*—and their movement, 'fundamentalism.'"[56]

Yet such engagement in the world was actually rather limited. Theological purity was often seen as more important than acting in the outside world. Cooperation with liberal or "inclusive" conservatives was treated with much bitterness by fundamentalists. From the 1920s onward, separatism and a very strong distaste for doctrinal compromise became even stronger. Rejecting the nineteenth-century's post-millennialism—which was seen as being connected to the more liberal Social Gospel movement[57]—the fundamentalists arrived at what was actually a more recent theological position, what has been called "pre-millennialist dispensationalism." This can be characterized in the following way:

> Premillennialism taught that history and society were—in God's plan—inevitably going to grow worse and worse until, just before things hit rock bottom, Christ would return to vindicate his faithful people and establish his kingdom on earth. This pessimistic view of history suggested that the only task left for the church was to remain separate from and unblemished by the world and to "win" as many souls to heaven before the damned ship of history went down. ... The perspective of many fundamentalists became: let the worldly intelligentsia, scholars, universities, media, cultural elite, politicians—all who spurned Christian truth and civilization—go to perdition.[58]

This constituted part of what has been described as the "Great Reversal": the rejection of the Social Gospel's emphasis on social reform rather than on saving lost souls through evangelism; the rise of a pessimistic eschatology such as premillennialism; and the turn to social and political conservatism.[59] Attempting to engage with the world and reform it, hence, was like polishing the brass on a doomed ship. The depth of the rejection of the reformist commitments behind the Social Gospel is perhaps nowhere stated more clearly than in the revivalist Billy Sunday's angry message that "We've had enough of this God-less social service nonsense."[60]

I do not want to overstate the fundamentalists' rejection of engagement in the world. Although many such conservative Christians took the path of resistance to modernity that led to withdrawal, a goodly number of others took a much more overtly militant and activist stance. As George Marsden, one of the leading scholars of the evangelical movement, tartly states when discussing this tendency, "A fundamentalist is an evangelical who is angry about something."[61] These "angry" evangelicals battled against the influence of modernity and liberalism both in the churches and the schools, again with Darwinism playing a large role in what they struggled against in the latter. Such militancy had its attractions and some victories. But ultimately a combination of factors—with the fear of schism and the humiliation of William Jennings Bryan at the 1925 Scopes trial being among the most important—led to a loss of widespread support for fundamentalism.[62]

The fundamentalists, then, ultimately lost ground. But a strong current of militant, inerrantist, antiliberal (and later on, aggressively anticommunist), and antisecular sentiment was kept alive. It was kept alive in churches and Bible institutes and seminaries. It was given constant transfusions of new blood in the writings and teachings of strongly conservative theologians such as Carl McIntire and others as well. Thus, the movement may have been in cultural "exile," but the flame of politicized resistance still burned—and grew—in the ensuing decades. In fact, as we shall see later on, the flame burned ever more brightly in the 1950s, 1960s, and 1970s with the growth of the New Right. But the roots of this have their genesis in the 1940s.

Although fundamentalists sought to protect what they believed was spiritual purity, by the 1940s a number of more "moderate" fundamentalists grew increasingly worried about its tendencies. In their minds, the separatist and judgmental character of fundamentalism had sacrificed one of its most important tasks, "evangelizing American society for Christ." Fundamentalism's tacit (and sometimes overt) anti-intellectualism, its pessimistic premillennial dispensationalism, its disengagement from the real social, political, and economic world—all of this needed to be overcome. For these new heirs to the evangelical legacy—among them Harold Okenga, J. Elwin Wright, Wilbur Smith, Edward Carnell, Carl Henry, Harold Lindsell, Charles Fuller, Gleason Archer, Everett Harrison, Bernard Ramm, and a name that would become even more significant, Billy Graham—such positions had to be replaced by an *engaged orthodoxy*. For them, one could be fully committed to promoting orthodox Protestant beliefs and practices and at the same time be equally vigorous in "bringing Christ to the world."[63]

This vision was institutionalized in the formation of a national movement, the National Association of Evangelicals. It both reached out beyond orthodox fundamentalists by stressing "the need for unity and love among different Protestant traditions for the sake of the Gospel and the world" and provided institutional support for the growing number of evangelical Christians who were convinced that "Jesus Christ was the answer for the world's social, economic, and political problems and wanted to see Christians making a real impact on the world."[64]

This "neoevangelical" movement combined many elements: orthodoxy and tradition, but with a concern for more intellectual respectability than that accorded to the earlier fundamentalists; social and political activism; and spreading the word of the Gospel while avoiding some of the behavioral rigidity of fundamentalism. This gave it more legitimacy and allowed it to spread. It also enabled people who were not as enamored with the anti-intellectual tendencies within previous conservative religious traditions to ground their beliefs in what seemed to be a more "rational" foundation. Neoevangelicalism spawned and in turn was itself spurred by the formation of other religious, educational, and cultural forms. For example, a number of theological seminaries were either founded or transformed into its own image. A considerable number of colleges aligned themselves with the movement. Evangelical missions and ministries saw steady growth—Youth for Christ, Campus Crusade for Christ, Inter-Varsity Christian Fellowship, Teen Challenge, Fellowship of Christian Athletes, the Overseas Missionary Fellowship, the World Evangelical Fellowship, the Evangelical Foreign Missions Fellowship, and the list goes on.

A considerable number of evangelical periodicals were published, accompanied by a growing list of evangelical publishing houses and music production and recording companies. Other aspects of the media and cultural apparatus were not ignored, with organizations such as the National Religious Broadcasters and the Evangelical Press Association being formed. In these ways, a "transdenominational" evangelicalism was both built and defended by networks of "parachurch agencies."[65]

For many of these churches and parachurch agencies, however, a specific kind of engaged orthodoxy came to dominate. Much of this combined particular and exceptionally conservative views on the family, on gender roles within the home and the outside world, on national and international politics, on militant Christianity, and often on race as well. Significant parts of these tendencies can only be explained if we look more deeply at the history of conservative evangelicalism in the South especially.

Southern Cross

We are used to hearing evangelicalism's call in a Southern voice. Although it is a truly national and international phenomenon, much of conservative evangelicalism grew from the soil of specifically Southern experiences at first. Oddly enough, far from dominating the South, throughout much of the eighteenth and nineteenth centuries evangelicals were viewed by most white Southerners as either odd or subversive.[66] Indeed, many Southern whites of all classes believed that evangelicalism would not strengthen, but instead weaken, community ties and eliminate many of the celebrations and social events that gave meaning to life in the region. In particular, evangelicalism's unremitting emphasis on "mankind's sinfulness, hell's torments, and Satan's wiles" had a telling effect. It "estranged men and women from the strong and decent parts of their personalities and plunged them into fathomless darkness."[67] For the majority of Southern whites, then, evangelicalism seemed to erase social identity and rupture communal bonds.

Yet, over time, the margin became the center as evangelicalism grew in strength. Partly this increase was a natural outgrowth of cultural elements that were already there—a belief in supernaturalism, in the foretelling power of dreams and portents, in the ability of spirits to take visible form. Thus, at the same time as Thomas Jefferson and other southern leaders helped usher in the "Age of Reason," it was not natural law that dominated the daily lives and beliefs of many southern whites. Rather, they already combined varied forms of supernaturalism with their Christian beliefs. Hence, sensing the "fullness of Satan's sway" was not that large a leap.[68] And evangelicalism enabled the making of that leap. As time passed, although evangelicals still listened to and connected with the region's strong traditions of supernaturalism, they toned down diabolism's (Satan's) terror in their discourse. This too increased their legitimacy across the South by attracting a wider swath of the population.[69]

As in the later periods I have already discussed, economic transformations and crises, immigration, the loss of a firm identity based on one's social location—all of these also had an impact. Yet something else was crucial. Evangelicals drew strength from the feeling that each and every one of them was participating in a cosmic drama. In the struggle between God and Satan, they were on the winning side. As Christine Leigh Heyrman recognized in her exceptional history of the growth of evangelicalism in the South, committing oneself to evangelical discipline did begin with a process of self-repentance, in essence of radical self-abasement. Yet it also brought with it a profound sense of individual importance. One's guilt, doubt, and fear—the hidden yet powerful emotions that become even more potent in times of crisis—became of great significance not only to you, but to an entire religious community as well. Individual and community are joined here. As Heyrman says, for many Southerners—"those who happened to be black in a society ruled by whites, poor in a society that bowed to wealth, female in a society dominated by males, young in a society that honored age"—being taken seriously was itself *serious*. It made evangelicalism nearly irresistible.[70]

Thus, evangelicalism had multiple roots, often among the least powerful. However, these democratic tendencies often caused a conservative backlash that profoundly changed evangelicalism over time and helped to make it into what it is today.

For example, the emergence of a distinctly African-American Christianity that fused elements of West African traditions with evangelical teachings is part of what must be told here.[71] In fact, evangelicalism in the South had elements that challenged racial superiority, that called for active not passive worship, and were less hierarchical than many other churches. Evangelical gatherings were also at times interracial and provided spaces for bringing in personal experience (and thus allowed for elements and memories of African cultural forms). Because of this, it is clear why many African-Americans saw it positively and transformed it for their own spiritual, cultural, and political purposes. (This theme of African-Americans using traditions that may originally have come from soil that oppressed them was visible as well in my discussion in Chapter 4 of the ways in which black activist groups attempt to transform neoliberal policies.)

This led many dominant whites to try to curb the behavior of many of these converts, attempts that in the long run proved less than successful.[72] But it also did not stop some conservative evangelicals who were worried about what would happen in a less racially stratified church and society from seeing African-Americans as the literal embodiment of the devil. The repulsively stereotypical grinning black face became the face of Satan as he came for children to bring them to Hell.[73] Indeed, in their constant search for greater "respectability" in the South, not only did many evangelical churches vigilantly monitor their "black brothers and sisters," but they began erecting barriers against interracial religious intimacy.[74] Dominant whites and slaveholders were increasingly moved to the center. In the words of one well-known evangelical leader, "I am called upon to suffer for Christ's sake, not for slavery."[75] This became the moral calculus for most white Southern evangelical leaders. As they themselves moved from margin to center, the margin was again rebuilt—and once again, African-Americans occupied it on the terrain of religion. For the evangelicals, then, reclaiming (white) souls was of the essence and "any concession to the South's ruling race could be justified in the name of that end."[76] This prefigures the often tense relationship many authoritarian populist religious activists currently have with people of color today.

The contradictory history of Southern evangelicalism—its partially democratic beginnings leading ultimately to a return to dominant forms—can be seen not only in its history of compromise over racial stratification. It is quite visible in the history of its changing vision of the family and gender hierarchies as well. It is ironic that conservative evangelicals—whose embrace of the "traditional family" is one of their identifying marks—were in the early years of their growth in the South in the 1800s among the most powerful forces that challenged traditional family solidarity and values. Those who converted to evangelical faiths had to renounce their previous sinfulness, including many of their family members who continued their "sinful ways." The *church* was one's new family. Criticism of the evangelicals' challenges to the rights of families is what ultimately led them to move toward sanctifying the "natural family." This, too, was deeply connected historically to issues of race. Evangelicals began their effort to bring their version of family values into accord with white Southern mores by retreating from their opposition to slavery.[77] Family values were to be upheld, but not necessarily for slaves.

Gender relations played a major role historically in this valorization of the natural family. Evangelicals showed their resourcefulness by suspending the usual southern belief that nothing good could come out of the North. They enthusiastically embraced a "new" form of patriarchal relations that had originated among middle-class Northern evangelicals, "the cult of domesticity." For its proponents, the home is a church. It constitutes an Edenic sanctuary that is tended by wives and mothers. In this Edenic home, religious and moral sensibility were seeds that were incubated in children. A "flowering of rectitude" ennobled husbands and fathers.[78]

Just as it did in the North, the compelling metaphor of home as church evoked powerful positive reactions. However, there were regional differences as to why it struck such a responsive chord. In the North, the growth of commerce and industry fostered the emergence of these new domestic ideals, especially within the middle class. Yankee men increasingly spent their days in offices, factories, and shops, thereby further sanctioning a definition of the public sphere as commercial and male and the private sphere as domestic and female.[79]

In the South, most husbands and fathers were farmers. The household was a workplace for both women and men. However, although homes in the antebellum South did not become only the sphere of women, Southern whites found the image of the home as a church more than a little appealing. It restored the moral authority of the "natural family." The evangelical embrace of the natural family, then, was a crucial tactical move. By changing its emphasis from supporting the idea that one's total loyalty must be to God and the church rather than to family and home, to one in which families and homes were created in God's image, tensions were eased and converts could be won. If the home *is* a church, then family claims and religious claims could be made one and the same.[80]

Behind these changes in evangelicalism was something more than the cementing of the bonds of family, household integrity, and order. As I have noted, these transformations over time were dependent on a revivification of gender and racial orders. They were harbingers of things to come. Heyrman summarizes these orders in a striking manner:

> Reinforcing these claims was something sterner—the absolute rule that husbands and fathers exercised over all their dependents—wives, children, and slaves. As a result, during the same years that evangelicals sought to persuade all white southerners that their churches ceded primacy to family solidarity and kinship loyalty, they also tailored their teachings to uphold, even more unequivocally, the authority of male heads of households, particularly over godly women. These ever more rigid teachings on gender roles, along with their changing messages about familial order and the prerogatives of age, transformed the early ... movements into the evangelical culture that later generations of Americans would identify as epitomizing "family values."[81]

Heyrman is quite insightful here. However, this can be interpreted as giving little agency to those people—women and people of color, for example—who were subjected to such authority. This is not necessarily the case, nor is it her position.

At the same time as evangelicals revivified patriarchal authority, historically the churches themselves provided a space for women to assert themselves as authoritative *in public*.[82] This paradox actually represented in the past and still represents in the present a major achievement on the part of religiously conservative women. In a family structure in which "God has willed" that the man is the head and in which women are to be submissive and/or helpmates, the evangelical churches provided a public arena for women to exercise intelligence, judgment, fortitude, and power. Historically, for women of the South— a region that had long had a culture steeped in misogyny "against which women had become schooled, as their best defense, in habits of submission"—the creation of such a public arena was a liberating force, no matter what its ideological content.[83] As I show in the next chapter, there is no doubt that this continues to this day, as many women in evangelical movements whose official beliefs center around God-given gender roles occupy that public space in creative and powerful ways.[84] In fact, in my mind this is one of the most significant ways in which the contradictions of patriarchal authority are solved within authoritarian populist religious movements. Women are *both* passive and active at the same time.

In this regard, we need to remember that gender relations are exactly that, relations. Thus, spaces for agency created by and for women necessarily imply changes in men's roles as well. And here, once again, evangelicalism wrought contradictory transformations in the past that live with us still today.

For instance, evangelicalism also had an effect on the prevailing definitions of masculinity, especially in the South, where white men were asked to forswear their culture's rigidly defined gender roles. Church fellowship seemed to be but a poor replacement for "swaggering male comraderie," but for many men it did provide a different model.[85] Although a mistrust of the church for its requirement that men submit to religious authority and God's judgment was widespread, such fears of "unmanly dependence" were assuaged by a vision of male authority in the family. These new forms of masculinity and male authority were also made more legitimate by the development of literature and stories about what might be called "warrior preachers." In these stories and sermons, real men could embrace evangelical faith without sacrificing their masculinity. The stories were extremely popular and often took the form of a confession. Swearing, fighting, gambling, hunting, and more were sins that were recounted in detail. All of them were forsworn on conversion for the mightier challenges and higher glory of becoming God's warrior. The message was clear. It took a tough man to make a tender Christian. For many of the nineteenth-century evangelical clergy and their converts, spreading the gospel was a military campaign requiring nerves of steel, agility, cunning, and courage. One was now a soldier in the army of Jesus.[86]

Thus, just as evangelicalism provided spaces for African-Americans' and white women's agency, it also allowed for a creative solution to the contradictory positions surrounding male authority, a solution still struggled over in such modern forms as the Promise Keepers with their emphasis on strong but godly men. Yet, in the process of creating these spaces, the solutions that were proposed did not—and do not—challenge the fundamental social hierarchies around race, gender, and class that dominated society in both the North and the South. Space was given, but the rules that constituted the social field of power on which it played remained the same. In the final analysis, the world of Southern evangelicals converged with the world of Southern white male masters. The "muscular Christianity" built in the nineteenth century both solved and recreated problems of power. It changed, but ultimately vindicated, the mastery of white men in the public and private spheres.[87]

There can be no doubt that, in comparison to many religious groups, in a number of ways the early evangelicals were considerably more democratic and egalitarian. Evangelicals were neither an undifferentiated mass, nor were their beliefs static and monolithic. In their early years, evangelical fellowships did promise the prospect of greater fulfillment and freedom to the most subordinated groups within the South—the poor, the female, the young, and the black. However, as the nineteenth century progressed, these very same churches retreated from these earlier promises in order to become more successful. Their energies were invested in upholding the honor and equality of all white men.[88] Present-day evangelicals live in the shadow of the values; theological, social, and educational commitments; and institutions of this legacy, with all its contradictions, strengths, and weaknesses. It is to the current embodiment of this legacy that I now turn.

CHAPTER 6

God, Morality, and Markets

Bringing God to the World

To understand the authoritarian populist religious right, it is crucial to complement the historical excavation of how and why such movements grew. Although the historical roots I traced out in Chapter 5 are important, we also have to look at the world through their eyes now. Before I begin, however, it is important to remember that strong religious convictions can go in many directions, including progressive ones. An example of the latter would be such things as base-community movements throughout Latin America and elsewhere.[1] Therefore, we need to realize that such convictions need not inexorably lead to conservative positions. At times, organizations form around considerably more progressive social and political issues. Indeed, some bear a striking resemblance to liberation theology in its taking up of concerns about social justice, poverty, racial segregation, and so on. However, the dominant tendencies of religious activism (at least those that get the most attention in the media), especially in the United States, move in conservative directions for reasons of theology, social position, temperament, and as we just saw, history.

As I demonstrated, after failing to sway the majority of mainline Protestants, fundamentalists largely withdrew. More liberal and "modern" forces flourished until the resurgence of more public forms of conservative evangelicalism in the 1940s and 1950s, stressing an agenda of moral reform and a less internally antagonistic outlook. Though still grounded in the traditional emphasis on private individual salvation, conservative evangelicalism increasingly came to concentrate on public civic issues—but not those that guided the more liberal Social Gospel movement. The emerging conservative bloc recognized that it was crucial to enter the political arena if they were to guarantee the conditions of sustaining the moral order they wished to protect and expand.[2] Indeed, the dispensationalist belief in the cosmic struggle between God and Satan clearly has contributed to the militancy of many conservative Christians.[3] Although many religious conservatives have historically objected to a focus on the political sphere, preferring to emphasize individual salvation, for a large portion of Christian right leaders today— such as Jerry Falwell, Pat Robertson, James Dobson, Tim and Beverly LaHaye—activism is utterly essential if we are to restore God's hand as our guide.[4]

This commitment to "bring God to the world" is partly the result of changes in the class composition of evangelicalism. The less overtly political stance of earlier periods was transformed and delegitimated by the growth in upwardly mobile middle-class converts to evangelicalism in the 1970s and 1980s. A new constituency of professional, technical, and businesspeople was formed. These individuals had a much greater interest in politics and social action than did their predecessors,[5] in part because they had come of age in an era of social ferment in which social activism was seen as a legitimate form of expression.

It would be deceptive to assume that because of these changes in class composition and outlook the Christian right is a unitary movement and that it speaks with one voice. Not only is it diverse organizationally, but it is also in constant motion. It is always "in formation," characterized by shifting alliances and tensions caused by changing events and social conditions.[6] However, there *are* central tendencies that push it in particular directions. Within these central tendencies, how do conservative evangelicals understand the world? How do they interpret their own actions? Do they see themselves as many others see them—as people who are attempting to impose their religious beliefs and values on others?

To answer these questions, we need to begin with an empirical question. What are some of the things we know about fundamentalists and conservative evangelicals? I shall direct most of my attention to evangelicals as they are a considerably larger group numerically and are more influential.

The empirical evidence is striking. Of all Christians in the United States, including fundamentalists, evangelicals have the strongest belief in traditional orthodoxy. Ninety-seven percent believe that the Bible is God-inspired and that it is without error. They adhere to a theologically orthodox vision of human nature. Even though we are "created in God's image," human beings are inherently sinful and need God's redemption and restoration. The only way to salvation is through a faith in Jesus Christ. Further, evangelicals—even more than fundamentalists—"are the most likely of all major Christian traditions to affirm a belief in moral absolutes." There is a firm rejection of moral relativism. Not human reason, but God and the Bible, provide the sources of direction for one's life.[7] Human and institutional authority are secondary to these more spiritual groundings.

Overall, though this may not always have been the case, evangelicals report that they are now "no more economically or educationally deprived than others in American society." Although they do not seem to believe that they more than others have suffered economically or in terms of status, they consistently voice powerful feelings about America's turn from "the ways of God." They believe that we are witnessing all around us the consequences—social and spiritual—of the nation's and the people's loss of a God-centered life.[8]

Empirically as well, the vast majority of evangelicals state that they *never* have doubts about their faith. In most ways, they seem to be immune to the undermining effects of uncertainty and skepticism—or perhaps the insistent and publicly professed lack of doubt is an armor that guards them from unconscious and dangerous feelings of grave doubt.

Yet it is not just the strength of belief and certainty that separates them from many others. They also exhibit a striking optimism about the probability that a Christian revival will sweep across the United States.[9]

The effects of this strong set of beliefs are not limited to the "private" sphere. For them, such beliefs must also permeate the world of paid work. A "Christian presence" must follow one everywhere, a point to which I return later. Occasionally a cost may be exacted at work for being "moral and honest," but it is still crucial to Christianize the workplace because "God knows more than I do about where my life is going."[10] Perhaps because of this, by and large evangelicals do not question the larger structures of the economy. Corporate behavior is determined not by the norms and structures of the economy, by class or race or gender relations, or by colonial and postcolonial histories. Rather, it is the goodness or badness of individuals who work in these businesses that is determinate.[11] Individual morality and honesty are the answers to economic problems; structural transformation is not a category even used by most conservative evangelicals. "Truth" will rule when moral people act in their businesses, homes, and communities in truthful ways.

It is not only that an unchanging and universal "truth" exists, but evangelicals often see themselves as the ones to whom God had revealed it. Again, empirically, they are much more likely than mainstream Protestants to hold that there are unchanging and absolute moral standards. They are more apt to hold that "Christian morality" should be the law of the land and less apt to believe that other people—even those who are not themselves Christians—should be able to choose their own moral standards. And, more than others, a significant fraction of them tend to believe that public schools must instruct children in distinctly Christian values. It is important to realize, however, that for evangelicals this is not a conscious attempt at dominating others. Rather, it is grounded in a deeply seated belief that the world would be a much better place if everyone followed "God's ways."[12]

This certainty is coupled with a powerful impulse to change American society, not only by example, but by conversion and by action in the political sphere. As Christian Smith puts it, "Talk ... is cheap. What about actions? ... Which Christian tradition is actually *doing* the work of trying to influence American society? ... The evidence suggests that it is the evangelicals who are mostly walking their talk."[13] The acts of "walking their talk" are varied. Compared with all other Christians and with nonreligious Americans, they are most likely by far to vote, to lobby political officials, to work hard to educate themselves about what they take to be important social and political issues, and to defend biblical worldviews in intellectual circles. While, like neoliberals who put their faith in the market and neoconservatives who emphasize character and "proper" values, they may usually be against government programs of assistance, in keeping with their emphasis on personal conduct they are also *most* likely to give money to the poor and the needy. They also are most likely to *personally* evangelize others and, among Christians, to participate in political protests and demonstrations. Furthermore, along with fundamentalists, they donate quite extensive amounts of money to Christian political candidates and organizations.[14]

This belief in moral superiority and following God's way, hence, extends well beyond the sphere of private life. For conservative evangelicals, religion is not a private matter. It is necessary to extend its voice and reach in the public debates over cultural, political, economic, and bodily practices and policies.[15] Although it may be grounded for some evangelicals in a relatively unself-conscious paternalism,[16] it is clearly connected to an extremely strong sense of social mission.

The Christianization of all parts of life can be seen in other ways as well. Not only do evangelicals participate in these political acts of influence, they also engage in more church-related activities than any other part of Christianity. Furthermore, they have exceptionally high rates of engaging in "parachurch" religious activities. For example, their rate of listening to Christian radio is nearly twice as much as even fundamentalists and nearly four times as much as members of more mainstream churches. Their rate of watching specifically Christian television programs exhibits similar tendencies.[17]

Politics and the Clergy

Much of this can be understood not only by examining the structure of beliefs of conservative Christians but also by asking who their ministers are and how these messages are reinforced in other ways. Thus, in many churches, one of the best predictors of political activism is how conservative the clergy are. The more conservative, the more active.[18]

Ministers who are younger and who went to Bible colleges are more apt to be conservative theologically. Ministers from working-class homes and with less-advanced education are also more likely to be conservative. Furthermore, there is an inverse correlation between having a liberal arts background and religious conservatism among ministers. The less background in liberal arts, the less likely one is to hold liberal theological positions.[19] The antipathy between conservative evangelicals toward a secular education, then, may have some of its roots not only in theological and cultural disputes, but in autobiographical ones as well.

Such backgrounds have an effect. Like their church members, conservative clergy insist that social reform comes not from altering social institutions, but from the "changed hearts" of individuals. In the words of a number of orthodox clergy, "Our problems are not drugs, divorce, abortion, greed, and so on, but the symptoms of a larger problem, that of alienation from God." Only through mass conversion to faith in Jesus Christ will there be social improvement. Thus, "Jesus is the answer to all problems: social, financial, health, national, international, civil, moral, and educational."[20]

That there are close theological connections between conservative clergy and their church members is important here. A comparison is helpful. Perhaps because of the pervasiveness of conservative discourses in public life, there is a growing gap between liberal clergy and their parishioners. Although differences often may exist between conservative clergy and the members of their churches, they are not as wide as those developing between more liberal ministers and their church members. On such things as the death penalty, gay rights, defense spending, school prayer, affirmative action, and similar issues, modernist clergy themselves have noticed growing differences between their parishioners and themselves.[21] This is a crucial fact, as it points to the inroads of a more conservative common sense even among members of more mainline churches.

The comparison is made more powerful by the fact that recent research also has indicated that members of evangelical churches are more likely to be in the pews on Sunday. They are the most accepting of clerical pronouncements and place a premium on pastoral leadership. Furthermore, they most often take as definitive their minister's "biblical warrant" for political preaching. This stands in stark contrast to more liberal congregations who attend less regularly, are less deferential to pastoral leadership, and may have more disagreement with their ministers in terms of their political views.[22] And although many liberal clergy remain involved in the social gospel, there is a growing trend among conservative clergy to be even more activist than their liberal counterparts in areas such as political and moral pronouncements, endorsing candidates, campaign activities, organizing petition drives, and sponsoring boycotts.[23] Thus, increasingly, political momentum is with the conservatives, sponsored mightily by their clergy.

The Electronic Clergy

Although clergy are quite influential in developing and responding to conservative sensibilities at the local level in churches and parachurch organizations, a good deal of the work of bringing God to the world is accomplished through the creative use of media by the Christian right. There has been a tendency to think of this as a recent development. However, the use of the media by Christian broadcasters is not a new phenomenon by any means. It has an exceedingly long history. In fact, in 1921 the first Christian radio broadcast was aired. Even though periods of rise and decline occurred over the next decades, and some tension between fundamentalist and modernizing Christian broadcasters emerged during this period, fundamentalist use of media such as radio was a very real presence on the airwaves by the early 1930s.

As an example, fundamentalist and conservative religious broadcasters accounted for 246 of the 290 weekly quarter-hours of Christian radio programming in Chicago in 1932. In 1939, Charles E. Fuller's "Old

Fashioned Revival Hour" had the most extensive prime-time distribution of any radio broadcast in the entire nation. It had airtime on 60 percent of all the licensed stations, with an estimated weekly audience of twenty million.[24] Radio and, later on, television were seen as essential to the New Testament missionary mandate to "go into the world and make disciples."[25]

This "making of disciples" was and is not only national but international as well. Through international networks such as HCJB (Heralding Christ Jesus' Blessings), FEBC (Far East Broadcasting Company), TWR (TransWorld Radio), and other outlets, there is a clear hope that "as many souls as possible" will be drawn to become "followers of Christ." This goal can perhaps best be seen in the joint pledge that HCJB, FEBC, and TWR made in the mid-1980s: "We are committed to provide every man, woman, and child on earth the opportunity to turn on their radio and hear the gospel of Jesus Christ in a language they can understand, so that they can become followers of Christ and responsible members of His church."[26]

A good example, but certainly not the only one, of the use of such media to both communicate and reinforce conservative religious and social worldviews is Pat Robertson's ministry of the air. Robertson, one of the most influential public figures on the conservative religious front and a former candidate for the presidency, is not your "ordinary" televangelist. Although there is a sense of rags-to-riches in his personal story, it is also true that his father, Willis A. Robertson, served in Congress for thirty-four years in both the House and the Senate, ultimately serving as chair of the Senate Banking Committee.[27] It is also true that Pat Robertson himself went to Yale Law School and became a minister only after failing the bar examination in New York State.[28]

Robertson's powerful television show, *The 700 Club,* began in 1963 with the idea of having seven hundred viewers contribute $10 per month, thereby enabling the television ministry to be self-sustaining.

This has been more than a little successful. As early as 1985, Robertson's annual budget was nearly $230 million. *The 700 Club* itself was broadcast on two hundred stations in the United States and syndicated for broadcast in another sixty countries. Money for the broadcasts comes not only from viewers but also from "sympathetic corporations" within the conservative movement.[29] One of Robertson's Christian Broadcasting Network's strokes of genius was to obtain the broadcasting rights to older, "family-friendly," situation comedies such as *I Love Lucy, Gilligan's Island,* and other shows. It reduced its overtly religious programming to 25 percent of its airtime and garnered an increasingly large audience, as well as selling airtime for commercials to a considerable number of major corporations.[30] This made the Christian Broadcasting Network (CBN) something of a media empire (although parts of it have been sold to a secular corporate media giant to provide Robertson and his allies with money for other evangelical work).

Showing family-friendly programs and evangelizing the world have not been the Christian broadcasting movement's only tasks. Politically conservative messages (often radically so) have been promoted side by side with religious and cultural themes. This has extended to "defending the freedom" of truly murderous regimes. For example, Robertson and CBN's stance on international politics not surprisingly has often been supportive of rightist and militaristic social alliances and governments. Thus, Robertson himself was strongly supportive of U.S. intervention in Nicaragua to aid the Contras. He found Roberto D'Aubuisson of El Salvador (widely considered to be the leader of rightist death squads there) to be a "very nice fellow." And he has consistently supported Israel's hard-line factions in their repression of Palestinians.[31]

My point is not to decry any use of media to bring one's case before the public. Indeed, the creative use of radio, television, and now the Internet by conservative evangelicals demonstrates how potent a force such media can be, something Rush Limbaugh, Pat Robertson, and other figures on the right have realized for years. Rather, I want us to think about the connections that make this possible. Linda Kintz is quite perceptive when she reminds us that this is not a level playing field. The conservative religious agenda, and its accompanying political and cultural attacks, articulated by Robertson, Ralph Reed, and others is massively overdetermined by its minutely organized electronic and grassroots networks, its media empire, and its ties to conservative and corporate funding and think tanks. Clearly, this way of looking at the world collapses local, national, and international politics into an absolutist Christian agenda based on the words of "our saviour, the central figure of all history, the risen Lord, sovereign over all." It is also the case, as these religious conservatives constantly remind us, that Martin Luther King Jr. and much of the civil rights movement constantly employed biblical language and metaphors to justify their actions and got a good deal of attention in the media. But it is essential to realize that Dr. King did "not have access to an entire political and corporate structure within which to make his language 'literal.'"[32]

A Christian Nation and Free Speech

The unquestioning support of imperial and antidemocratic tendencies internationally both in the media and in their other religious work has much to do with how the United States is seen by conservative evangelicals and how this fits directly into a view of the special nature of the chosen group's covenant with God. For the authoritarian populist religious right, the United States is a blessed nation. It has as its mission the spread of liberty and Christianity. In many ways, in the minds of many on the Christian right, this is linked to the purity and innocence of Eden, for America was something of a "new Eden." Robertson and other conservative religious leaders do not deny the realities of racial and class prejudice, of bigotry and injustice. These "moments" happened because our forefathers wandered from keeping "Christ's commission." As with many neoconservatives, our past, then, is not really shameful, no matter what has been done in terms of genocide and slavery. We need only recall the immensity of the positive achievements of America's Christian culture. The achievements of America as a Christian nation constitute a golden age that needs to be relearned and restored. This restorational vision plays an important part in justifying and maintaining the conservative view of America. In Watson's words:

> The assertion that "America is a Christian nation" is a statement of faith about God's special relationship to America. Faith in a national covenant with God, or in the providential role of America, can neither be proved nor disproved. Such assertions are not statements of historical fact, but part of a vision about the meaning of the national experience.[33]

For conservative evangelicals, it is exactly this providential status that is under threat, in much the same way as Eden was ultimately lost. For them, America was *founded* as a Christian nation. Yet it has "turned its back" on this. In fact, its major institutions have become anti-Christian. The result of this is moral degeneration; and the result of this is in turn social degeneration. Public schools, the mass media, political bodies, the courts, feminist and gay and lesbian rights movements, and so on—these have in essence mounted an attack on Christian values. Immorality and an "anything goes" ethic have led to a rot at the very center of American society. For many evangelicals, it started with the situation I discussed in the previous chapter, when Darwin and evolution took center stage and the Bible was taken out of the schools. This is not seen as only a moral crisis, but a threat to prosperity and freedom as well. America became great because it was based on God's laws and on Christian principles.[34] Turning one's back on these laws and principles can only lead to economic and moral disarray. Any forces inside this society such as these "immoral" movements around feminism and the politics of sexuality and toward "socialism" here in the United States must be overcome. Any external threats—communism, socialism, anti-imperialism, liberation struggles—these too must be fought, with immense military force if necessary.

Thus, there once was a nation that could be an Eden on earth. America was that nation, based on its covenant with God. Its historical role was and is to bring to the world of the unanointed the blessings of freedom. This restorational agenda can be seen in Pat Robertson's statement: "We want our history back. We want our tradition back. We want our constitution back. And we want God back in the schools of America."[35] For Robertson and others, only religion, especially that into which he has been anointed, can provide a secure basis for morality and for individual self-restraint. It is absolutely necessary for the continued survival of our government in a world dominated by the threat and reality of evil.[36] For those who might be worried about possible negative implications of this vision, Ralph Reed, the former spokesperson for the Christian Coalition and someone whose task until recently was to put a more personable and less threatening face to its political and moral agenda, continues this kind of argument in a more moderate public tone: "A secular government informed by sacred principles and open to the service of persons of faith not only poses no threat to the Constitution, it is essential to its survival."[37]

External threats are woven together with internal threats to religious freedom. This is deeply connected to the theme of persecution to which I pointed earlier. For many evangelicals, among the most obvious evidence of the threats they believe they face is their perception that the supposed openness of the United States—an openness they see themselves as defending against the infidels, liberals, socialists, and communists—is true for everyone but *them*. Existing cultural and political institutions do not give space or time for "the" Christian perspective. Schools, the media, politics, indeed nearly the entire society, have created the conditions for pushing evangelicals into a second-class position. The church is left out; Christian views are ignored; Christians are discriminated against. In sum, it is not a level playing field where Christians are concerned. What seems like value neutrality is actually the silencing of a committed Christian agenda and should be seen as an infringement of the right to free speech.

For some, this silencing is the result of an active, secular, anti-Christian "religion" that has come to dominate our society. Conspiratorial movements taking leadership from the devil are behind the turn from the Bible.[38] A spiritual battle must be waged throughout every institution in this society to root out the influence of homosexuality, atheism, liberalism, and secularism. For others, their interpretation may be less conspiratorial. But the feeling that Christian rights are being denied—much as the right of religious practice was denied under a number of state bureaucratic socialist regimes—is widespread. Only a lasting campaign of "engaged orthodoxy" can save the world and can restore the American covenant with God.

The issue of silencing is a vexed one for authoritarian populist religious conservatives. One of the claims made by them is that "liberals" have used the issue of censorship to create a situation in which the media focus all their attention on the right, not on what they perceive are the more widespread problems created by "secular humanists."[39] As Phyllis Schlafly puts it in her own usually biting way, "Like the thief who cries 'Stop thief' in order to distract attention from his own crime, many powerful liberals cry 'censorship' in order to hide the fact that *they* are the most ruthless censors of all."[40]

Schlafly, Robertson, and so many others, then, have found the path. Blocking that path is where "real" censorship lies. For them, following "God's way" is the only route to stability, morality, and prosperity nationally and internationally. Other roads inevitably lead to immorality and social disintegration. Powerful secular forces are denying evangelicals their God-given constitutional right to "tell the truth." Yet this very position of certainty creates a tension between their commitment to their religious beliefs and their sense that what makes America special is its legacy of religious, political, and economic freedom. This is an important point since it helps explain why they interpret their actions in particular ways.

A large portion of the evangelical community(ies) is influenced by a resilient voluntarism that mistrusts imposition, that valorizes the individual and her or his personal choice. Because of this, unlike many neoliberals, evangelicals' activism in bringing God to the world is given legitimacy in their minds because it is seen as *transcending self-interest*. Living out one's faith everywhere—in education, in the home, in the paid workplace, in politics—is grounded in "a genuine heartfelt burden for the state of the world, a tremendous sense of personal responsibility to change society."[41] In the words of one strongly committed evangelical woman, "We can't say, 'the world is always going to be a mess and there is nothing I can do about it.' We need to say, 'yes, it's a mess and what part do I play in dealing with that?'"[42] There is, hence, an evangelical *burden* of activism in all spheres of life. Echoing what I said earlier, the world as a whole is seen as an important mission field, from paid jobs to education and child-raising to politics. It is one's personal responsibility both to evangelize the "unsaved" and to bring the wisdom of the gospel to every sphere of life—"not coercively, but to share."[43]

The secular commitments of the dominant institutions of this society prevent such "selfless" sharing. Thus, the separation of public and private is largely rejected by the Christian right. What many people would consider the most private of all matters—one's religious and moral beliefs—are instead viewed as crucial resources for the moral reformation and "healing" of a society as a whole. How could anyone be against such selfless healing? In this way, part of its restorational project is to restore the *public* role and authority of evangelical beliefs, values, and morality in order to help everyone clean up the mess that should be visible to everyone in the nation.

What I discussed earlier is what might be called the Christian right's "offensive" agenda. Yet a "defensive" agenda exists as well, one that shows the paradox of the evangelical rejection of the separation of public and private. For these same conservatives, the separation of public and private is not wide enough. Thus, in issues of school prayer, abortion, the areas of education and family life, the public intrusion into private life in the form of government policies and regulations has to be resisted.[44] (This is one of the reasons in fact that some conservative evangelicals may often reject state imposed testing and the audit culture found in No Child Left Behind. I shall say more about this is my final chapter.)

Therefore, there is no simple dichotomy at work here—private is good; public is bad. Bringing the "private" into the public sphere around (their) religious values is good. Bringing "public" values into (their) private sphere is bad. Hence, public can be good, but only when it mirrors evangelical beliefs.

Godless Schools

One part of the public sphere, however, is *consistently* not good, but bad—the public school. It reflects all that is wrong with this godless society.

Education has been a primary arena of struggle because of this. Secularity, liberalism, "statism"—all of these have combined in schools to destroy the central place of religious beliefs. The educational theories advanced by the "public school cartel" have simply been a "vehicle for socialism and anti-religious cleansing."[45] The Christian right's hostility to public education is extended to teachers' organizations such as the National Education Association (NEA). They too are extremely dangerous. They are anti-Christian and radical leftist organizations whose prime thrust is to wean children away from loyalty to "the outdated religious superstitions, loyalty to family, loyalty to the United States, and beliefs in free market economics, and then introduce them to socialism and world citizenship."[46] How can our children be among the "saved," when their daily lives in schools teach them things that are of the "unsaved"?

The sense of difference, of we/they, of saved and unsaved, can lead to withdrawal from public institutions such as public schools and to a greater reliance on home schooling, about which I say more later on in this chapter and in the chapters that follow. However, when connected to the strong sense of mission that many religious conservatives have, it can just as often lead to a reinvigorated commitment to transform public schools. Such active engagement is quite visible in the commitment of some conservative evangelicals to keep their children in such schools, even though they know that some of the viewpoints there will be opposed to what they believe. In their minds, however, the school is a "mini-mission field."[47] Schools will not become more Christian if evangelical Christians and their children are not there.

If the existing public school system cannot be made to support such Christian beliefs, then neoliberal school choice programs such as vouchers—or failing that, charter schools—provide the keys for changing what children will learn and how they will be taught it. As a group that sees itself as being victimized by current laws and by the educational system, many authoritarian populists are convinced that their threatened cultural identity can only be maintained through the use of public money to establish and expand the rights of parents to school their children in any manner they see fit. Although some religious conservatives fear that these kinds of programs might actually expand the sphere of state influence into what should be private decisions, for the majority of conservative Christians, voucher plans would enable the cultural survival of their most deeply held beliefs and would ensure that their children adhere to these beliefs. I do not use the term "survival" lightly. In the minds of many of these parents, that is what is at stake, not only in terms of the beliefs and culture that their children are to be taught but in terms of what may happen to the nation and the world given the threat of godlessness and evil.

For leaders such as Pat Robertson (and not just him, of course), educational policies such as vouchers have additional benefits. Free markets are in essence "God's way." Of course, he would say, such competition would create better schools for everyone. But, even if "vouchers would spell the end of public schools in America," he has an answer: "To which we say, so what?"[48] If one believes as Robertson does that the schools in this country are "firmly in the grip of fanatical ideologues whose crackpot theories are fast destroying not only the public school system but an entire generation of our young,"[49] then even though such a response may strike many readers as disturbing, it is understandable in the face of such fears.

From these comments, it is easy to see why home schooling as well would seem to hold out hope for a safe and Christian future. Home schooling has been written about in a positive manner in the pages of many "mainstream" national publications and on television and radio, but it is truly glorified in publications such as the conservative magazine *Christianity Today*. One of the major benefits cited is that children schooled at home are more free from the pressures of peers than those at public schools. There are elements of good sense in this claim—and as we shall see in Chapters 7 and 8, in a number of other claims made by advocates of home schooling—because it is not only the religious right that has serious concerns about the influences of peer culture and the sometimes disturbing realities of life in our schools, especially after such things as the repeated shootings that have occurred in a number of schools.

It is what accompanies these elements of good sense that may make one pause, however. As the president of the Washington state branch of the Moral Majority put it, secular education is a "Godless monstrosity." Hence, "every born-again Christian in America [should] take their children out of public schools." He goes on, condemning the curriculum of public schools and urging the removal of "immoral" materials. "Just as I don't think a black kid should be forced to read Mark Twain because of the word 'nigger,' religious Christians shouldn't be forced to read books offensive to them." He singled out a number of examples of such dangerous books, among them *The Wonderful Wizard of Oz* and *The Diary of Anne Frank*. The first "condoned the practice of witchcraft," the second "promoted the belief that all paths lead to God."[50]

These fears, although perhaps articulated in a manner that might seem rather extreme to many less aggressively ideological evangelicals, may explain one of the reasons that recent research has found that James Dobson's extremely conservative Focus on the Family has emerged as the most popular organization among conservative Christian clergy.[51] In fact, Focus on the Family may now be even more influential in a number of ways than the weakened Christian Coalition. The fact that it brings in annual revenues of more than $100 million provides one indication of its widespread support.[52]

Focus on the Family is not alone by any means of course. Among others, Reverend Don Wildmon's American Family Association (what was once called the National Federation for Decency; notice as well the resonance of the word *family*) and its associated AFA Law Center have been active in bringing lawsuits against textbook publishers for their espousal of witchcraft and other "anti-Christian" beliefs. Along with Focus on the Family, the Eagle Forum, Citizens for Excellence in Education, and other groups, they have aggressively challenged textbooks, curricula, and school systems for their purportedly anti-Christian messages and for their own violations of the separation of church and state given these schools' and texts' promotion of secular humanist values.[53]

A good deal of this activism has its roots in the removal of publicly sponsored prayer in schools and in what is perceived to be the federal government's aforementioned attacks on privately run Christian academies that were supposedly only created to guarantee the teaching of proper morality. The removal of school prayer (although it was actually never removed from the daily activities of many schools who simply ignored the ruling) is seen as both a national loss and a cause of what ails the nation. The Supreme Court's decision to "take prayer out of the school" in the 1960s was "a sign of the lifting of God's blessing from our land" and a "major contributing cause of the moral breakup of society."[54] It not only led to social disorder and moral confusion but also brought down God's wrath. The result has been the degradation of Christian America. For Pat Robertson, this assault on Christian America is directed by Satan as part of Satan's plan for a world government that will be formed after the "Christian United States is out of the way."[55] Although not every conservative evangelical takes quite as seriously the "fact" that Satan is behind all of this, once again we can see the ways in which there is a suturing together of America's covenant with God, its special status granted by God, the ever present possibility of evil, the collapse of morality, and the saving grace of commitment to Christianity in all our institutions.

The issue of school prayer, like Darwinism and evolution, hence, cannot be seen in isolation. It is caught up in and related to a much larger assemblage of values, fears, and commitments. Challenges to any one of these is a challenge to all of the authoritarian populists' position. Yet the crisis over school prayer gets even more complicated when coupled with something I mentioned earlier—the establishment of largely all-white Christian academies in the South (and elsewhere in many cases) by conservative parents and churches. The federal government, after years of delay, finally sought to remove the tax exemption these schools had been originally given. In the eyes of the government, this amounted to a public subsidy both of religion and of segregation. In the eyes of the school supporters, this, too, was clearly a government attack on both parental freedom of choice and religious liberty.

Race, class, and religion were often mixed together here. Faced with the loss of their tax exemption as charitable institutions, many southerners argued that their religious academies (more than ten thousand of which had been founded nationally in the 1960s and 1970s) were not based on race. They were created to avoid secular humanism. Thus, the issue was not race, but religion. Because 60 percent of the students in southern academies came from working-class or lower-middle-class backgrounds, many families that were threatened with a doubling of their tuition bills were less than pleased with this government intervention for economic reasons as well. Reflecting on the situation, Jerry Falwell concluded that because of such intrusions, it is now "easier to open a massage parlor than a Christian school."[56]

This is obviously a complex situation phenomenologically. For the parents and the clergy, race issues (e.g., are my child's chances of mobility and better achievement compromised by attending schools with "low-achieving" minority students?) are coupled with economic worries. And these are in turn connected to religiously based fears about increasingly dominant secular messages and institutions. Antigovernment sentiment is partly understandable here. Once again, the religious right sews all these concerns together and enables racializing logics to be hidden under other themes that seem wholly meritorious—and not racist—to the people who believe that their and their children's lives and values are under severe threat. This makes it *no less* racist in its effects, but functional explanations should not be confused with intentional ones. For the parents and school leaders, their understandings of their behavior was and is that race plays little or no part. Of course, this is how the politics of whiteness usually plays itself out so that race is the absent presence whose overt absence masks its power in our daily lives,[57] a point to which I return in my concluding chapter.

We Are Not Doing Anything Different

Race, however, *does* play a large part in the overt arguments of authoritarian populist religious activists. The history of struggles over racism is consistently used to justify their actions.

Groups such as the Christian Coalition and similar more recent organizations that have evolved in its footsteps do not see themselves as asking for things that are out of the ordinary. Indeed, they see themselves as part of a long tradition of others who have successfully struggled over the politics of recognition. For them, just as African-Americans, Latino/as, Native Americans, Asian-Americans, and others have demanded recognition of their unique cultural identities, evangelicals believe that they ought to receive the same kind of differential recognition.[58]

For example, the Christian Coalition has been quite aggressive in its portrayal of conservative Christians as oppressed. The claiming of "victimhood" is a powerful rhetorical device. It enhances the legitimacy of a group at the same time as it calls out for redress. Thus, its role in building collectivity and providing "moral" justification for collective actions should not be underestimated. This gives meaning to the connections constantly being made between the civil rights movement and conservative Christians. Martin Luther King Jr.'s name, and the entire history of the civil rights movement, is invoked repeatedly by conservative evangelicals as justification for the battles against what are perceived as injustices. For them, this is exactly what conservative Protestants are doing as well. Once again, Pat Robertson provides a telling rhetorical example: "In the 1930s, African-Americans in the South were classified by bigots as 'niggers,' not worthy of respect; today it is evangelical Christians who are considered by the liberal media as 'niggers' and not worthy of respect."[59] And although Ralph Reed has been less blunt than Robertson, he, too, states: "It is no exaggeration that Christian bashing is the last acceptable form of prejudice in America."[60]

In the minds of such evangelicals, a clear double standard is applied to them differentially. If civil rights leaders such as Martin Luther King Jr. could move from the pulpit to the street and could employ religious and moral criteria and political activity to change unjust laws, why can't the Christian Coalition? Jerry Falwell makes this clear when he argues that the predecessor of the Moral Majority was the early civil rights movement. After all, King took his message "from the pulpit to the streets."[61] Aren't "we" doing exactly what liberals and African-American political activists have done for years? The fact that a much more affluent group, one that has *not* faced centuries of state-sanctioned apartheid and was not subject to murders, lynching, and overt degradation, does not see that there are very few parallels between its own experiences and those of the African-American population is actually what needs to be asked here.

In many ways, the example of King and the civil rights movement is employed for multiple purposes by the Christian right. By claiming, as they often do, that they are following in his footsteps in acting against a society that denies them their "freedom," they seek to take on his mantle. This both justifies their actions *and* it helps shield them from feeling racist because of the effects of the punitive welfare, education, and penal policies they consistently support—policies whose differential effects on the same black people whose leaders they supposedly wish to emulate are simply scandalous.

Ralph Reed also argues that what the Christian Coalition did—for example, in its voter education efforts to convince people to vote for conservative candidates—was no more than what any other movement has done. The only innovation was that each chapter of the Christian Coalition, through its liaisons with local churches, also focused on local elections, including most importantly those for school board.[62] Furthermore, by the very fact that local liaisons are usually not ministers but laypeople, these efforts more likely will be seen as a genuinely populist response. As Reed put it in 1990, "The Christian community got it backwards in the 1980s. We tried to change Washington when we should have been focusing on the states. The real battles of concern to Christians are in the neighborhoods, school boards, city councils, and state legislatures."[63] (The examples of textbook guidelines in Kansas and Alabama with which I began Chapter 5 lend credibility to this position.) Victories at a local level help cement a more conservative "profamily" set of policies into our daily lives—although this has not stopped conservative religious groups from maintaining a very real presence at the national level and in Washington, as evidenced by the example of their candidate screening process I gave earlier.

To the complaint by moderates that the Christian right has taken over the Republican Party, Reed has a direct answer. "The only crime that the Christian Right has committed is the crime of democracy."[64] To paraphrase him, licking envelopes and burning shoe leather are things everyone can do. Critics, however, are quick to point out that what seems to be a simple exercise of democracy is often instead a "stealth" campaign in which conservative religious activists specifically target "pro-family" voters in historically low-turnout elections such as those for school board.[65] Or they run on a platform of fiscal responsibility, hiding the rest of their more aggressive agenda until they have been elected. The use of such tactics is denied, but the Christian Coalition's field director in 1991 did not help their case when he argued that most people do not care about such elections and are not going to vote. Therefore, speaking to the majority of voters made little sense. Nor did it help when in the same year Ralph Reed himself suggested that rather than following Jerry Falwell's approach of large-scale media events and rallies, the Christian Coalition should engage in something like guerrilla warfare: "It's better to move quietly, with stealth, under cover of night."[66] Although Reed claimed that he was not speaking literally and that he was quoted out of context, the worries about stealth campaigning have persisted well after Reed left to form a political consulting firm.

Not only do authoritarian populist religious movements see parallels between themselves and civil rights and voter registration movements of the past, paradoxically given their positions on cultural restoration as a return to a golden past, they see parallels between what they do and the struggle over multiculturalism as well. Unlike the claims by disenfranchised Americans whose roots lie in Asia, Latin America, or Africa that their history has never been told, there is an even greater sense of loss among many evangelicals. To them, their history *was* central to the historical narrative of the United States and it now has been purged from its central location. "Campus gurus and thought police have attempted to strip from our society all references to our Christian heritage, to the faith of our fathers, to the artistic and literary achievements of Western Christian civilization."[67]

All this leads to another kind of paradox. What is it that such conservative religious activists want? A restoration of "Christian America"? Simply a recognition of their distinct cultural and religious heritage, values, and beliefs that would enable them to participate more fully in society's public life? The most credible answer is that they want both. "They want their 'place at the table' *and* they want everyone to agree with them. They want a Christian nation *and* religious freedom. As contradictory as it may seem, they want their cake *and* to eat it too."[68] It is this odd combination of an antipluralist set of beliefs (we are the chosen ones, the ones with the truth) and a belief that in the United States everyone's values should be responded to equally (we are an oppressed minority) that makes the case of authoritarian populists such a complex story. Recognition of the complexity should not lead us to ignore the very real dangers associated with its arrogance. But it does mean that we need to listen carefully to the elements of good sense packed into the elements of bad sense in their positions.

The Structures of Feeling of Authoritarian Populism

How do these contradictory sentiments work at the level of everyday life? The much discussed breakdown of community caused in part by economic demands and crises, by the concomitant creation of possessive individualism, by the mobility of a population, by the blurring of idealized gender roles, and so on has created a situation in which many people feel unmoored, anomic, and isolated. The church has historically provided a central place for building community. It takes on an even more central role for many people today. Conservative visions of homogeneity under God's laws and guidance not only assist in the construction of real social communities through the church; they also help create imagined communities, structures of feeling that connect you with unseen people throughout the nation who are "just like me."[69] As Raymond Williams reminded us, one of the most important underpinnings of social stability and social transformation is the production of "structures of feeling" that are not necessarily conscious, but presage important limits on and possibilities for social action.[70]

Authoritarian populist sentiments act in exactly this way. They do particular kinds of work for people who hold them. As in the past, for many women, for example, such conservatism holds the promise of community, of female agency, and of the security of responsible male behavior.[71] Rather than looking with ironic condescension on the appeal that conservative populism has to so many people, we need to continue the process that I started in earlier sections; we must get inside it. We need to ask why—in the face of conditions that might predict the opposite—large numbers of people have found in such positions answers to the problems they face in their daily lives.

Such conservatism rests on a structure of feeling that might be thought about as a set of concentric circles that are stacked on top of each other and that point upward to heaven: God, property, womb, family, church, free market, global mission, God.[72] In many of the iterations of these circles, the sense-making that lies behind them takes the form of apocalyptic narratives. History is a divinely predetermined totality. Extreme pessimism about the present is accompanied by a strong belief that a crisis is imminent. Yet, even though evil is present, God will eventually triumph over evil. In the words of Elaine Pagels, "The faith that Christ has conquered Satan assures Christians that in their own struggles the stakes are eternal, and victory is certain. Those who participate cannot lose."[73] These narratives hold a central place, for instance, in Pat Robertson's modernized apocalyptic vision and in Ralph Reed's version that has been sanitized for public consumption. For them and for their many followers, Christ is coming; but he can only return if born-again Christians, rather than waiting to be "raptured out of harm's way," prepare the conditions for the Second Coming.[74] Positions such as these create something of an unbridgeable binary—either the absolutism of conservative Christians or the nihilism of a society that is falling apart around us. God versus evil; there is no other choice.

Because the arguments of conservative religious activists are not presented in ways in which perhaps many readers are very comfortable politically or intellectually, we can overlook the very places where politics often matter the most—in our unconscious needs and fears, in our very bodies and emotions, and through faith. Ignoring these areas involves too truncated a definition of rationality. In the words of one of the most astute analysts of how secular processes of interpretation have all too often coded the spheres of feeling and spirituality as "irrational and feminized," it is important to remember that "part of what has happened is that absolutist Christianity has situated meaning in the heart of Christ rather than in the head of Man."[75] Yet this very act of situating meaning in this way has a long rhetorical tradition within religious discourse not only in the United States but in nations throughout the world.

In this narrative of "truth," God sent his son to redeem us. Thus, he gave up his own child for us. This sacrifice, in a time when so many people feel as if they must move earth and stars to keep their families intact economically and emotionally, creates a powerful imaginary connection. All things are linked together, with children often providing a key nexus, a set of connections that links to the restoration and legitimation of an imagined yet sacred past of family, religion, and nation in an almost sensual set of conjoined meanings and relations. It is Christianity, read as a story pregnant not only with past but fully present meanings, that joins one's intimate experiences of family life and its threats, gender relations, economic and emotional security, and so much more into a coherent framework.[76] Given the potent mix of biblical inerrancy (the Bible is correct) and the rich metaphors in which it is written (I can read it in such a way that I can find my own predicaments and ways of dealing with them in it), it is not at all surprising that considerable numbers of people find it powerful. Of course, these kinds of sensibilities can be found in the growth of particularly militant variants of Judaism and Islam, ones often stimulated by similar social conditions and structures of feeling.

But how does this power work in largely conservative ways for so many people in the current context? The issue of gender provides a prime example of how such narratives create structures of feeling that can feel so personally freeing and yet paradoxically support dominance.

At its most extreme, the religious right's position on feminism can be seen in Pat Robertson's 1992 statement: "The feminist agenda is not about equal rights for women. It is about a socialist, anti-family political movement that encourages women to leave their husbands, kill their children, practice witchcraft, destroy capitalism, and become lesbians."[77] It is exactly this kind of rhetoric that Ralph Reed tried to refashion so that the Christian right had a more moderate image.

Even with this kind of argument, however, there are contradictory tendencies in conservative evangelicals' positions on gender relations. For example, while evangelicals often cite Ephesians 5:22, which states

"Wives, submit to your husbands as to the Lord," at the same time conservative religious groups actively seek out women of faith to take on major roles in mobilizing for "spiritual warfare."[78] "Selfless women," in roles ordained by God, work for the cause, but they must never forget their true calling, a calling I shall delve into further in Chapter 8's discussion of the labor of home schooling. This tension is perhaps best exemplified in a quote from Beverly LaHaye, the founder of Concerned Women of America, when she argues that one of the most important things women can do is to help "restore righteousness."

> I believe that God has a particular task for every Christian woman to perform. Some may be called to be "salt and light" in their own church, fulfilling a need there. Others may be called to action in the local community, organizing an anti-abortion rally or protest against pornography being sold at a corner store. ... Others may fulfill God's purpose by being intercessors or letter writers. ...
>
> But let me caution those women who are, by nature, "activists." If you are married and have small children, you must know where your primary responsibility lies. ... Your "call" at this point in your life will be localized and centered within your family. If you travel and lose your own children, you have failed to fulfill God's primary purpose for you at this point—and that is to train your children.[79]

Therefore, for the most conservative of the authoritarian populist leaders such as LaHaye, women cannot serve both God and feminism. Nor, as we shall see, can they accept homosexuality or abortion. Any acceptance of such "immorality" is the result of the acceptance by this society of "Satan's biggest lie"—evolution. "God's truth is that we come from God's hand. ... By doubting God's truth about creation, we have set ourselves up for a tidal wave that will destroy our very foundations."[80]

Notice what is being said here. It directly connects to my earlier discussion in Chapter 5 of what stands behind the recent events in education in Kansas. It is not that evolution and its teaching is one element to which such conservatives object. In fundamental ways (excuse the double entendre), it is one of the most *central* foundations of their entire world. We are *made* from God's hand. What gives us value is this fact; it is what provides the underpinnings of our belief in scriptural authority. It determines our responsibilities to each other and to nature. Undercutting this does no less than challenge the very foundation of our entire world. "We know that God's truth is only found in God's word. We must defend that truth in our homes, in our schools, and in our country."[81]

How would I know what to do, how would I be guided through a time of chaos, fluidity, and danger, if God does not provide me—as a special creation—with the ethical principles that make me selfless, make me willing to sacrifice—as God's only child did—in my commitment to act as God's willing servant? For authoritarian populists, this selflessness, this feeling of being one who sacrifices, of having turned oneself over to God and his values, enables one to truly believe that she or he is not guilty of political manipulation, hatred, or racism. Selflessness and truth are fused in powerful ways in this couplet, ways that are even more powerful for many conservative women. Let me say more about this because the relations of all this to particular constructions of gender and women's roles are intricate and are integral to the structures of feeling that help establish identities within authoritarian populist religious communities.

The structure of motherhood is exemplary in this regard. Motherhood is a sacred trust. With the centuries of struggle by women both for recognition and redistribution, not only were there transformations in male identities (though not sufficient ones), but this created a crisis in the idealized identities of many traditional women. This crisis has opened a space for absolutist religion. A considerable number of women have turned religious to "satisfy the anguish, the suffering, and the hopes of mothers."[82] Not surprisingly, the (re)construction of religiously based visions of sacred motherhood is:

> constructed precisely where much of secular society's contempt and disgust have historically been focused, for mothers are at the same time idealized and despised. In this religious framework, children become the instruments of a guaranteed, sacred identity for women who have a deep and realistic fear that without such a guarantee, they will inevitably be judged against men and found lacking. Then they and their children will be left at great risk in a society based on masculine competition, whether built by free-market theorists or liberal institutions.[83]

This sense of sacred motherhood is also then employed as a set of intellectual and emotional resources to counter the move toward such things as institutionalized child care. Such arrangements for our children break the bonds of parents—especially mothers—and children and are largely in the interests of "yuppies" or the state's social engineers.[84] As Christian conservative Connie Marshner argues, such "social parenting" is "not in accord with God's plan for raising children." It may be the case that "social parenting has the power to assume a pleasing shape," but—using the words of Shakespeare—Marshner goes on to remind us that "the Devil hath the power to assume a pleasing shape as well."[85]

Sacred motherhood is itself dependent on the sacredness of the nuclear family, God's chosen unit. But the sacredness of motherhood and the sacredness of the family do not stand alone. They are a crucial counterbalance to something else that is divinely inspired and human nature. (Remember, we are created in God's image, so human nature is itself divine.) This additional element is free enterprise. Justification for this can be found, according to Pat Robertson, in the Eighth Commandment: "Thou shalt not steal." This embodies God's recognition of the sanctity of property. God "forbids a citizen to take what belongs to another citizen." The commandment tells us not to take from the rich and give to the poor. The biblical message is indeed clear: "What a man has accumulated [is] his. In God's order there are no schemes of wealth redistribution under which government forces productive citizens to give the fruit of their hard-earned labors to those who are nonproductive."[86]

Thus, for many of these people, corporations are a "natural extension" of God's law. Our moral and religious duty to the rest of the world is to export unregulated "free enterprise" around the globe. In this, as with other couplets that prove significant in conservative religious discourse, corporate and religious discourse are stitched together, each legitimating the other. Here, traditional family and religious values need to be globalized, and in God's plan this can only be accomplished through the advance of multinational capitalism. Corporate capitalism and the export of U.S. culture are now overtly and without apology defined as among the highest expressions of God's will, the missionary expansion of his culture to the rest of the globe.[87] Human nature *is* the market; and unbridled expansion of such a market to all the world's nations (and ultimately to schools as we have seen) is God's will. Identities and their accompanying beliefs and practices that are not disciplined according to market logic are, hence, in essence also ungodly. Many neoliberal ideas, then, can be easily connected to this range of sentiments since they are given a biblical warrant.

In the words of the conservative Catholic "moral economist" Michael Novak, who often finds himself in agreement with the beliefs of rightist Protestant evangelicals, "Personal economic initiative is a fundamental human right and to exercise that right is to fulfill the image of God inherent in every man and women."[88] For Novak, moral responsibility requires the creation of wealth, which is itself the only true guarantor of liberty and democracy. Hence, his advice to "intelligent, ambitious, and morally serious young Christians and Jews" is the following. "They will better save their souls and serve the cause of the Kingdom of God all around the world by restoring the liberty and power of the private sector than by working for the state."[89]

This is closely connected to something I discussed earlier, the politics of whiteness, for there is almost always a racial subtext here. This is evidenced in the fact that for many European Americans, being middle class is partly defined by not being black. The absence of African-Americans is what makes a neighborhood a "decent place to live."[90] "They" (blacks) tend to be wards of the state. They are neither efficient nor productive, while "we" are. Although all of us are God's children, some of us—especially particular people of color—can only be saved by setting the market loose on them. Here again, religion, markets, anti-statism, and racialized and racializing logics are all brought together in ways in which it is God's will that black, red, and brown poor are made into self-reliant citizens "just like us."[91] The fact that government subsidies and tax breaks to the middle class and the wealthy are *far more* extensive than all of the combined programs to support the poor is not part of this self-understanding.

If the Other is raced, she or he is also sexed. Thus, bodily politics provide another key element in this structure of feeling. Homosexuality is a threat to the sacred family, and to the God-given gender roles that constitute it. It can pollute children's minds and their identities as Christians. Schools, themselves, are sites of danger here, because they are clearly promoting a gay agenda. Resources that should be devoted to raising standards, preventing violence, ensuring that teachers are qualified, and so much more in our crisis-ridden schools are being siphoned away to support sex education and an agenda of immorality. This can only be stopped if sex education is devoted to one theme only—abstinence—and if such "private" matters are left to the family.[92] Valorizing the "private"—with all the contradictions this entails—becomes crucial in structuring one's interpretive frame.

However, the sanctity of private life is not extended to gays. They can be "cured," brought back into the fold of sacred gender relations defined by compulsory heterosexual norms and values. Rather than interpreting their actions as forms of bigotry and discrimination, the conservative activists who support such policies see themselves as acting in a wholly meritorious manner. They are acting out of deep love of children and out of a religious conviction that loving the "sinner" means bringing her or him back into a covenant with God, and as truly principled about the fate of the nation. It is exactly these sentiments that led to such a virulent set of reactions to the issue of gay marriage.

Like many of the sentiments of the religious right, this logic too is grounded in a strong commitment of "being fair to everyone." The "gay agenda" is seen as an attack on religious rights. Just as important, granting civil rights protections to gays and lesbians grants them the right to use the law to establish that homosexuals are a legitimate minority and deserve the protections accorded to racial minorities, women, and others. It would force schools to teach children that gays and lesbians are "good." In this way, the constitutional rights of parents and children who hold religious beliefs that find homosexuality abhorrent are themselves abrogated by schools.[93] A finely tuned sense of what they see as democratic justice provides an important element in this intellectual/emotional assemblage.

Understanding this sense of justice should not make us lose perspective on the hatefulness that guides much of it. Some of the antigay rhetoric gets quite extreme and can and has been used to justify murderous acts. Consider the following statement made by the antigay activist Paul Cameron on the Christian Broadcasting Network. Supposedly drawing on one of the nation's founders, Cameron said, "Think of Thomas Jefferson, one of our most liberal thinkers in the western world. He said in a considered statement that homosexuals ought to be castrated. He said that homosexual females ought to have a one-inch hole drilled through the cartilage of their nose."[94] Although other conservative evangelicals may take less of a violent position, and even Jerry Falwell has recently met with representatives of gay and lesbian movements to try to lessen the overt hostility, it is clear that for many conservative religious activists the "sin" of homosexuality needs to be punished and eradicated. Indeed, HIV/AIDS, for example, is seen not only as a punishment against gays, but also as a punishment from God against society as a whole because this society has tolerated the "perversion" of homosexuality. "We" (the church and "good" Christians) must fight the social acceptance of homosexuality, "not just in terms of pressing for testing or even quarantining of gays, but in terms of massive action to stop non-monogamous, non-heterosexual activity in its entirety."[95] We shall do this out of love for the homosexual and out of love for this society. How else can they and this society about which we care so much be saved?

A good deal of these structures of feeling center around what is perhaps best named "plain-folks Americanism," an identity with its roots in the populist and libertarian soil of the South and West. It also draws strength from Pentecostal traditions with their own grounding in the work ethic, personal responsibility, and traditional values. Although this plain-folks Americanism was often racist in earlier periods of populism, it also focused on a critique of elites. (Remember, for instance, my point that the now derogatory term *rednecks* had its origins in the fierce pride many farmers and working-class people in the South had in differentiating themselves from those who worked in jobs where their necks would not be reddened by the sun.) In the 1960s and 1970s, these critiques increasingly shifted to people of color, feminists, unions, urban elites, "liberals," and the state.[96] In fact, I do not think it is possible to understand the seductiveness of authoritarian populist messages unless we appreciate the undercurrent of a stern moral critique of elitism that works throughout it. This responds to a deep popular discontent over the directions our culture has taken,[97] a discontent that is itself part of the moral economy that feels righteous when it is expressed by religious conservatives.

From what I have said in this section, it should be clear that the structures of feeling underlying all of this are tense and contradictory, but they do provide meaning and emotional cement that give one a definite place in an uncertain world. They embody certain tendencies. First, there is the horror of mixing, a binary of purity and danger. Second, there is a fear of solitude. Third, there is intense anxiety over the possibility that equality will produce uniformity. These elements lead to an emotional economy in which specific kinds of "circuits of solidarity" are produced and reinforced. The world is to become a perpetual small town in which all know their place and where hierarchies are based on God's plan. But these are not just any circuits of solidarity; they are circuits of *preferential* solidarity. The limited absolutist vision of democracy under God's law turns democracy into an exclusive "patriotic religion."[98] Women, gays and lesbians, people of color, the poor, the dispossessed and oppressed—for them there is to be no recourse through the state. Faith will solve all. Perhaps Michelle LeDoeuff is right when she says that these structures of feeling support "structures of vassalage which are as undemocratic as possible."[99]

How Can Hate Seem So Nice?

Structures of vassalage can contain elements that create forms of misrecognition for those who participate in them, forms that make one feel *powerful* even in the face of the depowering of oneself and especially those whom such discourses position as the Other. For the majority of conservative evangelicals, they themselves are "nice" people, "real Americans" who stand for things that the rest of us have given up on.

They are the defenders of all of us. Their power, their willingness to strictly uphold moral principles, stands between us and what is certain to be a future that will be a disaster. Their very "niceness" serves as a major element of their misrecognition. Linda Kintz asks what is perhaps one of the most significant questions in this regard: "How can hate seem so nice?"[100]

Although it does not provide a complete explanation, Kelly argues that one of the reasons conservative religions have been growing is actually because of their strictness. The fact that they are so demanding means that they present people with a rich set of meanings. Less-demanding religious groups call forth less sacrifice and less discipline, and therefore are less able to seem relevant to every aspect of one's life.[101] This is true to some extent, but one of the signal accomplishments of modern conservative evangelicalism has been its strategic curbing of some of fundamentalism's rigid absolutism and its separateness from the world. By reducing the level of strictness, and by creating an atmosphere of what can be called "seeker-friendly" churches, evangelicalism enables one to walk the tightrope of religiosity in all parts of life. It helps one deal with the task of not remaining pure from the world, but advancing into it and transforming its very soul.[102]

These actions increase its vitality, its sense of being both traditional *and* modern. Its very lack of one single authoritative creed, guided by one central organizational form, enables conservative evangelicalism to create "a meaningful identity space." In the process, it also provides another kind of space. By its very nature as a transdenominational identity movement, it is characterized by a loose network that is wide open structurally. This enables the development of entrepreneurial and inventive leaders. But it also gives people subject positions, identities, that respond to people's definition of themselves as individuals who have made a personal choice to be reborn.[103] How can I interpret my actions as hateful and authoritarian when I am so strongly committed to personal choice and to seeking the "truth"?

Although large numbers of citizens may find such a position to be nothing short of arrogant and aggressive, paradoxically this confirms evangelicalism's correctness for its followers. Christian Smith argues that rather than threatening its growth, evangelicalism is actually made stronger by the tensions and conflicts that its engagement with the public world engenders. It is exactly this engagement that keeps it vital, that gives it its purpose and identity.[104] This is connected to the ways "self" and "others" are produced socially. "Collective identities depend heavily for existence on contrast and negation. Social groups know who they are in large measure by knowing who they are not."[105] Such identities are not necessarily stable. They are constantly being reproduced symbolically and socially by one's daily interactions, interactions that constantly mark the differences between insiders and outsiders, between "we" and "they." In Bourdieu's terms, nearly all cultural symbols and practices act to reproduce distinctions among collective actors. In the case of the growing conservative evangelical movement, these distinctions enable identities to be achieved and reinforced.[106]

> This has been described as something of the "cultural DNA" of evangelicalism. The evangelical tradition's entire history, theology, and self-identity reflects strong cultural boundaries with nonevangelicals; a zealous burden to convert and transform the world outside of oneself; and a keen perception of external threats and crises seen as menacing what it views to be true, good, and valuable.[107]

This means that evangelicalism depends for its very existence on having a "constitutive outside." Its very meaning and identity requires that there be those who are immoral, lazy, burdens on the state, evil, secular humanists, or unsaved. This very binary gives meaning to one's most fundamental sets of interpretive structures. It is one of the reasons that evangelicals have some very real sympathies with neoconservative positions on the importance of character and virtue (but I hasten to add not necessarily with the belief held by many neoconservatives that national and state curricula, standards, and tests are the way forward).

Do not take this as a negative statement about evangelical religion in general. It is not meant to imply that such religious affiliations are built around a false consciousness that somehow wrongly solves the tensions over identity in the modern/postmodern world.[108] There is nothing new in evangelicalism's attempt to do this. Nearly all religious movements have constantly attempted to create communities of meaning, memory, and belonging. This is one of the ways in which they provide a primary basis of making sense of the world. Just as in its early history, evangelicalism's activist rebirth comes about at a time when people are experiencing alienation and rootlessness, isolation, and feelings of insignificance.[109] What would have to be explained would be not the rebirth of activist evangelicalism, but if it had *not* occurred.

However, although much of this is to be expected, conservative evangelicalism has built on, extended, and in part transformed these earlier instances of religious mobilization in distinct ways. It has taken existing themes and creatively transmuted them in such a way that the conservative elements come to the fore. Such creative alterations—ones that are both connected to historical meanings and yet reworked in powerful ways—can be seen in the ways in which conservative evangelicalism resonates and connects with deep-seated American constructions of the embodiment of individualism in our daily lives. As I argued earlier, the forces of conservative restoration and of conservative modernization have been more than a little successful in altering our ideas about democracy and citizenship. They have partly depoliticized them (and then repoliticized them around extremely conservative visions), transforming earlier collective forms into the language of consumption and choice. Evangelicalism is itself both a response to this and a reproduction and extension of it. Just as we saw in my discussion of its earlier history, evangelicalism provides a collectivity, while at the same time making it a result of active individual *choice*. This is clear in the following:

> For … modern Americans the ultimate criteria of identity and lifestyle validity is individual choice. It is by choosing a product, a mate, a lifestyle, or an identity that one makes it one's very own, personal, special, meaningful—not "merely" something one inherits or assumes. In the value-epistemology of modern American culture, to believe, to want, or to do something simply because that is what one's parents believe, or what one's friends want, or what somebody else does is considered inferior and unauthentic. … That is parochial, acquiescent, and artificial. Rather every such thing must be personalized and substantiated through individual choice. Even if (as is often the case) one chooses what one was already inheriting or assuming, it is only through the observance of individual choice—whether actual or ritualized—that it becomes "real" and personally meaningful.[110]

In a faith-based movement where one of the most important acts is making a "personal decision for Christ," of being "reborn" through an experience of individual conversion, the power of such values can be seen.[111] Making a "choice for Christ" validates individualism (and hence cannot be oppressive to others since it is based on the fundamental value that supposedly guarantees freedom in the United States) and at the same time secures an identity within a larger movement. This is a profoundly creative way of dealing with the contradictions and tensions of authoritarian populist identities today. And it allows what is often based on hate to seem like love.

This is closely tied to another element of the structures of feeling that I described before, antielitism. This is not only a sociological outlook, but also an epistemological one. It reconstructs our understanding of "truth." Truth is simple and clear, unlike the opinions of the "plague of experts" in, say, government, law, the media, and education. This position works off of the populist hostility to experts and to their supposed belief that our problems are too complex for the common sense solutions held by average citizens.[112] Strategically, this element is more important than many of us might like to admit. Like the critical and deconstructionist tools employed by, say, critical multiculturalists, this view of truth as commonsense supplies a powerful vocabulary for describing and fighting against perceived oppressions. Yet, and this is crucial, whereas the social and cultural criticism of the former is based on what is often a new and difficult vocabulary taken from critical theory and postmodernism for example,[113] the Christian conservatives speak in familiar terms. They call on their constituency to employ tools that they *already possess*—a strong Christian faith and common sense. Whether we like it or not, this gives them a functional and tactical advantage.[114] This connects with the criticisms I made in Chapter 3 of the overly theoretical and rhetorical turn taken by many writers about "critical pedagogy." The tactical advantage that familiarity gives the authoritarian populist right needs to be thought about directly and strategically, not ignored.

Turning Straw into Gold

The implications of this "plain speaking" are not small by any stretch of the imagination. This advantage is not sitting unused. The religious right has not been and is not static. It is in constant motion, involved in "reclaiming and reinvigorating lost or dormant themes, traditions, and practices," at the same time as the Christian right often generates new themes and practices. In their interactions with the world and in their modes of interpretation, as I have demonstrated here these groups are often more than a little talented in "using quintessentially modern tools to strengthen and promote their traditional worldviews and ways of life."[115] In one commentator's clever words, evangelical religious movements are more than capable of taking these advantages and "turning the proverbial 'straw into gold.'"[116]

Although this talent should no longer surprise us, given what I have shown in these chapters, it should make us try even harder to understand the creative elements that underpin the structures of feelings and identities of this movement. If we do not, then the institutions in our society may embody a set of values that may not be filled with love— evangelical or any other kind. Although Pat Robertson does not speak for all of the many evangelical communities, conservative or otherwise, his statements about the place of religion in public life and in our schools help illuminate the reasons for concern. For him, the current separation of church and state is an "intellectual scandal." For the sake of our children, we must bring God back into the classrooms, homes, and businesses of America. The fact that nonbelievers have the right to citizenship should not be employed to argue that "the ninety-four percent of us who believe in God have any duty whatsoever to dismantle our entire public affirmation of faith in God just to please a tiny minority who don't believe in anything."[117] The tone of this statement gives much cause to worry.

Even with this rhetoric, however, we need to be fair. There are religious impulses that are even more conservative than those I have discussed so far. These range from the Reconstructionist movement to the utterly racist and at times quite violent far-right groups such as neo-Nazis, the followers of Christian Identity, the Order, and others.[118] Although in no way do I wish to minimize the dangers of radical paramilitary and racist groups—given the long and murderous history of such action in the United States and given the recent spate of racist killings here—their very presence makes the positions of ultraconservative religious groups seem more "mainstream." That is, their existence gives legitimacy to conservative religious groups that would otherwise be seen as beyond the boundaries of widespread public acceptability. A case in point here is Christian Reconstructionism.

The Reconstructionist movement is relatively small in numbers, but its language and principles have been increasingly influential among charismatic Christians, home-schoolers, and the religious right. The core of Reconstructionism centers around "presuppositionalism," the idea that the only way to understand reality is through the lens of the Bible. The Bible, hence, is *the* governing text in education, law, government, and all other areas of public and private life. Family, church, and government are under God's covenant. Under such a covenant, the nuclear family is the basic unit. Wives and children submit to the head, the husband. But he in turn submits to Jesus and to the laws of God as detailed in the Old Testament. All forms of civil government exist only to implement God's laws. Thus, family, church, and government are under God's law, "theonomy."[119] This biblical worldview, then, is not to be applied only to such contentious moral issues as pornography, homosexuality, abortion, or the knowledge that is declared official in schools. Rather, as one noted Reconstructionist theologian argues, as God's chosen people, "the Christian goal for the world is the universal development of Biblical theocratic republics, in which every area of life is redeemed and placed under the Lordship of Jesus Christ and the rule of God's Law."[120]

As one pastor puts it, "We have the word of God. ... Principle some-times takes precedent over silly laws."[121] In a similar vein, another leader of Concerned Women for America writes that the "separation of church and state is a bogus phrase. Our country was founded on Biblical prin-ciples and we need to turn back to God and his precepts."[122]

Although not alone in this belief, central to Reconstructionist call-ing is the attack on public schools. One of the most vocal of such critics is Gary North, who writes, "Until the vast majority of Christians pull their children out of public schools, there will be no possibility of creat-ing a theocratic republic."[123] For this wing of the movement, the task is not to improve public schools but—ultimately—to shut them down. Urging conservative Christians to pull their children out of school *and* run for their local school boards, the task once elected is to cut off funding for such schools and, finally, "to sink the ship."[124] At the very least, "our" task will be to return to the situation before 1837 when vir-tually all education in the country was Christian and private. Through Christian schools and home schooling, it is hoped that an entire gen-eration of people will be trained to understand that religious neutrality is, in essence, a fiction. In home school advocate Christopher Klicka's words, "Sending our children to public schools violates nearly every Biblical principle. ... It is tantamount to sending out our children to be trained by the enemy."[125]

Many religious conservatives have had to distance themselves from any public affiliation with Reconstructionism because it has become too controversial. For example, Pat Robertson has had to defend himself against charges that he wants to establish a theocracy. This is a charge that can be justified by some of his writings, but he has attempted to move away from some of his earlier more aggressive claims about this.[126] Even with such public disavowals, Reconstructionism has helped pull people even further toward the right. The influences that it and similar "biblical worldview" perspectives of this segment of the Christian right have are more widespread than are usually admitted, especially since many conservative evangelicals interact constantly both with figures from this movement and with the symbols to which it gives legitimacy.

For example, televangelist D. James Kennedy's weekly television program airs on over three hundred stations and is broadcast on the Armed Services Network. He hosts a yearly national political confer-ence on "Reclaiming America," which has drawn more than two thou-sand people, including such conservative luminaries as presidential hopeful Gary Bauer of the Family Research Council, Beverly LaHaye of Concerned Women of America, Bob Dugan of the National Association of Evangelicals, Robert Simonds of Citizens for Excellence in Education,

Russ Walton of the Plymouth Rock Foundation, George Grant, the even more ultraconservative Reconstructionist formerly of Coral Ridge Ministries, and others such as former vice president Dan Quayle. Aside from being a gathering ground for rightist religious figures, the conference is also notable for the participants' recitation of the pledge of allegiance to the "Christian flag." Thus, before Dan Quayle's speech to the assembly, the audience recited "I pledge allegiance to the Christian flag, and to the Saviour, for whose freedom it stands. One Saviour, crucified, risen and coming again, with life and liberty for those who believe."[127] It is probable that not everyone in the audience was fully committed to the principles of Reconstructionism. Yet this pledge shows the reach of its underlying premises.

It is still important to remember, however, that while many evangelicals do want to reassert the power and authority of their morality and beliefs in the public sphere, they have *not* consistently taken the even stronger stance advocated by the more radical Reconstructionist movement. As I documented, as postmillennialists, the Reconstructionists believe that God requires "man" to create the kingdom of God on earth. Rather than the premillennial assumption that time is running out soon, Reconstructionism advocates even more uncompromising and grassroots struggles that leave no room for false ideas of tolerance for other religions.[128] "Time is on our side." Christ is coming and "has willed our victory." Thus, there is no need for compromise and pluralism. Although Robertson and other conservative evangelicals may sound this way at times and undoubtedly want to change the world, only dominionists like the Reconstructionists insist that they, and they alone, must run it.[129]

This said, though, it should be absolutely clear that for Robertson, Reed, and so many other authoritarian populist religious leaders and spokespersons religious diversity and pluralism are certainly not things to be fully welcomed. For them, such things are among the ways the forces of secular humanism have engaged in the "de-Christianizing of America."[130] This does not mean that they are necessarily overtly anti-Semitic or anti-Catholic, although that border is sometimes crossed. Their major enemies are those whom they see as antireligion. They have been willing to compromise and to form alliances with conservatives within Judaism and Catholicism (but certainly not with Islam) in the restorational struggle.

In saying that authoritarian populists such as Robertson, Reed, and others are willing to compromise and that they are not quite as radical as, say, Reconstructionists in terms of seeking dominion over every institution so that a "theonomy" is established, I do not want to minimize their constant and often partly successful attempts to reconstruct our common sense. This actually may make them even more powerful, since their interest is not only in transforming a few laws but in transforming the structures of feeling of an entire culture.

> What Robertson and Reed want is a return to a supposed golden era in which it would not occur to anyone to question the propriety of school prayer, the Ten Commandments on the wall of a government building, unabashed mixtures of evangelical piety and patriotism, or the assertion that this is a Christian nation. Although this evangelical ethos was protected and reinforced in some ways by law, what Robertson and Reed hope for is more powerful and pervasive than mere legality—the restoration of a culture in which evangelicals are insiders, not outsiders.[131]

Of course, for them to be "insiders" means that there must be an extraordinary number of "outsiders." And who these people would be is unfortunately thoroughly predictable. Welcome to the outside.

CHAPTER 7

Away with All Teachers
The Cultural Politics of Home Schooling

Situating Home Schooling

Protecting religious identities and transforming both education and the larger world go hand in hand. One of the ways that the differentiation of inside from outside can be accomplished and maintained is through home schooling. If one of the marks of the growing acceptance of ideological changes is their positive presentation in the popular media, then home schooling has clearly found a place in our consciousness. It has been discussed in the national press, on television and radio, and in widely circulated magazines. Its usual presentation is that of a savior, a truly compelling alternative to a public school system that is presented by neoliberals and neoconservatives as a failure. Although the presentation of public schools as simply failures is deeply problematic,[1] given the arguments I have developed in the chapters that preceded this, it is the largely unqualified support of home schooling that concerns me in my next two chapters. I am considerably less sanguine.

Data on home schooling are not always accurate and are often difficult to compile. However, a sense of the extent of home schooling can be found in the fact that the National Home Education Research Institute has estimated that as of the 1997–1998 school year, 1.5 million children were being home schooled in the United States. The Institute also has suggested that there has been a growth of 15 percent annually in these numbers since 1990. These data are produced by an organization that is one of the strongest supporters of home schooling, but even given the possible inflation of these figures, this clearly is a considerable number of students,[2] a number that is constantly growing.

Given the range of reforms sponsored under the umbrella of conservative modernization, I cannot deal at length with all the many issues that could be raised about the home schooling movement. Nevertheless, I want to ask a number of critical questions about the dangers associated with it. Although it is quite probable that some specific children and families will gain from home schooling, my concerns are larger. As in my previous chapters, these concerns are connected to the more extensive restructuring of this society that I believe is quite dangerous and to the manner in which our very sense of public responsibility is withering in ways that will lead to even further social inequalities. To illuminate these dangers, I shall do a number of things: situate home schooling within the larger movement that provides much of its impetus; suggest its connections with other protectionist impulses; connect it to the history of and concerns about the growth of activist government; and, finally, point to how it may actually hurt many other students who are not home schooled.

At the very outset of this chapter, let me state as clearly as I can that any parents who care so much about the educational experiences of their children that they actively seek to be deeply involved are to be applauded, not chastised or simply dismissed. Let me also say that it is important not to stereotype individuals who reject public schooling[3] as unthinking promoters of ideological forms that are so deeply threatening that they are—automatically—to be seen as beyond the pale of legitimate concerns. Indeed, there are complicated reasons behind the growth of antischool sentiments. As I showed, such beliefs contain elements of "good" sense as well as "bad" sense. All too many school systems are overly bureaucratic, are apt not to listen carefully to parents' or community concerns, or act in overly defensive ways when questions are asked about what and whose knowledge is considered "official." In some ways, these kinds of criticisms are similar across the political spectrum, with both left and right often making similar claims about the politics of recognition.[4] Indeed, these very kinds of criticisms have led many progressive and activist educators to build more community-based and responsive models of curriculum and teaching in public schools.[5]

This said, however, it is still important to realize that although the intentions of critics such as home schoolers may be meritorious, the effects of their actions may be less so. Although many home schoolers have not made their decision based on religious convictions, a large proportion have.[6] As in the last two chapters, I focus largely on this group, in part because it constitutes some of the most committed parents and in part because ideologically it raises a number of important issues.[7]

As I noted, many home schoolers are guided by what they believe are biblical understandings of the family, gender relationships, legitimate knowledge, the importance of "tradition," the role of government, and the economy.[8] Whereas many home schoolers combine beliefs from three of the tendencies I have identified—neoliberalism, neoconservatism, and authoritarian populism—it is the last one that seems to drive a large portion of the movement. For this reason it is not hard to understand why they are often integrated within the tense alliance that has been built among various segments of "the public" in favor of particular policies in education and the larger social world.

Satan's Threat and the Fortress Home

As we saw, for many on the right, one of the key enemies is public education. Secular education is turning our children into "aliens" and, by teaching them to question our ideas, is turning them against us. What are often accurate concerns about public schooling that I noted earlier—its overly bureaucratic nature, its lack of curriculum coherence, its disconnection from the lives, hopes, and cultures of many of its communities, and more—are here often connected to more deep-seated and intimate worries. These worries echo Elaine Pagels's argument that Christianity has historically defined its most fearful satanic threats not from distant enemies, but in relation to very intimate ones.[9] "The most dangerous characteristic of the satanic enemy is that though he will look just like us, he will nevertheless have changed completely."[10]

Some of the roots of this can be found much earlier in the conservative activist Beverly LaHaye's call for the founding of an organization to counter the rising tide of feminism. In support of Concerned Women of America, she spoke of her concern for family, nation, and religion:

> I sincerely believe that God is calling the Christian women of America to draw together in a spirit of unity and purpose to protect the rights of the family. I believe that it is time for us to set aside our doctrinal differences to work for a spiritually renewed America. Who but a woman is as deeply concerned about her children and her home? Who but a women has the time, the intuition, and the drive to restore our nation? ... They

may call themselves feminists or humanists. The label makes little difference, because many of them are seeking the destruction of morality and human freedom.[11]

It is clear from the preceding quote what is seen as the satanic threat and what is at stake here. These fears about the nation, home, family, children's "innocence," religious values, and traditional views of gender relations are sutured together into a more general fear of the destruction of a moral compass and personal freedom. "Our" world is disintegrating around us. Its causes are not the economically destructive policies of the globalizing economy,[12] not the decisions of an economic elite, and not the ways in which, say, our kind of economy turns all things—including cherished traditions (and even our children)—into commodities for sale.[13] Rather, the causes are transferred onto those institutions and people who are themselves being constantly buffeted by the same forces—public sector institutions, schooling, poor people of color, other women who have struggled for centuries to build a society that is more responsive to the hopes and dreams of many people who have been denied participation in the public sphere, and so on.[14]

As I noted at the beginning of this chapter, however, it is important not to stereotype individuals involved in this movement. For example, a number of men and women who are activists in rightist movements believe that some elements of feminism did improve the conditions of women overall. By focusing on equal pay for equal work and opening up jobs and opportunities that had been traditionally denied to women who had to work for pay, women activists had benefited many people. However, as was developed in considerable detail in Chapters 5 and 6, for authoritarian populists, feminism and secular institutions in general still tend to break with God's law. They are much too individualistic and misinterpret the divine relationship between families and God. In so doing, many aspects of civil rights legislation, of the public schools' curricula, and so many other parts of secular society are simply wrong. Thus, for example, if one views the Constitution of the United States literally as divinely inspired, then it is not public institutions but the traditional family—as God's chosen unit—that is the core social unit that must be protected by the Constitution.[15] In a time of seeming cultural disintegration, when traditions are under threat and when the idealized family faces ever more externally produced dangers, protecting our families and our children are key elements in returning to God's grace.[16]

Even without these religious elements, a defensive posture is clear in much of the movement. In many ways, the movement toward home schooling mirrors the growth of privatized consciousness in other areas of society. It is an extension of the "suburbanization" of everyday life that is so evident all around us. In essence, it is the equivalent of gated communities and of the privatization of neighborhoods, recreation, parks, and so many other things. It provides a "security zone" both physically and ideologically. Linda Kintz describes it this way:

> As citizens worried about crime, taxes, poor municipal services, and poor schools abandon cities, the increasing popularity of gated communities, ... fortress communities, reflects people's desire to retreat.... They want to spend more of their tax dollars on themselves instead of others. Further, they take comfort in the social homogeneity of such communities, knowing that their neighbors act and think much as they do.[17]

This "cocooning" is not just about seeking an escape from the problems of the "city" (a metaphor for danger and heterogeneity). It is a rejection of the entire *idea* of the city. Cultural and intellectual diversity, complexity, ambiguity, uncertainly, and proximity to the Other, all these are to be shunned.[18] In place of the city is the engineered pastoral, the neat and well-planned universe where things (and people) are in their "rightful place" and reality is safe and predictable.

Yet in so many ways such a movement mirrors something else. It is a microcosm of the increasing segmentation of American society in general. As we move to a society segregated by residence, race, economic opportunity, and income, "purity" is increasingly more apt to be found in the fact that upper classes send their children to elite private schools; where neighborliness is determined by property values; where evangelical Christians, ultraorthodox Jews, and others only interact with each other and their children are schooled in private religious schools or schooled at home.[19] A world free of conflict, uncertainty, the voice and culture of the Other—in a word I used before, cocooning—is the ideal.[20] When conflict comes in the form of planes being used as weapons of mass murder, or bombs on public transportation systems, and by people who are now seen as the ultimate religious "Other," cocooning seems even more sensible.

Home schooling, thus, has many similarities with the Internet, a tool that I will take up in much more detail in my next chapter. It enables the creation of "virtual communities" that are perfect for those with specialized interests. It gives individuals a new ability to "personalize" information, to choose what they want to know or what they find personally interesting. However, as many commentators are beginning to recognize, unless we are extremely cautious, "customizing our lives" could radically undermine the strength of local communities, many of which are already woefully weak. As Andrew Shapiro puts it,

> Shared experience is an indisputably essential ingredient [in the formation of local communities]; without it there can be no chance for mutual understanding, empathy and social cohesion. And this is precisely what personalization threatens to delete. A lack of common information would deprive individuals of a starting point for democratic dialogue.[21]

Even with the evident shortcomings of many public schools, at the very least they provide "a kind of social glue, a common cultural reference point in our polyglot, increasingly multicultural society."[22] Yet, whether called personalizing or cocooning, it is exactly this common reference point that is rejected by many within the home schooling movement's pursuit of "freedom" and "choice."

This particular construction of the meaning of freedom is of considerable moment, since there is a curious contradiction within such conservatism's obsession with freedom. In many ways this emphasis on freedom is, paradoxically, based on a *fear* of freedom.[23] Freedom is valued, but also loathed as a site of danger, of "a world out of control." Many home schoolers reject public schooling out of concern for equal time for their beliefs. They want "equality." Yet they have a specific vision of equality, because coupled with their fear of things out of control is a powerful anxiety that the nation's usual understanding of equality will produce uniformity.[24] But this feared uniformity is not seen as the same as the religious and cultural homogeneity sponsored by the conservative project. It is a very different type of uniformity—one in which the fear that "we are all the same" actually speaks to a loss of religious particularity. Thus, again at the heart of this movement lies another paradox: we want everyone to be like "us" (this is a "Christian nation"; governments must bow before "a higher authority");[25] but we want the right to be different—a difference based on being God's elect group. Uniformity weakens our specialness. This tension between knowing one is a member of God's elect people and thus by definition different, and also being so certain that one is correct that the world needs to be changed to fit one's image, is one of the central paradoxes behind authoritarian populist impulses. For some home schoolers, the paradox is solved by withdrawal of one's children from the public sphere in order to maintain their difference. And for still others, this allows them to prepare themselves and their children with an armor of Christian beliefs that will enable them to go forth into the world later on to bring God's word to those who are not among the elect. Once again, let us declare our particularity, our difference, to better prepare ourselves to bring the unanointed world to our set of uniform beliefs.

Attacking the State

At the base of this fear both of the loss of specialness and of becoming uniform in the "wrong way" is a sense that the state is intervening in our daily lives in quite powerful ways, ways that are causing even more losses. It isn't possible to understand the growth of home schooling unless we connect it to the history of the attack on the public sphere in general and on the government (the state) in particular. To better comprehend the antistatist impulses that lie behind a good deal of the home schooling movement, I need to place these impulses in a longer historical and social context. Some history and theory is necessary here.

One of the keys to this feeling of antistatism is the development of what Clarke and Newman have called the "managerial state," the characteristics of which I detailed in Chapter 4.[26] This was an active state that combined bureaucratic administration and professionalism. The organization of the state centered on the application of specific rules of coordination. Routinization and predictability are among the hallmarks of such a state. This was to be coupled with a second desirable trait, that of social, political, and personal neutrality, rather than nepotism and favoritism. This bureaucratic routinization and predictability would be balanced by an emphasis on professional discretion. Here, bureaucratically regulated professionals such as teachers and administrators would still have an element of irreducible autonomy based on their training and qualifications. Their skills and judgment were to be trusted, if they acted fairly and impartially. Yet fairness and impartiality were not enough; the professional also personalized the managerial state. Professionals such as teachers made the state "approachable" not only by signifying neutrality but also by acting in nonanonymous ways to foster the "public good" and to "help" individuals and families.[27]

Of course, such bureaucratic and professional norms were there not only to benefit "clients." They acted to protect the state, by providing it with legitimacy. (The state is impartial, fair, and acts in the interests of everyone.) They also served to insulate professional judgments from critical scrutiny. (As holders of expert knowledge, we—teachers, social workers, state employees—are the ones who are to be trusted since we know best.)

Thus, from the end of World War II until approximately the mid-1970s, there was a "settlement," a compromise, in which an activist welfare state was seen as legitimate. It was sustained by a triple legitimacy.

There was (largely) bipartisan support for the state to provide and manage a larger part of social life, a fact that often put it above a good deal of party politics. Bureaucratic administration promised to act impartially for the benefit of everyone. And professionals employed by the state, such as teachers and other educators, were there to apply expert knowledge to serve the public.[28] This compromise was widely accepted and provided public schools and other public institutions with a strong measure of support since by and large the vast majority of people continued to believe that schools and other state agencies did in fact act professionally and impartially in the public good.

This compromise came under severe attack as the fiscal crisis deepened and as competition over scarce economic, political, and cultural resources grew more heated in the 1970s and beyond. The political forces of conservative movements used this crisis, often in quite cynical and manipulative—and well-funded—ways. The state was criticized for denying the opportunity for consumers to exercise choice. The welfare state was seen as gouging the citizen (as a taxpayer) to pay for public handouts for those who ignored personal responsibility for their actions. These "scroungers" from the underclass were seen as sexually promiscuous, immoral, and lazy as opposed to the "rest of us" who were hardworking, industrious, and moral. They supposedly are a drain on all of us economically, and state-sponsored support of them leads to the collapse of the family and traditional morality.[29] These arguments may not have been totally accurate, but they were effective.[30]

This blending together of neoliberal and neoconservative attacks led to a particular set of critiques against the state, critiques that connected dramatically with the authoritarian populist mistrust of elites. For many people, the state was no longer the legitimate and neutral upholder of the public good. Instead the welfare state was an active agent of national decline, as well as an economic drain on the country's (and the family's) resources. In the words of Clarke and Newman:

> Bureaucrats were identified as actively hostile to the public—
> hiding behind the impersonality of regulations and "red tape"
> to deny choice, building bureaucratic empires at the expense of
> providing service, and insulated from the "real world" pressures
> of competition by their monopolistic position. Professionals
> were arraigned as motivated by self-interest, exercising power
> over would-be customers, denying choice through the dubious
> claim that "professionals know best." Worse still, ... liberalism

... was viewed as undermining personal responsibility and family authority and as prone to trendy excesses such as egalitarianism, anti-discrimination policies, moral relativism or child-centeredness.[31]

These moral, political, and economic concerns were easily transferred to public schooling, since for many people the school was and is the public institution closest to them in their daily life. Hence, public schooling and the teaching and curricula found within it became central targets of attack. Curricula and teachers were not impartial, but elitist. School systems were imposing the Other's morality on "us." And "real Americans" who were patriotic, religious, and moral—as opposed to everyone else—were suffering and were the new oppressed.[32] Although this position fits into a long history of the paranoid style of American cultural politics and it was often based on quite inaccurate stereotypes, it does point to a profound sense of alienation that many people feel.

Much of this antistatism of course was fueled by the constant attention given in the media and in public pronouncements to "incompetent" teachers who are overpaid and have short working days and long vacations.[33] We should not minimize the effects of the conservative attacks on schools for their supposed inefficiency, wasting of financial resources, and lack of connection to the economy. After years of well-orchestrated attacks, it would be extremely odd if one did not find that the effects on popular consciousness were real. And these effects are made ever more powerful by the constant publicity surrounding our supposedly failing public schools through No Child Left Behind and similar mechanisms of what might be called "deviance amplification." The fact that a number of these criticisms may be *partly* accurate should not be dismissed. There undoubtedly is a small group of teachers who treat teaching as simply a job that gives them many holidays and free time in the summer. Administrative costs and bureaucratic requirements in schools have risen. Parents and local communities do have a justifiable right to worry about whether their daughters and sons will have decent jobs when they leave school, especially in a time when our supposedly booming economy has left millions of people behind and many of the jobs being created are anything but fulfilling and secure.[34] (The fact that the school has very little to do with this is important.)

Yet it is not only worries about teachers that fuel this movement. As I showed, public schools themselves are seen as extremely dangerous places. These schools were institutions that threatened one's very soul. Temptations and godlessness were everywhere within them. God's truths were expunged from the curriculum and God's voice could no longer be heard. Prayers were now illegal and all of the activities that bound one's life to scriptural realities were seen as deviant.

Even with the negative powerful emotions that such senses of loss and disconnection create, an additional element has entered into the emotional economy being created here with a crushing force. For an increasingly large number of parents, public schools are now seen as threatening in an even more powerful way. They are dangerous bodily; that is, they are seen as filled with physical dangers to the very life of one's children. The spate of shootings in schools in the United States has had a major impact on the feelings of insecurity that parents have about their children. Stories of violence-ridden schools, ones that were worrisome but were seen as largely an "urban problem" involving the poor and children of color, were already creating an antipublic school sentiment among many conservative parents. The horrors of seeing students shoot other students, and now not in those supposedly troubled urban schools but in the suburban areas that had grown after people fled the city, exacerbated the situation. If even the schools of affluent suburbia were sites of danger, then the *only* remaining safe haven was the fortress home.[35]

Fears, no matter how powerful they are or whether they are justified or not, are not enough, however. That a person will act on her or his fears is made more or less probable by the availability of resources to support taking action. It is an almost taken-for-granted point, but important nonetheless, that the growth of home schooling has been stimulated by the wider accessibility to tools that make it easier for parents to engage in it. Among the most important is the Internet.[36] Scores of Web sites are available that give advice, that provide technical and emotional support, that tell the stories of successful home schoolers, and that are more than willing to sell material at a profit. The fact that, like the conservative evangelical movement in general, a larger portion of home schoolers than before seem to have the economic resources to afford computers means that economic capital can be mobilized in antischool strategies in more flexible and dynamic ways than in earlier periods of the home schooling movement.[37]

Because home schooling is often done using the Web, whereas I will spend much more time on this in Chapter 8 it is still useful here to see what some of the sites say. The Teaching Home, based in Portland, Oregon, is one of the central resources for conservative Christians who wish to home school.[38] On its Web site, after the following general statement on the question "Why do families home school?" a number of answers are given:

Many Christian parents are committed to educating their children at home because of their conviction that this is God's will for their family. They are concerned for the spiritual training and character development as well as the social and academic welfare of their children.

Among the advantages listed are:

Parents can present all academic subjects from a biblical perspective and include spiritual training.

"The fear of the LORD is the beginning of wisdom, and the knowledge of the Holy One is understanding" (Prov. 9:10 NAS).

Home schooling makes quality time available to train and influence children in all areas in an integrated way.

Each child receives individual attention and has his unique needs met.

Parents can control destructive influences such as various temptations, false teachings (including secular humanism and occult influences of the New Age movement), negative peer pressure, and unsafe environments.

Children gain respect for their parents as teachers.

The family experiences unity, closeness, and mutual enjoyment of one another as they spend more time working together.

Children develop confidence and independent thinking away from the peer pressure to conform and in the security of their own home.

Children have time to explore new interests and to think.

Communication between different age groups is enhanced.

Tutorial-style education helps each child achieve his full educational potential.

Flexible scheduling can accommodate parents' work and vacation times and allow time for many activities.

This list is broader than might be allowed in some of the stereotypes of what home schooling advocates—particularly religiously conservative ones—are like. There is a focus on wanting their children to explore, to achieve their full academic potential, to have "his" needs met. Yet, in this diverse list of advantages, certain themes come to the fore, themes that resonate deeply with those I described in the prior two chapters. At the top is biblical authority, with knowledge and understanding connected with "fear of the LORD." "Real" knowledge is grounded in what the Holy One has ordained. The role of the parent is largely one of "training," of influencing one's children in all areas so that they are safe from the outside influences of a secular society. God/home/family is pure; the rest of the world—secular humanism, peers, popular culture—are forms of pollution, temptations, dangers. That the male pronoun is used throughout is indicative of God's wish for the man of the house to be God's chosen leader.[39]

Yet saying these things must not be used as an excuse to deny the elements of concern that parents such as these express. They are *deeply* worried about the lives and futures of their children, children for whom they are fully willing to sacrifice an immense amount. They do want there to be a caring environment for their children, one in which all family members respect and care for each other. There are powerful positive moments in these statements. In a time when many groups of varying religious and political sentiments express the concern that children are ignored in this society, that they are simply seen as present and future consumers by people who only care whether a profit is made off of them, that our major institutions are less responsive than they should be, and that there are elements of popular culture that are negative as well as positive—all these sentiments are central to the concerns of home schoolers as well.

Given what I have just said, once again we do need to recognize that there are elements of good sense in the critique of the state made by both the left and the right, such as the home schoolers I have discussed above. The government has assumed all too often that the only true holders of expertise in education, social welfare, and so on are those in positions of formal authority. This has led to a situation of overbureaucratization. Furthermore, as I showed in Chapter 4, it has also led to the state being partly "colonized" by a particular fraction of the new middle class that seeks to ensure its own mobility and its own positions by employing the state for its own purposes.[40] Some schools have become sites of danger given the levels of alienation and meaninglessness in this society—and the dominance of violence as an "imaginary solution" in the "popular" media. However, there is a world of difference between, say, acknowledging that the state has some historical tendencies to become overly bureaucratic and to not listen carefully enough to the expressed needs of the people it is supposed to serve and a blanket rejection of public control and public institutions such as schools. This has not only led to cocooning, but it threatens the gains made by large groups of disadvantaged people for whom the possible destruction of public schooling is nothing short of a disaster. The final section of my analysis turns to a discussion of this.

Public and Private

We need to think *relationally* when we ask who will be the major beneficiaries of the attack on the state and the movement toward home schooling. What if gains that are made by one group of people come at the expense of other, even more culturally and economically oppressed groups? As we shall see, this is not an inconsequential worry in this instance.

A helpful distinction here is that between a politics of redistribution and a politics of recognition. In the first (redistribution), the concern is for socioeconomic injustice. Here, the political-economic system of a society creates conditions that lead to exploitation (having the fruits of your labor appropriated for the benefit of others), or economic marginalization (having one's paid work confined to poorly paid and undesirable jobs or having no real access to the routes to serious and better paying jobs), or deprivation (being constantly denied the material that would lead to an adequate standard of living). All these socioeconomic injustices lead to arguments about whether this is a just or fair society and whether identifiable groups of people actually have equality of resources.[41]

The second dynamic (recognition) is often related to redistribution in the real world, but it has its own specific history and differential power relations as well. It is related to the politics of culture and symbols. In this case, injustice is rooted in a society's social patterns of representation and interpretation. Examples of this include cultural domination (being constantly subjected to patterns of interpretation or cultural representation that are alien to one's own or even hostile to it), nonrecognition (basically being rendered invisible in the dominant cultural forms in the society), and disrespect (having oneself routinely stereotyped or maligned in public representations in the media, schools, government policies, or in everyday conduct).[42] These kinds of issues surrounding the politics of recognition are central to the identities and sense of injustice of many home schoolers. Indeed, they provide the organizing framework for their critique of public schooling and their demand that they be allowed to teach their children outside of such state control.

Although both forms of injustice are important, it is absolutely crucial that we recognize that an adequate response to one must not lead to the exacerbation of the other. That is, responding to the claims of injustice in recognition by one group (say religious conservatives) must not make the conditions that lead to exploitation, economic marginalization, and deprivation more likely to occur for other groups. Nor must it lead to the denial of recognition to those who are even more oppressed. Unfortunately, this may be the case for some of the latent effects of home schooling.

Because of this, it is vitally important not to separate the possible effects of home schooling from what we are beginning to know about the possible consequences of neoliberal policies in general in education. As I argued earlier and as Whitty, Power, and Halpin have shown in their review of the international research on voucher and choice plans, one of the latent effects of such policies has been the reproduction of traditional hierarchies of class and race. That is, the programs clearly have differential benefits in which those who already possess economic and cultural capital reap significantly more benefits than those who do not.[43] This is patterned in very much the same ways as the stratification of economic, political, and cultural power produces inequalities in nearly every socioeconomic sphere.[44] One of the hidden consequences that is emerging from the expanding conservative critique of public institutions, including schools, is a growing antitax movement in which those who have chosen to place their children in privatized, marketized, and home schools do not want to pay taxes to support the schooling of the Other.[45]

The wider results of this are becoming clear—a declining tax base for schooling, social services, health care, housing, and anything "public" for those populations (usually in the most economically depressed urban and rural areas) who suffer the most from the economic dislocations and inequalities that so deeply characterize this nation. Thus, a politics of recognition—I want to guarantee "choice" for my children based on my identity and special needs—has begun to have extremely negative effects on the politics of redistribution. It is absolutely crucial that we recognize this. If it is the case that the emergence of educational markets has consistently benefited the most-advantaged parents and students and has consistently disadvantaged both economically poor parents and students, and parents and students of color,[46] then we need to critically examine the latent effects of the growth of home schooling in the same light. Will it be the case that social justice loses in this equation just as it did and does in many of the other highly publicized programs of "choice"?

We now have emerging evidence to this effect, evidence that points to the fact that social justice often does lose with the expansion of home schooling in some states. A case in point is the way in which the ongoing debate over the use of public money for religious purposes in education is often subverted through manipulation of loopholes that are only available to particular groups. Religiously motivated home schoolers are currently engaged in exploiting public funding not only in ways that are hidden, but also in ways that raise serious questions about the drain on economic resources during a time of severe budget crises in all too many school districts.

Let me say more about this, since it provides an important instance of my argument that gains in recognition for some groups (say, home schoolers) can have decidedly negative effects in other spheres such as the politics of redistribution and in claims to recognition by other groups. In California, for example, charter schools have been used as a mechanism to gain public money for home schoolers. Charter school legislation in California has been employed in very "interesting" ways to accomplish this. In one recent study, for example, 50 percent of charter schools were serving home schoolers. "Independent study" charter schools (a creative pseudonym for computer-linked home schooling) have been used by both school districts and parents to gain money that otherwise might not have been available. While this does demonstrate the ability of school districts to strategically use charter school legislation to get money that might have been lost when parents withdraw their children to home school them, it also signifies something else. In this and other cases, the money given to parents for enrolling in such independent study charter schools was used by the parents to purchase religious material produced and sold by Bob Jones University, one of the most conservative religious schools in the entire nation.[47]

Although I will return to this kind of example in Chapter 8, it is important to realize what is happening here. In this case, public money not legally available for overtly sectarian material is used to purchase religious curricula under the auspices of charter school legislation. Yet unlike all curricula used in public schools that *must* be publicly accountable in terms of its content and costs, the material purchased for home schooling has no public accountability whatsoever. Although this does give greater choice to home schoolers and does enable them to act on a politics of recognition, it not only takes money away from other students who do not have the economic resources to afford computers in the home, but it denies them a say in what the community's children will learn about themselves and their cultures, histories, values, and so on. Given that a number of textbooks used in fundamentalist religious schools expressly state such things as Islam is a false religion and embody similar claims that many citizens would find deeply offensive,[48] serious questions can be raised about whether it is appropriate for public money to be used to teach such content without any public accountability.

Thus, two things are going on here. Money is being drained from already hard-pressed school districts to support home schooling. Just as important, curricular materials that support the identities of religiously motivated groups are being paid for by the public *without* any accountability, even though these materials may act in such a way as to deny the claims for recognition of one of the fastest-growing religions in the nation, Islam. This raises more general and quite serious issues about how the claims for recognition by religious conservatives can be financially supported when they may at times actually support discriminatory teaching. Here, one form of recognition politics interferes with another group's justifiable claims to recognition and legitimacy, and especially a group (Islam) that has suffered immensely from both stereotyping and discrimination in the United States and elsewhere.

I don't wish to be totally negative here. After all, this is a complicated issue in which there may be justifiable worries among home schoolers that their culture and values are not being listened to. But it must be openly discussed, not lost in the simple statement that we should support a politics of recognition of religiously motivated home schoolers because their culture seems to them to be not sufficiently recognized in public institutions. At the very least, the possible dangers to the public good need to be recognized and publicly debated.

Conclusion

In this chapter, I have raised a number of critical questions about the economic, social, and ideological tendencies that often stand behind significant parts of the home schooling movement. In the process, I have situated it within larger social movements that I and many others believe can have quite negative effects on our sense of community, on the health of the public sphere, and on our commitment to building a society that is less economically and racially stratified. I have suggested that issues need to be raised about the effects of its commitment to "cocooning," its attack on the state, and its growing use of public funding with no public accountability. Yet I have also argued that there are clear elements of good sense in the home schooling movement's criticisms of the bureaucratic nature of all too many of our institutions, in its worries about the managerial state, and in its devotion to being active in the education of its children. The fact that home schoolers show a particular disdain toward the professional and managerial middle class may provide some interesting tensions in maintaining the alliance supporting conservative modernization, for example.

In my mind, the task is to disentangle the elements of good sense evident in these concerns from the selfish and antipublic agenda that has been pushing concerned parents and community members into the arms of the conservative restoration. The task of public schools is to listen much more carefully (but still *critically* when necessary) to the complaints of parents such as these and to rebuild our institutions in much more responsive ways. As I have argued earlier, all too often public schools push concerned parents who are not originally part of conservative cultural and political movements into the arms of such alliances by their defensiveness and lack of responsiveness and by their silencing of democratic discussion and criticism. Of course, sometimes these criticisms are unjustified or are politically motivated by undemocratic agendas. However, this must not serve as an excuse for a failure to open the doors of our schools to the intense public debate that makes public education a living and vital part of our democracy.[49] Whether those drawn to home schooling for conservative ideological reasons will listen, given not only their commitments but also their identities as the new oppressed, as "subaltern," is important.[50] But let us not use this as an excuse for not continuing our own struggles to rebuild our institutions so that they mirror our own commitments to a truly "thick" democracy, not the eviscerated "thin" versions of neoliberals or the repressive ones envisioned by the champions of the only faith that "got it right."

CHAPTER 8

Doing the Work of Home Schooling
Gender, Technology, and Curriculum

Introduction[1]

In the last three chapters, I spent a good deal of time detailing the world as seen through the eyes of authoritarian populists, the conservative groups of religious fundamentalists and evangelicals whose voices in the debates over social and educational policies are now increasingly powerful.[2] I critically analyzed the ways in which they construct themselves as the "new oppressed," as people whose identities and cultures are ignored by or attacked in schools and the media. As I showed, in many ways, they have taken on subaltern identities and have (very selectively) reappropriated the discourses and practices of figures such as Dr. Martin Luther King Jr. to lay claim to the fact that they are the last truly dispossessed groups.

In this chapter, I examine in considerably more detail than the last the ways in which the claim to subaltern status has led to a partial withdrawal from state-run institutions and to a practice of schooling that is meant to equip the children of authoritarian populist parents both with an armor to defend what these groups believe is their threatened culture and with a set of skills and values that will change the world so that it reflects the conservative religious commitments that are so central to their lives. I shall focus on the ways in which new technologies such as the Internet have become essential resources in what authoritarian populists see as a counterhegemonic struggle against secular humanism and a world that no longer "listens to God's word." Much of my discussion will center around the place of gender in these movements, as it was clear in the previous chapters that women play a key role here. I want to illuminate the fact that conservative women have multiple identities within these movements, simultaneously able to claim subaltern status based on the history of dominant gender regimes and having dominant status given their positioning in relationship to other oppressed groups.

Resources and the Growth of Social Movements

There has been an explosion of analyses of the Internet in education, cultural studies, sociology, the social studies of technology and science, and elsewhere. Much of this material has been of considerable interest and has led to a good deal of discussion of the use, benefits, history, and status of such technologies.[3] However, much of this debate is carried on with limited reference to the contexts in which the Internet is actually used; or the context is mentioned as an issue but remains relatively unexamined. As one of the more perceptive writers on the social uses and benefits of the Internet has said, "We can only understand the impact of the Internet on modern culture if we see that symbolic content and online interaction are embedded in social and historical contexts of various kinds."[4] As Manuel Castells reminds us, rather than having a unitary meaning and use, the new communications networks that are being created "are made of many cultures, many values, many projects, that cross through the minds and inform the strategies of the various participants."[5]

New technologies have both been stimulated by and have themselves stimulated three overlapping dynamics: the intensification of globalization; the detraditionalizing of society; and the intensification of social reflexivity.[6] In the process, technologies such as the Internet have provided the basis for new forms of solidarity as groups of people seek to deal with the transformations brought about by these dynamics. Yet, the search for such forms of solidarity that would restore or defend "tradition" and authority can itself lead to the production of new forms of social *disintegration* at one and the same time.[7]

In this chapter, I examine a growing instance of this paradoxical process of solidarity and disintegration. By focusing on the social uses of the Internet by a new but increasingly powerful group of educational activists—the conservative Christian evangelical home schoolers I discussed in Chapter 7—I want to contribute both to our understanding of how populist conservative movements grow and support themselves ideologically and to the complex ways in which technological resources can serve a multitude of social agendas. I argue that only by placing these technologies back into the social and ideological context of their use by *specific* communities (and by specific people within these communities) can we understand the meaning and function of new technologies in society and in education. In order to accomplish this, I build on my analysis in the previous chapter. But in this one I also focus on the labor of home schooling, on how it is organized, on new definitions of legitimate knowledge, and on how all this has been partly transformed by the ways in which technological markets are being created.

Technology and the Growth of Home Schooling

The connections between conservative evangelical forms and technologies are not new by any means. Earlier in the book, I pointed to the creative use of electronic ministries both nationally and internationally by the authoritarian populist religious right. As I showed, technological resources such as television and radio have been employed to expand the influence of conservative religious impulses and to make "the word of God" available to believers and "those who are yet to believe" alike.[8] Although understanding the increasing range and impact of such efforts is crucial, here I am less interested in such things. I want to point to more mundane but growing uses of technologies such as the Internet in supporting evangelical efforts that are closer to home. And, once again, I do mean "home" literally.

As we saw, home schooling is growing rapidly. But it is not simply the result of additive forces. It is not simply an atomistic phenomenon in which, one by one, isolated parents decide to reject organized public schools and teach their children at home. Home schooling is a *social movement*. It is a collective project, one with a history and a set of organizational and material supports.[9]

Although many educators devote a good deal of their attention to reforms such as charter schools, and such schools have received a good deal of positive press, there are many fewer children in charter schools than there are being home schooled. Given the almost reverential and rather romantic coverage in national and local media of home schooling (with the *New York Times* and *Time* providing a large amount of very positive coverage, for example),[10] the numbers may in fact be much higher than this and as I noted the growth curve undoubtedly is increasing. As I know from personal experience, the numbers of home schooled children are growing outside the United States, with increasing numbers of parents choosing to pull their children out of public schools in England, Germany, Scandinavia, and elsewhere.

The home schooling movement is not homogeneous. It includes people of a wide spectrum of political/ideological, religious, and educational beliefs. It cuts across racial and class lines. For example, in a number of cities African-American parents have decided that they cannot allow their children to go to what they see as the destructive environments found in public schools. For them, home schooling is the only way that their children can be protected. As the father of a black child myself, I have a good deal of sympathy for their struggles.

As Stevens notes, there are in essence two general groupings within the home school movement, "Christian" and "inclusive." There are some things that are shared across these fault lines, however: a sense that the standardized education offered by mainstream schooling interferes with their children's potential; that there is a serious danger when the state intrudes into the life of the family; that experts and bureaucracies are apt to impose their beliefs and are unable to meet the needs of families and children.[11] These worries tap currents that are widespread within American culture and they too cut across particular social and cultural divides.

Yet, it would be wrong to interpret the mistrust of experts by many home schoolers as simply a continuation of the current of "anti-intellectualism" that seems to run deep in parts of the history of the United States. The mistrust of science, government experts, and "rationality" became much more general as a result of the Vietnam War, when the attacks on scientists for their inhumanity, on government for lying, and on particular forms of instrumental rationality for their loss of values and ethics spread into the common sense of society. This was often coupled with a mistrust of authority in general.[12] Home schoolers are not only not immune to such tendencies, but combine them in creative ways with other elements of popular consciousness concerning the importance of education in times of rapid change and economic, cultural, and moral threat.

Demographic information on home schoolers is limited, but like the data on the evangelical community, in general home schoolers seem to be somewhat better educated, slightly more affluent, and considerably more likely to be white than the population in the state in which they reside.[13] Although it is important to recognize the diversity of the movement, it is just as crucial to understand that the largest group of people who home school are what I pictured in Chapter 7. They have conservative religious commitments and are authoritarian populists. Given the dominance of conservative Christians in the home schooling movement, this picture does match the overall demographic patterns of evangelical Christians in general.[14]

Based on a belief that schooling itself is a very troubled institution (but often with widely divergent interpretations of what has caused these troubles), home schoolers have created mechanisms where "horror stories" about schools are shared, as are stories of successful home schooling practices. The metaphors that describe what goes on in public schools and the dangers associated with them, especially those used by many conservative evangelical home schoolers, are telling. Stevens puts it in the following way:

> Invoking the rhetoric of illness ("cancer," "contagion") to describe the dangers of uncontrolled peer interaction, believers frame the child-world of school as a kind of jungle where parents send their kids only at risk of infection. The solution: keep them at home, away from that environment altogether.[15]

Given these perceived dangers, through groups that have been formed at both regional and national levels, home schooling advocates press departments of education and legislatures to guarantee their rights to home school their children. They have established communicative networks—newsletters, magazines, and increasingly the Internet—to build and maintain a community of fellow believers, a community that is often supported by ministries that reinforce the "wisdom" (and very often godliness) of their choice. And as we shall see, increasingly as well the business community has begun to realize that this can be a lucrative market.[16] Religious publishers, for-profit publishing houses large and small, conservative colleges and universities, Internet entrepreneurs, and others have understood that a market in cultural goods—classroom materials, lesson plans, textbooks, religious material, CDs, and so forth—has been created. They have rushed to both respond to the expressed needs and to stimulate needs that are not yet recognized as needs themselves. But the market would not be there unless what created the opportunity for such a market—the successful identity work of the evangelical movement itself—had not provided the space in which such a market could operate.

Understanding Social Movements

As I demonstrated, conservative Christian home schoolers are part of a larger evangelical movement that has been increasingly influential in education, politics, and in cultural institutions such as the media.[17] Nationally, white evangelicals constitute at least 25 percent of the adult population in the United States.[18] The evangelical population is growing steadily and undoubtedly is increasing over time as it actively provides subject positions and new identities for people who feel unmoored in a world where, for them, "all that is sacred is profaned" and where the tensions and structures of feeling of advanced capitalism do not provide either a satisfying emotional or spiritual life.[19] The search for a "return"—in the face of major threats to what they see as accepted relations of gender/sex, of authority and tradition, of nation and family—is the guiding impulse behind the growth of this increasingly powerful social movement.

Social movements often have multiple goals that may or may not be reached. Yet, it is also important to understand that they also can produce consequences that are much broader than their avowed goals and that are not always foreseen. Thus, social movements that aim at structural transformations in state policies may produce profound changes in the realms of culture, everyday life, and identity. The mobilizations around specific goals as well can strengthen internal solidarities, cement individual and collective identity shifts in place, create a new common sense, and ultimately lead to perceptible shifts in public attitudes about a given issue.[20] They also create "innovative action repertoires" and have an influence on the practices and culture of mainstream organizations.[21] As we shall see, this is exactly what is happening both within the lives of home schoolers, but also in the ways in which organized public school systems have responded to the perceived threat to their financial well-being by a growing home school population.

A key to all this is something I mentioned above—the importance of identity politics. For social movements to prosper, they must provide identities that constantly revivify the reasons for participating in them. They must, hence, have an emotional economy in which the costs of being "different" are balanced by the intense meanings and satisfactions of acting in opposition to dominant social norms and values. This doesn't happen all at once. People are changed by participating in oppositional movements such as home schooling. As social movements theorists have widely recognized, there are crucial biographical impacts of participating in movements. People become transformed in the process.[22] This point is clearly made by Meyer:

By engaging in the social life of a challenging movement, an individual's experience of the world is mediated by a shared vision of the way the world works and, importantly, the individual's position in it. By engaging in activism, an individual creates himself or herself as a subject, rather than simply an object, in history and … is unlikely to retreat to passive acceptance of the world as it is.[23]

Technology and Doing Home Schooling

Like the neoliberals I discussed earlier, but with an ethical/cultural edge that is more biting, as I said a large portion of social movement activity targets the state,[24] and this is especially the case with the home schooling movement where the edge is more than a little visible. Although there is often a fundamental mistrust of the state among many religiously conservative home schoolers, interestingly there are a considerable number of such people who are willing to compromise with the state. But they employ state programs and funds for their own tactical advantage. One of the clearest examples of this is something I pointed out in Chapter 7, the growing home schooling/charter school movement in states such as California. Even though many of the parents involved in such programs believe that they do not want their children to be "brainwashed by a group of educators" and do not want to "leave [their] children off somewhere like a classroom and have them influenced and taught by someone that I am not familiar with,"[25] a growing number of Christian conservative parents have become quite adept at taking advantage of government resources for their own benefit. By taking advantage of home school charter programs that connect independent families through the use of the Internet and the Web, they are able to use public funding to support schooling that they had previously had to pay for privately.[26]

But it is not only the conservative evangelical parents who are using the home schooling charter possibilities for their own benefit. School districts themselves are actively strategizing, employing such technological connections to enhance their revenue flow but maintaining existing enrolments or by actively recruiting home school parents to join a home school charter.

For example, by creating a home school charter, one financially pressed small California school district was able to solve a good deal of its economic problems. Over the first two years of its operation, the charter school grew from 80 students to 750.[27] The results were striking:

Along with the many new students came a surge of state revenue to the small district, increasing the district's budget by more than 300 percent. [The home schooling charter] garnered home school families by providing them with a wealth of materials and instructional support. In exchange for resources, families would mail monthly student learning records to the school. Learning records are the lifeline of the school and serve a dual purpose—outlining the academic content completed by students and serving also as an attendance roster from which [the charter school staff] can calculate average daily attendance. ... Thus, parents' self-reported enrollment data permit [the school district] to receive full capitation grants from the state.[28]

In this way, by complying with the minimal reporting requirements, conservative Christian parents are able to act on their desire to keep government and secular influences at a distance; and at the very same time, school districts are able to maintain that the children of these families are enrolled in public schooling and meeting the requirements of secular schooling.

Yet, we should be cautious of using the word "secular" here. It is clear from the learning records that the parents submit that there is a widespread use of religious materials in all of the content. Bible readings, devotional lessons, moral teachings directly from online vendors, and so on were widely integrated by the parents within the "secular" resources provided by the school. "Write and read Luke 1:37, memorize Luke 1:37, prayer journal" are among the many very nonsecular parts of the sample learning records submitted by the parents.[29]

Such content, and the lack of accountability over it, raises serious question about the use of public funding for overtly conservative religious purposes. It documents the power of Huerta's claim that "In an attempt to recast its authority in an era of fewer bureaucratic controls over schools, the state largely drops its pursuit of the common good as public authority is devolved to local families."[30] In the process, technologically linked homes are reconstituted as a "public" school, but a school in which the very meaning of public had been radically transformed so that it mirrors the needs of conservative religious form and content.

Home Schooling as Gendered Labor

Even with the strategic use of state resources to assist their efforts, home schooling takes hard work. But to go further we need to ask an important question: *Who* does the labor? Much of this labor is hidden from view. Finding and organizing materials, teaching, charting progress, establishing and maintaining a "proper" environment, the emotional labor of caring for as well as instructing children—and the list goes on—all of this requires considerable effort. And most of this effort is done by *women*.[31]

Because home schooling is largely women's work, it combines an extraordinary amount of physical, cultural, and emotional labor.[32] It constitutes an intensification of women's work in the home, because it is added on to the already extensive responsibilities that women have within the home, and especially within conservative religious homes with their division of labor in which men may be active, but are seen as "helpers" of their wives who carry the primary responsibility within the domestic sphere. The demands of such intensified labor have consistently led women to engage in quite creative ways of dealing with their lives. New technologies, as labor-saving devices, have played key roles in such creative responses.[33]

This labor and the meanings attached to it by women themselves need to be situated into a much longer history and a much larger context. A number of people have argued that many women see rightist religious and social positions and the groups that support them as providing a nonthreatening, familiar framework of discourse and practice that centers directly on what they perceive to be issues of vital and personal concern: immorality, social disorder, crime, the family, and schools. Yet, the feelings of personal connection are not sufficient. Rightist action in both the "public" and the "private" spheres empowers them as women.[34] Depending on the context, they are positioned as "respectable, selfless agents of change deemed necessary, or as independent rebels."[35]

Historically, as I noted in earlier chapters, right-wing women have consistently exalted the family. It is seen as a privileged site of women's self-realization and power, but one that is threatened by a host of internal and external "Others." It is "the" family that is the pillar of society, the foundation of a society's security, order, and naturalized hierarchy that is given by God.[36]

Usually, fundamentalist and evangelical women are depicted as essentially dedicated to acting on and furthering the goals of religiously conservative men.[37] This is much too simplistic. Rather, the message is more complex and compelling—and connected to a very clear understanding of the realities of many women's lives. Very much like the women I discussed in my treatment of the Southern roots of a good deal of evangelical movements, women are to have not a passive but a very active engagement in their family life and the world that impinges on it.

They can and must "shape their husband's actions and alter disruptive family behaviors." The latter tasks are becoming especially important since this is a time when all too many men are abdicating their family responsibilities, often impoverishing women and their dependent children.[38] Furthermore, only a strong woman could mediate the pressures and the often intensely competitive norms and values that men brought home with them from the "world of work." Capitalism may be "God's economy," but allowing its norms to dominate the home could be truly destructive. Women, in concert with "responsible" men, could provide the alternative but complementary assemblage of values so necessary to keep the world at bay and to use the family as the foundation for both protecting core religious values and sending forth children armed against the dangers of a secular and profane world.

To conservative religious women, what from the outside may look like a restrictive life guided by patriarchal norms, feels very different on the inside. It provides an identity that is embraced precisely because it improves their ability to direct the course of their lives and empowers them in their relationships with others. Thus, as I argued in the previous chapters, intense religiosity is a source of considerable power for many women.[39]

Based on her extensive research on conservative Christian women, Brasher is very clear on this. As she puts it,

> [Although such women] insistently claimed that the proper relationship between a woman and her husband is one of submission, they consistently declared that this submission is done out of obedience to God not men and is supposed to be mutual, a relational norm observed by both spouses rather than a capitulation of one to the other. ... Submission increases rather than decreases a woman's power within the marital relationship.[40]

Divine creation has ordained that women and men are different types of beings. Although they complement each other, each has distinctly different tasks to perform. Such sacred gender walls are experienced not as barriers, but as providing and legitimating a space for women's action and power. Interfering with such action and power in this sphere is also interfering in God's plan.[41]

Echoes of this can be found in other times and in other nations. Thus, an activist within the British Union of Fascists—an anti-Semitic and proto-Nazi group before World War II—looked back on her activity and said that her active membership demonstrated that she had always been "an independent, free thinking individual."[42] This vision of independence and of what might be called "counterhegemonic thinking" is crucial not just then but now as well. It connects with today's belief among conservative religiously motivated home schoolers that the world and the school have become too "PC." Bringing conservative evangelical religion back to the core of schooling positions secular schooling as hegemonic. It enables rightist women to interpret their own actions as independent and free thinking—but always in the service of God. Let me say more about this here.

Solving Contradictions

One of the elements that keeps the Christian right such a vital and growing social movement is the distinctive internal structure of evangelical Protestantism. As we saw, evangelicalism combines orthodox Christian beliefs with an intense individualism.[43]

This is a key to understanding the ways in which what looks like never-ending and intensified domestic labor from the outside is interpreted in very different ways from the point of view of conservative religious women who willingly take on the labor of home schooling and add it to their already considerable responsibilities in the domestic sphere. Such conservative ideological forms do see women as subservient to men and as having the primary responsibility of building and defending a vibrant godly "fortress-home" as part of "God's plan." Yet, it would be wrong to see women in rightist religious or ideological movements as only being called on to submit to authority per se. Once again, such "obedience" is also grounded in a call to act on their duty as women.[44] This is what might best be seen as *activist selflessness,* one in which the supposedly submerged self reemerges in the activist role of defender of one's home, family, children, and God's plan. Lives are made meaningful and satisfying—and identities supported—in the now reconstituted private and public sphere in this way.

There is an extremely long history in the United States and other nations of connecting religious activism and domesticity.[45] This has consistently led to mobilizations that cut across political lines that bridge the public and private spheres. In Koven and Michel's words:

> Essential to this mobilization was the rise of domestic ideologies stressing women's differences from men, humanitarian concerns for the conditions of child life and labor, and the emergence of activist interpretations of the gospel ... [including] evangelicalism, Christian socialism, social Catholicism, and the social gospel. Women's moral vision, compassion, and capacity to nurture came increasingly to be linked to motherliness.[46]

Often guided by a sense of moral superiority, when coupled with a strong element of political commitment, this became a powerful force. Maternalism could be both progressive and retrogressive, often at the same time. Although it is the conservative elements of this ideological construction that have come to the fore today, forms of maternalism also had a major impact on many of the progressive programs and legislation that currently exist.[47]

The restorative powers of domesticity and "female spirituality" could be combined with a strong commitment both to democratic principles and education and opportunities for women.[48] The key was and is how democracy—a sliding signifier—is *defined,* an issue that has been at the center of much of my discussion throughout this book.

Protecting and educating one's children, caring for the intimate and increasingly fragile bonds of community and family life, worries about personal safety, and all of this in an exploitative and often disrespectful society—these themes are not only the province of the right and should not be only the province of women. Yet, we have to ask how identifiable people are mobilized around and by these themes, and by whom.

The use of a kind of "maternalist" discourse and a focus on women's role as "mother" and as someone whose primary responsibility is in the home and the domestic sphere does not necessarily prevent women from exercising power in the public sphere. In fact, it can serve as a powerful justification for such action and actually *reconstitutes* the public sphere. Educating one's children at home so that they are given armor to equip them to transform their and others' lives outside the home, establishes the home as a perfect model for religiously motivated ethical conduct for all sets of social institutions. This tradition, what has been called "social housekeeping," can then claim responsibility for nonfamilial social spaces and can extend the idealized mothering role of women well beyond the home. In Marijke du Toit's words, it was and can still be used to forge "a new, more inclusive definition of the political."[49]

Such maternalism historically enabled women to argue for a measure of direct power in the redefined public arena. One could extol the virtues of domesticity and expand what counts as a home at the same time. Thus, the state and many institutions in the public sphere were "a household where women should exercise their ... superior skills to create [both] order [and a better society]."[50]

All of this helps us make sense of why many of the most visible home school advocates devote a good deal of their attention to "making sense of the social category of motherhood." As a key part of "a larger script of idealized family relations, motherhood is a lead role in God's plan" for authoritarian populist religious conservatives.[51] Again in Stevens' words, "One of the things that home schooling offers, then, is a renovated domesticity—a full-time motherhood made richer by the tasks of teaching, and [by] some of the status that goes along with those tasks."[52]

Yet it is not only the work internal to the home that is important here. Home schooling is outward looking as well in terms of women's tasks. In many instances, home schooling is a collective project. It requires organizational skills to coordinate connections and cooperative activities (support groups, field trips, play groups, time off from the responsibilities that mothers have, etc.) and to keep the movement itself vibrant at local and regional levels. Here, too, women do the largest amount of the work. This had led to other opportunities for women as advocates and entrepreneurs. Thus, the development and marketing of some of the most popular curriculum packages, management guides, self-help and devotional materials, and so on has been done by women. Indeed, the materials reflect the fact that home schooling is women's work, with a considerable number of the pictures in the texts and promotional material showing mothers and children together.[53] A considerable number of the national advocates for evangelically based home schooling are activist women as well.

Marketing God

Advocacy is one thing, being able to put the advocated policy into practice is quite another. In order to actually *do* home schooling a large array of plans, materials, advice, and even solace must be made available. "Godly schooling" creates a market, in a manner similar to the ways in which No Child Left Behind has created a lucrative space for firms to market expertise and material to help school districts manage its seemingly endless demands. Even with the burgeoning market for all kinds of home schooling, it is clear that conservative evangelicals and fundamentalists have the most to choose from in terms of educational and religious (the separation is often fictional) curricula, lessons, books, and inspirational material.[54] Such materials not only augment the lessons that home schooling parents develop, but increasingly they become *the* lessons in mathematics, literacy, science, social studies, and all of the other subjects that are taught. This kind of material also usually includes homework assignments and tests as well as all of the actual instructional material. Thus, a complete "package" can be assembled or purchased whole in a way that enables committed parents to create an entire universe of educational experiences that is both rigorously sequenced and tightly controlled—and prevents unwanted "pollution" from the outside world.

The A Beka Book program provides a clear example. An offshoot of Pensacola Christian College, it markets material for nursery school up to the end of secondary school. It offers the home schooler a curriculum in which Christian teachings are woven into every aspect of knowledge. Little is left to chance. Preschool children learn through the use of Bible story flannelgraphs. At the age of five, they begin a complete "Bible Curriculum" and as they move up in age their texts include *Bible Doctrines for Today* and *Managing Your Life Under God*. The elementary-level science textbooks, *God's World*, are based in an inerrantist approach to the Bible and a literalist reading of Genesis and creation, one in which evolution is dismissed. The difference between right and wrong is seen as answerable only through reference to biblical teachings.[55]

Easily ordered on the Web, similar kinds of material are made available by other religiously based publishers—Bob Jones University Press, Christian Liberty Academy, Alpha Omega Publications, KONOS, the Weaver Curriculum Series, and a number of others. Although there are pedagogic differences among these sets of materials, all of them are deeply committed to integrating biblical messages, values, and training throughout the entire curriculum. Most not only reproduce the particular biblically based worldviews of the parents, but they also create an educational environment that relies on a particular vision of "appropriate" schooling, one that is organized around highly sequenced formal lessons that have an expressly moral aim. Technological resources such as videos are marketed that both provide the home schooler with a model of how education should be done and the resources for actually carrying it out.[56]

The *organizational form* that is produced here is very important. As I argued earlier, since much of the religiously conservative home schooling movement has a sense of purity and danger in which all elements of the world have a set place, such an organization of both knowledge and pedagogy embodies the ideological structure underlying the evangelical universe. As Bernstein reminds us, it is often in the form of the curriculum that the social cement that organizes our consciousness at its most basic level is reproduced.[57]

Although the form of the curriculum is clearly a collection code in key ways, the content is partly integrated.[58] Project methods are also used in many conservative home schoolers' practices. For example, at the same time as parents may use the detailed sequential curriculum purchased from The Weaver Curriculum Series because it enables lessons to be related as well to a sequential reading of the Bible, these same parents also approve of the ways in which such curricular material includes creative ideas for student projects. Thus, one parent had her children engage in brick-making as part of the study of the Tower of Babel. She also used the genealogies of the Old Testament to stimulate her children's study of their family tree.[59]

This kind of integration is found in nearly all of the widely used material. Stevens clearly describes a common situation.

> By creative elaboration, curriculum authors spin out a wide range of lessons from biblical passages. Every word and phrase can be a metaphor for a revered character trait, a starting point for a science lesson. In this instance the first line of the first verse of the Sermon on the Mount, "Seeing the crowds, he went up the mountain," commences lessons on sight, light, and the biological structure of the eye, as well as character studies on the virtues of alertness. [The parent] noted that her children's "entire curriculum will be Matthew 5, 6, and 7. Through high school." Detailed lesson plans provide project descriptions and learning guides for children of various ages, so that the whole family can do the same lesson at once. "Our part in this," [the parent] explained, "is to read through the booklet."[60]

This sense of the importance of structured educational experiences that are infused with strong moral messages is not surprising given the view of a secular world filled with possible sins, temptations, and dangers. The emphasis then on equipping children with an armor of strong belief supports a pedagogical belief that *training* is a crucial pedagogic act. Although children's interests have to be considered, these are less important than preparing children for living in a world where God's word rules. This commitment to giving an armor of "right beliefs" "nourishes demands for school material."[61] A market for curriculum materials, workbooks, lesson plans, rewards for doing fine work such as merit badges, videotapes and CDs, and so many other things that make home schooling seem more doable is created not only out of a strategy of aggressive marketing and of using the Internet as a major mechanism for such marketing; but it is also created and stimulated because of the ideological and emotional elements that underpin the structures of feeling that help organize the conservative evangelical home schooler's world.

Emotional Labor and the Daily Life of Curriculum and Teaching

Of course, parents are not puppets. Although the parent may purchase or download material that is highly structured and inflexible, by the very nature of home schooling parents are constantly faced with the realities of their children's lives, their boredom, their changing interests. Here, chat rooms and Internet resources become even more important. Advice manuals, prayers, suggestions for how one should deal with recalcitrant children, and biblically inspired inspirational messages about how important the hard work of parenting is and how one can develop the patience to keep doing it—all of this provides ways of dealing with the immense amount of educational and especially *emotional* labor that home schooling requires.

The technology enables women who may be rather isolated in the home due to the intense responsibilities of home schooling to have virtual but still intimate emotional connections. It also requires skill, something that ratifies the vision of self that often accompanies home schooling parents. We don't need "experts"; with hard work and creative searching we can engage in a serious and disciplined education by ourselves. Thus, the technology provides for solace, acknowledging and praying for each other's psychic wounds and tensions—and at the same time enhances one's identity as someone who is intellectually worthy, who can wisely choose appropriate knowledge and values. What, hence, may seem like a form of anti-intellectualism is in many ways exactly the opposite. Its rejection of the secular expertise of the school and the state is instead based on a vision of knowledgeable parents and especially mothers who have a kind of knowledge taken from the ultimate source—God.

Thus, one of the most popular of the evangelically oriented Web sites that markets products for home schoolers sells such things as "The Go-to-the-Ant Chart." The wall chart contains pictures of common situations and biblical passages that speak to them. A list of the topics that the chart covers speaks to the realities that home schooling parents often face—serving God, gratefulness, honesty, perseverance, obedience, thoroughness, responsibility, initiative, consideration, and redeeming time. In language that not only home schooling parents will understand, it says:

> This chart arms parents with Scripture for working with the easily distracted or "less than diligent" child. The chart covers every area of laziness we could think of, plus a Bible verse for each problem for easy reference when they are driving you crazy! Take your child to the chart, identify his slothful action or attitude, read what God says about it, and pray for His strength to obey.[62]

It is important to note that the Internet is not only an effective tool for marketing and for movement building, and as I have just noted, for dealing with the emotional and intellectual labor home schooling requires. Just as importantly, it has become an extremely powerful tool for advocacy work and lobbying. Thus, the Home School Legal Defense Association has been at the forefront of not only home schooling, but in active and aggressive efforts to coordinate lobbyists inside and outside the Washington "Beltway." The HSLDA's Congressional Action Program has proven how powerful and responsive a tool such as the Internet can be in mobilizing for and against congressional and state laws and in defending the interests of its conservative positions.[63] However, once again, such mobilizing about home schooling needs to be situated within its larger context if we are not to miss some crucial connections between conservative-oriented home schooling and the more extensive authoritarian movement of which it is a key part. In this regard, it is worthwhile remembering what I noted earlier—that one of the most visible leaders of the home school movement nationally is Michael Farris. Farris plays a crucial leadership role in the HSLDA and is the President of Patrick Henry College.[64] Patrick Henry is a college largely for religiously conservative home schooled students and it has one major—*government*. The principles that animate its educational activities are quite clear in the following description:

> The Vision of Patrick Henry College is to aid in the transformation of American society by training Christian students to serve God and mankind with a passion for righteousness, justice and mercy, through careers of public service and cultural influence.

> The Distinctives of Patrick Henry College include practical apprenticeship methodology; a deliberate outreach to home schooled students; financial independence; a general education core based on the classical liberal arts; a dedication to mentoring and disciplining Christian students; and a community life that promotes virtue, leadership, and strong, life-long commitments to God, family and society.

> The Mission of the Department of Government is to promote practical application of biblical principles and the original intent of the founding documents of the American republic, while preparing students for lives of public service, advocacy and citizen leadership.[65]

These aims are both laudable and yet worrisome. Create an environment in which students learn to play active roles in reconstructing both their lives and the larger society. But make certain that the society they wish to build is based wholly on principles that themselves are not open to social criticism by nonbelievers.[66] Only those anointed by their particular version of God and only a society built upon the vision held by the anointed is legitimate. All else is sinful.

Thus, for all of its creative uses of technology, its understanding of "market needs" and how to fill them, its personal sacrifices, the immense labor of the mostly women who are engaged in the work of actually doing it, and its rapid growth fostered by good press and creative mobilizing strategies, a good deal of home schooling speaks the language of authoritarian populism. There's an inside and an outside. And for many authoritarian populists, the only way to protect the inside is to change the outside so that it mirrors the religious impulses and commitments of the inside. Doing this is hard political, educational, and emotional work. And new technologies clearly are playing a growing role in such personal and social labor.

Conclusion: Children and Living the "Right" Life

In the last two chapters, I have examined a number of the complexities involved in the cultural and political efforts within a rapidly growing movement that has claimed subaltern status. This has involved critically analyzing a set of technological resources—the Internet—and situating it within the social context of its use within a specific community and by specific people within that community. In so doing, I have suggested that in order to understand the social meaning and uses of these technologies, we need to examine the social movement that provides the context for their use and the identities that are being constructed within that social movement. I have also argued that we need to critically analyze the kind of labor that is required in home schooling, *who* is engaged in such labor, and how such labor is interpreted by the actors who perform it. Only in this way can we understand the lived problems such technologies actually solve. And I have pointed to how the space for production of such "solutions" is increasingly occupied by ideological and/or commercial interests who have responded to and enlarged a market to "fill the needs" of religiously conservative home schoolers.

A good deal of my focus has been on the work of mothers, of "Godly women" who have actively created new identities for themselves (and their children and husbands)[67] and have found in new technologies solutions to a huge array of difficult personal and political problems in their daily lives. Such Godly women are not that much different from any of us. But they are "dedicated to securing for themselves and their families a thoroughly religious and conservative life."[68] And they do this with uncommon sacrifice and creativity.

The picture I have presented is complicated; but then so, too, is reality. On the one hand, one of the dynamics we are seeing is social disintegration, that is the loss of legitimacy of a dominant institution that supposedly bound us together—the common school. Yet, on the other hand, and very importantly, what we are also witnessing is the use of the Internet not to "detraditionalize" society, but in the cases I have examined here, to *retraditionalize* parts of it. However, to call this phenomenon simply retraditionalization is to miss the ways in which such technologies are also embedded not only in traditional values and structures of feeling. They are also participating in a more "modern" project, one in which self-actualized individualism intersects with the history of social maternalism, which itself intersects with the reconstitution of masculinities as well.

But such maternalism needs to be seen as both positive and negative, and not only in its partial revivification of elements of patriarchal relations—although obviously this set of issues must not be ignored in any way. We need to respect the labor and the significant sacrifices of home schooling mothers (and the fathers as well since the question of altered masculinities in home schooling families is an important topic that needs to be focused upon in a way that complements what I have done here). This sensitivity to the complexities and contradictions that are so deeply involved in what these religiously motivated parents are attempting is perhaps best seen in the words of Jean Hardisty when she reflects on populist rightist movements in general.

> I continue to believe that, within that movement, there are people who are decent and capable of great caring, who are creating community and finding coping strategies that are enabling them to lead functional lives in a cruel and uncaring late capitalist environment.[69]

However, recognizing such caring, labor, and sacrifice—and the creative uses of technologies that accompany them—should not make us lose sight of what this labor and these sacrifices also produce. Godly technologies, godly schooling, and godly identities can be personally satisfying and make life personally meaningful in a world in which traditions are either destroyed or commodified. But at what cost to those who don't share the ideological vision that seems so certain in the minds of those who produce it?

As I argued at the end of the previous chapter, dealing with all of this requires a serious understanding of what motivates home schoolers. But it also requires listening carefully to the partial insights in their worries about the children, about a world where even children can be bought and sold, and about a society that destroys valued traditions unless they can be commodified and turned into saleable objects. It also requires that schools continue their efforts to reach out to communities, to become less apt to dismiss complaints. I am not romantic about this. It won't be easy—and some attacks on schools, policies, teachers, and curricula simply cannot be mediated. Nor can or should they be accepted when the agenda that may be behind them is so powerfully conservative religiously and economically that the agenda itself must be fought with all of the resources at our disposal.

Yet, my arguments also assume that connecting with communities in ways that are not limited to the publication of test scores and to the lamentable policies of NCLB need to be continued in *genuine and nonmanipulative* ways.[70] This is not an "engineering" problem, but involves the kinds of commitments to powerful and substantive public debate and struggle to which I pointed at the end of Chapter 4.

We are not starting anew here. Indeed, we have models for doing exactly these kinds of things, as my points about the democratic schools movement in earlier chapters demonstrate. While I do not want to be overly romantic here, I argue in more detail in my concluding chapter that there are models of curricula and teaching that are related to community sentiment, that are committed to social justice and fairness, and that are based in schools where both teachers and students want to be. If schools do not do this, all too many parents may be pushed in the direction of antischool sentiment. This would be a tragedy both for the public school system and for our already withered sense of community that is increasingly under threat. Even though state-supported schools have often served as arenas through which powerful social divisions are partly reproduced, at least in the United States such schools have also served as powerful sites for the mobilization of collective action and for the preservation of the very possibility of democratic struggle.[71] As one of the few remaining institutions that are still public, struggles over it are crucial.

This is obviously a tightrope we need to negotiate. How do we uphold the vision of a truly public institution at the same time as we rigorously criticize its functioning? In the United States, this is one of the tasks that the critical educators involved in *Democratic Schools* and the National Coalition of Education Activists have set for themselves. They have recognized that schools have both contradictory impulses and pressures on them, especially in a time of conservative modernization. It is not romantic to actively work on and through those contradictions so that the collective memory of earlier and partly successful struggles is not lost. Nor is it romantic to engage in what I have called elsewhere "nonreformist reforms," reforms whose aim is to expand the space of counterhegemonic action in public institutions.[72] Yet, to do this, it is necessary to defend the public nature of such public spaces.

Raymond Williams may have expressed it best when—positioning himself as an optimist without any illusions—he reminded us of the importance of the mutual determination of the meanings and values that should guide our social life. In expressing his commitment toward "the long revolution," his words are worth remembering. "We must speak for hope, as long as it doesn't mean suppressing the nature of the danger."[73] There are identifiable dangers to identifiable groups of people in public schooling as we know it. But the privatizing alternatives may be much worse. This tension between realism and hope forms the context for my concluding chapter.

CHAPTER 9

Righting Wrongs and Interrupting the Right

Culture Counts

My task in this book has not simply been to castigate the right, although there is a bit of fun in doing so. Rather, in each chapter I have also sought to illuminate the elements of good sense, not only bad sense, that are found within the various factions of the rightist alliance. I have several reasons for doing so. First, people who find certain elements of conservative modernization relevant to their lives are not puppets. They are not dupes who have little understanding of the "real" relations of this society. This smacks of earlier reductive analyses that were based in ideas of "false consciousness." My position is very different. I maintain that the reason that some of the arguments coming from the various factions of this new hegemonic bloc are listened to is because they are connected to aspects of the realities that people experience. The tense alliance of neoliberals, neoconservatives, authoritarian populist religious activists, and the professional and managerial new middle class only works because there has been a very creative articulation of themes that resonate deeply with the experiences, fears, hopes, and dreams of people as they go about their daily lives. The right has often been more than a little manipulative in its articulation of these themes. It has integrated them within racist nativist discourses, within economically dominant forms of understanding, and within a problematic sense of "tradition." But this integration could only occur if they were organized around people's understanding of their real material and cultural lives.

The second reason I have stressed the tension between good and bad sense—aside from my profound respect for Antonio Gramsci's writings about this—has to do with my belief that we have witnessed a major educational accomplishment over the past three decades in many countries. All too often, we assume that educational and cultural struggles are epiphenomenal. The real battles occur in the paid workplace—the "economy." Of course, the economy is an absolutely critical sphere of action. But not only is this position often guided by a strikingly reductive sense of what the economy is (its focus on paid, not unpaid, work; its neglect of the fact that, say, cultural institutions such as schools are also places where paid work goes on, etc.),[1] it also ignores what the right has actually done. Conservative modernization has radically reshaped the common sense of society. It has worked in every sphere—the economic, the political, and the cultural—to alter the basic categories we use to evaluate our institutions and our public and private lives. It has established new identities. It has recognized that to win in the state, you must win in civil society. The accomplishment of such a vast educational project has many implications. It shows how important cultural struggles are. And, oddly enough, it gives reason for hope. It forces us to ask a significant question. If the right can do this, why can't we?

I do not mean this as a rhetorical question. As I have argued throughout this book, the right has shown how powerful the struggle over meaning and identity can be. Although we should not want to emulate rightist groups' often cynical and manipulative processes, the fact that they have had such success in pulling people under their ideological umbrella has much to teach us. Granted, there are real differences in money and power between the forces of conservative modernization and those whose lives are being tragically altered by the policies and practices coming from the alliance. But the right wasn't as powerful thirty years ago as it is now. It collectively organized. It created a decentered unity, one where each element sacrificed some of its particular agenda to push forward on those areas that bound them together. Can't we do the same?

I believe that we can, but only if we face up to the realities and dynamics of power in unromantic ways. As I argued in Chapter 3, the

romantic possibilitarian rhetoric of some of the writers on critical pedagogy is not sufficiently based on a tactical or strategic analysis of the
current situation nor is it sufficiently grounded in its understanding
of the reconstructions of discourse and movements that are occurring
in all too many places. Here I follow Cameron McCarthy, who wisely
reminds us, "We must think possibility within constraint; that is the
condition of our time."[2]

As I have been at pains to show in this book, cultural struggles are
not epiphenomenal. They are not substitutes for action on the economy; but they count, and they count in institutions throughout society.
For dominant groups to exercise leadership, large numbers of people
must be convinced that the maps of reality circulated by those with
the most economic, political, and cultural power are indeed wiser than
other alternatives. Dominant groups do this by attaching these maps to
the elements of good sense that people have and by changing the very
meaning of the key concepts and their accompanying structures of feeling that provide the centers of gravity for our hopes, fears, and dreams
about this society. The right has been much more successful in doing
this than the left, in part because it has been able to craft—through
hard and lengthy economic, political, and cultural efforts—a tense but
still successful alliance that has shifted the major debates over education and economic and social policy onto its own terrain.

Evidence of this is all around us in the terms we use, in the arguments
in which we engage, indeed even in many of the cultural resources we
employ to imagine alternative futures. For example, as I was complet-
ing the writing of the first edition of this book, one of the top-selling
books on the *New York Times* fiction list was Tim LaHaye (yes, the
same Tim LaHaye) and Jerry Jenkins's *The Indwelling,* the seventh of
a series of books about "true believers" who confront the "Antichrist."[3]
The imagined future is a time of "rapture" where the good are taken
up to heaven and the bad are condemned to eternal damnation. The
identity of each of these groups is predictable, given what I described in
the previous four chapters. In a number of ways, then, the authoritarian
populist "outside" has indeed moved to become the inside. It has creatively learned how to use the codes of popular adventure and science
fiction novels to build an imaginative space of possibility, and a "muscular" yet sensitive Christianity, that gives meaning to people's daily
lives and hopes.[4]

Just as these spaces create imagined futures, so, too, do they help
create identities. Neoliberalism creates policies and practices that
embody the enterprising and constantly strategizing entrepreneur
out of the possessive individualism it establishes as the ideal citizen.

Neoconservatism creates imagined pasts as the framework for imagined and stable futures, futures in which identities are based on people knowing the knowledge and values that neoconservatives themselves have decided "have stood the test of time." Authoritarian populist religious conservatives also have an imagined past where a society, based on God's knowledge and values, has pregiven identities that enable women and men to rearticulate the neoliberal ideology of "choice" and to act in what are seen as godly ways toward bringing society to God. And managerialism establishes new identities for the professional and managerial middle class, identities that give new meaning to their lives and enable them to recapture their feelings of worthiness and efficacy. Out of all these multiple spaces and identities, and the conflicts, tensions, and compromises that their interactions generate, policies evolve. These policies are almost never purely from only one of the elements within this bloc. Rather, they often embody a rich mix that somehow must accommodate as many themes as possible from within the multiple forces of conservative modernization—without alienating those groups believed to be significant who are not yet integrated under the hegemonic umbrella of the right but who the right would like to bring under its leadership in the future.

This is a truly difficult task, and it is filled with contradictory impulses. Yet, even with this movement's contradictions and tensions, it has moved the balance of forces significantly to the right. Educational policies have been part of that move. In fact, education not only has been drawn along by the pressure of these rightist waves, it has actually played a major role in building these waves. The conservative alliance has paid attention to education—both formal and informal—and it has paid off for them. As I showed in Chapter 3, even in my critical deconstruction of the effects of neoliberal, neoconservative, and managerial policies and practices in a number of countries, it is their policies that have provided the outlines of the debates in which we engage.

Contradictory Reforms

Throughout this book, I have demonstrated that policies often have strikingly unforeseen consequences. Reforms that are instituted with good intentions may have hidden effects that are more than a little problematic. I have shown that the effects of some of the favorite reforms of neoliberals, neoconservatives, and new middle-class managerialists, for instance—voucher plans, national or statewide curricula, and national or statewide testing can serve as examples—quite often reproduce or even worsen inequalities. Thus, we should be very cautious about accepting what may seem to be meritorious intentions at face value. Intentions are too often contradicted by how reforms may function in practice. This is true not only for large-scale transformations of educational policies and governance, but also about moves to change the ways curriculum and teaching go on in schools.

The framework I have employed to understand these tendencies is grounded in what in cultural theory is called the act of repositioning. It in essence says that the best way to understand what any set of institutions, policies, and practices does is to see it from the standpoint of those who have the least power.[5] That is, every institution, policy, and practice—and especially those that now dominate education and the larger society—establish relations of power in which some voices are heard and some are not. Although it is not preordained that those voices that will be heard most clearly are also those who have the most economic, cultural, and social capital, it is most likely that this will be the case. After all, we do not exist on a level playing field. Many economic, social, and educational policies when actually put in place tend to benefit those who already have advantages.

These points may seem overly rhetorical and too abstract, but unfortunately there is no small amount of truth in them. For example, in a time when all too much of the discourse around educational reform is focused on vouchers and choice plans on the one hand and on proposals for national or state curricula, standards, and testing on the other, as I have shown throughout this volume a good deal of national and international evidence now indicates that such policies may actually reproduce or even worsen class, gender, and race inequalities. Thus, existing structures of economic and cultural power often lead to a situation in which what may have started out in some educators' or legislators' minds as an attempt to make things better, in the end is all too usually transformed into another set of mechanisms for social stratification.

Although much of this situation is a result of the ways in which race, gender, class, and "ability" act as structural realities in this society, some of it is related to the hesitancy of policy makers to take seriously enough the complicated ways in which education is itself a political act. These very politics and the structurally generated inequalities that stand behind them provide much of the substance underpinning the organizational principles of this volume.

Near the end of the introductory section of a recent volume on the politics of educational policies and practices, *Learning as a Political Act*, the editors state that as progressives they are committed to an "intellectual solidarity that seeks to lay bare the ideas and histories of groups that have been silenced in mainstream educational arenas."[6] There are several key concepts in this quote—intellectual solidarity, laying bare, silencing. Each speaks to a complicated history, and each phrase again says something about the position from which this book has been written. These, too, are what I called "key words" in Chapter 1. They come from a very different tradition than that provided by the linguistic mapping of markets. They also speak to a different politics of official knowledge.

Over the past decade, it has become increasingly clear that the school curriculum has become a battleground. Stimulated in large part by neoliberal complaints about "economically useless" knowledge, neoconservative laments about the supposed loss of discipline and lack of "real knowledge," and by religious authoritarian populists' relentless attacks on schools for their supposed loss of God-given "traditional" values, discussions of what should be taught in schools and how it should be taught are now as contentious as at any time in our history.

Evidence of this is not hard to find. In his repeated call for a return to a curriculum of "facts," E. D. Hirsch Jr. argues that schools have been taken over by progressive educators from Rousseau to Dewey,[7] a claim that has almost no empirical warrant at all and largely demonstrates how disconnected Hirsch is from the daily life of schools. Most schooling in the United States is already fact-driven. In addition, school districts throughout the country are constantly looking over their shoulders, worried that their reading, social studies, or mathematics programs will be challenged by the forces of the authoritarian religious right[8]—although as I demonstrate in *Cultural Politics and Education*, sometimes school systems themselves create the conditions for the growth of rightist antischool movements in their own communities by being less than democratic in their involvement of the community.[9] Other evidence of such contentiousness is visible in the fact that the contents of the mathematics curriculum was even recently debated in the editorial pages of the *New York Times,* in which spokespersons for constructivist and traditional curricula went head to head. Many more instances might be cited, including the continuing saga in Kansas and other states where the battles over evolution, "creation science," "intelligent design," sexuality education, and "secular humanist" curricula in general have reemerged in powerful ways.[10] But clearly the debate over "what knowledge is of most worth" has taken on more than a few political overtones.[11]

Much of the debate over this goes on with little empirical substance. For example, the argument that we must "return" to teaching, say, mathematics in "traditional" ways is obviously partly an ideological one.

(We need to restore discipline; students have too much freedom; "bad" knowledge has pushed "good" knowledge to the sidelines.) Yet it is also based on a claim that such a return will lead to higher achievement and ultimately to a more competitive economy. Here, neoliberal and neo-conservative emphases are joined with authoritarian populist mistrust of child-centeredness. (Remember, Dewey's *Democracy and Education* was high on the list of dangerous books I noted in my Preface.) This is where Jo Boaler's recent richly detailed qualitative and quantitative comparison of mathematics curricula and teaching enters.[12]

Boaler engages in a fine-grained analysis of two secondary schools with decidedly different emphases. Although her book is based on data from England, as in my analysis of the international literature in Chapter 3 its implications are again profound for debates over curriculum and teaching in the United States and elsewhere as well. Both schools are largely working class, with some minority and middle-class populations as well. Both sets of students had attended our equivalent of middle schools that were dominated by more traditional academic methods. And both had similar achievement profiles. One school overtly focused on preparing its students for national tests. Its program was almost totally teacher directed, organized around textbooks that were geared to the national tests, ability grouped, and run in such a way that speed and accuracy of computations and the learning of procedural rules for dealing with mathematical problems were highly valued—all those things that traditionalists here say are currently missing in mathematics instruction. Furthermore, the boundary between mathematics and both the real world and other subjects was strong.[13] The other school did not group by ability. It was decidedly more "progressive" both in its attitude toward students (there was a more relaxed communication style between teachers and students; student input was sought on the curriculum) and in its mathematics program. In this second school, the instruction was project-based, with a minimum of textbook-based teaching and a maximum of cooperative work among the students. The boundary between mathematics and "real-world" problems was weak.

The first school was quiet, on task, well organized—the very embodiment of the dream of nearly all elements of conservative modernization. The second was more noisy, students were not always fully on task, and had very flexible time schedules. Both schools had dedicated and hardworking teachers. Yet the differences in the results were striking, both in terms of overall achievement and in terms of the differential effects of each orientation on the students themselves.

The more traditional school, with its driving concern for "covering material" that would be on the test, stressed textbook knowledge and moved relatively rapidly from topic to topic. The more student centered approach of the second school sacrificed some coverage, but it also enabled students to more fully understand the material. By and large, students in the first school actually did less well on the standardized tests than the second, especially but not only on those parts of the tests that needed them to actually think mathematically, in large part because they could not generalize to new contexts as well as did those students who had used their mathematics in more varied (though more time-consuming) projects. Furthermore—and of great importance for equity—young women in the second school did consistently better in a more cooperative atmosphere that stressed understanding and use rather than coverage. The same held true for social class. Working-class students were consistently disadvantaged in the more pressured and text- and test-based agenda of traditional mathematics instruction.

This is a complex situation and Boaler is talking about general tendencies here. But her overall conclusions are clear and are supported by a very nice combination of data. In sum, the claim that a return to (actually, given the fact that most mathematics instruction is still chalk and talk and textbook based, it would be much more honest to say the continuation of) the traditional mathematics programs that the critics are demanding neither increases students' mathematical competence nor their ability to use their mathematical knowledge in productive ways. Although it may keep classrooms quiet and students under control, it may also systematically disadvantage young women—including, as Boaler shows, the brightest young women—and economically disadvantaged students, results that mirror much of what I reported in my discussion of Texas and NCLB in Chapter 4.[14] Finally, it may have one other effect, a strengthening of students' dislike of mathematics and their feelings that it is simply irrelevant for their future. If this is true for mathematics, it is worth considering the hidden negative effects of the more general policies being proposed by neoconservative reformers who wish to return to what they have constructed, rather romantically, as "the tradition" in all subjects.

If Boaler's conclusions are even partly generalizable, as I think they may very well be, the hidden effects of certain reform movements may not be what we had in mind. Tighter control over the curriculum, the tail of the test wagging the dog of the teacher and the curriculum, more pressure, more reductive accountability plans—all this may lead to less equitable results, not more. Boredom, alienation, and increased inequalities are not the ideal results of schooling. Once again, looking outside of our usual all-too-limited and parochial boundaries can be more than a little beneficial. The careful research underpinning Boaler's volume, research that is ratified by Eric Gutstein's engaging analysis of socially committed mathematics curricula and teaching,[15] needs to be taken seriously by anyone who assumes that in our unequal society there is a direct relationship between policy intentions and policy results. There isn't.

One of the most important tasks of critical education, therefore, is an empirical one. Just as Boaler did, we need to make research public not only on the negative effects of the policies of conservative modernization, but just as importantly on the positive effects of more socially and educationally critical alternatives. A good example of this is the SAGE program in Wisconsin, where significantly reducing class size within schools that historically have served a larger portion of dispossessed people has had much more robust results than, say, marketization and voucher plans.[16] And once again, the very interesting research on teaching mathematics for social justice by Gutstein shows similar effects.[17] This is one form of interrupting dominant discourses and policies, and much more of it needs to be done. However, in doing this we cannot simply rely on the dominant forms of what counts as evidence. In Linda Tuhiwai Smith's words, we need "decolonizing methodologies."[18] I return to the issue of making such things as alternative policies and practices public later on in this concluding chapter.

"Racing" toward Educational Reform

How else can these retrogressive movements be interrupted? Let me first speak relatively generally about facing the realities of differential power head on and what this means. The commitment to face such reality rests once again on what I argued at the outset of this chapter—the act of repositioning, of seeing the world through the eyes of the most oppressed of our fellow citizens.

In a number of other books, I have brought together data demonstrating the nature of the structured inequalities that characterize this society. I shall not rehearse them here. Suffice it to say that in spite of our overly individualized discourses to describe the society in which we live, class, race, and gender structures and dynamics are powerfully significant.[19] These structures and dynamics are not simply abstractions, but they inflect even the most mundane aspects of our daily lives. Although too many people have either ignored or given up on the power of class analysis, a neglect I have fought consistently for years,[20] perhaps some of my more general points can best be grasped by focusing on race. In so doing, let me remind us of some of what I argued in Chapter 4.

In their exceptional analysis of the way the discourses of race have operated in the United States, Omi and Winant argue that race is not an "add-on," but is truly constitutive of many of our most taken-for-granted daily experiences, a point I have reiterated in my discussions of the elements of conservative modernization throughout this book:

> In the U.S., race is present in every institution, every relationship, every individual. This is the case not only for the way society is organized—spatially, culturally, in terms of stratification, etc.—but also for our perceptions and understandings of personal experience. Thus as we watch the videotape of Rodney King being beaten, compare real estate prices in different neighborhoods, size up a potential client, neighbor, or teacher, stand in line at the unemployment office, or carry out a thousand other normal tasks, we are compelled to think racially, to use racial categories and meaning systems in which we have been socialized. Despite exhortations both sincere and hypocritical, it is not possible or even desirable to be "color-blind."[21]

Not only is it not possible to be color-blind, as they go on to say "opposing race requires that we notice race, not ignore it." Only by noticing race can we challenge it, "with its ever-more-absurd reduction of human experience to an essence attributed to all without regard for historical or social context." By placing race squarely in front of us, "we can challenge the state, the institutions of civil society, and ourselves as individuals to combat the legacy of inequality and injustice inherited from the past" and continually reproduced in the present.[22]

Although Omi and Winant were analyzing racial dynamics in the United States, I would hope that by now it is equally clear that their claims extend well beyond these geographical borders to include the United Kingdom and many other nations. It would not be possible to understand the history, current status, and multiple effects of educational policy in a large array of nations without placing race as a core element of one's analysis.[23]

Placing race at the center is less easy than one might expect, for one must do this with due recognition of its complexity. Race is not a stable category. What it means, how it is used, by whom, how it is mobilized in public discourse, and its role in educational and more general social policy—all this is contingent and historical. Indeed, it would be misleading to talk of race as an "it." "It" is not a thing, a reified object that can be measured as if it were a simple biological entity. Race is a construction, a set of fully social relationships. This unfortunately does not stop people from talking about race in simplistic ways that ignore the realities of differential power and histories.[24] Yet complexity needs to be recognized here as well. Racial dynamics have their own histories and are relatively autonomous. But they also participate in, form and are formed by, other relatively autonomous dynamics involving, say, class, colonial and postcolonial realities, and so on—all of which are implicated in and related to the social construction of race. Furthermore, racial dynamics can operate in subtle and powerful ways even when they are not overtly on the minds of the actors involved.

We can make a distinction between intentional and functional explanations here. Intentional explanations are those self-conscious aims that guide our policies and practices. Functional explanations, on the other hand, are concerned with the latent effects of policies and practices.[25] In my mind, the latter are more powerful than the former.

In essence, this rightly turns what is called the genetic fallacy in logic on its head, so to speak. Let me be specific here. We are apt to think of the genetic fallacy in particular ways. We tend to castigate authors who assume that the import and meaning of any position is totally determined by its original grounding. Thus, for example, it is clear that E. L. Thorndike—one of the founders of educational psychology—was a confirmed eugenicist and was deeply committed to the project of "race betterment" and had a vision of education that was inherently undemocratic. Yet one is on shaky ground if one concluded that every aspect of his work is totally "polluted" by his (repugnant) social beliefs. Thorndike's research program may have been epistemologically and empirically problematic, but a different kind of evidence and a more complex analysis is required to debunk all of it than to simply claim (correctly) that he was often racist, sexist, and elitist.[26] Indeed, it is not difficult to find progressive educators drawing on Thorndike's work for support of what were then seen to be radical positions.

When we are talking about racism and reform in current policies, we need to turn the genetic fallacy around. The overt motivations of the sponsors of New Labour's policies in the United Kingdom or of the proposals for education such as the establishment of voucher programs or national and state testing in the United States embodied in No Child Left Behind and similar proposals may not have been about race (or rather may not have been overtly racist) or may have assumed that such proposals would "level the playing field" for everyone. Their intentions may have been self-consciously "meritorious." (I very much mean this play on words.) Yet, as I have shown repeatedly throughout this book, conscious originating motives do not guarantee at all how arguments and policies will be employed, what their multiple and determinate functions and effects will be, whose interests they will ultimately serve, and what identifiable patterns of differential benefits will emerge, given existing and unequal relations of economic, cultural, and social capital and given unequal strategies of converting one form of capital to another in our societies. Indeed, race gets a good deal of its power through its very hiddenness. Nowhere is this more true than in the discourse of markets and standards.

For example, although some commentators may be correct that "the competitive schools market in the U.K. as envisioned by neo-liberals was created without reference to implications for ethnic minorities,"[27] this may be true only at the level of conscious intentions. While race talk may be overtly absent in the discourse of markets—except as a form of legitimation talk[28]—it remains an absent presence that I believe is fully implicated in the goals and concerns surrounding support for the marketization of education. The sense of economic and educational decline, the belief that private is good and public is bad, and so on is coupled with an often unarticulated sense of loss, a feeling that things are out of control, an anomic feeling that is connected to a sense of loss of one's "rightful place" in the world (an "empire" now in decline), and a fear of the culture and body of the Other. The "private" is the sphere of smooth-running and efficient organizations, of autonomy and individual choice. The "public" is out of control, messy, heterogenous. "We" must protect "our" individual choice from those who are the controllers or the "polluters" (whose cultures and very bodies are either exoticized or dangerous). Thus, I believe that there are very close connections between support for neoliberal visions of markets and free individuals; the concerns of neoconservatives with their clear worries about standards, "excellence," and decline; the worries of authoritarian populists that lead to home schooling; and the emphasis on certainty, testing, and control that plays such a large part in new middle-class managerialism.

In this regard, I believe that it is also the case that under current conditions national and state standards and curricula all too often actually represent a step backward in antiracist education (although we should never romanticize the situation before; not all that much antiracist education was actually going on I fear). This is clear in Linda McNeil's important research I mentioned earlier on the destructive effects of the move toward standardized and state-mandated curricula and testing—especially among schools with high concentrations of African-American and Latino/a students that had made major gains in building curricula and teaching that were responsive to and respectful of local cultures, values, and knowledge and that also had led to increased achievement and school attendance.[29] Isn't it odd that just as gains were being made in decentering dominant narratives, dominance returns in the form of legislation such as No Child Left Behind with its covert and overt national and state curricula (and national and state testing) that specify—often in distressing detail—what "we" are all like?[30] Of course, as I stated, in many nations the attempts at building national curricula and/or national standards were and are forced to compromise, to go beyond the mere mentioning of the culture and histories of the Other. (Certainly, this was and is the case in the United States.) And it is in such compromises that we see hegemonic discourse at its most creative best.

I hope you will forgive me if I once again repeat myself here, but I can think of no better indication of what I am describing. Take again the example I mentioned in an earlier chapter, the new national history standards in the United States and the attempt in textbooks to respond to the standards' creation of a multicultural narrative that binds "us" all together, to create that elusive "we." As I noted, such a discourse, while having a number of progressive-sounding elements, demonstrates how hegemonic narratives creatively erase historic memory and the specificities of difference and oppression. Although all too many textbooks in our schools construct the history of the United States as the story of "immigrants," such a story totally misconstrues the different conditions that existed. As I stated, some "immigrants" came in chains, were enslaved, and faced centuries of repression and state-mandated apartheid. Others were subjected to death and forced enclosure as official policies. And there is a world of difference here between the creation of (an artificial) "we" and the destruction of historical experience and memory.

This destruction and how it is accomplished is again related to how race functions as an absent (at least for some people) presence in our societies. This can be made clearer by directing our attention to the invisibility of whiteness. Indeed, I want to suggest that those who are deeply committed to interrupting the forces of conservative modernization and are equally committed to antiracist curricula and teaching need to place much more of their focus on white identity.

It may be unfortunate, but it is still true that many whites believe that there is a social cost not to being a person of color but to being white. For them, whites are the "new losers" in a playing field that they believe has been leveled now that the United States is a supposedly basically egalitarian, color-blind society. Because "times are tough for everybody," policies to assist "underrepresented groups"—such as affirmative action—are unfairly supporting "nonwhites." Thus, whites can now claim the status of victims, in much the same way as conservative evangelicals claimed to be oppressed, even though for some of them there is a loss of collective memory of how in the early years of the movement in the South a conscious choice was made to become less integrated in order to become part of a dominant racial order.[31] These feelings are of considerable importance in the politics of education in the United States as well as in many other nations. As it is being shaped by the conservative restoration, whiteness as an explicit cultural product is taking on a life of its own. In the arguments of the conservative discourses now so powerfully circulating, the barriers to social equality and equal opportunity have been removed. Whites, hence, have no privilege. Much of this is untrue, of course. Although undercut by other dynamics of power, there is still considerable advantage to "being white" in this society.[32] However, it is not the truth or falsity of these claims that are at issue here. Rather, it is the production of retrogressive white identities.

The implications of all this are profound politically and culturally. For, given the right's rather cynical use of racial anxieties, given the economic fears and realities many citizens experience, and given the historic power of race on the U.S. psyche and on the formation of identities in so many other nations, many members of these societies may develop forms of solidarity based on their "whiteness." To say the least, this is not inconsequential in terms of struggles over meaning, identity, and the characteristics and control of our major institutions.

How do we interrupt these ideological formations? How do we develop antiracist pedagogic practices that recognize white identities and yet do not lead to retrogressive formations? These are complex ideological and pedagogical questions. Yet these issues cannot be dealt with unless we focus directly on the differential power relations that have created and been created by the educational terrain on which we operate. And this requires an insistent focus on the role of the state, on state policies, on the shift to the right in government policies and by political parties in so many nations, and on the reconstruction of common sense in which the right has successfully engaged.

If we were to be true to the historical record, whiteness is certainly not something we have just discovered. The politics of whiteness has been enormously, and often terrifyingly, effective in the formation of coalitions that unite people across cultural differences, across class and gender relations, and against their best interests.[33] It would not be possible to write the history of "our" economic, political, legal, health, educational, indeed all of our institutions, without centering the politics of whiteness either consciously or unconsciously as a core dynamic. Of course, I am saying little that is new here. As critical race theorists and postcolonial writers have documented, racial forms and identities have been and are constitutive building blocks of the structures of our daily lives, imagined and real communities, and cultural processes and products.[34]

Let us look at this situation a bit more closely. Race as a category is usually applied to "nonwhite" peoples. White people are usually not seen and named. They are centered as the human norm. "Others" are raced; "we" are just people.[35] Richard Dyer speaks to this in his telling book, *White:*

> There is no more powerful position than that of being "just" human. The claim to power is the claim to speak for the commonality of humanity. Raced people can't do that—they can only speak for their race. But non-raced people can, for they do not represent the interests of a race. The point of seeing the racing of whites is to dislodge them/us from the position of power, with all of the inequities, oppression, privileges, and sufferings in its train, dislodging them/us by undercutting the authority with which they/we speak and act in and on the world.[36]

"Our" very language speaks to the invisibility of power relations in our ordinary talk about whiteness. "We" speak of a sheet of white paper as "blank." A room painted all white is seen as perhaps "needing a bit of color." Other examples could be multiplied. But the idea of whiteness as neutrality, as a there that is not there, is ideally suited for designating that social group that is to be taken as the "human ordinary."[37]

In the face of this, in the face of something that might best be called an absent presence, a crucial political, cultural, and ultimately pedagogic project then is making whiteness strange.[38] Thus, part of our task in terms of pedagogy and political awareness and mobilization is to tell ourselves and teach our students that identities are historically conferred. We need to recognize that "subjects are produced through multiple identifications." We should see our project as not reifying identity, but both understanding its production as an ongoing process of differentiation, and most importantly as subject to redefinition, resistance, and change.[39] There are dangers in doing this, of course. Having whites focus on whiteness can have contradictory effects, ones we need to be well aware of. It can enable one to acknowledge differential power and the raced nature of everyone—and this is all to the good. Yet it can also serve other purposes than challenging the authority of, say, the white West. As I argue in *Cultural Politics and Education*, it can just as easily run the risk of lapsing into the possessive individualism that is so powerful in this society. That is, such a process can serve the chilling function of simply saying "But enough about you, let me tell you about me." Unless we are very careful and reflexive, it can still wind up privileging the white, middle-class woman's or man's need for self-display. This is a seemingly endless need among many people. Scholars within the critical educational community will not always be immune to these tensions. Thus, we must be on our guard to ensure that a focus on whiteness doesn't become one more excuse to recenter dominant voices and to ignore the voices and testimony of those groups of people whose dreams, hopes, lives, and their very bodies are shattered by current relations of exploitation and domination.

Furthermore, focusing on whiteness and the complex roles it plays in current "reforms" can simply generate white guilt, hostility, or feelings of powerlessness. It can actually prevent the creation of those "decentered unities" that speak across differences and that can lead to broad coalitions that challenge dominant cultural, political, and economic relations. Thus, doing this requires an immense sensitivity, a clear sense of multiple power dynamics in any situation, and a nuanced and (at times risky) pedagogy.[40]

Issues of whiteness may seem overly theoretical to some readers or one more "trendy" topic that has found its way to the surface of the critical educational agenda. This would be a grave mistake. What counts as "official knowledge" consistently bears the imprint of tensions, struggles, and compromises in which race plays a substantial role.[41] Furthermore, as Steven Selden has so clearly shown in his history of the close connections between eugenics and educational policy and practice, almost every current dominant practice in education—standards, testing, systematized models of curriculum planning, gifted education, and so much more—has its roots in such concerns as "race betterment," fear of the Other, and so on.[42] And these concerns were themselves grounded in the gaze of whiteness as the unacknowledged norm. Thus, issues of whiteness lie at the very core of educational policy and practice. We ignore them at our risk.

Of course, this is partly an issue of the politics of "identity," and increasing attention has been paid over the past decade to questions of identity in education and cultural studies. However, one of the major failures of research on identity is its failure to adequately address the hegemonic politics of the right. As I have been at pains to show here and elsewhere, the conservative restoration has been more than a little successful in creating active subject positions that incorporate varied groups under the umbrella of a new hegemonic alliance. It has been able to engage in a politics inside and outside of education in which a fear of the racialized Other is connected to fears of nation, culture, control, and decline—and to intensely personal fears about the future of one's children in an economy in crisis. All of these are knit together in tense but creative and complex ways. Given this, those of us who are committed to antiracist educational policies and practices and who are engaged in bearing witness to the actual functioning of existing and newly proposed educational "reforms" would be wise to direct our attention not only to the racial effects of markets and standards, but just as much to the creative ways neoliberal and neoconservative (and in the United States and a number of other nations, authoritarian populist religious conservative) movements work to convince so many people (including many of the leaders of the Labour Party in the United Kingdom and in the Democratic and Republican parties in the United States) that these policies are merely neutral technologies. They're not.

Making Challenges Public

My arguments in the previous section of this concluding chapter have been at a relatively general level because I did not want us to lose sight of the larger picture. Let me now get more specific and tactical, since as I am convinced that it is important to interrupt rightist claims immediately, within the media, in academic and professional publications, and in daily life.

One crucial example of such interruption is found in the Educational Policy Project originally formed under the auspices of the Center for Education Research, Analysis, and Innovation at the University of Wisconsin, Milwaukee, but now housed at Arizona State University. This involves the ongoing construction of an organized group of people who are committed to responding very rapidly to material published by the right. This group includes a number of well-known educators and activists who are deeply concerned that the right has successfully used the media to foster its own ideological agenda, just as it has devoted a considerable amount of resources to getting its message to the public. For example, a number of conservative foundations have full-time staff members whose responsibility it is, for example, to fax synopses of reports to national media, to newspapers, and to widely read journals of opinion and to keep conservative positions in the public eye. Progressives have been much less successful in comparison, in part because they have not devoted themselves to the task as rigorously or because they have not learned to work at many levels, from the academic to the popular, simultaneously. In recognition of this, a group of socially and educationally critical educators met first in Milwaukee and has been continuously meeting to generate an organized response to conservative reports, articles, research, and media presentations.

A full-time staff member was hired by the Center to focus on conservative material, to identify what needs to be responded to, and to help edit responses written by individual members of the group. A Web site has been developed that publishes these responses and/or original publications of more progressive research and arguments. The project also focuses on writing "op-ed" pieces, letters to the editor, and other similar material and on making all of this available to the media. This requires establishing contacts with journals, newspapers, radio, and television, and so on. This is exactly what the right did. We can and must do similar things. It requires hard work, but the Educational Policy Project is the beginning of what we hope will be a larger effort involving many more people. The reader can see the kinds of things that have been done by going to the following Web site for the Educational Policy Studies Laboratory at Arizona State University: http://www.asu.edu/educ/epsl/.

To give a sense of the kinds of pieces that are being produced and widely circulated, I am including my response to Gary Rosen's arguments for vouchers that he published in the neoconservative journal *Commentary*.[43]

ARE VOUCHERS REALLY DEMOCRATIC?
A RESPONSE TO "ARE SCHOOL VOUCHERS UN-AMERICAN?"
BY GARY ROSEN
BY MICHAEL W. APPLE
FEBRUARY 2000

Over the past decade, conservative groups in particular have been pressing for public funding for private and religious schools. At the forefront of this movement have been voucher plans. Voucher proponents argue that only by forcing schools onto a competitive market will there be any improvement. Writing in the neo-conservative journal *Commentary*, Gary Rosen attempts to synthesize the arguments for vouchers and against public schools and teachers.[1] Voucher proposals do not stand alone. They are connected to other widespread attacks on public institutions and public employees. This more extensive agenda—often not available for scrutiny—shows itself when one looks carefully at Rosen's position.

Rosen seeks to rebut arguments that vouchers for religious schools violate the US constitutional principle of church-state separation, and arguments that they would have a corrosive effect on common public education and therefore would undermine national identity and unity. Such arguments by public school partisans, Rosen asserts, are self-serving; private schools, he claims, do a better job of civic education and are more racially integrated than public schools. Private school vouchers, he concludes, can reverse a trend in which growing numbers of minority inner city teenagers emerge unprepared from today's urban public schools—by providing some of those students an alternative, while goading public schools to improve for the rest. "What could be more democratic—or more American—than this?"[2]

While he is very selective in those arguments against vouchers to which he chooses to respond, Rosen presents them as simply a tool to improve the lives of inner city students. While that may be the aim of some voucher advocates, it ignores the realities of the larger voucher movement, which has a much more ambitious agenda. In Wisconsin, Polly Williams, a Democratic, African American legislator, allied with the Republican governor a decade ago to craft a voucher plan limited to poor children in inner city schools in Milwaukee. She assumed that its aim, as Rosen states, was to give African American and poor parents the right to exit public schools. Yet once the State Supreme Court, in a close vote, ruled the program was constitutional, conservative proponents of the program began calling for its expansion to include all parents—a clear, direct attack on public schools while providing public money to support even affluent parents who wished to pull their children out of public education. Ms. Williams, though still a supporter of vouchers targeted only to low-income families, attacked her erstwhile allies, accusing them of not having the interests of her constituents at the heart of their policies.[3]

The issue is not simply one of competing social beliefs, though. It is also about what research actually says. Voucher proponents are extremely selective in their use of data to support their cause, and Rosen in his essay is no exception. Rosen points to Paul E. Peterson's data on the "success" of vouchers and then quotes from the recent long term study of these programs by John Witte to further bolster the argument. Yet, Rosen does not report Witte's own conclusion that vouchers are not necessarily effective in raising achievement and that the research does not clearly support vouchers at all.[4] At best, the available research is still quite unclear. It cannot be used to give a ringing endorsement to vouchers. Witte's cautions are not alone here, though. Internationally, a number of studies have powerfully demonstrated the effects of policies to privatize schools and turn education into a market-driven institution. Study after study has shown that, except for a very limited group of students, placing schools on a market merely reinforces existing hierarchies, further stratifying education.[5] Poor and working class children are even more marginalized. While a small number of children of color do get the right to exit, the vast majority of these same children either gain no benefits whatsoever, or they and their schools are left in even worse condition than before.

The data also indicate worrisome effects on teachers and administrators. While Rosen, without supporting data, claims that vouchers do not cause added hardship for schools, an extensive body of international research on placing schools in a competitive market can lead to exactly the opposite conclusion. Much more time is spent on maintaining the image of a "good" school, with much less time spent by teachers and administrators on curricular substance. Since it is comparative test scores that determine whether a school is "good" or "bad," children who do perform well on such reductive tests are seen as welcome. Those who do not are often discouraged or are marginalized. Once again, the vast majority of children harmed by such reforms are exactly those whom Rosen and others state they are supporting. These conditions exist not because teachers do not already work extremely hard or are uncaring. Rather, markets in schools seem to worsen, rather than improve, work load, pressure, and access to resources.

The issue of teachers is significant. Rosen's essay not only fails to report much of the countervailing data, but it is clearly an attack on teachers and on teachers' unions. Words and phrases such as teachers' "mock concern" and "disingenuous" behavior point to a powerful antipathy to public employees. This is unfortunate, since any institution that acts in dismissive and undemocratic ways to the employees who work every day in it cannot be considered democratic.

Much of the literature in support of vouchers assumes that the root cause of the supposed decline in education is directly related to unprepared teachers and overly bureaucratic schools. There undoubtedly are some ill-prepared teachers and there are school districts that are overly bureaucratic. To place the blame only on teachers and schools, however, ignores the larger structural realities that have nearly destroyed public services in our inner cities. It is simply not possible to understand what has happened in education unless we honestly link schooling to the growth of poverty. One of the most consistent research findings over the past decades has been that income inequality and other social and economic factors—not type of school—have the most power in determining success in schools.[6] This is not to ignore the role of schooling in enhancing mobility, but it does ask us to be very honest. It was not schools that caused the massive decline of respectful jobs with decent pay in our inner cities, thereby creating a crisis in faith about the future among generations of parents and children. It was not schools that caused capital flight as factories fled to non-unionized, lower paid parts of the world. And it was not schools that led to the willful neglect of the families, health care, and decent housing in these inner cities. To blame teachers for this is to live in a world divorced from reality.

Yet, even given the unfortunate relationship between schooling and an unequal economy, there are things that can be done and that have been proven to work. Effective schooling does not necessarily mean turning our schools over to a market. There are other, and even more proven, choices. The democratic schools movement growing throughout the country shows how educators and local communities can jointly build responsive and effective education that makes a real difference in the lives of children, teachers, and communities. Schools such as Central Park East in New York, Fratney Street School in Milwaukee, and the Rindge School of Technical Arts in the Boston area all provide telling examples of public schools that treat their teachers, students, and local communities with the respect they deserve.[7] Programs in Tennessee and Wisconsin to reduce class size have shown a much more robust set of results than any of those reported for voucher plans.[8]

Most of the debates about vouchers have been conducted around one issue, whether or not they raise scores on standardized tests. There are other crucial issues that must not be ignored, however. Voucher plans, like all market-driven and privatized models, are part of a larger and quite aggressive ideological movement to change how we think about our society and our participation in it. They assume without question that public is by definition bad and private is by definition good. Instead of collectively building and rebuilding our institutions, voucher plans are part of the larger effort by conservatives to change the very meaning of citizenship. Citizenship is now to be defined as simply consumer choice. The unattached individual makes choices about her or his life, without caring what its effects are on the rest of society.[9] The reduction of democracy to selfish individualism may in fact be Un-American. I doubt that this is what we as a society want.

Notes

1. Gary Rosen, "Are School Vouchers Un-American?" *Commentary*, Vol. 109, No. 2, February 2000, pp. 26–31.
2. Ibid.
3. It is important to understand as well that many of the same foundations that are pouring money into the campaign for voucher plans are those which provided financial and logistical support for such volumes as Richard Herrnstein and Charles Murray, *The Bell Curve* (New York: Free Press, 1994). Widely discredited in the scientific literature, the volume claimed that African Americans were on the whole less intelligent than European Americans. While this does not discredit all of the arguments in favor of vouchers, it should make us extremely cautious about how voucher plans fit into the larger sets of social commitments that guide many of their proponents.
4. John Witte, *The Market Approach to Education: An Analysis of America's First Voucher Program* (Princeton, N.J.: Princeton University Press, 2000).
5. See the following: Geoff Whitty, Sally Power, and David Halpin, *Devolution and Choice in Education* (Philadelphia: Open University Press, 1998). Hugh Lauder and David Hughes, *Trading in Futures: Why Markets in Education Don't Work* (Philadelphia: Open University Press, 1999). David Gillborn and Deborah Youdell, *Rationing Education: Policy, Practice, Reform, and Equity* (Philadelphia: Open University Press, 2000). Sharon Gewirtz, Stephen Ball, and Richard Bowe, *Markets, Choice, and Equity in Education* (Philadelphia: Open University Press, 1995).
6. Grace Kao, Marta Tienda, and Barbara Schneider, "Race and Ethnic Variation in Academic Performance," *Research in Sociology of Education and Socialization* 11:263–297. 1996.

7. Michael W. Apple and James A. Beane, eds. *Democratic Schools* (Alexandria, Va.: Association for Supervision and Curriculum Development, 1995).
8. The entire issue of *Educational Evaluation and Policy Analysis* 21, 2 (Summer 1999) is devoted to evaluating various programs that lower class size.
9. Michael W. Apple, *Cultural Politics and Education* (New York: Teachers College Press, 1996).

This is just one example of one strategy for bringing what we know to parts of the public in more popular forms. Many other examples are posted on the Web site and published as reports, responses in journals, letters to the editor, and op-ed pieces. Although this project is relatively new, it shows considerable promise. In combination with the use of talk radio, call-in shows, and similar media strategies in multiple languages,[44] these kinds of activities are part of a larger strategy to bring both more public attention to what the dangers are in the "solutions" proposed by the right and to what the workable alternatives to them might be. Integrating the educational interventions within a larger focus on the media is absolutely crucial.[45] This is just one of the reasons that the existence of liberal talk radio such as Air America is such an interesting phenomenon.

Learning from Other Nations

During one of the times I was working in Brazil with Paulo Freire, I remember him repeatedly saying to me that education must begin in critical dialogue. These last two words were crucial to him. Education both must hold our dominant institutions in education and the larger society up to rigorous questioning and at the same time this questioning must deeply involve those who benefit least from the ways these institutions now function. Both conditions were necessary, since the first without the second was simply insufficient to the task of democratizing education.

Of course, many committed educators already know that the transformation of educational policies and practices—or the defense of democratic gains in our schools and local communities—is inherently political. Indeed, this is constantly registered in the fact that rightist movements have made teaching and curricula the targets of concerted attacks for years. One of the claims of these rightist forces is that schools are "out of touch" with parents and communities. Although there are elements of insight in such criticisms, we need to find ways of connecting our educational efforts to local communities, especially those members of these communities with less power, that are more truly democratic than those envisioned by the right. I talked earlier on, in Chapter 1, about the efficacy of turning to the experiences of other nations to learn what the effects of neoliberal and neoconservative policies and practices actually are. Yet we can learn many more things from other nations' struggles. For example, currently in Porto Alegre, Brazil, the policies of participatory budgeting are helping to build support for more progressive and democratic policies there in the face of the growing power of neoliberal movements at a national level. The Workers Party ("PT" as it is known there) was able to increase its majority even among people who had previously voted in favor of parties with much more conservative educational and social programs because it has been committed to enabling even the poorest of its citizens to participate in deliberations over the policies themselves and over where and how money should be spent. By paying attention to more substantive forms of collective participation and, just as important, by devoting resources to encourage such participation, Porto Alegre has demonstrated that it is possible to have a thicker democracy, even in times of both economic crisis and ideological attacks from neoliberal parties and from the conservative press. Even though PT has been challenged in Porto Alegre and has recently suffered electoral losses, programs such as the "Citizen School" and the sharing of real power with those who live in "favelas" (slums) provide ample evidence that thick democracy offers realistic alternatives to the eviscerated version of thin democracy found under neoliberalism.[46] Just as important is the pedagogic function of these programs. They develop the collective capacities among people to enable them to continue to engage in the democratic administration and control of their lives.[47] This is time-consuming, but time spent in such things now has proven to pay off dramatically later on.

A similar story can be told about another part of Brazil. In Belem, a "Youth Participatory Budget" process was instituted. It provided resources and space for the participation of many thousands of youth in the deliberations over what programs for youth needed to be developed, how money should be spent, and over creating a set of political forums that could be used by youth to make public their needs and desires. This is very different from most of the ways youth are dealt with in all too many countries, where youth are seen as a "problem" not as a resource.[48] A similar instance is found in New Zealand, where under the original leadership of the International Research Institute on Maori and Indigenous Education, multiracial groups of youth are formed in communities to publicly discuss the ways in which youth see their realities and advance proposals for dealing with these realities.[49] In this way, alliances that begin to cut across race, class, and age are being built. There are models, then, of real participation that we can learn from and that challenge the eviscerated vision of democracy advanced by neoliberals by putting in place more substantive and active models of actually "living our freedoms." The issue is not the existence of such models; it is ensuring that they are made widely visible.

Thinking Heretically

To build counterhegemonic alliances, we may have to think more creatively than before—and, in fact, may have to engage in some nearly heretical rethinking. Let me give an example. I would like us to engage in a thought-experiment. I believe that the right has been able to take certain elements that many people hold dear and connect them with other issues in ways that might not often occur "naturally" if these issues were less politicized. Thus, for instance, one of the reasons populist religious groups are pulled into an alliance with the right is because such groups believe that the state is totally against the values that give meaning to their lives. They are sutured into an alliance in which other elements of rightist discourse are then able to slowly connect with their own. Thus, they believe that the state is antireligious. Others also say that the state seeks to impose its will on white working-class parents by giving "special treatment" to people of color and ignoring poor white people. These two elements do not necessarily have to combine. But they slowly begin to be seen as homologous.

Is it possible that by taking, say, religion out of the mix that some parts of the religious community that currently find collective identities on the right would be less susceptible to such a call if more religious content were found in school? If religious studies had a more central place within the curriculum, is it less likely that people who find in religion the ultimate answers to why they are here would be less mistrustful of the state, less apt to be attracted to a position that public is bad and private is good? I am uncertain that this would be the case. But I strongly believe that we need to entertain this possibility.

Do not misunderstand me. I am decidedly not taking the position that we should use vouchers to fund private religious schools, nor am I saying that the authoritarian populist religious right should be pandered to. Rather, I am taking a position similar to that espoused by Warren Nord that I noted in Chapter 1. Our failure to provide a clear place for the study of religion in the curriculum makes us "illiberal." Yet I do not want to end with Nord's position. Rather, I see it as a starting point. In earlier books and here, I have argued that at times people "become right" because of the lack of responsiveness of public institutions to meanings and concerns that are central to their lives. Teaching more about, not for, religion doesn't just make us more "liberal" in Nord's words. It may also help interrupt the formation of antipublic identities. This has important implications for it can point to strategic moves that can be made to counter the integration of large numbers of people under the umbrella of conservative modernization.

As I have demonstrated elsewhere, people often become right at a local level, not through plots by rightist groups but because of local issues and sentiments. Making schools more responsive to religious sentiments may seem like a simple step, but it can have echoes that are profound since it may undercut one of the major reasons some populist groups who are also religious find their way under the umbrella of rightist attacks on schools and on the public sphere.

I am not a romantic about this. I do think that it could be dangerous and could be exploited by the religious right. After all, some of them do have little interest in "teaching about" and may hold positions on Christianity and other religions that both construct and leave little room for the Other. Yet the centrality of religious sentiments need not get pushed toward neoliberalism. (In fact, in my work in a number of nations that are witnessing religious revivals, and occasionally surges in Islamic, Jewish, Christian, and Hindu fundamentalisms, at times people who are deeply religious and might be seen as "fundamentalist" may also be just as committed to the struggle against neoliberal policies. Let's not romanticize the dangers of fundamentalism and aggressive evangelizing, but let's also not see people who adhere to such things as having little insight into the realities of globalizing capitalist relations.) Religious sentiments need not be connected to a belief that public schools and teachers are so totally against religious people that marketization and privatization are the only answers.

Thus, I'd like us to think seriously—and very cautiously—about the possible ways members of some of the groups currently found under the umbrella of the conservative alliance might actually be pried loose from it and might work off the elements of good sense they possess. In saying this, I am guided by a serious question. In what ways can religious commitments be mobilized for socially progressive ends? Our (often justifiable) worries about religious influences in the public sphere may have the latent effect of preventing such a mobilization by alienating many people who have deep religious commitments and who might otherwise be involved in such struggles. If many evangelicals do commit themselves to helping the poor, for example, in what ways can these sentiments be disarticulated from seeing capitalism as "God's economy" and from only helping the "deserving poor" and rearticulated toward greater social and economic transformation? It would seem well worth studying the recent histories of religious involvement in, say, the anti-WTO struggles to understand this better. At the very least, we cannot act as if religious beliefs about social and educational justice are outside the pale of progressive action, as too many critical educators do. A combination of caution, openness, and creativity is required here.

Yet another example is to take advantage of the shared elements of good sense among groups who usually have very different agendas in order to work against specific policies and programs that are being instituted by other elements within the new hegemonic alliance. That is, there are real tensions within conservative modernization that provide important spaces for joint action.

This possibility is already being recognized. Because of this, for example, some truly odd political couplings are emerging today. Both the populist right and the populist left are occasionally joining forces to make strategic alliances against some neoliberal incursions into the school. For instance, Ralph Nader's group Commercial Alert and Phyllis Schlafly's organization the Eagle Forum are building an alliance against Channel One. Both are deeply committed to fight the selling of children in schools as a captive audience for commercials. They are not alone. The Southern Baptist Convention has passed a resolution opposing Channel One. Groups such as Donald Wildmon's American Family Association, and even more important, James Dobson's powerful organization Focus on the Family, have been working with Nader's groups to remove Channel One from schools and to keep it out of schools where it is not already established. This tactical alliance has also joined together to support antigambling initiatives in a number of states and to oppose one of the fastest-growing commercial technology initiatives in education—ZapMe! Corp. ZapMe! has provided free computers to schools at the cost of collecting demographic data on students, which it then uses to target advertising specifically at these children.[50]

The tactical agreement is often based on different ideological positions. Although the progressive positions are strongly anticorporate, the conservative positions are grounded in a distaste for the subversion of traditional values, "the exploiting of children for profit," and a growing rightist populist tension over the decisions that corporations make that do not consider the "real folks" in America. This latter sentiment is what the rightist populist and nativist Pat Buchanan has worked off of for years. In the words of Ron Reno, a researcher at Focus on the Family, we need to fight "a handful of individuals exploiting the populace of America to make a buck."

This teaming up on specific causes is approached more than a little cautiously on both sides, as you would imagine. As Ralph Nader says, "You have to be very careful because you can start tempering your positions. You can be too solicitous. You have to enter and leave on your own terms. You tell them, 'Here's what we're doing, if you want to join us fine. If not, fine.'"

Phyllis Schlafly portrays her own reasons this way. "[Nader and I] agree that the public schools should not be used for commercial purposes. A captive audience of students should not be sold for profit. I agree with that. I don't recall his objection to the content of the news, which is what stirs up a lot of conservatives."[51] Schlafly's comments show the differences as well as similarities in the right-left division here. Although for many people across the divide, there is a strong distaste for selling our children as commodities, divisions reappear in other areas. For one group, the problem is a "handful of individuals" who lack proper moral values. For the other, the structural forces driving our economy create pressures to buy and sell children as a captive audience. For conservatives, the content of the news on Channel One is too "liberal"; it deals with issues such as drugs, sexuality, and similar topics. Yet, as I have shown in my own analysis of what counts as news in the major media and in Channel One, even though there is some cautious treatment of controversial issues, the content and coding of what counts as news is more than a little conservative and predominantly reinforces dominant interpretations.[52]

These differences should not detract from my basic point. Tactical alliances are still possible, especially where populist impulses and anticorporate sentiments overlap. These must be approached extremely carefully, however, since the grounding of much of the populism of the right is also in a racist nativism, a very dangerous tendency that has had murderous consequences. A recognition, however, of the anticorporate tendencies that do exist here is significant, because it also points to cracks in the alliance supporting some aspects of conservative modernization in general and to similar fissures within the ranks of authoritarian populism itself. For example, the fact that Ralph Reed was hired as a consultant to burnish Channel One's image has also created a number of tensions within the authoritarian populist ranks.[53]

Another area that is ripe for such coalitions is that of national and state curricula and testing. Neither the populist right nor the populist left believe that such policies leave room for the cultures, histories, or visions of legitimate knowledge that they are so deeply committed to. Although the specific content of such knowledge is decidedly dissimilar for each of these groups, the fact that there is agreement both on a generally antielitist position and on the fact that the very processes involved are antidemocratic provides room for tactical alliances not only against these processes but as a block against even further incursions of managerialism into schools. In addition, given the ideological segregation that currently exists in this society, working (carefully) with such groups has the advantage of reducing stereotypes that they may hold (and perhaps that we might also hold?). It increases the possibility that the populist right will see that progressives may in fact be able to provide solutions to serious issues that are so distressing in populist movements of multiple orientations. This benefit should not be minimized.

My position here, hence, embodies a dual strategy. We can and must build tactical alliances where this is possible and where there is mutual benefit—and where such an alliance does not jeopardize the core of progressive beliefs and values. At the same time, we need to continue to build on more progressive alliances between our core constituencies around issues such as class, race, gender, sexuality, ability, globalization and economic exploitation, and the environment. That such a dual strategy can be used to organize both within already existing alliances and to work across differences is made clear in the anti-WTO mobilizations in Seattle, in Washington, and in a number of other cities throughout the world.

Can Alliances Be Built across the Religious and Secular Divide?

I need to say more about the possibility of such alliances and the ways in which religious forms play into them. Throughout this book, I have critically analyzed the creative ways in which conservative modernization and the complicated alliance that stands behind it has pulled society to the right. One of the effects of this is that the current dominance of rightist discourse enables the unsayable to now become sayable in so many areas that it's hard to keep track. Thus, for example, this has become a time of an unapologetic claim of an American "Empire." As William Kristol openly states, "If people want to say we're an imperial power, fine."[54] What is not in question is the sincerity of the belief that "we are the best" and hence have a duty to bring what we believe is best to the rest of the world. But when this is connected, as it now so clearly is, to a belief that "God is on our side" (and no one else's) and we are in essence doing God's will, this becomes simply an act of hubris. Theology is used to support a national and international ideology of U.S. dominance. And it is bad theology as well.[55] As Jim Wallis reminds us, "God bless America" is found nowhere in the Bible.[56]

Coupled with such imperial ambitions and claims is a dangerous position about the religions that many people throughout the world, and here in the United States, find compelling and profoundly meaningful. The case of Islam provides a powerful example. Many rightist evangelical leaders see Islam as an embodiment of evil, both in terms of the acts of some Islamic fundamentalists and in terms of its religious convictions. This is not only immensely arrogant, but it is all too often done in ignorance of the multiple traditions within Islam and of Islam's exceptional history of tolerance and its commitment to social justice.[57]

But religious movements *do not* have to be imperial and conservative. Many of the most powerful movements for social change in the United States have been fueled by progressive religious impulses.[58] The complex politics of the Bible and the differing ways it has been used can be seen in the fact that slave owners in the South gave their captives the Bible so that they would supposedly look to heaven rather than focus on their plight on earth. Yet, that same Bible enabled enslaved people to find Moses and Jesus and often became one of the foundations for liberation struggles.[59] It is in the latter view of Bible that a number of evangelicals find the strength to challenge the relations of dominance and subordination that are so powerful today.

It is worth quoting Jim Wallis, one of the most articulate members of the progressive evangelical community, at length here.

> Today we face two related vision problems. One is the lack of vision in public life. ... But the other is when political leaders have a clear vision—but the wrong one. When politics is shaped by visions that defend wealth and power, rather than opening up more opportunity; that are more exclusionary than inclusive; that pursue policies that destabilize families and communities; that exalt private interests over the common good; that simply leave too many people behind; that seek national or corporate self-interest over international peace and justice; or that increase conflict rather than reducing it—then such political vision can be as having no vision at all. ... Neither will suffice. ... And neither is faithful to the compelling public visions contained in both our best religious and democratic traditions.[60]

For those like Wallis, "allowing the right to decide what is a religious issue has become a moral and political tragedy."[61] Hence, for example, "a budget based on a windfall of benefits for the wealthy and harsh cuts for poor families and children is an unbiblical budget."[62] One well-known pastor from Riverside Church in New York City puts it this way: "Nobody gets into heaven without a letter of reference from the poor."[63] The deepening of poverty, the millions of people without health care, the elderly who must choose either to eat or to pay for their medicines, the little discussed massive under-funding of medical care for thousands of wounded veterans who are returning from "our" wars in Iraq and Afghanistan, the attacks on and destruction of our very sense of the "public" and of the common good—all of these are moral and religious issues. Thus, we need to remember that budgets are not simply about numbers and tables or about cost and benefit ratios. They are *moral* documents. When there are record deficits brought on by tax cuts to the richest people in the United States, when the cost of a war means as well that there must be destructive cuts in funding for education, health care, child care, housing, and so many more programs that recognize a society's commitment to the least advantaged among us, then these documents demonstrate a government's ethical commitments.[64] In Wallis's words again, such monetary priorities are again actually "unbiblical." As he might put it, we do need a faith-based initiative, but one that argues against budgets that are attacks on the poor.[65]

One of the claims made by Wallis that is worth taking seriously is that social location often determines biblical interpretation.[66] In a society in which the geography of racial segregation is ever more intense—the destruction of urban economies, white flight, gated communities, "cocooning," a politics of "not in my backyard," and so on—many rightist evangelicals are distant from the poor in the most significant way. They don't interact with them. And as I mentioned earlier, given the increasingly comparatively affluent nature of evangelicals, class location may at times influence the reading of biblical texts.[67]

In Wallis and others, we see a very different sense of "calling," one in which biblical injunctions are taken in a very different direction than those advanced by the right. Thus, for these religious figures, how a government deals with poverty is a religious issue. An administration's failure to support poor working families should be called a religious failure as well. The same must be said for its environmental policies, since neglect and destruction of the environmental is a denial of stewardship,[68] something I about which I shall say more shortly.

Wallis's challenge is the following. Progressives should not shun religious discourse and "God talk," but instead should be arguing on both moral and religious grounds that all Americans should have economic security, health care, and educational opportunity. "True faith" must involve a deep-seated compassionate concern for those who have been marginalized in this society—and it requires sets of policies that demonstrate that such concern is not simply rhetorical.[69]

Stereotypes exist that may prevent alliances against the right from being built. Thus, listening carefully to religiously committed people would also demonstrate that not all religiously inspired groups see the state as a mission field; nor do they necessarily intend to destroy the boundaries between church and state. A large proportion of them do not support state-sanctioned prayer in schools or see the necessity of having large granite blocks with the Ten Commandments standing in front of every courthouse in the land.[70] Given this, it is healthy for a critical and ever moving democracy to have religiously committed groups and individuals bring these commitments into the public arena and to engage in public debate as long as there is a commitment to the common good, not to a proselytizing project or to what is often now a religious takeover of the mechanisms of the state. Thus, religious people can participate *as citizens,* ones who have the right "to bring their deepest moral convictions to the public square for the democratic discourse on the most important values and directions that will shape our society."[71] Bringing convictions about social and racial justice, gender equity, respect for the power of love and same-sex relationships, stewardship of the environment, peacemaking, international accords, full funding of educational needs and institutions—all of these are crucial resources within the public arena.[72] And if they are generated out of deep religious understandings and sentiments, then they can become even more powerful in cutting through some of the divides that currently separate people who may actually have similar intuitions about many of the distressing conditions within this society. A similar point is implied by Jean Anyon when she traces out the history of some of the most powerful movements for racial justice in the United States.[73]

Indeed, there are groups within the Christian evangelical, as well as within Jewish and Islamic, communities (the plural is important here) who have challenged religious people to make the reduction of poverty, comprehensive economic justice, the combating of HIV/AIDs, dealing with the close connections between poverty and race, and similar things core parts of their agenda. Their moral and religious commitments put them clearly at odds with much of the agenda of the evangelical right wing.[74] This is evident in recent efforts within evangelical communities to combat global warming. For them, global warming is a Christian issue because the Bible mandates "stewardship of God's creation." The vice president of governmental affairs for the National Association of Evangelicals, Rev. Rich Cizik, has been outspoken about this. As he says, "I don't think that God is going to ask us how he created the earth, but he will ask us what we did with what he created."[75] This is connected as well to the growing commitment among these groups of evangelicals to taking poverty seriously. Rev. Jim Ball of the Evangelical Environmental Network put it this way. "Christ said, 'What you do to the least of these you do to me. ... And so caring for the poor by reducing the threat of global warming is caring for Jesus Christ."[76]

We should not assume that this means that there will be agreement between secular progressives and evangelicals on all issues—and this is why I urge us to approach the possibilities I am discussing in this section with appropriate caution. There is still a profound distrust of government intervention and regulation, and of secularity in general at work here. Further, the connections between this newly emerging environmentalism and what are often hallmark conservative causes are still more than a little visible. The complexities and tensions are visible, for instance, in Rev. Cizik's statement that "We're not adverse to government-mandated prohibitions on behavioral sin such as abortion. ... We try to restrict it. So why, if we're social tinkering to protect the sanctity of human life, ought we not be for a little tinkering to protect the environment."[77] Add to this the fact that many of these evangelicals groups are also "pro-business environmentalists" and one can sense the difficulty of creating alliances on other issues across the divide.[78]

Let me say more about this here. There have been attempts among evangelicals to bridge the fault lines that are so present in the evangelical world through the publication of such documents as "For the Health of the Nation: An Evangelical Call to Civic Responsibility."[79] Although this is an opportunity, it also creates a divide. At a luncheon held in Washington to discuss the paper, the vice president of Focus on the Family said that he was opposed to a focus on global warming. For him, "the issues of marriage, the issues of pro-life are the issues that define us to this day."[80] Some more "progressive" evangelical activists—including an African-American speaker who may oppose abortion but wants a clearer focus on poverty and racism—feel that a consensus needs to be reached that would enable evangelicals to work on such issues together. For others, however, the attempt to have the religious right and the religious left reach agreement on such things is not viable. Any attempt by progressives to mobilize the religious left is doomed because the "religious left is political smoke and mirrors."[81]

But the fact remains that there is a growing sentiment that an entire range of problems that have been relatively low on the list of priorities advanced by religiously conservative groups have now become much more visible and are being acted upon. This will require much more thought, much less stereotyping, and much more creative action on the part of progressives if we wish to interrupt parts of the agendas of conservative modernization, especially that of neoliberalism.

Think for instance of the following kinds of questions. Can a different kind of religious populism emerge, one that is not authoritarian in nature? Could the (im)moral effects of our economy and the ways in which our economically driven materialism affects our families, our sense of well-being, personal relations, our time commitments, the loss of a sense of purpose other than "getting more" and "getting ahead" become central concerns of the curricula and discussions in Sunday schools, in temples and mosques? Could the concerns about the scandals over corporate pay, over the lack of social and community responsibility of these very same corporations, over tax policies that create even more inequalities in these same communities, over campaign financing, over torture and the loss of civil liberties, and over so much more become more central to the religious discussions in these religious institutions?[82] I am not sanguine that this will automatically occur. But if Wallis and others like him are even partly correct—as I think they may be—then we may begin to see cracks in the ways in which religious impulses are now pulled to the right.[83] And we may see the emergence of conditions in which tactical alliances can be constructed across the religious and secular fault lines that now divide us.

Thus, just as there may be possibilities in the area of environmental politics, so too may there be similar tactical alliances in education over policies such as those found in No Child Left Behind. The strong regimes of accountability and testing and of an increasingly interventionist national state is definitely not something on which authoritarian populist religious conservatives look fondly. Is this a place where critical educators and religious groups that would otherwise (literally) shun each other can cooperate? It is worth considering. The fact that people such as myself and those involved with Phyllis Schlafly are already joining forces to challenge Channel One in schools makes it even more of a possibility.

In saying all of this, however, I do not mean to exclude the millions of people in the United States and elsewhere who do not ground their ethical and political sensibilities within a recognized religious framework or institution. One of the responsibilities that religious communities themselves must take on is to recognize that it is possible to powerfully justify strong ethical and political positions on other bases than religious texts. There is an element of disrespect in this lack of recognition that once again can, and sometimes does, border on arrogance. This is a two-way street; and although I do want to argue that the left needs to be much less dismissive of religious visions and beliefs, religiously committed people must reciprocate as well.

I have been discussing both alliances based on shared principles and those that are "simply" tactical. Once the issue of tactical alliances specifically in education is raised, however, it is nearly impossible to ignore charter schools. For a number of people on both the left and the right, charter schools have been seen as a compromise that can satisfy some of the demands of each group. Here, however, I would urge even more caution. Much of the discussion of these schools has been more than a little romantic. It has accepted the rhetoric of "debureaucratization," experimentation, and diversity as the reality. Yet, as Amy Stuart Wells and her colleagues have demonstrated, charter schools can and do often serve less meritorious ends. As I showed in Chapter 8, they can be manipulated to provide public funding for ideologically, religiously, and educationally problematic programs, with little public accountability. Beneath the statistics of racial equality they supposedly produce, they can exacerbate white flight and can be captured by groups who actually have little interest in the culture and futures of those whom they assume are the Other. They are used as the "constitutive outside" in attacks on public schooling for the majority of children in schools throughout the United States, by deflecting attention to what must be done there. Thus, they often can and do act to deflect attention from our lack of commitment to provide sufficient resources and support for schools in urban and rural areas. And in a number of ways they threaten to become an opening wedge for voucher plans.[84]

Having said this, however, I do not believe that charter schools will go away.[85] Indeed, during the many periods of time when I have lectured and engaged in educational and political work in countries in, say, Latin America and Asia, it has become ever more clear to me that there is considerable interest in the charter school movement. This is especially the case in those nations that have a history of strong states and strong central control over the curriculum, teaching, and evaluation and where the state has been inflexible, highly bureaucratic, and unresponsive. Given this situation, it is absolutely crucial that the terrain of charter schools not be occupied by the forces within the conservative alliance. If charter schools become, as they threaten to, primarily a site where their function is to deflect attention from schools where the vast majority of students go, if they are allowed to be used as vouchers "incognito," if they serve to legitimate concerted attacks on teachers and other educators, then the effects will not be limited to the United States. This will be a worldwide tragedy. For these very reasons, it is crucial that some of our empirical, educational, and political energy goes into guaranteeing that charter schools are a much more progressively inclined set of possibilities than they are today. We need to work so that the elements of good sense in the movement are not lost by it being integrated under the umbrella of conservative modernization.[86]

Making Critical Educational Practices Practical

You will notice that I said "some" of our energy in the previous paragraph. Once again we need to be extremely cautious that by focusing our energies on "alternatives" such as charter schools we are not tacitly enhancing the very real possibility that progressives will spend so much of their attention on them that action in the vast majority of schools will take a back seat. While all of the tactical and strategic foci I have mentioned are important, I believe that one area in particular should be at the center of our concerns as educators—providing real answers to real practical problems in education. I noted this in Chapter 4, but it needs to be stressed again. By showing successful struggles to build a critical and democratic education in real schools and real communities with real teachers and students today, attention is refocused on action not only in charter schools but on local elementary, middle, and secondary schools in communities much like those in which most of us spend our lives. Thus, publicizing such "stories" makes critical education seem actually "doable," not merely a utopian vision dreamed up by "critical theorists" in education.

For this very reason, as I have stressed repeatedly throughout this book, political/educational interventions such as the popular and widely translated book *Democratic Schools* and the increasingly influential journal *Rethinking Schools* become even more important.[87] As I showed in Chapters 3 and 4, this is crucial if we are indeed to interrupt the right. Because the right does have an advantage of speaking in "common sense" and in "plain-folks Americanism"—and peoples' common sense does have elements of good and bad sense within itself—we can also use these progressively inclined elements to show that it is not only the right that has answers to what are real and important issues of educational practice.

For example, the specific vocational and academic programs in which curricula and teaching are linked to paid work and to the economy in socially progressive ways in the Rindge School of Technical Arts in the Boston area powerfully demonstrate that those students and parents who are (justifiably) deeply concerned about their economic futures do not have to turn to neoliberal policies to find practical answers to their questions.[88] I can think of little that is more important than this.

The forces of conservative modernization have colonized the space of practice and of providing answers to the question of "What do I do on Monday?" in part not because the right has all the answers, but because the left has too often evacuated that space.

Here again, we have much to learn from the right. Although we do not need progressive imitators of, say, E. D. Hirsch, we do need to be much more active in actually attempting to provide answers to teachers, community members, and an increasingly skeptical public that pose questions such as what will I teach, how will I teach it, how will I evaluate its success—in essence, all those practical questions that people have a right to ask and to which they are entitled to get sensible answers—so that they are taken very seriously. In the absence of this, we are left standing on the sidelines while the right reconstructs not only common sense but the schools that help produce it.

This is where the work engaged in by several critically inclined practicing educators has proven to be so important. Debbie Meier and her colleagues at Central Park East School in New York and at Mission Hill School in Boston; Bob Peterson, Rita Tenorio, and their colleagues at Fratney Street School in Milwaukee; the staff at Rindge School; and many other educators, such as Barbara Brodhagen, in similar schools throughout the country provide critical models of answering the day-to-day questions that I have noted. They also directly respond to the arguments that are made by neoliberals, neoconservatives, and authoritarian populists. They do this not only by defending the very idea of a truly public school (although they are very good at marshaling such a defense),[89] but also by demonstrating workable alternatives that are based both on high expectations for their diverse students and on a deep-seated respect for the cultures, histories, and experiences of these students and their parents and local communities.[90] Only in this way can the neoliberal, neoconservative, and managerial factions of the new alliance be undercut at the level of the school.

Hope as a Resource

Much more could be said about interrupting the right and about building workable alternatives, but there is a limit to what can be done in any one book. I have written this book to contribute to an ongoing set of crucial debates about the means and ends of our educational institutions and about their connections to larger institutions and power relations. Keeping such debates alive and vibrant is one of the best ways of challenging "the curriculum of the dead." To stimulate such discussion, I want to continue a practice that I began in *Official Knowledge* by again giving my postal and e-mail address for people to raise questions about or affirm my arguments here, or to send your own stories about successful interruptions of the conservative tendencies now so powerful in education. I can be reached at the University of Wisconsin, Department of Curriculum and Instruction, 225 North Mills Street, Madison, WI 53706, USA, or at the following e-mail address: apple@education.wisc.edu. Building and defending a truly democratic and critical education is a collective project. We have much to learn from each other.

Let me end with something that I always want to keep in the forefront of my own consciousness when times are difficult. Sustained political and cultural transformations are impossible "without the hope of a better society that we can, in principle and in outline, imagine."[91] One of my hopes is that this volume will contribute to the larger movement that is struggling to loosen the grip of the narrow concepts of "reality" and "democracy" that have been circulated by neoliberals and neoconservatives in education and so much else over the past decades. As I showed in Chapter 1, there historically have been alternatives to the limited and increasingly hypocritical conception of democracy that, unfortunately, even social democratic parties (under the label of the "third way") in many nations have come to accept. In the words of Panitch and Leys, we need "to insist on a far fuller and richer democracy than anything now available. It is time to reject the prevailing disparagement of anything collective as 'unrealistic' and to insist on the moral and practical rightness, as well as the necessity, of egalitarian social and economic arrangements." As they go on to say, this requires "the development of popular democratic capacities and the structures that nurture rather than stifle or trivialize them."[92] The movements I have analyzed in Educating the "Right" Way may be "wrong," not "right." They may in fact "stifle or trivialize" a vision of democracy that is based on the common good. But they certainly don't have trivial effects, not only on my former student Joseph but on millions of people all over the world. Our children, our teachers, and our communities deserve something better. And people who are deeply committed to doing something about it, like many of you, are neither "creeps" nor "a disgrace to the American flag." Indeed, we might say that their and your actions in demanding that this society take seriously, not simply rhetorically, its responsibilities toward our children and to challenging the structures of inequality that are so pervasive here makes them and you true patriots.

Notes

Preface

1. Michael W. Apple and James A. Beane, eds., *Democratic Schools* (Alexandria, Va.: Association for Supervision and Curriculum Development, 1995).
2. See Michael W. Apple, et al., *The State and the Politics of Knowledge* (New York: RoutledgeFalmer, 2003).
3. I have purposely put the word "Americans" in quotation marks for a specific reason. Perhaps because I have spent a good deal of time working on democratizing educational policy and practice throughout Central and South America, it is clear to me these, too, are "America." There is something arrogant about the fact that the word American has been taken over by one nation out of the many more that actually exist in the Americas.
4. Michael W. Apple, *Ideology and Curriculum* (Boston: Routledge and Kegan Paul, 1979). See also Michael W. Apple, *Ideology and Curriculum,* 3rd ed. (New York: RoutledgeFalmer, 2004).
5. "Ten Most Harmful Books of the 19th and 20th Centuries," *Human Events,* May 31, 2005. I am indebted to Catherine Bernard for bringing this list to my attention.
6. See my discussion of this in Apple, *Ideology and Curriculum,* 3rd ed., especially Chapter 9.
7. Jane Smiley, "Stable Relationships," *The Guardian Review,* October 16, 2004, 4.
8. One of many examples of this is described in James Dao, "Sleepy Election is Jolted by Evolution," *New York Times,* May 17, 2005, A12. See also

Amy Binder, *Contentious Curricula: Afrocentrism and Creationism in American Public Schools* (Princeton, N.J.: Princeton University Press, 2002). Conservative leaders within Catholicism have recently become more active in the debate over "intelligent design" and evolution, offering public support for theories of intelligent design as "truth." See Cornelia Dean, "Scientists Ask Pope For Clarification On Evolution Stance," *New York Times,* July 13, 2005, A18.

9. See David Cohen and Heather Hill, *Learning Policy: When State Education Reform Works* (New Haven, Conn.: Yale University Press, 2001).

10. For a popular, but quite telling, analysis of this process, see Thomas Frank, *What's the Matter With Kansas: How Conservatives Won the Heart of America* (New York: Metropolitan Books, 2004).

11. Michael W. Apple, *Cultural Politics and Education* (New York: Teachers College Press, 1996).

12. Raymond Williams, *Resources of Hope* (New York: Verso, 1989), 19.

13. Ibid., 322.

14. See Jean Anyon, *Radical Possibilities* (New York: Routledge, 2005); Eric Gutstein, *Reading and Writing the World With Mathematics* (New York: Routledge, 2006); Wolff-Michael Roth and Angela Barton, *Rethinking Scientific Literacy* (New York: RoutledgeFalmer, 2004); Apple, et al., *The State and the Politics of Knowledge;* and Michael W. Apple and Kristen Buras, eds., *The Subaltern Speak* (New York: Routledge, 2006).

Chapter 1

1. For a discussion of this and of the problems of using this dichotomy between phonics and whole language, see Gerald Coles, *Reading Lessons* (New York: Hill & Wang, 1998).

2. I have demonstrated these connections in a number of places. See, for example, Michael W. Apple, *Ideology and Curriculum,* 3rd ed. (New York: RoutledgeFalmer, 2004); Michael W. Apple, *Education and Power,* 2d ed. (New York: Routledge, 1995); Michael W. Apple, *Teachers and Texts* (New York: Routledge, 1988); and Michael W. Apple, *Official Knowledge,* 2d ed. (New York: Routledge, 2000). See also James Loewen, *Lies My Teacher Told Me* (New York: The New Press, 1995).

3. See Stephen Ball, *Education Reform: A Critical and Post-Structural Approach* (Buckingham, England: Open University Press, 1994).

4. An articulate and thoughtful analysis of these relations is Jean Anyon's *Ghetto Schooling: A Political Economy of Urban Educational Reform* (New York: Teachers College Press, 1997). See also Grace Kao, Marta Tienda, and Barbara Schneider, "Race and Ethnic Variation in Academic Performance," in *Research in Sociology of Education and Socialization, Volume 11,* ed. Aaron Pallas (Greenwich, Conn.: JAI Press, 1996), 263–97.

5. This is described in considerably more detail in Michael W. Apple, *Cultural Politics and Education* (New York: Teachers College Press, 1996), 68–90.

6. Edward Wyatt, "Investors See Room for Profit in the Demand for Education," *New York Times*, November 4, 1999, A1.

7. Ibid.

8. Ibid.

9. Richard Rorty, *Achieving Our Country: Leftist Thought in Twentieth-Century America* (Cambridge, Mass.: Harvard University Press, 1998), 14.

10. See, for example, Michael W. Apple and James A. Beane, eds., *Democratic Schools* (Alexandria, Va.: Association for Supervision and Curriculum Development, 1995) and Michael W. Apple and James A. Beane, eds., *Democratic Schools: Lessons from the Chalk Face* (Buckingham, England: Open University Press, 1999).

11. Noam Chomsky, *Profits Over People: Neoliberalism and the Global Order* (New York: Seven Stories Press, 1999), 145.

12. See, for example, Raymond Williams, *Keywords: A Vocabulary of Culture and Society* (New York: Oxford University Press, 1983).

13. Eric Hobsbawm, *The Age of Extremes: A History of the World, 1914–1991* (New York: Pantheon, 1994), 3.

14. Eric Foner, *The Story of American Freedom* (New York: W. W. Norton, 1998), 4.

15. Ibid.

16. Ibid., 4.

17. Ibid., 7–8.

18. Ibid., 8.

19. Ibid., 9. See also Nancy Fraser and Linda Gordon, "A Genealogy of Dependency," *Signs* 19 (Winter 1994): 309–36.

20. Foner, *Story of American Freedom*, 10.

21. Ibid., xx. Foner's book is absolutely essential for anyone interested in the continuing struggle over what freedom means and how it has been embodied in our daily life.

22. Ibid., 264.

23. Ibid., 269.

24. Ibid., 308–9.

25. William Bennett, Chester E. Finn Jr., and John T. E. Cribb Jr., *The Educated Child* (New York: The Free Press, 1999) and William Bennett, *Our Children and Our Country* (New York: Simon & Schuster, 1988).

26. Foner, *Story of American Freedom*, 310–11.

27. Thomas Frank, *What's the Matter With Kansas: How Conservatives Won the Heart of America* (New York: Metropolitan Books, 2004).

28. Foner, *Story of American Freedom*, 317–18.

29. Charles W. Mills argues insightfully that nearly all of our economic, political, and cultural/educational institutions in the past and today are undergirded by what he calls "the racial contract" that marginalizes people of color. See Charles W. Mills, *The Racial Contract* (Ithaca, N.Y.: Cornell University Press, 1997).

30. Robert McChesney, "Introduction" to Noam Chomsky, *Profit Over People: Neoliberalism and the Global Order* (New York: Seven Stories Press, 1999), 7.

31. Ibid., 8.

32. Apple, *Cultural Politics and Education*.

33. McChesney, "Introduction," 11.

34. Chomsky, *Profit Over People,* 39.

35. Adam Smith, *The Wealth of Nations* (Oxford: Clarendon Press, 1976), 709–10.

36. Stuart Hall, "The Problem of Ideology: Marxism without Guarantees," in *Stuart Hall: Critical Dialogues in Cultural Studies,* ed. David Morley and Kuan-Hsing Chen (New York: Routledge, 1996), 40.

37. For more on this, see Michael W. Apple, Jane Kenway, and Michael Singh, eds., *Globalizing Education: Policies, Pedagogies, and Politics* (New York: Peter Lang, 2005).

38. Hall, "The Problem of Ideology," 37.

39. Apple, *Cultural Politics and Education;* see especially 68–90.

40. Jorge Larrain, "Stuart Hall and the Marxist Concept of Ideology," in *Stuart Hall: Critical Dialogues in Cultural Studies,* ed. David Morley and Kuan-Hsing Chen (New York: Routledge, 1996), 68.

41. See Gilles Kepel, *Jihad: The Trial of Political Islam* (Cambridge, Mass.: Belknap Press of Harvard University Press, 2002) and Gilles Kepel, *Allah in the West: Islamic Movements in America and Europe* (Stanford, Calif.: Stanford University Press, 1997) for a more complicated sense of the United States' role in supporting a number of the movements that we now see as "threats to civilization" and for a better sense of the various Islamic tendencies in the West.

42. Foner, *Story of American Freedom,* 119.

43. Ibid., 121.

44. Ibid., 134.

45. I have discussed this at greater length in Michael W. Apple, *Ideology and Curriculum*, 3rd ed. (New York: RoutledgeFalmer, 2004).

46. Such forced allegiance had a long history in Europe as well of course. See, for example, Janet Liebman Jacobs, *Hidden Heritage: The Legacy of the Crypto-Jews* (Berkeley: University of California Press, 2002).

47. Foner, *Story of American Freedom,* 26.

48. Ibid., 26–27.

49. Warren A. Nord, *Religion and American Education: Rethinking a National Dilemma* (Chapel Hill: University of North Carolina Press, 1995), 8.

50. Ibid.

51. See Steven Vryhof, *Between Memory and Vision: The Case for Faith-Based Schooling* (Grand Rapids, Mich.: William B. Eerdmans Publishing Co., 2004) for further discussion of this from the point of view of one of the advocates of faith-based schooling.

52. Nord, *Religion and American Education,* 32.

53. Karl Marx and Friedrich Engels, *Manifesto of the Communist Party,* in *Marx and Engels: Basic Writings on Politics and Philosophy,* ed. Lewis S.

Feuer (New York: Anchor Books, 1959), 10. For a more personal account of what this meant to Marx, see Francis Wheen, *Karl Marx: A Life* (New York: W. W. Norton, 1999).

54. The writings on this issue are vast and filled with a good deal of empirical and theoretical debate. For a brief overview, see, for example, James A. Beckford, *Religion and Advanced Industrial Society* (New York: Routledge, 1989).

55. Nord, *Religion and American Education,* 50.

56. Ibid., 51.

57. Ibid., 65.

58. Ibid., 65.

59. Ibid., 67.

60. Beckford, *Religion and Advanced Industrial Society,* 25.

61. Ibid., 18.

62. Ibid., 6–7.

63. Ibid., 89–105.

64. Michel Foucault, "The Subject and Power," in *Michel Foucault: Beyond Structuralism and Hermeneutics,* ed. Herbert Dreyfus and Paul Rabinow (Chicago: University of Chicago Press, 1982), 215.

65. Beckford, *Religion and Industrial Society,* 132–33.

66. Ibid., 142. See also Stuart Hall and Lawrence Grossberg, "On Postmodernism and Articulation: An Interview with Stuart Hall," in *Stuart Hall: Critical Dialogues in Cultural Studies,* ed. David Morley and Kuan-Hsing Chen (New York: Routledge, 1996), 142.

67. John Clarke and Janet Newman, *The Managerial State* (Thousand Oaks, Calif.: Sage, 1997), 27–28.

68. Ibid., 93.

69. See the analysis of managerial discourse in James Paul Gee, Glynda Hull, and Colin Lankshear, *The New Work Order: Behind the Language of the New Capitalism* (Boulder, Colo.: Westview Press, 1996).

70. Clarke and Newman, *The Managerial State,* 76. Clarke and Newman argue that corporate missions have moved from the bare pursuit of efficiency to the pursuit of "excellence" and the achievement of continuous improvement. In their words, there has been an "epidemic of quality." There is of course nothing necessarily wrong with pursuing quality, but much of this represents the colonization of professional discourse by corporate models whose ultimate concern is not quality, but profit.

71. Ibid., 30.

72. Jennifer Daryl Slack, "The Theory and Method of Articulation in Cultural Studies," in *Stuart Hall: Critical Dialogues in Cultural Studies,* ed. David Morley and Kuan-Hsing Chen (New York: Routledge, 1996), 113.

73. Ibid.

Chapter 2

1. Madeleine Arnot, "Schooling for Social Justice," unpublished paper, University of Cambridge, Department of Education, 1990.

2. William Greider, *One World, Ready or Not* (New York: Simon & Schuster, 1997).

3. See Michael W. Apple, *Cultural Politics and Education* (New York: Teachers College Press, 1996) and Michael W. Apple, *Official Knowledge*, 2d ed. (New York: Routledge, 2000).

4. I am drawing upon Roger Dale, "The Thatcherite Project in Education," *Critical Social Policy* 9 (Winter 1989/1990): 4–19. Because of the size and complexity of the United States, I cannot focus on all the policy issues and initiatives now being debated or implemented. For further descriptions, see the chapters on policy research in William Pink and George Noblit, eds., *Continuity and Contradiction: The Futures of the Sociology of Education* (Cresskill, N.J.: Hampton Press, 1995).

5. Apple, *Cultural Politics and Education* and Ted Honderich, *Conservatism* (Boulder, Colo.: Westview Press, 1990).

6. Given the current emphasis on this by neoliberals, it may be the case that although Bowles and Gintis's book on the relationship between education and capitalism, *Schooling in Capitalist America,* was reductive, economistic, and essentializing when it first appeared in 1976, oddly it may be more accurate today. See Samuel Bowles and Herbert Gintis, *Schooling in Capitalist America* (New York: Basic Books, 1976). For criticism of their position, see Michael W. Apple, *Teachers and Texts* (New York: Routledge, 1988); Michael W. Apple, *Education and Power*, 2d ed. (New York: Routledge, 1995); and Mike Cole, ed., *Bowles and Gintis Revisited* (New York: Falmer Press, 1988).

7. See Michael W. Apple, *Ideology and Curriculum,* 3rd ed. (New York: RoutledgeFalmer, 2004).

8. Stephen Ball, *Education Reform* (Philadelphia: Open University Press, 1994) and Apple, *Cultural Politics and Education.*

9. Apple, *Teachers and Texts,* 31–78 and Sandra Acker, "Gender and Teachers' Work," in *Review of Research in Education, Volume 21,* ed. Michael W. Apple (Washington, D.C.: American Educational Research Association, 1995), 99–162. A number of the larger gender implications of neoliberalism in education and the economy can be seen in Jacky Brine, *Under-Educating Women; Globalizing Inequality* (Philadelphia: Open University Press, 1992) and Madeleine Arnot, Miriam David, and Gaby Weiner, *Closing the Gender Gap: Postwar Education and Social Change* (Cambridge, England: Polity Press, 1999).

10. John Chubb and Terry Moe, *Politics, Markets, and America's Schools* (Washington, D.C.: The Brookings Institution, 1990). See also Ernest House, *Schools for Sale* (New York: Teachers College Press, 1998).

11. See the discussion of these arguments in Kristen L. Buras and Michael W. Apple, "School Choice, Neoliberal Promises, and Unpromising Evidence," *Educational Policy* 19 (July 2005): 550–64.

12. See Amy Stuart Wells, *Time to Choose* (New York: Hill & Wang, 1993); Jeffrey Henig, *Rethinking School Choice* (Princeton, N.J.: Princeton University Press, 1994); Kevin Smith and Kenneth Meier, eds., *The Case Against School Choice* (Armonk, N.Y.: M. E. Sharpe, 1995); Bruce Fuller,

Elizabeth Burr, Luis Huerta, Susan Puryear, and Edward Wexler, *School Choice: Abundant Hopes, Scarce Evidence of Results* (Berkeley and Stanford: Policy Analysis for California Education, University of California at Berkeley and Stanford University, 1999); and John F. Witte, *The Market Approach to Education* (Princeton, N.J.: Princeton University Press, 2000).

13. Geoff Whitty, "Creating Quasi-Markets in Education," in *Review of Research in Education, Volume 22,* ed. Michael W. Apple (Washington, DC: American Educational Research Association, 1997), 17. See also Chubb and Moe, *Politics, Markets, and America's Schools* and Gary Rosen, "Are School Vouchers Un-American?" *Commentary* 109 (February 2000): 26–31.

14. Quoted in Whitty, "Creating Quasi-Markets in Education," 17.

15. See, for example, Geoff Whitty, Sally Power, and David Halpin, *Devolution and Choice in Education* (Philadelphia: Open University Press, 1998) and Hugh Lauder and David Hughes, *Trading in Futures: Why Markets in Education Don't Work* (Philadelphia: Open University Press, 1999).

16. See Apple, *Cultural Politics and Education,* especially Chapter 4, for a description of the ways in which many current social and educational policies often widen racial gaps.

17. Whitty, "Creating Quasi-Markets in Education," 58.

18. Henig, *Rethinking School Choice,* 22.

19. See Whitty, "Creating Quasi-Markets in Education," Lauder and Hughes, *Trading in Futures,* and Apple, *Cultural Politics and Education.*

20. Many times, however, these initiatives are actually "unfunded mandates." That is, requirements such as these are made mandatory, but no additional funding is provided to accomplish them. The intensification of teachers' labor at all levels of the education system that results from this situation is very visible. On the history of education for employment, see Herbert Kliebard, *Schooled to Work: Vocationalism and the American Curriculum, 1876–1946* (New York: Teachers College Press, 1999). For clear and thoughtful analyses of other effects on higher education, see Geoffrey White, ed., *Campus, Inc.* (Amherst, N.Y.: Prometheus Books, 2000) and Sheila Slaughter and Larry L. Leslie, *Academic Capitalism* (Baltimore: Johns Hopkins University Press, 1997).

21. For further discussion of the powerful forces of commercialism in schools, see Alex Molnar, *School Commercialism* (New York: Routledge, 2005).

22. I have engaged in a much more detailed analysis of Channel One in Apple, *Official Knowledge,* 89–112. See also Alex Molnar, *Giving Kids the Business* (Boulder, Colo.: Westview Press, 1996). A good example as well is provided by financially troubled ZapMe!, which gives free computer equipment in return for demographic information on children in schools. Of course, there is a history of resistance to things such as Channel One. UNPLUG, a student-led group, has been in the forefront of contesting the commercialization of schools. Further, as I discuss in

my final chapter, both conservative and progressive groups have joined forces to act against Channel One.

23. Apple, *Cultural Politics and Education,* 68–90 and Greider, *One World, Ready or Not.*

24. Ibid. See also, Christopher Cook, "Temps Demand a New Deal," *The Nation,* March 27, 2000, 13–19.

25. Nancy Fraser, *Unruly Practices* (Minneapolis: University of Minnesota Press, 1989), 168.

26. Ibid., 172. See also the discussion of how gains in one sphere of social life can be "transported" into another sphere in Samuel Bowles and Herbert Gintis, *Democracy and Capitalism* (New York: Basic Books, 1986) and Apple, *Teachers and Texts.* On the history of such positions in health care, see Sandra Opdycke, *No One Was Turned Away* (New York: Oxford University Press, 1999).

27. Fraser, *Unruly Practices,* 172.

28. Roger Dale, *The State and Education Policy* (Philadelphia: Open University Press, 1989).

29. For further discussion of residual and emergent ideological forms, see Raymond Williams, *Marxism and Literature* (New York: Oxford University Press, 1977).

30. See Allen Hunter, *Children in the Service of Conservatism* (Madison: University of Wisconsin, Institute for Legal Studies, 1988) and Apple, *Cultural Politics and Education.*

31. See, for example, E. D. Hirsch Jr., *The Schools We Need and Why We Don't Have Them* (New York: Doubleday, 1996). For an insightful critique of Hirsch's position, see Kristen L. Buras, "Questioning Core Assumptions: A Critical Reading of E. D. Hirsch's *The Schools We Need and Why We Don't Have Them,*" *Harvard Educational Review* 69 (Spring 1999): 67–93. See also Susan Ohanian, *One Size Fits Few: The Folly of Educational Standards* (Portsmouth, N.H.: Heinemann, 1999).

32. William Bennett, *The Book of Virtues* (New York: Simon & Schuster, 1994).

33. William Bennett, *Our Children and Our Country* (New York: Simon & Schuster, 1988), 8–10.

34. See Amy Stuart Wells, *Beyond the Rhetoric of Charter School Reform* (Los Angeles: University of California at Los Angeles, Graduate School of Education and Information Studies, 1999).

35. Mary Douglas, *Purity and Danger* (London: Routledge, 1966).

36. See, for example, Cameron McCarthy and Warren Crichlow, eds., *Race, Identity, and Representation in Education* (New York: Routledge, 1994).

37. See, for example, Diane Ravitch, *Left Back* (New York: Simon & Schuster, 2000). See my response to Ravitch in Michael W. Apple, "Standards, Subject Matter, and a Romantic Past," *Educational Policy* 15 (May 2001): 7–36.

38. This is treated in greater depth in Apple, *Ideology and Curriculum.*

39. Lawrence Levine, *The Opening of the American Mind* (Boston: Beacon Press, 1996), 20.

40. Ibid.

41. Ibid., 15. See also Apple, *Ideology and Curriculum* and Herbert Kliebard, *The Struggle for the American Curriculum,* 2d ed. (New York: Routledge, 1995).

42. Levine, *The Opening of the American Mind,* 15.

43. Catherine Cornbleth and Dexter Waugh, *The Great Speckled Bird* (New York: St. Martin's Press, 1995).

44. For a counternarrative on the history of the United States, see Howard Zinn, *A People's History of the United States* (New York: HarperCollins, 1999). See also Howard Zinn, *The Howard Zinn Reader* (New York: Seven Stories Press, 1997) and Howard Zinn, *The Future of History* (Monroe, Maine: Common Courage Press, 1999).

45. This is often done through a process of "mentioning" where texts and curricula include material on the contributions of women and "minority" groups but never allow the reader to see the world through the eyes of oppressed groups. Or as is the case in the discourse of "we are all immigrants," compromises are made so that the myth of historical similarity is constructed at the same time as economic divides among groups grow worse and worse. See Apple, *Official Knowledge,* 42–60.

46. Diane Ravitch, *National Standards in American Education* (Washington, D.C.: The Brookings Institution, 1995).

47. In the face of concerted criticism, the NCTM recently has officially voted to return to more of an emphasis on traditional mathematical concerns and methods of teaching. See Anemona Hartocollis, "Math Teachers Back Return of Education to Basic Skills," *New York Times,* April 15, 2000, A16.

48. This is discussed in more detail in Michael W. Apple, *Power, Meaning, and Identity* (New York: Peter Lang, 1999) and Apple, *Cultural Politics and Education.* See also Ohanian, *One Size Fits Few.*

49. This distinction is developed in more depth in Dale, *The State and Education Policy.*

50. For a detailed critical discussion of the effects of this on curricula, teaching, and evaluation, see Linda McNeil, *Contradictions of School Reform* (New York: Routledge, 2000).

51. See Apple, *Education and Power;* Apple, *Teachers and Texts;* and Acker, "Gender and Teachers' Work." Clear gender and class antagonisms are at work here, ones that have a long history. Analyses of the ways in which race intersects with these dynamics and helps construct the history and labor process of teaching has been somewhat less developed. However, the ongoing work of Michelle Foster and Michael Fultz is quite helpful in this regard.

52. Richard Herrnstein and Charles Murray, *The Bell Curve* (New York: Free Press, 1994).

53. See Michael Omi and Howard Winant, *Racial Formation in the United States,* 2d ed. (New York: Routledge, 1994) and Steven Selden, *Inheriting Shame* (New York: Teachers College Press, 1999). Selden's book in particular demonstrates how very prevalent constructions of race were in a

wide range of educational policies and practices, including many programs and individuals whose participation in, say, the popular eugenics movement is little known.

54. Ibid. See also Richard Dyer, *White* (New York: Routledge, 1997) and Cornel West, *Race Matters* (New York: Vintage Books, 1994).

55. Rebecca Klatch, *Women of the New Right* (Philadelphia: Temple University Press, 1987). For criticism of some of these positions, and especially those espoused by Herrnstein and Murray, see Joe Kincheloe, Shirley Steinberg, and Aaron D. Gresson, eds., *Measured Lies* (New York: St. Martin's Press, 1996).

56. For further discussion of this, see Apple, *Cultural Politics and Education,* 11–13.

57. Hunter, *Children in the Service of Conservatism,* 15.

58. Quoted in Ibid., 57.

59. Ibid.

60. The power of the text and its contradictory impulses have been detailed in Apple, *Teachers and Texts* and Apple, *Official Knowledge*. For more discussion of the ways in which struggles over the textbook help mobilize conservative activists, see Apple, *Cultural Politics and Education,* 42–67.

61. Delfattore, *What Johnny Shouldn't Read,* 123.

62. Ibid., 139.

63. The history and influence of the state's role in defining official knowledge and in textbooks is developed in much more depth in Apple, *Teachers and Texts* and Apple, *Official Knowledge*. See also Cornbleth and Waugh, *The Great Speckled Bird.*

64. See Alexandra S. Dimick and Michael W. Apple, "Texas and the Politics of Abstinence-Only Textbooks," *Teachers College Record*, May 2, 2005.

65. See Delfattore, *What Johnny Shouldn't Read;* Ralph Reed, *After the Revolution* (Dallas: Word Publishing, 1996); and Fritz Detwiler, *Standing on the Premises of God* (New York: New York University Press, 1999).

66. Anita Oliver and I provide an analysis of a concrete instance of this in Apple, *Cultural Politics and Education,* 42–67.

67. Although he limits himself to a discussion of the nation as an "imagined community," I am extending Benedict Anderson's metaphor to include religious communities as well since many of the attributes are the same. See Benedict Anderson, *Imagined Communities* (New York: Verso, 1991).

68. Fraser, *Unruly Practices,* 172–73.

69. Basil Bernstein makes an important distinction between those fractions of the new middle class who work for the state and those who work in the private sector. They may have different ideological and educational commitments. See Basil Bernstein, *The Structuring of Pedagogic Discourse* (New York: Routledge, 1990). For more on the ways "intermediate" classes and class fractions operate and interpret their worlds, see Erik Olin Wright, ed., *The Debate on Classes* (New York: Verso, 1998); Erik Olin Wright, *Classes* (New York: Verso, 1985); Erik Olin Wright, *Class Counts*

(New York: Cambridge University Press, 1997); and Pierre Bourdieu, *Distinction* (Cambridge, Mass.: Harvard University Press, 1984).

70. See Bourdieu, *Distinction;* Pierre Bourdieu, *Homo Academicus* (Stanford, Calif.: Stanford University Press, 1988); and Pierre Bourdieu, *The State Nobility* (Stanford, Calif.: Stanford University Press, 1996).

71. A combination of the work of Bernstein, Wright, and Bourdieu would be useful in understanding this class. A satirical, but still interesting, analysis of a segment of this class can be found in the work of the conservative commentator David Brooks. See David Brooks, *Bobos in Paradise* (New York: Simon & Schuster, 2000).

72. See Apple, *Cultural Politics and Education,* 22–41.

73. See especially Michael W. Apple and James A. Beane, eds., *Democratic Schools* (Alexandria, Va.: Association for Supervision and Curriculum Development, 1995); Michael W. Apple and James A. Beane, eds., *Democratic Schools: Lessons from the Chalk Face* (Buckingham, England: Open University Press, 1999); and Gregory Smith, *Public Schools That Work* (New York: Routledge, 1993). Also of considerable interest here is the work on detracking and educational reform by Jeannie Oakes. See Jeannie Oakes, Karen H. Quartz, Steve Ryan, and Martin Lipton, *Becoming Good American Schools* (San Francisco: Jossey-Bass, 2000).

74. See Jacques Steinberg, "Blue Books Closed, Students Boycott Standardized Tests," *New York Times,* April 13, 2000, A1, A22. It remains to be seen whether this will grow. It is also unclear whether children of the poor and culturally and economically disenfranchised will participate widely in this. After all, affluent children *do* have options and can compensate for not having tests scores. This may not be the case for the children of those this society calls the "Other."

75. See, for example, the journal *Rethinking Schools.* It is one of the very best indicators of progressive struggles, policies, and practices in education. Information can be obtained from Rethinking Schools, 1001 E. Keefe Avenue, Milwaukee, WI 53212, USA or via its Web site at http://www.rethinkingschools.org.

Chapter 3

1. Geoff Whitty, "Sociology and the Problem of Radical Educational Change," in *Educability, Schools, and Ideology,* ed. Michael Flude and John Ahier (London: Halstead Press, 1974), 112–37.

2. Pierre Bourdieu, *Distinction* (Cambridge, Mass.: Harvard University Press, 1984).

3. Herbert Kliebard, *The Struggle for the American Curriculum,* 2d ed. (New York: Routledge, 1995).

4. John Rury and Jeffrey Mirel, "The Political Economy of Urban Education," in *Review of Research in Education, Volume 22,* ed. Michael W. Apple (Washington, D.C.: American Educational Research Association, 1997), 49–110; Kenneth Teitelbaum, *Schooling for Good Rebels* (New York:

Teachers College Press, 1996); and Steven Selden, *Inheriting Shame* (New York: Teachers College Press, 1999).

5. Michael W. Apple, *Official Knowledge,* 2d ed. (New York: Routledge, 2000) and Michael W. Apple, *Cultural Politics and Education* (New York: Teachers College Press, 1996).

6. Richard Herrnstein and Charles Murray, *The Bell Curve* (New York: Free Press, 1994). See also Joe Kincheloe, Shirley Steinberg, and Aaron D. Gresson, eds., *Measured Lies* (New York: St. Martin's Press, 1997).

7. Apple, *Cultural Politics and Education,* 22–41.

8. Stuart Ranson, "Theorizing Educational Policy," *Journal of Education Policy* 10 (July 1995): 427.

9. David Gillborn, "Race, Nation, and Education," unpublished paper, Institute of Education, University of London, 1997, 2.

10. Gary McCulloch, "Privatising the Past," *British Journal of Educational Studies* 45 (March 1997): 80.

11. See E. D. Hirsch Jr., *The Schools We Need and Why We Don't Have Them* (New York: Doubleday, 1996).

12. Quoted in McCulloch, "Privatising the Past," 78.

13. Ibid.

14. Ibid.

15. John Chubb and Terry Moe, *Politics, Markets, and American Schools* (Washington, D.C.: The Brookings Institution, 1990) and Geoff Whitty, "Creating Quasi-Markets in Education," in *Review of Research in Education, Volume 22,* ed. Michael W. Apple (Washington, D.C.: American Educational Research Association, 1997), 3–47.

16. David Gillborn, "Racism and Reform," *British Educational Research Journal* 23 (June 1997): 357.

17. Michael W. Apple, *Power, Meaning, and Identity* (New York: Peter Lang, 1999) and Michael W. Apple, *Teachers and Texts* (New York: Routledge, 1988). Of course, there has been a considerable amount of literature on the question of "clarity" in critical educational writings, with contributions on both sides made by Burbules, Giroux, Lather, Gitlin, myself, and a number of others. My own position on this is that such a debate is essential and that while there is a danger in sacrificing theoretical elegance and the richness and subtlety of language in our attempts to be clear, there is still a good deal of arrogance and truly sloppy and merely rhetorical writing within the multiple communities of critical educational work. Obviously, there is a need to respond to complexity, but there is also a need not to marginalize sympathetic readers.

18. Gillborn, "Racism and Reform," 353.

19. Ibid.

20. Herrnstein and Murray, *The Bell Curve* and Hirsch, *The Schools We Need and Why We Don't Have Them.*

21. Roger Dale quoted in Ian Menter, Yolande Muschamp, Peter Nicholls, Jenny Ozga, with Andrew Pollard, *Work and Identity in the Primary School* (Philadelphia: Open University Press, 1997), 27.

22. Menter et al., *Work and Identity in the Primary School,* 27.

23. See Whitty, "Creating Quasi-Markets in Education." See also Geoff Whitty, Tony Edwards, and Sharon Gewirtz, *Specialization and Choice in Urban Education* (London: Routledge, 1993) and Apple, *Cultural Politics and Education.* The integration of markets, standards, and performance indicators is clearly expressed in David Stearns and James Harvey, *A Legacy of Learning: Your Stake in Standards and New Kinds of Public Schools* (Washington, D.C.: The Brookings Institution, 2000). This book is an intriguing example of "plain talk" and manages to strike a series of populist notes while at the same time placing the needs of the economy and efficiency at the very center of its proposals for "democracy."

24. Chubb and Moe, *Politics, Markets, and American Schools.*

25. Sally Power, David Halpin, and John Fitz, "Underpinning Choice and Diversity," in *Educational Reform and Its Consequences,* ed. Sally Tomlinson (London: IPPR/Rivers Oram Press, 1994), 27.

26. Whether there have been significant changes in this regard given the victory by "New Labour" over the Conservatives in the last election is open to question. Certain aspects of neoliberal and neoconservative policies have already been accepted by Labour, such as stringent cost controls on spending put in place by the previous Conservative government and an aggressive focus on "raising standards" in association with strict performance indicators. See, for example, David Gillborn and Deborah Youdell, *Rationing Education* (Philadelphia: Open University Press, 2000).

27. See Power, Halpin, and Fitz, "Underpinning Choice and Diversity" and Gillborn and Youdell, *Rationing Education.*

28. Stephen Ball, Richard Bowe, and Sharon Gewirtz, "Market Forces and Parental Choice," in *Educational Reform and Its Consequences,* ed. Sally Tomlinson (London: IPPR/Rivers Oram Press, 1994), 39.

29. Ibid., 17–19.

30. Mark Olssen, "In Defense of the Welfare State and of Publicly Provided Education," *Journal of Education Policy* 11 (May 1996): 340.

31. See Sally Power, Tony Edwards, Geoff Whitty, and Valerie Wigfall, *Education and the Middle Class* (Philadelphia: Open University Press, 2003) and Stephen Ball *Class Strategies and the Education Market* (London: RoutledgeFalmer, 2003).

32. Ball, Bowe, and Gewirtz, "Market Forces and Parental Choice," 19.

33. See the discussion of the racial state in Michael Omi and Howard Winant, *Racial Formation in the United States* (New York: Routledge, 1994) and the analyses of race and representation in Cameron McCarthy and Warren Crichlow, eds., *Race, Identity, and Representation in Education* (New York: Routledge, 1994) and Cameron McCarthy, *The Uses of Culture* (New York: Routledge, 1998).

34. Bourdieu, *Distinction.*

35. Ball, Bowe, and Gewirtz, "Market Forces and Parental Choice," 20–22.

36. Michelle Fine and Lois Weis, *The Unknown City* (Boston: Beacon Press, 1998) and Mitchell Duneier, *Sidewalk* (New York: Farrar, Straus & Giroux, 1999).

37. Pierre Bourdieu, *The State Nobility* (Stanford, Calif.: Stanford University Press, 1996) and David Swartz, *Culture and Power* (Chicago: University of Chicago Press, 1997).

38. Apple, *Teachers and Texts* and Apple, *Official Knowledge,* 113–36.

39. Whitty, Power, and Halpin, *Devolution and Choice in Education,* 12–13.

40. Ibid., 36.

41. Olssen, "In Defense of the Welfare State and Publicly Provided Education."

42. Whitty, Power, and Halpin, *Devolution and Choice in Education,* 37–38. See also the discussion of managerialism and the state in John Clarke and Janet Newman, *The Managerial State* (Thousand Oaks, Calif.: Sage, 1997).

43. This is discussed in greater detail in Michael W. Apple, *Education and Power,* 2d ed. (New York: Routledge, 1995).

44. See Omi and Winant, *Racial Formation in the United States;* Debbie Epstein and Richard Johnson, *Schooling Sexualities* (Philadelphia: Open University Press, 1998); and Sue Middleton, *Disciplining Sexualities* (New York: Teachers College Press, 1998).

45. Whitty, Power, and Halpin, *Devolution and Choice in Education,* 60–62.

46. Among the best work here is Nancy Fraser, *Unruly Practices* (Minneapolis: University of Minnesota Press, 1989) and Nancy Fraser, *Justice Interruptis* (New York: Routledge, 1997).

47. Whitty, Power, and Halpin, *Devolution and Choice in Education,* 63.

48. Ibid., 67–68. See also Gillborn and Youdell, *Rationing Education.*

49. Youdell and Gillborn's *Rationing Education* demonstrates this clearly. What is also important here is that this has consistently happened even in the face of overt attempts to use such policies to alter existing inequalities. See also Whitty, Power, and Halpin, *Devolution and Choice in Education,* 119–20.

50. Whitty, Power, and Halpin, *Devolution and Choice in Education,* 80.

51. Ibid. See also Gillborn and Youdell, *Rationing Education* and Sharon Gewirtz, Stephen Ball, and Richard Bowe, *Markets, Choice, and Equity in Education* (Philadelphia: Open University Press, 1995). We need to be very cautious of employing these data to legitimate the "model minority" stereotype of Asian students. See Stacey Lee, *Unraveling the Model-Minority Stereotype* (New York: Teachers College Press, 1996).

52. Hugh Lauder and David Hughes, *Trading in Futures* (Philadelphia: Open University Press, 1999), 2.

53. Ibid., 29. See also Phil Brown, "Cultural Capital and Social Exclusion," in *Education: Culture, Economy, and Society,* ed. A. H. Halsey, Hugh Lauder, Phil Brown, and Amy Stuart Wells (New York: Oxford University Press, 1997), 736–49.

54. Lauder and Hughes, *Trading in Futures,* 101.

55. Ibid., 132.

56. See Michael W. Apple, et al., *The State and the Politics of Knowledge* (New York: RoutledgeFalmer, 2003), 109–47.

57. On the issue of a racial contract that underpins nearly all social arrangements in our kind of society, see Charles W. Mills, *The Racial Contract* (Ithaca, N.Y.: Cornell University Press, 1997). I am drawing as well on Benedict Anderson's position that nations are themselves based on "imagined communities." See Benedict Anderson, Imagined Communities (New York: Verso, 1991).

58. See, for example, the analysis of the gender dynamics surrounding neoliberal policies in Madeleine Arnot, Miriam David, and Gaby Weiner, *Closing the Gender Gap* (Cambridge: Polity Press, 1999). The ways in which neoconservative policies act on and through the politics of sexuality and the body as well are nicely described in Epstein and Johnson, *Schooling Sexualities*.

59. Whitty, Power, and Halpin, *Devolution and Choice in Education*, 98. See also Amy Stuart Wells, *Beyond the Rhetoric of Charter School Reform* (Los Angeles: University of California at Los Angeles, Graduate School of Education and Information Studies, 1999).

60. Whitty, Power, and Halpin, *Devolution and Choice in Education*, 112–13.

61. Ibid., 14.

62. Ibid., 42.

63. Jeffrey R. Henig, *Rethinking School Choice: Limits of a Market Metaphor* (Princeton, N.J.: Princeton University Press, 1994), 222. See also some of the comments in Michael Engel, *The Struggle to Control Public Education* (Philadelphia: Temple University Press, 2000).

64. See Jean Anyon, *Radical Possibilities* (New York: Routledge, 2005).

65. See especially the discussion of the role of the state in this in Bourdieu, *The State Nobility*.

66. Loic Wacquant, "Foreword" to Bourdieu, *The State Nobility*, xiii.

67. Bourdieu, *The State Nobility*, 273.

68. Ball, Bowe, and Gewirtz, "Market Forces and Parental Choice," 24.

69. Menter et al., *Work and Identity*, 8.

70. Ibid., 57. The work of Susan Robertson on the global effects of these transformations, especially on teachers, is exceptional. See, for example, Susan Robertson, *A Class Act: Changing Teachers' Work, the State, and Globalization* (New York: Falmer Press, 2000).

71. Ibid., 9.

72. Ibid., 24.

73. Ibid.

74. Apple, *Cultural Politics and Education*, 22–41.

75. Ball, Bowe, and Gewirtz, "Market Forces and Parental Choice," 23.

76. Power, Halpin, and Fitz, "Underpinning Choice and Diversity," 38.

77. Ranson, "Theorizing Educational Policy," 436.

78. Ibid. See also Misook Kim Cho and Michael W. Apple, "Schooling, Work, and Subjectivity," *British Journal of Sociology of Education* 19 (Summer 1998): 269–90.

79. Ranson, "Theorizing Educational Policy," 437.

80. Richard Hatcher and Barry Troyna quoted in ibid., 438.

81. Ranson, "Theorizing Educational Policy," 438.

82. Philip O'Hear, "An Alternative National Curriculum," in *Educational Reform and Its Consequences*, ed. Sally Tomlinson (London: IPPR/Rivers Oram Press, 1994), 66.

83. Ibid., 55–57.

84. Ibid., 68.

85. Ibid., 65–66.

86. Caroline Gipps and Patricia Murphy, *A Fair Test?* (Philadelphia: Open University Press, 1994), 204.

87. See Basil Bernstein, *The Structuring of Pedagogic Discourse* (New York: Routledge, 1990); Basil Bernstein, *Pedagogy, Symbolic Control, and Identity* (Bristol, Pa.: Taylor & Francis, 1996); and Apple, *Official Knowledge*, 61–88.

88. John Evans and Dawn Penney, "The Politics of Pedagogy," *Journal of Education Policy* 10 (January 1995): 27–44. See also Apple, et al., *The State and the Politics of Knowledge*, 81–107.

89. Evans and Penney, "The Politics of Pedagogy," 41–42.

90. See, for example, Robert Linn, "Assessment and Accountability," *Educational Researcher* 29 (March 2000): 4–16; Jeannie Oakes, "Can Tracking Research Inform Practice?" *Educational Researcher* 21 (March 1992): 12–21; Jeannie Oakes, Amy Stuart Wells, Makeba Jones, and Amanda Datnow, "Detracking: The Social Construction of Ability, Cultural Politics, and Resistance to Reform," *Teachers College Record* 98 (Spring 1997): 482–510; and Amy Stuart Wells, Alejandra Lopez, Janelle Scott, and Jennifer Holme, "Charter Schools as Postmodern Paradox: Rethinking Social Stratification in an Age of Deregulated School Choice," *Harvard Educational Review* 69 (Summer 1999): 172–204.

91. See, for example, Michael W. Apple and James A. Beane, eds., *Democratic Schools* (Alexandria, Va.: Association for Supervision and Curriculum Development, 1995).

92. For more disuccion of this, see Pauline Lipman, *High Stakes Education* (New York: RoutledgeFalmer, 2004) and Mary Lee Smith, with Linda Miller-Kahn, Walter Heinecke, and Patricia Jarvis, *Political Spectacle and the Fate of American Schools* (New York: RoutledgeFalmer, 2004).

93. Gillborn and Youdell, *Rationing Education*.

94. See, for example, Stephen Jay Gould, *The Mismeasure of Man* (New York: W. W. Norton, 1981) and Steven Selden, *Inheriting Shame* (New York: Teachers College Press, 1999).

95. Gillborn and Youdell, *Rationing Education*, 194.

96. Ibid., 195.

97. Linda McNeil, *Contradictions of School Reform* (New York: Routledge, 2000).

98. Lipman, *High Stakes Education*.

99. See Glen Y. Wilson, "Effects on Funding Equity of the Arizona Tax Credit Law," paper presented at the annual meeting of the American Educational Research Association, New Orleans, April 2000 and Michele S. Moses, "The Arizona Tax Credit and Hidden Considerations of Justice," paper

presented at the annual meeting of the American Educational Research Association, New Orleans, April 2000. See also Mary Lee Smith, Walter Heinecke, and Audrey Noble, "Assessment Policy and Political Spectacle," *Teachers College Record* 101 (Winter 1999): 157–91.

100. Terri Seddon, "Markets and the English," *British Journal of Sociology of Education* 18 (June 1997): 165–66.

101. Alan Luke, "Series Editor's Introduction" to Jay Lemke, *Textual Politics* (Bristol, Pa.: Taylor & Francis, 1995), vi–vii.

102. Rethinking Schools is one of the best examples of the ways critical academics, elementary/middle/high school teachers, students, and community activists can work together in nonelitist ways. Information can be obtained from Rethinking Schools, 1001 E. Keefe Avenue, Milwaukee, Wisc. 53212, USA. For faxes, the number is 414–964–7220. The Web site is http://www.rethinkingschools.org. For an articulate discussion of Freire's work and of the complexities of putting it into practice in schools, see Maria Pilar O'Cadiz, Pia Lindquist Wong, and Carlos Alberto Torres, *Education and Democracy: Paulo Freire, Social Movements, and Educational Reform in Sao Paulo* (Boulder, Colo.: Westview Press, 1998). Freire's work, however, has too often been appropriated in rhetorical and/ or depoliticized ways in the United States. See my discussion of this in Michael W. Apple, *Power, Meaning, and Identity* (New York: Routledge, 1999).

103. Apple and Beane, eds., *Democratic Schools.*

104. Translations of this volume have been or are due to be published in Japan, Argentina, Brazil, Spain, Portugal, and elsewhere. A Commonwealth edition for the UK, Australia, New Zealand, and other nations has also recently appeared. See Michael W. Apple and James A. Beane, eds., *Democratic Schools: Lessons from the Chalk Face* (Buckingham, England: Open University Press, 1999). Thus, it is clear that providing critical answers to the pressing issues of "What do I do on Monday?" is seen as crucial in a number of nations.

105. Apple, *Teachers and Texts* and Apple, *Power, Meaning, and Identity.*

106. Dennis Carlson and Michael W. Apple, "Critical Educational Theory in Unsettling Times," in *Power/Knowledge/Pedagogy*, ed. Dennis Carlson and Michael W. Apple (Boulder, Colo.: Westview Press, 1998), 1–38.

107. Henry Giroux, *Border Crossings* (Routledge, 1992), 219.

108. One of the clearest discussion of the ethical and political dilemmas of doing critical theoretical and empirical work with due recognition of the importance of connecting this work to the lived culture of social actors in their everyday lives can be found in Fine and Weis, *The Unknown City*, 264–88. See also Carlson and Apple, *Power/Knowledge/Pedagogy* and Linda Tuhiwai Smith, *Decolonizing Methodologies* (New York: ZedBooks, 1999).

Chapter 4

1. Jack Jennings, "From the White House to the School House," in William Lowe Boyd and Debra Mitetzky, eds., *American Educational Governance on Trial* (Chicago: University of Chicago Press, 2003), 291–309.
2. My description here draws on Jennings' clear exposition of the major elements of No Child Left Behind. See ibid., 299–302.
3. Mary Lee Smith, et al., *Political Spectacle and the Fate of American Schools* (New York: RoutledgeFalmer, 2004).
4. Sam Dillon, "Teachers' Union and Districts Sue Over Bush Law," *New York Times,* April 21, 2005, A19.
5. Deborah Meier and George Wood, eds., *Many Children Left Behind: How No Child Left Behind is Damaging Our Children and Our Schools* (Boston: Beacon Press, 2004).
6. See Sam Dillon, " President's Education Law is Finding Few Fans in Utah," *New York Times,* March 6, 2005, 21 and Sam Dillon, "Utah Vote Rejects Parts of Education Law," *New York Times,* April 20, 2005, A14.
7. See Meier and Woods, *Many Children Left Behind* and David Berliner, "The Near Impossibility of Testing for Teacher Quality," *Journal of Teacher Education* 3 (May/June 2005), 205–13.
8. Michael W. Apple, *Official Knowledge: Democratic Education in a Conservative Age,* 2d ed. (New York: Routledge, 2000). In addition, one little recognized aspect of the law is its opening up of schools to further militarization, as the important ongoing work of Ross Collin demonstrates. See note 10.
9. Angela Valenzuela, ed., *Leaving Children Behind: How "Texas-style Accountability Fails Latino Youth* (Albany: State University of New York Press, 2005). See also Linda McNeil, *The Contradictions of School Reform* (New York: Routledge, 2000) and Pauline Lipman, *High Stakes Education* (New York: Routledge, 2004).
10. The ongoing work of Ross Collin at the University of Wisconsin, Madison is exemplary in its analysis of the history of such school related programs and issues. See, for example, Ross Collin, "Symbolic Struggles: The Junior Reserve Officer Training Corps, the Los Angeles Uprising of 1992, and the 1992 Presidential Election," unpublished paper, Department of Curriculum and Instruction, University of Wisconsin, Madison, 2005.
11. Michael W. Apple, "What Can We Learn from Texas About No Child Left Behind?" *Educational Policy,* in press.
12. Angela Valenzuela, "Accountability and the Privatization Agenda," in Valenzuela, *Leaving Children Behind,* 263–94.
13. Raymond Padilla, "High-Stakes Testing and Educational Accountability as Social Construction Across Cultures," in Valenzuela, ed., *Leaving Children Behind,* 257.
14. Valenzuela, ed., *Leaving Children Behind.*
15. Angela Valenzuela, "Introduction: The Accountability Debate in Texas," in Valenzuela, *Leaving Children Behind,* 1.
16. Ibid., 2.

17. See Linda McNeil and Angela Valenzuela, "The Harmful Impact of the TASS System of Testing in Texas: Beneath the Accountability Rhetoric," in Gary Orfield and M. Kornhaber, eds., *Raising Standards or Raising Barriers: Inequality and High-Stakes Testing in Public Education,* 127–150 (Cambridge, Mass.: Harvard Civil Rights Project, 2001) and Linda McNeil, "Faking Equity: High-Stakes Testing and the Education of Latino Youth," in Valenzuela, *Leaving Children Behind,* 57–111.

18. Valenzuela, "Introduction," 4.

19. McNeil, "Faking Equity."

20. Jorge Ruiz de Velasco, "Performance-Based School Reforms and the Federal Role in Helping Schools that Serve Language-Minority Students," in Valenzuela, *Leaving Children Behind,* 48–49.

21. McNeil, "Faking Equity," 58.

22. Ibid.

23. Ibid.

24. Ibid., 91–92.

25. Ibid., 92.

26. Much of the rhetoric behind NCLB is about fairness to poor children of color. Yet, this is partly disingenuous given the nature of the unfounded mandates that accompany its policies and given the tax breaks and other funding priorities under neoliberal economic and social policies which are creating even more impoverishment and inequalities. These results are often covered up by other rhetorical moves by the right, including saying that NCLB represents a way in which suburban schools were pressured to focus on the poor children of color in their communities. This may be the case as a slogan, but even as an intention the reality of how it has worked *in conjunction with* these other economic and social policies is nearly laughable. For a statement of justification of NCLB and suburbia as seen through the eyes of the vice president of the conservative Fordham Foundation, see Michael J. Petrilli, "School Reform Moves to the Suburbs," *New York Times,* July 11, 2005, A21.

27. See Jean Anyon, *Radical Possibilities* (New York: Routledge, 2005) and Michael W. Apple, *Education and Power,* 2d ed. (New York: Routledge, 1995).

28. Bob Jessop, *The Future of the Capitalist State* (Cambridge, Mass.: Polity Press, 2002).

29. Colin Leys, *Market-Driven Politics: Neoliberal Democracy and the Public Interest* (New York: Verso, 2003), 3.

30. John Chubb and Terry Moe, *Politics, Markets, and American Schools* (Washington, D.C.: Brookings Institution, 1990). See also Sheila Slaughter and Larry Leslie, *Academic Capitalism* (Baltimore: Johns Hopkins University Press, 1999); Sheila Slaughter and Gary Rhoades, *Academic Capitalism and the New Economy* (Baltimore: Johns Hopkins University Press, 2004); and Robert Rhoads and Carlos Alberto Torres, eds., *The Political Economy of Higher Education in America* (Stanford, Calif.: Stanford University Press, in press) for thoughtful discussions

of the effects of marketization and competitive economic pressures on universities.

31. Leys, *Market-Driven Politics*, 4.
32. Ibid.
33. See Emily Van Dunk and Anneliese Dickman, *School Choice and the Question of Accountability* (New Haven, Conn.: Yale University Press, 2003) for how this works, and doesn't work, in plans to marketize education.
34. Apple, *Official Knowledge*; Leys, *Market-Driven Politics*, 4.
35. Leys, *Market-Driven Politics*, 4.
36. Jurgen Habermas, *Knowledge and Human Interests* (Boston: Beacon Press, 1971).
37. Jessop, *The Future of the Capitalist State*; Apple et al., *The State and the Politics of Knowledge*.
38. Leys, *Market-Driven Politics*, 35–36.
39. Ibid., 42. See also Michael B. Katz, *The Price of Citizenship* (New York: Metropolitan Books, 2001); David Shipler, *The Working Poor* (New York: Knopf, 2004).
40. Mark Olssen, "In Defense of the Welfare State and of Publicly Provided Education," *Journal of Education Policy* 11 (May 1996), 340.
41. Leys, *Market-Driven Politics*, 70.
42. Ibid.
43. Ibid., 71.
44. Ibid., 73.
45. See Daniel Liston and Kenneth Zeichner, *Teacher Education and the Social Conditions of Schooling* (New York: Routledge, 1991); Dale Johnson, et al., *Trivializing Teacher Education* (New York: Rowman and Littlefield, 2005).
46. John Clarke and Janet Newman, *The Managerial State* (Thousand Oaks, Calif.: Sage, 1997).
47. Of course, this is a differentiated experience. In the United States, supermarkets are less apt to even be found in inner-city neighborhoods populated by poor persons of color.
48. See Lois Andre-Bechely, *Couldn't It Be Otherwise? Parents and the Inequalities of Public School Choice* (New York: Routledge, 2005) for an insightful discussion of the ways in which information is differentially distributed and of the amount of labor that it requires for poor parents to decipher it and to make sense of school choice plans.
49. Stephen Ball, *Education Reform* (Buckingham: Open University Press, 1994).
50. Leys, *Market-Driven Politics*, 108.
51. Michael W. Apple, *Education and Power*, 2d ed. (New York: Routledge, 1995); Apple, *Official Knowledge*.
52. Lipman, *High Stakes Education*.
53. See Apple, *Official Knowledge*; David Hogan, "Education and Class Formation," in *Cultural and Economic Reproduction in Education*, ed., Michael W. Apple (Boston: Routledge and Kegan Paul, 1983). For

the ways in which race has been and is a crucial dynamic, see Charles Mills, *The Racial Contract* (Ithaca, N.Y.: Cornell University Press, 1997); Cameron McCarthy, Warren Crichlow, Greg Dimitriadis, and Nadine Dolby, eds., *Race, Identity, and Representation in Education,* 2d ed. (New York: Routledge, 2005); Gloria Ladson-Billings and David Gillborn (eds.), *The RoutledgeFalmer Reader in Multicultural Education* (London: RoutlegeFalmer, 2004); Michelle Fine, Lois Weis, Linda Powell, and L. Mun Wong, eds., *Off White,* 2d ed. (New York: Routledge, 2005).

54. Leys, *Market-Driven Politics,* 211–12.

55. Apple, *Official Knowledge.*

56. Patricia Burch's ongoing research on this is particularly important. See Patricia Burch, "The New Educational Privatization: Educational Contracting and High Stakes Accountability," *Teachers College Record,* in press. 34.

57. Ibid.

58. David Marquand, *The Progressive Dilemma* (London: Phoenix Books, 2000), 212–213.

59. Theda Skocpol, *Diminished Democracy* (Norman: University of Oklahoma Press, 2003).

60. Katz, *The Price of Citizenship.*

61. Nancy Fraser, *Unruly Practices* (Minneapolis: University of Minnesota Press, 1989); Robin D. G. Kelly, "We Are Not What We Seem: Rethinking Black Working Class Opposition in the Jim Crow South," *The Journal of American History* 80 (June 1993): 75–112; See also Michael W. Apple and Thomas Pedroni, "Conservative Alliance Building and African American Support for Voucher Plans," *Teachers College Record,* 107 (September 2005): 2068–2105, however, on how oppressed people attempt to tactically take up the subject position of the consumer and rearticulate it to further their own collective interests.

62. Leys, *Market-Driven Politics,* 220.

63. Apple et al., *The State and the Politics of Knowledge.*

64. Skocpol, *Diminished Democracy.*

65. See, for example, Michael W. Apple, Jane Kenway, and Michael Singh, eds., *Globalizing Education* (New York: Peter Lang, 2005).

66. Basil Bernstein, *Pedagogy, Symbolic Control and Identity* (Philadelphia: Taylor & Francis, 1996).

67. Apple, *Ideology and Curriculum.*

68. Clarke and Newman, *The Managerial State.*

69. Bourdieu, *Distinction.*

70. See Bourdieu, *Distinction;* Pierre Bourdieu, *Homo Academicus* (Stanford, Calif.: Stanford University Press, 1988); Pierre Bourdieu, *The State Nobility* (Stanford, Calif.: Stanford University Press, 1996).

71. Sally Power, Tony Edwards, Geoff Whitty, and Valerie Wigfall, *Education and the Middle Class* (Buckingham: Open University Press, 2003); Stephen Ball, *Class Strategies and the Education Market* (London: RoutledgeFalmer, 2003).

72. See David Gillborn and Deborah Youdell, *Rationing Education* (Buckingham: Open University Press, 2000); McNeil, *The Contradictions of School Reform;* Lipman, *High Stakes Education;* Apple, *Cultural Politics and Education;* Apple, *Official Knowledge.* On whether these are more effective than other strategies, see Luis Benveniste, Martin Carnoy, and Richard Rothstein, *All Else Equal: Are Public and Private Schools Different?* (New York: RoutledgeFalmer, 2003).

73. Ball, *Class Strategies and the Education Market.* See also the very thoughtful discussion in Power, Edwards, Whitty, and Wigfall, *Education and the Middle Class.*

74. Mills, *The Racial Contract.* See also Michael Omi and Howard Winant, *Racial Formation in the United States* (New York: Routledge, 1994).

75. Gloria Ladson-Billings, "Just What is Critical Race Theory and What is it Doing in a Nice Field Like Education?" in Gloria Ladson-Billings and David Gillborn, eds., *The RoutledgeFalmer Reader in Multicultural Education* (New York: RoutledgeFalmer, 2004), 51.

76. See Gillborn and Youdell, *Rationing Education,* and Whitty, Power, and Halpin, *Devolution and Choice in Education* for discussions of this.

77. Much of the material in this section is based on joint work done with Thomas Pedroni. See Apple and Pedroni, "Conservative Alliance Building and African American Support for Vouchers." A number of the conceptual and empirical claims are advanced in Thomas Pedroni's crucial study, *Strange Bedfellows in the Milwaukee "Parental Choice" Debate,* unpublished Ph.D. dissertation, University of Wisconsin, Madison, 2003.

78. "Progressive" traditions in the United States were not free of such racializing and racist logics. See, for example, Steven Selden, *Inheriting Shame* (New York: Teachers College Press, 1999).

79. That, say, a number of African-American groups, ones that are making alliances with distinctly conservative movements, exist and are growing says something very important about the fascination with identity politics among many progressive scholars and activists in education and elsewhere. Too often writing on identity (wrongly) assumes that identity politics is a "good thing," and that people inexorably move in progressive directions as they pursue what Nancy Fraser would call a politics of recognition. See Fraser, *Justice Interruptus.* Yet, any serious study of rightist movements demonstrates that identity politics is just as apt to take, say, angry and retrogressive forms—antigay, racist nativism, antiwomen, and so on. For many such people, "we" are the new oppressed, with that "we" not including most people of color, feminists, "sexual deviants," immigrants, and so on. However, as I noted earlier, even people within these "despised" groups themselves may take on such retrogressive identities. For more discussion of these issues, see Michael W. Apple and Kristen Buras, eds., *The Subaltern Speak* (New York: Routledge, 2006).

80. See, for example, Terry Moe, *Schools, Vouchers, and the American Public* (Washington, D.C.: Brookings Institution, 2001).

81. See Valenzuela, *Leaving Children Behind,* 263–94.

82. Paul Willis, *Common Culture* (Boulder, Colo.: Westview, 1990).

83. Richard Hernnstein and Charles Murray, *The Bell Curve* (New York: The Free Press, 1994).

84. In this regard, Tom Pedroni's ongoing research on BAEO and similar groups is of considerable importance. See Pedroni, *Strange Bedfellows in the Milwaukee "Parental Choice" Debate*. See also, Apple and Pedroni, "Conservative Alliance Building and African American Support for Vouchers."

85. David Levering Lewis, *W.E.B. DuBois: Biography of a Race, 1868–1919* (New York: Henry Holt, 1993) and David Levering Lewis, *W.E.B. DuBois: The Fight for Equality and the American Century* (New York: Henry Holt, 2000).

86. Pedroni, *Strange Bedfellows in the Milwaukee "Parental Choice" Debate*.

87. Angela Dillard, *Guess Who's Coming to Dinner Now?* (New York: New York University Press, 2001).

88. David Hogan, "Education and Class Formation," in Michael W. Apple, ed., *Cultural and Economic Reproduction in Education* (Boston: Routledge and Kegan Paul, 1982) and Apple, et al., *The State and the Politics of Knowledge*.

89. Ball, *Education Reform*.

90. Apple, *Official Knowledge*.

91. Gillborn and Youdell, *Rationing Education;* Lipman, *High Stakes Education;* McNeil, *The Contradictions of School Reform;* and Valenzuela, *Leaving Children Behind*.

92. See Anyon, *Radical Possibilities* and Apple, *Official Knowledge*.

93. Ibid. Angela Dillard is very fair in her assessment of what the implications of such support may be. She nicely shows the contradictions of the arguments and logic of the people she focuses upon. In doing so, she draws on some of the more cogent analyses of the relationship between democracy and the maintenance of the public sphere on the one hand and an expansive and rich understanding of what it means to be a citizen on the other. Readers of her discussion would also be well served to connect her arguments to the historical struggles over the very meanings of our concepts of democracy, freedom, and citizenship such as that found in Foner's illuminating book, *The Story of American Freedom*, but Dillard's discussion is substantive and useful. See Eric Foner, *The Story of American Freedom* (New York: Norton, 1998).

94. Van Dunk and Dickman, *School Choice and the Question of Accountability*.

95. Apple and Pedroni, "Conservative Alliance Building and African American Support for Vouchers" and Pedroni, *Strange Bedfellows in the Milwaukee "Parental Choice" Debate*.

96. Michael B. Katz, *The Price of Citizenship* (New York: Metropolitan Books, 2001).

97. See Ball, *Class Strategies and the Education Market*; Power, Edwards, Whitty, and Wigfall, *Education and the Middle Class*; and Gillborn and Youdell, *Rationing Education*.

98. Alison Griffith and Dorothy Smith, *Mothering for Schooling* (New York: Routledge, 2005).

99. There has been some discussion of the dangers of voucher plans by African American nationalist activists and scholars. See Lawson Bush V, "Access, School Choice, and Independent Black Institutions," *Journal of Black Studies* 34 (2004): 386–401. On black activism and the ways in which consumer struggles have led to positive effects both within dominant white controlled economic and political institutions and within black mobilizations as well, see Stacy Kinlock Sewell, "The 'Not-Buying' Power of the Black Community," *Journal of African American History* 89 (2004): 135–51.

100. Apple and Pedroni, "Conservative Alliance Building and African American Support for Vouchers."

101. For more on this, see Valenzuela, *Leaving Children Behind* and Michael W. Apple, "What Can We Learn from Texas About No Child Left Behind?"

102. Valenzuela, "Introduction," 12.

103. Apple, et al., *The State and the Politics of Knowledge*.

104. Valenzuela, "Introduction," 13.

105. Ibid., 17. See also Michael W. Apple and James A. Beane, eds., *Democratic Schools* (Alexandria, Va.: Association for Supervision and Curriculum Development, 1995) and Eric Gutstein, *Reading and Writing the World With Mathematics* (New York: Routledge, 2006).

106. Stuart Ranson, "Public Accountability in the Age of Neo-Liberal Governance," *Journal of Education Policy* 18 (September–October 2003): 470.

107. Fraser, *Unruly Practices*; Mills, *The Racial Contract*.

108. Nancy Fraser, *Justice Interruptus* (New York: Routledge, 1997).

109. See Raymond Williams, *Resources of Hope* (New York: Verso, 1989).

110. Ranson, "Public Accountability in the Age of Neo-Liberal Governance," 476.

111. Ibid. For some cautions on seeing this as simply a liberal model of "deliberation," see James Avis, "Re-thinking Trust in a Performative Culture: The Case of Education," *Journal of Education Policy* 18 (May–June 2003): 315–32.

112. An account of a continuing attempt to organize core aspects of university life and work around these concerns can be found in Apple, *Official Knowledge*.

113. See Apple, et al., *The State and the Politics of Knowledge*, 193–219.

114. Within the field of education, the journal *Teaching Education* has attempted to institutionalize this task by consistently publishing accounts of critical teaching within undergraduate classes in teacher education and in graduate classes as well. See note 117 for even more resources that are crucial in this regard.

115. Gloria Ladson-Billings, *The Dreamkeepers* (San Francisco: Jossey-Bass, 1994).

116. Apple and Beane, *Democratic Schools.*

117. See Eric Gutstein, *Reading and Writing the World With Mathematics* (New York: Routledge, 2006); Eric Gutstein and Bob Peterson, eds. *Rethinking Mathematics: Teaching Social Justice by the Numbers* (Milwaukee: Rethinking Schools, 2005); Wolff-Michael Roth and Angela Barton, *Rethinking Scientific Literacy* (New York: RoutledgeFalmer, 2004); Deborah Meier, *The Power of their Ideas* (Boston: Beacon Press, 1995); and Deborah Meier, *In Schools We Trust: Creating Communities of Learning in an Era of Testing and Standardization* (Boston: Beacon Press, 2002).

118. Morva MacDonald, *Teacher Education for Social Justice* (New York: Routledge, in press).

Chapter 5

1. Joan Delfattore, *What Johnny Shouldn't Read* (New Haven, Conn.: Yale University Press, 1992), 93.

2. Pam Belluck, "Board for Kansas Deletes Evolution From the Curriculum," *New York Times*, August 12, 1999, A1, A13. The Board allowed the teaching of microevolution—genetic adaptation and natural selection *within* a species. Macroevolution—the origin of species—was purged.

3. Belluck, "Board for Kansas Deletes Evolution From Curriculum," A13.

4. Cornelia Dean, "Evolution Takes a Back Seat in U.S. Classes," *New York Times*, February 1, 2005, D1.

5. Ibid., D6.

6. Belluck, "Board for Kansas Deletes Evolution From Curriculum," A13.

7. Ibid.

8. For further discussion of the political economy of publishing, see Michael W. Apple, *Teachers and Texts* (New York: Routledge, 1988) and Michael W. Apple, *Official Knowledge*, 2d ed. (New York: Routledge, 2000).

9. Delfattore, *What Johnny Shouldn't Read,* 120.

10. Ronald L. Numbers, *Darwinism Comes to America* (Cambridge, Mass.: Harvard University Press, 1998), 8–10.

11. Ibid., 10.

12. Dean, "Evolution Takes a Back Seat in U.S. Classes," D6.

13. Numbers, *Darwinism Comes to America*, 9.

14. Ibid., 9–11. See also Ronald L. Numbers and John Stenhouse, "Antievolutionism in the Antipodes: From Protesting Evolution to Promoting Creationism in New Zealand," *British Journal for the History of Science,* in press, and Ronald L. Numbers, "Creationists and Their Critics in Australia," unpublished paper, Department of the History of Medicine, University of Wisconsin, Madison.

15. See Ronald L. Numbers, *The Creationists* (New York: Knopf, 1992) for more on the historical roots of such positions.

16. Numbers, *Darwinism Comes to America,* 109.

17. Ibid., 2.

18. Ibid.

19. Ibid., 3.

20. For more on this era and the conflicts that led to it, see John Rudolph, *Scientists in the Classroom: The Cold War Reconstruction of American Science Education* (New York: Palgrave, 2002).

21. Numbers, *Darwinism Comes to America*, 4.

22. Ibid., 5–6.

23. In *Cultural Politics and Education,* for instance, I show how the battle over textbooks doesn't just reflect, but helps form, rightist movements at a local level. See Michael W. Apple, *Cultural Politics and Education* (New York: Teachers College Press, 1996), 42–67.

24. Numbers, *Darwinism Comes to America*, 6.

25. Ibid., 55–56.

26. See Edward Larson, *Trial and Error: The American Controversy over Creation and Evolution* (New York: Oxford University Press, 1989).

27. For a perceptive and detailed analysis of the Scopes trial, see Edward Larson, *Summer of the Gods: The Scopes Trial and America's Continuing Debate over Science and Religion* (New York: Basic Books, 1997). Additional material can be found in Numbers, *Darwinism Comes to America*.

28. Numbers, *Darwinism Comes to America*, 74.

29. I discuss this at greater length in Apple, *Official Knowledge.*

30. Numbers, *Darwinism Comes to America*, 91.

31. Justin Watson, *The Christian Coalition: Dreams of Restoration, Demands for Recognition* (New York: St. Martin's Press, 1997), 27.

32. Richard Berke, "Conservatives Look For Believers Amid G.O.P. Presidential Field," *New York Times,* February 4, 1999, A19.

33. Laurie Goodstein, "Coalition's Woes May Hinder Goals of Christian Right," *New York Times,* August 2, 1999, A1.

34. Apple, *Official Knowledge,* especially Chapter 2.

35. Kenneth J. Heineman, *God is a Conservative: Religion, Politics, and Morality in Contemporary America* (New York: New York University Press, 1998), 265.

36. Delfattore, *What Johnny Shouldn't Read,* 4.

37. Ibid., 14.

38. Ibid., 21.

39. Ibid., 32.

40. Ibid., 82.

41. Ibid., 6.

42. Pat Robertson, *The Secret Kingdom* (Nashville: Thomas Nelson Publishers, 1982), 44.

43. James L. Guth, John C. Green, Corwin E. Smidt, Lyman A. Kellstedt, and Margaret Poloma, *The Bully Pulpit: The Politics of Protestant Clergy* (Lawrence: The University of Kansas Press, 1997), 2.

44. Watson, *The Christian Coalition,* 20.

45. Ibid., 3.

46. Ibid., 12–13.
47. Christian Smith, *American Evangelicalism: Embattled and Thriving* (Chicago: University of Chicago Press, 1998), 1.
48. Ibid., 2.
49. Ibid.
50. Ibid.
51. Ibid., 3.
52. Ibid.
53. Ibid., 5.
54. Ibid., 7.
55. Ibid., 6.
56. Ibid.
57. Ibid., 8.
58. Ibid.
59. Watson, *The Christian Coalition,* 17. Fundamentalists found evidence for Christ's imminent return to establish a thousand-year period of holiness in Revelation chapter 20.
60. Ibid., 17.
61. George Marsden, *Understanding Fundamentalism and Evangelicalism* (Grand Rapids, Mich.: Eerdmans, 1991), 1.
62. Ibid., 14. However, the initial sense among fundamentalists was that Bryan and the anti-Darwinian cause had totally vanquished their opponents. See, for example, Numbers, *Darwinism Comes to America.*
63. Christian Smith, *American Evangelicalism,* 10.
64. Ibid., 10–11.
65. Ibid., 12–13.
66. Christine Leigh Heyrman, *Southern Cross: The Beginnings of the Bible Belt* (New York: Knopf, 1997), 6.
67. Ibid., 33.
68. Ibid., 61.
69. Ibid., 73.
70. Ibid., 41.
71. Ibid., 6. See also Cornel West, *Prophesy Deliverance!* (Philadelphia: Westminster Press, 1982) for a discussion of the socially and religiously progressive tendencies within the African-American churches historically and currently.
72. Heyrman, *Southern Cross,* 46–53.
73. Ibid., 56.
74. Ibid., 68–69.
75. Ibid., 76.
76. Ibid.
77. Ibid., 155.
78. Ibid., 158.
79. Useful documents on the "cult of domesticity" can be found in Nancy Cott, ed., *Roots of Bitterness: Documents of the Social History of Women* (New York: E. P. Dutton, 1972). Of course, these positions were both class and race specific and were not accepted passively. They were mediated,

contested constantly, and actively used for other purposes by women in quite complex and contradictory ways. See Carroll Smith-Rosenberg, *Disorderly Conduct: Visions of Gender in Victorian America* (New York: Oxford University Press, 1985) and Alice Kessler-Harris, *Out to Work: A History of Wage-Earning Women in the United States* (New York: Oxford University Press, 1982).

80. Heyrman, *Southern Cross*, 159–160. This too was class and race specific. See Catherine Clinton, *The Plantation Mistress: Woman's World in the Old South* (New York: Pantheon Books, 1982).

81. Heyrman, *Southern Cross*, 160.

82. Ibid., 166.

83. Ibid., 173. This did create tensions among men over male authority, however. See ibid., 189.

84. See, for example, Rebecca Klatch, *Women of the New Right* (Philadelphia: Temple University Press, 1987).

85. Heyrman, *Southern Cross*, 214.

86. Ibid., 214, 232–39.

87. Ibid., 248–52.

88. Ibid., 254–55.

Chapter 6

1. See, for example, Johannes Van Vught, *Democratic Organizations for Social Change: Latin American Christian Base Communities and Literacy Campaigns* (New York: Bergin & Garvey, 1991).

2. James L. Guth, John C. Green, Corwin E. Smidt, Lyman A. Kellstedt, and Margaret Poloma, *The Bully Pulpit* (Lawrence: University Press of Kansas, 1997), 13–14. This public agenda of moral reform was, of course, not new. A focus on gambling, drinking, prostitution, and education has consistently characterized conservative religious activists historically, as well as activists in more progressive causes.

3. Ibid., 46.

4. Ibid., 63–65.

5. Ibid., 20.

6. Justin Watson, *The Christian Coalition* (New York: St. Martin's Press, 1997), 6.

7. Christian Smith, *American Evangelicalism* (Chicago: University of Chicago Press, 1998), 23–24. Smith also found that there were no generational differences among evangelicals. Younger evangelicals were equally orthodox. See p. 26.

8. Ibid., 84.

9. Ibid., 31.

10. Ibid.

11. Ibid., 206–10.

12. Ibid., 127–29.

13. Ibid., 39. Stress in original.

14. Ibid., 39–43. The relative lack of activism among "liberal" Christians is striking in comparison. See p. 43.

15. This is increasingly visible in the military as well, where conservative evangelicals have been accused of creating an atmosphere of intolerance for those of other religious and ethical beliefs. See Laurie Goodstein, "Evangelicals are a Growing Force in the Military Chaplain Corps," *New York Times*, July 12, 2005, A1, A20.

16. Smith, *American Evangelicalism*, 132–33.

17. Ibid., 34–35.

18. Guth et al., *The Bully Pulpit*, 137.

19. Ibid., 54–55. The connection between evangelical ministries and youth is not new. See, for example, Christine Leigh Heyrman, *Southern Cross* (New York: Knopf, 1997), 77–116.

20. Guth et al., *The Bully Pulpit*, 59.

21. Ibid., 112. This can and does go both ways, of course. There have been moves toward more liberal social beliefs within some churches as well. See ibid., 121.

22. Ibid., 143–44.

23. Ibid., 183.

24. Sara Diamond, *Spiritual Warfare: The Politics of the Christian Right* (Boston: South End Press, 1989), 3.

25. Ibid., 4.

26. Ibid., 10.

27. Ibid., 12.

28. For more on Robertson's biography, see Watson, *The Christian Coalition*.

29. Ibid., 13.

30. Ibid., 20.

31. Ibid., 17–18.

32. Linda Kintz, *Between Jesus and the Market: The Emotions That Matter in Right-Wing America* (Durham, N.C.: Duke University Press, 1997), 106.

33. Watson, *The Christian Coalition*, 91. Of course, many neoconservative commentators would part with the authoritarian populists' position that this is a "Christian nation." For neoconservative Jewish commentators, it is the history of openness, cultural pluralism, and "making it" economically that sets the United States aside as the special nation. See, for example, Norman Podheretz, *My Love Affair with America: The Cautionary Tale of a Cheerful Conservative* (New York: Free Press, 2000).

34. Smith, *American Evangelicalism*, 136–40.

35. Pat Robertson, "Law Must Embrace Morality," *Christian America*, April 1995, 17.

36. Watson, *The Christian Coalition*, 107.

37. Ralph Reed, *Politically Incorrect* (Dallas: Word Publishing, 1994), 79.

38. Smith, *American Evangelicalism*, 140–43.

39. The supposed "fact" that the media are dominated by liberals is argued repeatedly by conservative pundits and spokespersons. As Eric Alterman demonstrates, this claim is wildly overstated. See Eric Alterman, *What*

Liberal Media? The Truth About Bias and the News (New York: Basic Books, 2003).

40. Phyllis Schlafly, "Fact and Fiction About Censorship" (Washington, D.C.: National Defense Committee, National Society, Daughters of the American Revolution, 1984), 1. See also Eugene F. Provenzo Jr., *Religious Fundamentalism and American Education* (Albany: State University of New York Press, 1990).

41. Smith, *American Evangelicalism*, 44.

42. Ibid.

43. Ibid., 50.

44. Heyrman, *Southern Cross*, 21.

45. Pat Robertson, *The Turning Tide* (Dallas: Word Publishing, 1993), 227–28.

46. Pat Robertson, *The New Millennium* (Dallas: Word Publishing, 1990), 174–75.

47. Smith, *American Evangelicalism*, 136.

48. Robertson, *The Turning Tide*, 239.

49. Ibid.

50. Kenneth J. Heineman, *God Is a Conservative: Religion, Politics, and Morality in Contemporary America* (New York: New York University Press, 1998), 161–62.

51. Guth et al., *The Bully Pulpit*, 166. Another interesting finding here is that significant levels of support for Dobson's emphases were found among somewhat less conservative clergy as well. Obviously, the fear for one's children's future permeates a much larger swath of the population than the religious right.

52. Frederick Clarkson, *Eternal Hostility: The Struggle Between Theocracy and Democracy* (Monroe, Maine: Common Courage Press, 1997), viii.

53. Ibid., 39.

54. Robertson, *The Turning Tide*, 233.

55. Pat Robertson, *The New World Order* (Dallas: Word Publishing, 1991), 250.

56. Heineman, *God Is a Conservative*, 100.

57. See Michelle Fine, Lois Weis, Linda C. Powell, and L. Mun Wong, eds., *Off White* (New York: Routledge, 1997); Richard Dyer, *White* (New York: Routledge, 1997); and Michael W. Apple, "The Absent Presence of Race in Educational Reform," *Race, Ethnicity, and Education* 2 (March 1999): 9–16.

58. Watson, *The Christian Coalition*, 171.

59. Robertson, *The Turning Tide*, 144. Robertson also makes reference to the suffering of the Jews and draws parallels between the oppression of Jews under the Nazis and the contemporary experiences of evangelicals. Yet he often has anti-Semitic subtexts within his own writings.

60. Ralph Reed, "Putting a Friendly Face on the Pro-family Movement," *Christianity Today*, April 1993, 28.

61. Heineman, *God Is a Conservative*, 146.

62. Watson, *The Christian Coalition*, 59.

63. Ibid., 63.
64. Ibid., 64.
65. Ibid.
66. Ibid., 64–65.
67. Pat Robertson, *The Secret Kingdom*, 2d ed. (Dallas: Word Publishing, 1992), 60.
68. Watson, *The Christian Coalition*, 175.
69. See Benedict Anderson, *Imagined Communities* (New York: Verso, 1991).
70. Raymond Williams, *Marxism and Literature* (New York: Oxford University Press, 1977). In some ways this is similar to Bourdieu's concept of habitus. See Pierre Bourdieu, *Distinction* (Cambridge, Mass.: Harvard University Press, 1984).
71. Kintz, *Between Jesus and the Market*, 3.
72. Ibid., 6.
73. Elaine Pagels, *The Origins of Satan* (New York: Random House, 1995), 181. See also Michael O'Leary, *Arguing the Apocalypse* (New York: Oxford University Press, 1994).
74. Kintz, *Between Jesus and the Market*, 9.
75. Ibid., 18.
76. Ibid., 30.
77. Watson, *The Christian Coalition*, 77.
78. Diamond, *Spiritual Warfare*, 104–5.
79. Beverly LaHaye, "Women Restoring Righteousness," in *Judgement at the Gate: A Call to Awaken the Church*, ed. Richie Martin (Westchester, Ill.: Crossway Books, 1986), 35, 38.
80. Kintz, *Between Jesus and the Market*, 37.
81. Ibid.
82. Julie Kristeva, "Women's Time," *Signs* 7 (Autumn 1981): 13–35.
83. Kintz, *Between Jesus and the Market*, 39–40.
84. Ibid., 41.
85. Connie Marshner, *Can Motherhood Survive?* (Brentwood, Ind.: Wolgemuth & Hyatt, 1990), 2.
86. Robertson, *The New World Order*, 241. See also, Kintz, *Between Jesus and the Market*, 43.
87. Kintz, *Between Jesus and the Market*, 219.
88. Michael Novak, *This Hemisphere of Liberty* (Washington, D.C.: American Enterprise Institute, 1992), 33.
89. Michael Novak, *Toward a Theology of the Corporation* (Washington, D.C.: American Enterprise Institute, 1981), 34.
90. Kintz, *Between Jesus and the Market*, 44.
91. As I argue in *Cultural Politics and Education*, having paid work is the identificatory sign of full citizenship in this society, unless one is a white mother. See Michael W. Apple, *Cultural Politics and Education* (New York: Teachers College Press, 1996).
92. Alexandra Dimick and Michael W. Apple, "Texas and the Politics of Abstinence-Only Textbooks," *Teachers College Record*, May 2, 2005.

93. Apple, *Cultural Politics and Education*, 99.

94. Diamond, *Spiritual Warfare*, 102.

95. Ibid., 103.

96. Kintz, *Between Jesus and the Market*, 22.

97. Allen Hertzke, *Echoes of Discontent* (Washington, D.C.: Congressional Quarterly Press, 1992), xv.

98. Kintz, *Between Jesus and the Market*, 185–86.

99. Michelle LeDoeuff, *Hipparchia's Choice* (Cambridge, Mass.: Blackwell, 1991), 313.

100. Kintz, *Between Jesus and the Market*, 271.

101. Dean Kelly, *Why Conservative Churches Are Growing* (New York: Harper & Row, 1972).

102. Ibid., 85.

103. Ibid., 87.

104. Christian Smith, *American Evangelicalism*, 89.

105. Ibid., 91.

106. Bourdieu, *Distinction*. See also Smith, *American Evangelicalism*, 96–97.

107. Smith, *American Evangelicalism*, 121.

108. I have devoted a good deal of time to specifically arguing against the conceptual and political uses of ideas such as false consciousness. See, for example, Michael W. Apple, *Education and Power*, 2d ed. (New York: Routledge, 1995) and Michael W. Apple, *Official Knowledge*, 2d ed. (New York: Routledge, 2000).

109. Smith, *American Evangelicalism*, 117.

110. Ibid., 103.

111. Ibid., 104.

112. Watson, *The Christian Coalition*, 146.

113. See, for example, Peter McLaren, *Revolutionary Multiculturalism* (Boulder, Colo.: Westview Press, 1997).

114. Watson, *The Christian Coalition*, 148.

115. Smith, *American Evangelicalism*, 100.

116. Ibid.

117. Watson, *The Christian Coalition*, 38.

118. For a close-up portrayal of the people involved in such racist and militia groups, see Raphael Ezekiel, *The Racist Mind* (New York: Penguin, 1995).

119. Clarkson, *Eternal Hostility*, 78–79.

120. Ibid., 78. Among the most important figures in this movement are the following: Rousas John Rushdoony, author of the defining text, *The Institutes of Biblical Law* (Phillipsburgh, N.J.: Presbyterian and Reformed Publishing, 1973); Gary North of the Institute for Christian Economics; and Gary De Mar, president of the Reconstructionist publishing house American Vision, which publishes books primarily for use in Christian schools and for home schoolers. Rushdoony is one of the guiding ideological forces behind the ultrarightist U.S. Taxpayers Party and is on the board of Howard Phillips' Conservative Caucus. The hidden connections

between rightist political mobilizations around taxes and unquestioned support of privatization and far-right religious groups is important.

121. Clarkson, *Eternal Hostility*, 8.

122. Ibid., 17.

123. Ibid., 119.

124. See Robert Therburn, *The Children Trap: Biblical Principles for Education* (Fort Worth, Tex.: Dominion Press and Thomas Nelson Publishers, 1986), 171–72.

125. Christopher Klicka, *The Right Choice: The Incredible Failure of Public Education and the Rising Hope of Home Schooling* (Gresham, Ore.: Noble Publishing Associates, 1992), 109.

126. See, for example, Watson, *The Christian Coalition*, 109–19.

127. Ibid., 37.

128. Ibid., 112.

129. See Bruce Barron, *Heaven on Earth? The Social and Political Agendas of Dominion Theology* (Grand Rapids, Mich.: Zondervan, 1992), 144–46.

130. Robertson, *The New Millennium*, 64.

131. Watson, *The Christian Coalition*, 121.

Chapter 7

1. It is important that we remember that public schools were and are a victory. They constituted a gain for the majority of people who were denied access to advancement and to valued cultural capital in a stratified society. This is not to claim that the public school did not and does not have differential effects. Indeed, I have devoted many books to uncovering the connections between formal education and the re-creation of inequalities. It is to say that public schooling is a site of conflict, but one that also has been a site of major victories by popular groups. Thus, conservatives would not be so angry at schools if public schools had not had a number of progressive tendencies cemented in them. For more on the victories as well as defeats, see William Reese, *Power and the Promise of School Reform* (New York: Routledge, 1986). On the ways in which many people continued to struggle over the content and processes of schooling, even when they partly lost, see Kenneth Teitelbaum, *Schooling for Good Rebels* (New York: Teachers College Press, 1996).

2. For further information on the National Home Education Research Institute and on its data on home schooling, see the following Web site: http://www.nheri.org.

3. In the United States—unlike, say, England—the term "public" schooling refers only to those schools that are organized, funded, and controlled by the state. All other schools are considered "private" or "religious." Different linguistic meanings provide important insights into the ways language is mobilized in historical conflicts. See Raymond Williams, *Keywords* (New York: Oxford University Press, 1985).

4. See Michael W. Apple, *Cultural Politics and Education* (New York: Teachers College Press, 1996) and Nancy Fraser, *Justice Interruptus* (New York: Routledge, 1997).

5. See, for example, Michael W. Apple and James A. Beane, eds., *Democratic Schools* (Alexandria, Va.: Association for Supervision and Curriculum Development, 1995) and Michael W. Apple and James A. Beane, eds., *Democratic Schools: Lessons from the Chalk Face* (Buckingham, England: Open University Press, 1999).

6. See Fritz Detwiler, *Standing on the Premises of God* (New York: New York University Press, 1999) and Brian Ray, *Home Schooling on the Threshold* (Salem, Ore.: National Home Education Research Institute, 1999).

7. Although I focus on authoritarian populist home schoolers, it is important to recognize the diversity among home schoolers. Among the parents who are home schooling their children are also libertarians, environmentalists, progressives who are concerned about an overly standardized and uncreative curriculum, parents of color who wish to protect their children from the destructive effects of racism in schools, and others.

8. Detwiler, *Standing on the Premises of God* and Linda Kintz, *Between Jesus and the Market* (Durham, N.C.: Duke University Press, 1997). In part, the attractiveness of home schooling among religiously motivated parents is also due to a structural difference between schools in the United States and those in many other nations. Historically, although at times mythical, the separation between state-supported schooling and an officially defined state religion has been a distinctive feature of education here. Thus, the absence of particular kinds of religious instruction in schools has been a source of tension among many groups and has generated even more antischool sentiment. See Warren Nord, *Religion and American Education* (Chapel Hill: University of North Carolina Press, 1995). The idea that there has always been a religious substratum—largely white and "mainstream" Protestant—has been advanced in interesting ways in Randall Collins, *The Credential Society* (New York: Academic Press, 1979).

9. Elaine Pagels, *The Origin of Satan* (New York: Random House, 1995).

10. Ibid., 49.

11. Quoted in Kintz, *Between Jesus and the Market,* 80.

12. See William Greider, *One World, Ready or Not* (New York: Simon & Schuster, 1997).

13. I am thinking here of Channel One, the for-profit commercial television show that is in an increasingly large percentage of our middle and secondary schools. In this "reform," students are sold as a captive audience to corporations intent on marketing their products to our children in schools. See Michael W. Apple, *Official Knowledge,* 2d ed. (New York: Routledge, 2000) and Alex Molnar, *Giving Kids the Business* (Boulder, Colo.: Westview Press, 1996).

14. Of course, the very distinction between "public" and "private" spheres has strong connections to the history of patriarchal assumptions. See

Nancy Fraser, *Unruly Practices* (Minneapolis: University of Minnesota Press, 1989).

15. Kintz, *Between Jesus and the Market,* 97.

16. This is a *particular* construction of the family. As Coontz has shown in her history of the family in the United States, it has had a very varied form, with the nuclear family that is so important to conservative formulations merely being one of many. See Stephanie Coontz, *The Way We Never Were* (New York: Basic Books, 1992).

17. Kintz, *Between Jesus and the Market,* 107.

18. Ibid.

19. Ibid., 108.

20. Of course, it is important to realize that there may be good reasons for some groups to engage in cocooning. Take the example of indigenous or colonized groups. Given the destruction of cultures (and bodies) of oppressed peoples, it is clear that for many of them a form of cocooning is one of the only ways in which cultures and languages can be preserved. Since dominant groups already have cultural and economic power, the relative lack of such power by oppressed peoples creates protective needs. Thus, in cases such as this, cocooning may have a more positive valence.

21. Andrew Shapiro, "The Net That Binds," *The Nation,* 21 (June 1999), 168.

22. Ibid.

23. Kintz, *Between Jesus and the Market,* 168.

24. Ibid., 186.

25. Christian Smith, *American Evangelicalism* (Chicago: University of Chicago Press, 1998).

26. John Clarke and Janet Newman, *The Managerial State* (Thousand Oaks, Calif.: Sage, 1997).

27. Ibid., 5–7.

28. Ibid., 8.

29. See Apple, *Official Knowledge,* especially Chapter 2.

30. For a much less stereotypical picture, one that shows the complexities and struggles of poor and working-class people, see Michelle Fine and Lois Weis, *The Unknown City* (Boston: Beacon Press, 1998).

31. Clarke and Newman, *The Managerial State,* 15.

32. For parts of how this has affected debates over schooling and the curriculum, see Joan Delfattore, *What Johnny Shouldn't Read* (New Haven, Conn.: Yale University Press, 1992).

33. Antiteacher discourse has a long history, especially in the United States. It was often employed to legitimate centralized and standardized curricula and centralizing decision making about textbooks within the state. See, for example, my discussion of the growth of state textbook adoption policies in Apple, *Official Knowledge.*

34. Apple, *Cultural Politics and Education,* 68–90.

35. A number of highly publicized shootings in schools have occurred in the past few years in the United States. The most well known occurred in Columbine High School in a relatively affluent community in Colorado

in which two alienated students killed a teacher and twelve other students and also planted pipe bombs throughout the building. This followed on other shootings in suburban schools. In a recent instance in a suburban but much less affluent community in Michigan, a six-year-old boy killed a six-year-old girl classmate after an altercation on the playground. The threat of violence is now seen as a very real possibility in schools throughout the United States. It is crucial to understand that violence, both symbolic and material, is wreaked on communities, especially poor ones, *every day*. When families and entire communities are destroyed by job loss, the lack of health care and decent housing, poor or nonexistent child care, and so on, this society is apt to ignore it until what is officially labeled as violence erupts. Millions of more lives are affected by these "unofficial" forms of violence, but because it has somehow become "naturalized," we as a society seem unwilling to deal with it in any serious and long-term way.

36. For a discussion of the larger issues surrounding technology and the contradictions embodied in it, see Hank Bromley and Michael W. Apple, eds., *Education/Technology/Power* (Albany: State University of New York Press, 1998).

37. These changing demographic characteristics are dealt with in more detail in Smith, *American Evangelicalism*.

38. This and other similar material can be found at the following Web site address for The Teaching Home. See http://www.teachinghome.com/qa/why/htm.

39. For more on the vision of gender relations underpinning the home, see Kintz, *Between Jesus and the Market*.

40. Class dynamics within the state are quite complicated. See Pierre Bourdieu, *The State Nobility* (Stanford, Calif.: Stanford University Press, 1996). On the gender specificities within the state and its policies, see Madeleine Arnot, Miriam David, and Gaby Weiner, *Closing the Gender Gap* (Cambridge, Mass.: Polity Press, 1999) and Suzanne Franzway, Diane Court, and R. W. Connell, *Staking a Claim: Feminism, Bureaucracy, and the State* (Boston: Allen & Unwin, 1989).

41. Fraser, *Justice Interruptus,* 13.

42. Ibid., 14.

43. For a review of some of these recent data, see Kristen L. Buras and Michael W. Apple, "School Choice, Neoliberal Promises, and Unpromising Evidence," *Educational Policy* 19 (July 2005): 550–64.

44. See Geoff Whitty, Sally Power, and David Halpin, *Devolution and Choice in Education* (Philadelphia: Open University Press, 1998).

45. Apple, *Cultural Politics and Education*.

46. See Whitty, Power, and Halpin, *Devolution and Choice in Education* and Hugh Lauder and David Hughes, *Trading in Futures* (Philadelphia: Open University Press, 1999).

47. Amy Stuart Wells, personal communication. For more on the ways charter schools have provided such mechanisms, see Amy Stuart Wells,

Beyond the Rhetoric of Charter School Reform (Los Angeles: Graduate School of Education and Information Studies, UCLA, 1999).

48. See Moshe Re'em, *Young Minds in Motion: Teaching and Learning About Difference in Formal and Non-formal Settings,* unpublished doctoral dissertation, University of Wisconsin, Madison, 1998, for an interesting analysis of some of this content.

49. I have gone into considerably more detail on these points in Apple, *Cultural Politics and Education* and Michael W. Apple, *Power, Meaning, and Identity* (New York: Peter Lang, 1999).

50. For further discussion of the politics of claiming subaltern status, see Michael W. Apple and Kristen Buras, eds., *The Subaltern Speak: Curriculum, Power, and Educational Struggles* (New York: Routledge, 2006).

Chapter 8

1. I would like to thank Harry Brighouse, Kurt Squire, and the members of the Friday Seminar for their comments on this chapter. An earlier draft was presented at the Wisconsin/London/Melbourne Joint Seminar on New Technologies, Madison, Wisconsin, October 6, 2003.

2. In many ways, these chapters also have been a response to Gerald Grace's articulate call for sociologists of education to pay much more attention to the religious dimensions of society in their analyses of the relationship between power and education. See Gerald Grace, "Making Connections for Future Directions: Taking Religion Seriously in the Sociology of Education," *International Studies in Sociology of Education* 14 (number 1, 2004): 47–56.

3. See, for example, Hank Bromley and Michael W. Apple, *Education/ Technology/Power* (Albany: State University of New York Press, 1998); Larry Cuban, *Oversold and Underused* (Cambridge, Mass.: Harvard University Press, 2001); Mike Godwin, *Cyber Rights* (Cambridge, Mass.: MIT Press, 2003); David Hakken, *Cyborgs@Cyberspace* (New York: Routledge, 1999); and Tim Jordan, *Cyberpower* (New York: Routledge, 1999).

4. James Slevin, *The Internet and Society* (Cambridge, Mass.: Polity Press, 2000), ix.

5. Manuel Castells, *The Rise of Network Society, Volume 1* (New York: Oxford University Press, 1996), 199.

6. Slevin, *The Internet and Society*, 5.

7. Ibid., 5–6.

8. The right has been in the forefront of the use of the Internet, not only in creating linkages among existing members on key issues of concern. In understanding that youth are among the heaviest users of the Internet, conservative organizations have creatively employed such technology to build sophisticated Web sites whose form and content appeal to youth. See Jean Hardisty, *Mobilizing Resentment* (Boston: Beacon Press, 1999), 46.

9. Mitchell Stevens, *Kingdom of Children* (Princeton, N.J.: Princeton University Press, 2001), 4.

10. The relatively uncritical support of home schooling and of its religious imperatives can be seen as well in articles found in popular magazines. See, for example, Michelle Dugan with Andrea Cooper, "Count Our Blessings," *Parents*, September 2003, 161–64. I would like to thank Denise Oen for bringing this to my attention.

11. Ibid., 4–7.

12. Kelly Moore, "Political Protest and Institutional Change," in Marco Giugni, Doug McAdam, and Charles Tilly, eds., *How Social Movements Matter* (Minneapolis: University of Minnesota Press, 1999), 109.

13. Stevens, *Kingdom of Children*, 11.

14. Christian Smith, *American Evangelicalism* (Chicago: University of Chicago Press, 1998).

15. Stevens, *Kingdom of Children*, 53.

16. Ibid., 4.

17. See also Amy Binder, *Contentious Curricula* (Princeton, N.J.: Princeton University Press, 2002).

18. John Green, "The Christian Right and the 1998 Elections," in John Green, Mark Rozell, and Clyde Wilcox, eds., *Prayers in the Precincts* (Washington, D.C.: Georgetown University Press, 2000), 2.

19. Smith, *American Evangelicalism*.

20. Marco Giugni, "How Social Movements Matter: Past Research, Present Problems, and Future Developments," in Marco Giugni, Doug McAdam, and Charles Tilly, eds., *How Social Movements Matter* (Minneapolis: University of Minnesota Press, 1999), xxi–xxiii.

21. Edward Amenta and Michael P. Young, "Making an Impact: Conceptual and Methodological Implications of the Collective Goods Criterion," in Marco Guigni, Doug McAdam, and Charles Tilly, eds., *How Social Movements Matter*, 34.

22. See Doug McAdam, "The Biographical Impact of Activism," in Marco Giugni, Doug McAdam, and Charles Tilly, eds., *How Social Movements Matter*, 119–46.

23. David S. Meyer, "How the Cold War Was Really Won: The Effects of the Antinuclear Movements of the 1980s," in Marco Giugni, Doug McAdam, and Charles Tilly, eds., *How Social Movements Matter*, 186.

24. Armenta and Young, "Making an Impact," 30.

25. Luis Huerta, "Losing Public Accountability: A Home Schooling Charter," in Bruce Fuller, ed., *Inside Charter Schools* (Cambridge, Mass.: Harvard University Press, 2000), 177.

26. Ibid., 179–80.

27. Ibid., 180.

28. Ibid.

29. Ibid., 188.

30. Ibid., 192.

31. Stevens, *Kingdom of Children*, 15.

32. One of the most thoughtful discussions of how we might best think about our assumptions on gender relations and the realities of both school choice and the labor of women as "mothers and caretakers" can be found in Amy Stambach and Miriam David, "Feminist Theory and Educational Policy: How Gender Has Been 'Involved' in Family School Choice Debates," *Signs* 30 (Winter, 2005), 1633–58. In many other religious forms as well, women are seen as the carriers of tradition, especially when it is perceived as something that is under persistent threat. See, for example, Janet Liebman Jacobs, *Hidden Heritage: The Legacy of the Crypto-Jews* (Berkeley: University of California Press, 2002).

33. Actually, many of these technologies in fact were *not* labor saving ultimately. See Ruth Schwartz Cowan, *More Work for Mother* (New York: Basic Books, 1983) and Susan Strasser, *Never Done* (New York: Pantheon, 1982).

34. See Nancy Fraser, *Unruly Practices* (Minneapolis: University of Minnesota Press, 1989), regarding how these concepts themselves are fully implicated in the history of gendered realities, differential power, and struggles.

35. Paola Bacchetta and Margaret Power, "Introduction," in Paola Baccetta and Margaret Power, eds., *Right-Wing Women* (New York: Routledge, 2002), 6.

36. Ibid., 8.

37. Brenda Brasher, *Godly Women* (New Brunswick, N.J.: Rutgers University Press, 1998), 3.

38. Ibid., 3.

39. Ibid., 4–5.

40. Ibid., 6.

41. Ibid., 12–13.

42. Julie Gottlieb, "Female 'Fanatics,'" in Paola Bacchetta and Margaret Power, eds., *Right-Wing Women*, 40.

43. Green, "The Christian Right and the 1998 Elections," 2.

44. Victoria Enders, "And We Ate Up the World," in Paola Bacchetta and Margaret Power, eds., *Right-Wing Women*, 89.

45. Much of this literature, however, draws on the experiences of *white* women. The meaning of domesticity and the discourses of motherhood among black women cannot be understood from the standpoint of dominant groups. For more on this crucial point, see Eileen Boris, "The Power of Motherhood: Black and White Activist Women Redefine the 'Political',' in Seth Koven and Sonya Michel, eds., *Mothers of a New World* (New York: Routledge, 1993). Because the vast majority of right-wing home schoolers are indeed *white*, I have drawn on a literature that is based in their experiences. However, much more work needs to be done on people of color. This does not mean that we should not critically examine the ways in which the discourses of race constantly provide an absent presence within white communities, including not only that of home schooling parents but professional ones as well. See, for example, Laura Briggs, "The Race of Hysteria: 'Overcivilization' and the 'Savage' Woman in Late

Nineteenth-Century Obstetrics and Gynecology," *American Quarterly* 52 (June 2000), 246–73. I would like to thank Rima D. Apple for this point.

46. See Seth Koven and Sonya Michel, "Introduction: 'Mother Worlds'," in Seth Koven and Sonya Michel, eds., *Mothers of a New World* (New York: Routledge, 1993), 10.

47. Ibid. See also Alice Kessler-Harris, *In Pursuit of Equity* (New York: Oxford University Press, 2001) and Molly Ladd-Taylor, *Mother-Work* (Urbana: University of Illinois Press, 1994).

48. Koven and Michel, 17.

49. Marijke du Toit, "Framing Volksmoeders," in Paola Bacchetta and Margaret Power, eds., *Right-Wing Women*, 67.

50. Ibid. I would like to thank Rima D. Apple for her very helpful comments on this section.

51. Stevens, *Kingdom of Children*, 76.

52. Ibid., 83.

53. Ibid., 83-96. See Rima D. Apple, *Perfect Motherhood: Science and Childrearing in America* (New Brunswick, NJ: Rutgers University Press, 2006) for a detailed examination of the ways in which motherhood has been "marketed" both by business and "experts."

54. Stephens, *Kingdom of Children*, 54.

55. Ibid., 55.

56. Ibid., 56.

57. Basil Bernstein, *Class, Codes, and Control Volume 3*, 2d ed. (London: Routledge and Kegan Paul, 1977).

58. Ibid.

59. Stevens, *Kingdom of Children*, 58.

60. Ibid., 58–9.

61. Ibid., 60.

62. See http://doorposts.net/go_to_ant.htm.

63. Stevens, *Kingdom of Children*, 178–79. One of the most powerful figures in HSLDA is Michael Farris. He acts as both a public spokesperson for conservative home schoolers and as a legal advocate in court cases around the country. Farris has a long history of rightist activism. He ran for lieutenant governor of Virginia in 1993 on a strikingly conservative platform. Interestingly enough, he did not receive the endorsement of a number of other conservative Christian groups and national figures who believed that his public positions might alienate swing voters and actually harm the rightist cause. See Mark Rozell and Clyde Wilcox, *Second Coming* (Baltimore: Johns Hopkins University Press, 1996).

64. See John Green, Mark Rozell, and Clyde Wilcox, eds., *Prayers in the Precincts* (Washington, DC: Georgetown University Press, 2000).

65. See http://www.phc.edu/about/FundamentalStatements.asp.

66. One can get a sense of how close the students are to the seat of power in the United States from the little known fact that interns from Patrick Henry College are working in Karl Rove's office in the White House. See Hanna Rosin, "God and County," *The New Yorker*, June 27, 2005, 44–49.

67. I am not assuming the normative heterosexual family here. There is no literature on gay and lesbian home schoolers. Given the ideological position that the vast majority of conservative evangelicals take on the question of sexuality, I am simply reflecting their own assumptions.

68. Brasher, *Godly Women*, 29.

69. Hardisty, *Mobilizing Resentment*, 2–3.

70. For a powerful example, see Michael W. Apple, et al. *The State and the Politics of Knowledge* (New York: RoutledgeFalmer, 2003), especially Chapter 8.

71. See Jean Anyon, *Radical Possibilities* (New York: Routledge, 2005) and William Reese, *Power and the Promise of School Reform* (New York: Routledge, 1986).

72. Michael W. Apple, *Education and Power*, 2d ed. (New York: Routledge, 1995).

73. Raymond Williams, *Resources of Hope* (New York: Verso, 1989), 322.

Chapter 9

1. Michael W. Apple, *Teachers and Texts: A Political Economy of Class and Gender Relations in Education* (New York: Routledge, 1988).

2. Cameron McCarthy, unpublished lecture given at the International Sociology of Education Conference, University of Sheffield, Sheffield, England, January 2000.

3. Tim LaHaye and Jerry B. Jenkins, *The Indwelling* (New York: Tyndale, 2000). Tim LaHaye is the husband of Beverly LaHaye. As I noted in previous chapters, they are both deeply involved in ultraconservative political and cultural causes.

4. Of course, people read all kinds of fiction and are not compelled to follow its precepts. Thus, people can read hard-boiled detective novels in which women and men detectives often engage in violent acts of retribution. This does not necessarily mean that the readers are in favor of such acts. The politics of pleasure follows its own relatively autonomous logic. Most people engage in what have been called "guilty pleasures" and reading books such as *The Indwelling* may fall under that category for many readers. However, the fact that it is a national best-seller still has considerable importance.

5. The parallels between this position and standpoint epistemology should be obvious. However, this claim has a long history that goes back many years before the development of even more nuanced positions within feminist discourse. See Sandra Harding, *Whose Science? Whose Knowledge? Thinking from Women's Lives* (Ithaca, N.Y.: Cornell University Press, 1991) and Gyorgy Lukacs, *History and Class Consciousness* (Cambridge, Mass.: MIT Press, 1971).

6. Jose Segarra and Ricardo Dobles, eds., *Learning as a Political Act: Struggles for Learning and Learning from Struggles* (Cambridge, Mass.: Harvard Educational Review Reprint Series No. 33, 1999), xiii.

7. E. D. Hirsch Jr., *The Schools We Need and Why We Don't Have Them* (New York: Doubleday, 1996). See also the powerful criticism of Hirsch in Kristen Buras, "Questioning Core Assumptions: A Critical Reading and Response to E. D. Hirsch, *The Schools We Need and Why We Don't Have Them*," *Harvard Educational Review* 69 (Spring 1999): 67–93.

8. See the debate between Hirsch and myself in Diane Ravitch, ed., *Brookings Papers on Education Policy* (Washington, D.C.: Brookings Institution, 2005).

9. Michael W. Apple, *Cultural Politics and Education* (New York: Teachers College Press, 1996).

10. Cornelia Dean, "Opting Out in the Debate On Evolution," *New York Times*, June 21, 2005, D1, D6. Dean indicates that many scientists are refusing to participate in the hearings in Kansas and elsewhere, as they believe that this gives the creationist position more credibility than it deserves. In my opinion, this is self-defeating and a very bad move strategically. One should not assume that religious and other parents have actually been exposed to the best of scientific arguments about evolution. These hearings provide an important opportunity for scientists. Absent their participation, all that parents and the general public will hear will be the voices of advocates for creationism and "intelligent design." We need to take the shifting relations of power seriously. Otherwise, we may win in the scientific arena and lose in the schools.

11. Of course, in actuality the content and form of curricula and teaching have always been political issues. See Michael W. Apple, *Ideology and Curriculum*, 3rd ed. (New York: RoutledgeFalmer, 2004). On some of the recent curriculum struggles in England and Wales, see Richard Hatcher and Ken Jones, eds., *Education After the Conservatives* (Stoke-on-Trent, England: Trentham Books, 1996).

12. Jo Boaler, *Experiencing School Mathematics* (Philadelphia: Open University Press, 1998).

13. In Basil Bernstein's terminology, we could say the curriculum and teaching in this instance were strongly classified and strongly framed. See Basil Bernstein, *Class, Codes, and Control*, volume 3, 2d ed. (London: Routledge, 1977).

14. The focus on keeping youth "under control" is connected to a long history of the fear of youth and of seeing them as constantly in need of regulation. For an insightful discussion of this history, see Nancy Lesko, *Act Your Age!* (New York: Routledge, 2001).

15. See Eric Gutstein, *Reading and Writing the World With Mathematics* (New York: Routledge, 2006).

16. See Alex Molnar, Philip Smith, John Zahorik, Amanda Palmer, Anke Halbach, and Karen Ehrle, "Evaluating the SAGE Program," *Educational Evaluation and Policy Analysis* 21 (Summer 1999): 165–77. See also Alex Molnar, *Vouchers, Class Size Reduction, and Student Achievement* (Bloomington, Ind.: Phi Delta Kappa Education Foundation, 2000).

17. Gutstein, *Reading and Writing the World with Mathematics.*

18. Linda Tuhiwai Smith, *Decolonizing Methodologies* (New York: Zed Books, 1999). See also Andrew Gitlin, ed., *Power and Method* (New York: Routledge, 1994).

19. A large amount of data are synthesized in Apple, *Cultural Politics and Education*, 68–90.

20. See, for example, Michael W. Apple, *Power, Meaning, and Identity* (New York: Peter Lang, 1999). The debate over class analysis and over how it might be done can be found in Erik Olin Wright, ed., *The Debate on Classes* (New York: Verso, 1989) and Erik Olin Wright, *Class Counts: Comparative Studies in Class Analysis* (New York: Cambridge University Press, 1997).

21. Michael Omi and Howard Winant, *Racial Formation in the United States* (New York: Routledge, 1994), 158–59.

22. Ibid., 159.

23. See David Gillborn, "Education Policy as an Act of White Supremacy: Whiteness, Critical Race Theory, and Education Reform," *Journal of Education Policy* 20 (July 2005): 485–505.

24. I am thinking of Richard Herrnstein and Charles Murray's *The Bell Curve* (New York: Free Press, 1994).

25. See Daniel Liston, *Capitalist Schools* (New York: Routledge, 1988).

26. See, for example, Stephen Jay Gould, *The Mismeasure of Man* (New York: W. W. Norton, 1981) and Donna Harraway, *Primate Visions* (New York: Routledge, 1989).

27. Sally Tomlinson, "New Inequalities: Educational Markets and Ethnic Minorities," paper presented at the symposium on Racism and Reform in the United Kingdom at the annual meeting of the American Educational Research Association, San Diego, April 1998.

28. See, for example, the pro-voucher arguments advanced by Gary Rosen where he argues that vouchers are the only way African-Americans can have the possibility of a "real" education. See Gary Rosen, "Are School Vouchers Un-American?" *Commentary* 109 (February 2000): 26–31.

29. Linda McNeil, *Contradictions of School Reform* (New York: Routledge, 2000); Angela Valenzuela, ed., *Leaving Children Behind* (Albany: State University of New York Press, 2005); Pauline Lipman, *High Stakes Education* (New York: RoutledgeFalmer, 2004).

30. For more on this, see Valenzuela, ed., *Leaving Children Behind*.

31. Charles Gallagher, "White Reconstruction in the University," *Socialist Review* 94, nos. 1 and 2 (1995): 194.

32. On the historical advantages of being white, and especially on the historical disadvantages of being, say, African American, see Michael B. Katz, Mark J. Stern, and Jamie J. Fader, "The New African American Inequality," *The Journal of American History* 92 (June 2005): 75–108 and George Lipsitz, *The Possessive Investment in Whiteness* (Philadelphia: Temple University Press, 1998).

33. Richard Dyer, *White* (New York: Routledge, 1997), 19.

34. There is a vast literature here. See, for example, Omi and Winant, *Racial Formation in the United States*; Cameron McCarthy and Warren

Crichlow, eds., *Race, Identity, and Representation in Education* (New York: Routledge, 1994); William Tate, "Critical Race Theory and Education," in *Review of Research in Education, Volume 22*, ed. Michael W. Apple (Washington, D.C.: American Educational Research Association, 1997), 195–247; Michelle Fine, Lois Weis, Linda Powell, and L. Mun Wong, eds., *Off White* (New York: Routledge, 1997); and Cameron McCarthy, *The Uses of Culture* (New York: Routledge, 1998), to name just a few.

35. Dyer, *White*, 1.

36. Ibid., 2.

37. Ibid., 47.

38. Ibid., 4.

39. Joan Scott, "Multiculturalism and the Politics of Identity," in *The Identity in Question*, ed. John Rajchman (New York: Routledge, 1995), 11.

40. See Joe Kincheloe and Shirley Steinberg, eds., *White Reign: Deploying Whiteness in America* (New York: St. Martin's Press, 1998).

41. Michael W. Apple, *Official Knowledge*, 2d ed. (New York: Routledge, 2000).

42. Steven Selden, *Inheriting Shame* (New York: Teachers College Press, 1999).

43. Rosen, "Are School Vouchers Un-American?" An edited version of my response, along with many others that were critical of Rosen's position, was published in the journal in the next issue. See Michael W. Apple, "Response to Gary Rosen," *Commentary* 109 (June 2000): 20.

44. For example, in one of the "teach-ins" in which I participated in preparation for the anti-WTO mobilizations in Seattle and Washington, D.C., very few people had thought about the integration of Spanish language newspapers, television, radio, and Web sites in building support for the movement. Yet these are among the fastest-growing media in the United States, and they reach an audience that is suffering deeply from the effects of globalization and economic exploitation.

45. For analyses of the unequal ways the media are now controlled and for proposals to reconstruct these processes, see Robert McChesney, Ellen Meiksins Wood, and John Bellamy Foster, eds., *Capitalism and the Information Age* (New York: Monthly Review Press, 1998). See also Douglas Kellner, *Media Culture* (New York: Routledge, 1995). A useful guide on how to employ talk radio for progressive purposes is Ellen Ratner, *101 Ways to Get Your Progressive Issues on Talk Radio* (Washington, D.C.: National Press Books, 1997). Discussions of the roles that "public intellectuals" can play here have been varied. Among the more interesting recent discussions is Pierre Bourdieu, *Acts of Resistance* (Cambridge, Mass.: Polity Press, 1998). Talk radio is not alone here, of course. Once again, creative uses of the World Wide Web can be very useful. The Institute for Public Accuracy, for example, acts as a central link to a large number of progressive reports, media, and activists. Its e-mail address is institute@igc.org.

46. This is described in Porto Alegre City Secretariat of Education, "Cycles of Formation: Politic-Pedagogical Proposal for the Citizen's School," *Cadernos Pedagogicos* 9 (April 1999): 1–111.

47. Diane Elson, "Socializing Markets, Not Market Socialism," in *Necessary and Unnecessary Utopias*, ed. Leo Panitch and Colin Leys (New York: Monthly Review Press, 1999), 67–85. Elson's entire essay on the criteria that should be used to socialize markets is very thoughtful.

48. See, for example, the discussion in Lesko, *Act Your Age!*

49. Material on this can be obtained from the International Research Institute on Maori and Indigenous Education at the University of Auckland, Auckland, New Zealand.

50. Ruth Coniff, "Left–Right Romance," *The Progressive*, May 2000, 12–15.

51. Ibid., 13.

52. See Apple, *Official Knowledge*, 89–112.

53. Coniff, "Left–Right Romance," 13.

54. Jim Wallis, *God's Politics* (New York: HarperCollins, 2005), 138.

55. Ibid., 143.

56. Ibid., 4.

57. A readable introduction on parts of this can be found in Roger Du Pasquier, *Unveiling Islam* (Cambridge, Mass.: The Islamic Texts Society, 1992).

58. Wallis, *God's Politics*, 19. See also Irving Howe, *World of Our Fathers* (New York: Harcourt Brace Javonovitch, 1976).

59. Wallis, *God's Politics*, 66-67.

60. Ibid., 29.

61. Ibid., 61.

62. Ibid., 12.

63. Ibid., 16.

64. Ibid., 222–42.

65. Ibid., 250.

66. Ibid., 211.

67. Although it is a little too reductive in its analysis, Coreno does provide some interesting evidence of the class based nature of some evangelical and fundamentalist forms. See Thaddeus Coreno, "Fundamentalism as a Class Culture," *Sociology of Religion* 63 (2002): 335–60.

68. Wallis, *God's Politics*, 59.

69. Ibid.

70. Ibid., 70. Interestingly, many of these "large blocks of granite" with the Ten Commandments inscribed on them have a paradoxical history. When Cecil B. DeMille's epic film, *The Ten Commandments*, was about to be released, DeMille came up with a brilliant publicity scheme. In cooperation with the Fraternal Order of Eagles, "a nationwide association of civic-minded clubs founded by theater owners," he sponsored the construction of several thousand Ten Commandment monuments throughout the country to ensure that the movie was widely publicized. A number of the stars of of the movie—including Yul Brynner and Charlton Heston—participated in the unveiling of many of these monuments. One

of the most politically contentious of these granite monuments, the one placed on the grounds of the Texas Capitol in Austin, has its genesis in DeMille's publicity campaign. See Frank Rich, "The God Racket, From DeMille to DeLay," *New York Times*, March 27, 2005, AR1, AR30.

71. Ibid., 71.

72. Ibid., 74.

73. Jean Anyon, *Radical Possibilities* (New York: Routledge, 2005).

74. Wallis, *God's Politics,* 83.

75. Laurie Goodstein, "Evangelical Leaders Swing Influence Behind Effort to Combat Global Warming," *New York Times*, Thursday, March 10, 2005, A14.

76. Ibid.

77. Ibid.

78. Ibid.

79. National Association of Evangelicals, "For the Health of the Nation: An Evangelical Call for Civic Resposibility," available online at http://www.nae.net/images/civic_responsibility2.pdf.

80. Laura Goodstein, "Evangelicals Open Debate on Widening Policy Questions," *New York Times*, March 11, 2005, A14.

81. Ibid.

82. Wallis, *God's Politics,* 269.

83. Interestingly, there is some emerging evidence that there may be cracks in the opposition toward feminism within evangelical groups. This, too, might provide spaces for collective work. See Sally Gallagher, "Where are the Antifeminist Evangelicals?" *Gender and Society* 18 (August 2004): 451–472.

84. For an interesting discussion of these and other issues, see Amy Stuart Wells, Alejandra Lopez, Janelle Scoot, and Jennifer Holme, "Charter Schools as Postmodern Paradox: Rethinking Social Stratification in an Age of Deregulated Choice," *Harvard Educational Review* 69 (Summer 1999): 172–204. Recent research on the ways charter schools and "reforms" surrounding school finance have functioned in Arizona, for instance, should make us extremely wary of the connections between rhetoric and reality. See, for example, Michele Moses, "The Arizona Tax Credit and Hidden Considerations of Justice," paper presented at the annual meeting of the American Educational Research Association, New Orleans, April 2000 and Glen Y. Wilson, "Effects on Funding Equity of Arizona Tax Law," paper presented at the annual meeting of the American Educational Research Association, New Orleans, 2000.

85. In a number of school districts, there is renewed interest in charter schools and some schools that were established specifically to attract vouchers have reconstituted themselves as charter schools. See Sam Dillon, "For Parents Seeking a Choice, Charter Schools Prove More Popular Than Vouchers," *New York Times*, July 13, 2005, A23.

86. See the interesting arguments in Jonathan Schorr, "Giving Charter Schools a Chance," *The Nation*, June 5, 2000, 19–23. I am still not totally convinced that Schorr's arguments in support of the progressive

possibilities of charter schools can overcome the conservative context in which charter schools are actually situated. However, Schorr's points need to be taken seriously and should not be rejected out of hand.

87. Michael W. Apple and James A. Beane, eds., *Democratic Schools* (Alexandria, Va.: Association for Supervision and Curriculum Development, 1995) and Michael W. Apple and James A. Beane, eds., *Democratic Schools: Lessons from the Chalk Face* (Buckingham, England: Open University Press, 1998). The book has been translated into multiple languages including Spanish, Portuguese, and Japanese, and has served as a focal point for more democratic practices in many nations.

88. See Larry Rosenstock and Adria Steinberg, "Beyond the Shop: Reinventing Vocational Education," in Apple and Beane, *Democratic Schools*, 41–57.

89. See, for example, Deborah Meier, Theodore Sizer, Linda Nathan, and Abigail Thernstrom, *Will Standards Save Public Education?* (Boston: Beacon Press, 2000) and David Levine, Robert Lowe, Bob Peterson, and Rita Tenorio, eds., *Rethinking Schools: An Agenda for Change* (New York: New Press, 1995). See also Robert Lowe and Barbara Miner, eds., *Selling Out Our Schools: Vouchers, Markets, and the Future of Public Education* (Milwaukee, Wisc.: Rethinking Schools, 1996) and Robert Lowe and Barbara Miner, eds., *False Choices: Why School Vouchers Threaten Our Children's Future* (Milwaukee, Wisc.: Rethinking Schools, 1992).

90. For an account of these practices, see Apple and Beane, *Democratic Schools* and Gloria Ladson-Billings, *The Dreamkeepers* (San Francisco: Jossey-Bass, 1994). See also Meier, et al., *Will Standards Save American Education?*

91. Leo Panitch and Colin Leys, "Preface," in *Necessary and Unnecessary Utopias*, ed. Leo Panitch and Colin Leys (New York: Monthly Review Press, 1999), vii.

92. Ibid., viii.

Bibliography

Aasen, Petter. "What Happened to Social Democratic Progressivism in Scandinavia?: Restructuring Education in Sweden and Norway." Unpublished paper, Department of Education, Norwegian University of Science and Technology, Trondheim, Norway, 1998.

Acker, Sandra. "Gender and Teachers' Work." In *Review of Research in Education Volume 21,* ed. Michael W. Apple, 99–162. Washington, D.C.: American Educational Research Association, 1995.

Alterman, Eric. *What Liberal Media? The Truth About Bias and the News.* New York: Basic Books, 2003.

Amenta, Edward, and Michael P. Young, "Making an Impact: Conceptual and Methodological Implications of the Collective Goods Criterion." In *How Social Movements Matter,* eds. Marco Guigni, Doug McAdam, and Charles Tilly, 22–41. Minneapolis: University of Minnesota Press, 1999.

Anderson, Benedict. *Imagined Communities.* New York: Verso, 1991.

Andre-Bechely, Lois. *Couldn't It Be Otherwise? Parents and the Inequalities of Public School Choice.* New York: Routledge, 2005.

Anyon, Jean. *Ghetto Schooling: A Political Economy of Urban Educational Reform.* New York: Teachers College Press, 1997.

_____. *Radical Possibilities.* New York: Routledge, 2005.

Apple, Michael W., ed. *Cultural and Economic Reproduction in Education.* Boston: Routledge, 1982.

_____. *Teachers and Texts: A Political Economy of Class and Gender Relations in Education.* New York: Routledge, 1988.

_____. *Ideology and Curriculum,* 2d ed. New York: Routledge, 1990.

_____. *Education and Power,* 2d ed. New York: Routledge, 1995.

_____. *Cultural Politics and Education.* New York: Teachers College Press, 1996.

_____. *Power, Meaning and Identity.* New York: Peter Lang, 1999.

_____. "The Absent Presence of Race in Educational Reform." *Race, Ethnicity, and Education* 2 (March 1999): 9–16.

_____. *Official Knowledge: Democratic Education in a Conservative Age,* 2d ed. New York: Routledge, 2000.

_____. "Are School Vouchers the Answer: A Response to Gary Rosen." *Commentary* 109 (June 2000): 20.

_____. "Standards, Subject Matter, and a Romantic Past," *Educational Policy* 15 (May 2001): 7–36.

_____, et al. *The State and the Politics of Knowledge.* New York: RoutledgeFalmer, 2003.

_____. *Ideology and Curriculum,* 25th Anniversary 3rd Edition. New York: Routledge, 2004.

_____. "What Can We Learn from Texas About No Child Left Behind?" *Educational Policy,* in press.

Apple, Michael W., and James A. Beane, eds. *Democratic Schools.* Alexandria, Va.: Association for Supervision and Curriculum Development, 1995.

_____. *Democratic Schools: Lessons from the Chalk Face.* Buckingham, England: Open University Press, 1999.

Apple, Michael W., and Kristen Buras, eds. *The Subaltern Speak.* New York: Routledge, 2006.

Apple, Michael W., Jane Kenway, and Michael Singh, eds. *Globalizing Education.* New York: Peter Lang, 2005.

Apple, Michael W., and Thomas Pedroni. "Conservative Alliance Building and African American Support for Voucher Plans," *Teachers College Record,* 107 (September 2005): 2068–2105.

Apple, Rima D. *Perfect Motherhood: Science and Childrearing in America.* New Brunswick, N.J.: Rutgers University Press, 2006.

Arnot, Madeleine. "Schooling for Social Justice." Unpublished paper, Department of Education, University of Cambridge, 1990.

Arnot, Madeleine, Miriam David, and Gaby Weiner. *Closing the Gender Gap.* Cambridge, Mass.: Polity Press, 1999.

Avis, James. "Re-thinking Trust in a Performative Culture: The Case of Education," *Journal of Education Policy* 18 (May-June 2003): 315–332.

Bacchetta, Paola, and Margaret Power. "Introduction." In *Right Wing Women,* eds. Paola Baccetta and Margaret Power, 1–15. New York: Routledge, 2002.

Ball, Stephen. *Education Reform: A Critical and Post-Structural Approach.* Buckingham, England: Open University Press, 1994.

_____. *Class Strategies and the Education Market.* London: RoutledgeFalmer, 2003.

Ball, Stephen, Richard Bowe, and Sharon Gewirtz. "Market Forces and Parental Choice." In *Educational Reform and Its Consequences,* ed. Sally Tomlinson, 13–25. London: IPPR/Rivers Oram Press, 1994.

Barron, Bruce. *Heaven on Earth? The Social and Political Agendas of Dominion Theology.* Grand Rapids, Mich.: Zondervan, 1992.

Beckford, James A. *Religion and Advanced Industrial Society*. New York: Routledge, 1989.

Belluck, Pam. "Board for Kansas Deletes Evolution from the Curriculum." *New York Times*, August 12, 1999, A1–A13.

Bennett, William. *Our Children and Our Country*. New York: Simon & Schuster, 1988.

_____. *The Book of Virtues*. New York: Simon & Schuster, 1994.

Bennett, William, Chester E. Finn Jr., and John T. E. Cribb Jr. *The Educated Child*. New York: Free Press, 1999.

Benveniste, Luis, Martin Carnoy, and Richard Rothstein. *All Else Equal: Are Public and Private Schools Different?* New York: RoutledgeFalmer, 2003.

Berke, Richard. "Conservatives Look for Believers Amid G.O.P. Presidential Field." *New York Times*, February 4, 1999, A19.

Berliner, David. "The Near Impossibility of Testing for Teacher Quality," *Journal of Teacher Education* 3 (May/June 2005): 205–213.

Bernstein, Basil. *Class, Codes, and Control, Volume 3*, 2d ed. London: Routledge, 1977.

_____. *The Structuring of Pedagogic Discourse*. New York: Routledge, 1990.

_____. *Pedagogy, Symbolic Control, and Identity*. Bristol, PA: Taylor & Francis, 1996.

Binder, Amy. *Contentious Curricula: Afrocentrism and Creationism in American Public Schools*. Princeton, N.J.: Princeton University Press, 2002.

Boaler, Jo. *Experiencing School Mathematics*. Philadelphia: Open University Press, 1998.

Boris, Eileen. "The Power of Motherhood: Black and White Activist Women Redefine the 'Political.'" In *Mothers of a New World*, eds. Seth Koven and Sonya Michel, 213–245. New York: Routledge, 1993.

Bourdieu, Pierre. *Distinction*. Cambridge, Mass.: Harvard University Press, 1984.

_____. *Homo Academicus*. Stanford, Calif.: Stanford University Press, 1988.

_____. *The State Nobility*. Stanford, Calif.: Stanford University Press, 1996.

_____. *Acts of Resistance*. Cambridge, Mass.: Polity Press, 1998.

Bowles, Samuel, and Herbert Gintis. *Schooling in Capitalist America*. New York: Basic Books, 1976.

_____. *Democracy and Capitalism*. New York: Basic Books, 1986.

Brasher, Brenda. *Godly Women*. New Brunswick, N.J.: Rutgers University Press, 1998.

Briggs, Laura. "The Race of Hysteria: 'Overcivilization' and the 'Savage' Woman in Late Nineteenth-Century Obstetrics and Gynecology," *American Quarterly* 52 (June 2000): 246–273.

Brine, Jacky. *Under-Educating Women: Globalizing Inequality*. Philadelphia: Open University Press, 1999.

Bromley, Hank, and Michael W. Apple, eds. *Education/Technology/Power*. Albany: State University of New York Press, 1998.

Brooks, David. *Bobos in Paradise*. New York: Simon & Schuster, 2000.

Brown, Phillip. "Cultural Capital and Social Exclusion." In *Education: Culture, Economy, and Society*, ed. A. H. Halsey, Hugh Lauder, Phil

Brown, and Amy Stuart Wells, 736–749. New York: Oxford University Press, 1997.

Buras, Kristen L. "Questioning Core Assumptions: A Critical Reading of and Response to E. D. Hirsch's *The Schools We Need and Why We Don't Have Them." Harvard Educational Review* 69 (Spring 1999): 67–93.

Buras, Kristen L., and Michael W. Apple. "School Choice, Neoliberal Promises, and Unpromising Evidence," *Educational Policy* 19 (July 2005): 550–564.

Burch, Patricia. "The New Educational Privatization: Educational Contracting and High Stakes Accountability." *Teachers College Record,* in press.

Bush, Lawson. "Access, School Choice, and Independent Black Institutions," *Journal of Black Studies* 34 (January 2004): 386–401.

Carlson, Dennis, and Michael W. Apple. "Critical Educational Theory in Unsettling Times." In *Power/Knowledge/Pedagogy,* eds. Dennis Carlson and Michael W. Apple, 1–38. Boulder, Colo.: Westview Press, 1998.

_____, eds. *Power/Knowledge/Pedagogy.* Boulder, Colo.: Westview Press, 1998.

Castells, Manuel. *The Rise of Network Society, Volume 1.* New York: Oxford University Press, 1996.

Cho, Misook K., and Michael W. Apple. "Schooling, Work, and Subjectivity." *British Journal of Sociology of Education* 19 (Summer 1998): 269–290.

Chomsky, Noam. *Profit Over People: Neoliberalism and the Global Order.* New York: Seven Stories Press, 1999.

Chubb, John, and Terry Moe. *Politics, Markets, and America's Schools.* Washington, D.C.: The Brookings Institution, 1990.

Clarke, John, and Janet Newman. *The Managerial State.* Thousand Oaks, Calif.: Sage, 1997.

Clarkson, Frederick. *Eternal Hostility: The Struggle Between Theocracy and Democracy.* Monroe, Maine: Common Courage Press, 1997.

Clinton, Catherine. *The Plantation Mistress: Woman's World in the Old South.* New York: Pantheon Books, 1982.

Cohen, David, and Heather Hill. *Learning Policy: When State Education Reform Works.* New Haven, Conn.: Yale University Press, 2001.

Cole, Mike, ed. *Bowles and Gintis Revisited.* New York: Falmer Press, 1988.

Coles, Gerald. *Reading Lessons: The Debate Over Literacy.* New York: Hill & Wang, 1998.

Collin, Ross. "Symbolic Struggles: The Junior Reserve Officer Training Corps, the Los Angeles Uprising of 1992, and the 1992 Presidential Election," unpublished paper, Department of Curriculum and Instruction, University of Wisconsin, Madison, 2005.

Collins, Randall. *The Credential Society.* New York: Academic Press, 1979.

Coniff, Ruth. "Left–Right Romance." *The Progressive* (May 2000): 12–15.

Connell, Robert W. *Masculinities.* Cambridge, Mass.: Polity Press, 1995.

Cook, Christopher. "Temps Demand a New Deal," *The Nation,* March 27, 2000, 13–19.

Coontz, Stephanie. *The Way We Never Were.* New York: Basic Books, 1992.

Coreno, Thaddeus. "Fundamentalism as a Class Culture," *Sociology of Religion* 63, no. 3 (2002): 335–360.

Cornbleth, Catherine, and Dexter Waugh. *The Great Speckled Bird.* New York: St. Martin's Press, 1995.

Cott, Nancy, ed. *Roots of Bitterness: Documents of the Social History of Women.* New York: E. P. Dutton, 1972.

Cuban, Larry. *Oversold and Underused.* Cambridge, Mass.: Harvard University Press, 2001.

Dale, Roger. *The State and Education Policy.* Philadelphia: Open University Press, 1989.

_____. "The Thatcherite Project in Education: The Case of the City Technology Colleges." *Critical Social Policy* 9 (Winter 1989/1990): 4–19.

Dao, James. "Sleepy Election is Jolted by Evolution." *New York Times,* May 17, 2005, A12.

Dean, Cornelia. "Opting Out in the Debate On Evolution." *New York Times,* June 21, 2005, D1, D6.

_____. "Scientists Ask Pope for Clarification on Evolution Stance." *New York Times,* July 13, 2005, A18.

Delfattore, Joan. *What Johnny Shouldn't Read.* New Haven, Conn.: Yale University Press, 1992.

Della Porta, Donatella. "Protest, Protesters, and Protest Policing." In *How Social Movements Matter,* eds. Marco Giugni, Doug McAdam, and Charles Tilly, 66–96. Minneapolis: University of Minnesota Press, 1999.

Detwiler, Fritz. *Standing on the Premises of God.* New York: New York University Press, 1999.

Diamond, Sara. *Spiritual Warfare: The Politics of the Christian Right.* Boston: South End Press, 1989.

Dillard, Angela. *Guess Who's Coming to Dinner Now?* New York: New York University Press, 2001.

Dillon, Sam. "President's Education Law is Finding Few Fans in Utah." *New York Times,* March 6, 2005, 21.

_____. "Utah Vote Rejects Parts of Education Law." *New York Times,* April 20, 2005, A14.

_____. "Teachers' Union and Districts Sue Over Bush Law." *New York Times,* April 21, 2005, A19.

_____. "For Parents Seeking a Choice, Charter Schools Prove More Popular Than Vouchers." *New York Times,* July 13, 2005, A23.

Dimick, Alexandra S., and Michael W. Apple. "Texas and the Politics of Abstinence-Only Textbooks," *Teachers College Record,* May 2, 2005

Douglas, Mary. *Purity and Danger: An Analysis of Concepts of Pollution and Taboo.* London: Routledge and Kegan Paul, 1966.

Dugan, Michelle with Andrea Cooper. "Count Our Blessings," *Parents,* September 2003, 161–164.

Duneier, Mitchell. *Sidewalk.* New York: Farrar, Straus & Giroux, 1999.

DuPasquier, Roger. *Unveiling Islam.* Cambridge, Mass.: The Islamic Texts Society, 1992.

du Toit, Marijke. "Framing Volksmoeders." In *Right-Wing Women*, eds. Paola Bacchetta and Margaret Power, 57–70. New York: Routledge, 2002.

Dyer, Richard. *White*. New York: Routledge, 1997.

Elson, Diane. "Socializing Markets, Not Market Socialism." In *Necessary and Unnecessary Utopias*, eds. Leo Panitch and Colin Leys, 67–85. New York: Monthly Review Press, 1999.

Enders, Victoria. "And We Ate Up the World." In *Right-Wing Women*, eds. Paola Bacchetta and Margaret Power, 85–98. New York: Routledge, 2002.

Engel, Michael. *The Struggle for Control of Public Education*. Philadelphia: Temple University Press, 1999.

Epstein, Debbie, and Richard Johnson. *Schooling Sexualities*. Philadelphia: Open University Press, 1998.

Evans, John, and Dawn Penney. "The Politics of Pedagogy: Making a National Curriculum in Physical Education." *Journal of Education Policy* 10 (January 1995): 27–44.

Ezekiel, Raphael. *The Racist Mind: Portraits of American Neo-Nazis and Klansmen*. New York: Penguin, 1995.

Fine, Michelle, and Lois Weis. *The Unknown City: Lives of Poor and Working Class Young Adults*. Boston: Beacon Press, 1998.

Fine, Michelle, Lois Weis, Linda Powell, and L. Mun Wong, eds. *Off White: Readings on Race, Power, and Society*. New York: Routledge, 1997.

_____. *Off White*, 2d ed. New York: Routledge, 2005.

Foner, Eric. *The Story of American Freedom*. New York: Norton, 1998.

Foucault, Michel. "The Subject and Power." In *Michel Foucault: Beyond Structuralism and Hermeneutics*, ed. Herbert Dreyfus and Paul Rabinow, 208–26. Chicago: University of Chicago Press, 1982.

Frank, Thomas. *What's the Matter With Kansas: How Conservatives Won the Heart of America*. New York: Metropolitan Books, 2004.

Franzway, Suzanne, Diane Court, and R. W. Connell. *Staking a Claim: Feminism, Bureaucracy, and the State*. Boston: Allen & Unwin, 1989.

Fraser, Nancy. *Unruly Practices: Power, Discourse, and Gender in Contemporary Social Theory*. Minneapolis: University of Minnesota Press, 1989.

_____. *Justice Interruptus: Critical Reflections on the "Postsocialist" Condition*. New York: Routledge, 1997.

Fraser, Nancy, and Linda Gordon. "A Genealogy of Dependency." *Signs* 19 (Winter 1994): 309–36.

Fuller, Bruce, ed. *Inside Charter Schools*. Cambridge, Mass.: Harvard University Press, 2000.

Fuller, Bruce, Elizabeth Burr, Luis Huerta, Susan Puryear, and Edward Wexler. *School Choice: Abundant Hopes, Scarce Evidence of Results*. Berkeley and Stanford: University of California, Berkeley and Stanford University, Policy Analysis for California Education, 1999.

Gallagher, Charles. "White Reconstruction in the University." *Socialist Review* 24, nos. 1 and 2 (1995): 165–187.

Gallagher, Sally. "Where are the Antifeminist Evangelicals?" *Gender and Society* 18 (August 2004): 451–472.

Gee, James P., Glynda Hull, and Colin Lankshear. *The New Work Order: Behind the Language of the New Capitalism.* Boulder, Colo.: Westview Press, 1996.

Gewirtz, Sharon, Stephen Ball, and Richard Bowe. *Markets, Choice, and Equity in Education.* Philadelphia: Open University Press, 1995.

Gillborn, David. "Racism and Reform." *British Educational Research Journal* 23 (June 1997): 345–60.

_____. "Race, Nation, and Education." Unpublished paper, Institute of Education, University of London, 1997.

_____. "Education Policy as an Act of White Supremacy: Whiteness, Critical Race Theory and Education Reform." *Journal of Education Policy* 20 (July 2005): 485–505.

Gillborn, David, and Deborah Youdell. *Rationing Education: Policy, Practice, Reform, and Equity.* Philadelphia: Open University Press, 2000.

Gipps, Caroline, and Patricia Murphy. *A Fair Test?: Assessment, Achievement and Equity.* Philadelphia, Open University Press, 1994.

Giroux, Henry. *Border Crossings: Cultural Workers and the Politics of Education.* New York: Routledge, 1992.

Gitlin, Andrew, ed. *Power and Method.* New York: Routledge, 1994.

Giugni, Marco. "How Social Movements Matter: Past Research, Present Problems, and Future Developments." In *How Social Movements Matter,* eds. Marco Giugni, Doug McAdam, and Charles Tilly, xiii–xxxiii. Minneapolis: University of Minnesota Press, 1999.

Godwin, Mike. *Cyber Rights.* Cambridge, Mass.: MIT Press, 2003.

Goodstein, Laurie. "Coalition's Woes May Hinder Goals of Christian Right." *New York Times,* August 2, 1999, A1.

_____. "Evangelicals are a Growing Force in the Military Chaplain Corps," *New York Times,* July 12, 2005, A1, A20.

Gottlieb, Julie. "Female 'Fanatics.'" In *Right-Wing Women,* eds. Paola Bacchetta and Margaret Power, 29–41. New York: Routledge, 2002.

Gould, Steven J. *The Mismeasure of Man.* New York: Norton, 1981.

Grace, Gerald. "Making Connections for Future Directions: Taking Religion Seriously in the Sociology of Education." *International Studies in Sociology of Education* 14, no. 1 (2004): 47–56.

Green, John. "The Christian Right and the 1998 Elections." In *Prayers in the Precincts,* eds. John Green, Mark Rozell, and Clyde Wilcox, 1–19. Washington, D.C.: Georgetown University Press, 2000.

Greider, William. *One World, Ready or Not.* New York: Simon & Schuster, 1997.

Griffith, Alison, and Dorothy Smith. *Mothering for Schooling.* New York: Routledge, 2005.

Guth, James L., John C. Green, Corwin E. Smidt, Lyman A. Kellstedt, and Margaret Poloma. *The Bully Pulpit: The Politics of Protestant Clergy.* Lawrence, Kans.: The University of Kansas Press, 1997.

Gutstein, Eric. *Reading and Writing the World With Mathematics.* New York: Routledge, 2006.

Gutstein, Eric, and Bob Peterson, eds. *Rethinking Mathematics: Teaching Social Justice by the Numbers.* Milwaukee: Rethinking Schools, 2005.

Habermas, Jurgen. *Knowledge and Human Interests.* Boston: Beacon Press, 1971.

Hakken, David. *Cyborgs@Cyberspace.* New York: Routledge, 1999.

Hall, Stuart. "The Problem of Ideology: Marxism Without Guarantees." In *Stuart Hall: Critical Dialogues in Cultural Studies,* ed. David Morley and Kuan-Hsing Chen, 25–46. New York: Routledge, 1996.

Hall, Stuart, and Lawrence Grossberg. "On Postmodernism and Articulation: An Interview with Stuart Hall." In *Stuart Hall: Critical Dialogues in Cultural Studies,* ed. David Morley and Kuan-Hsing Chen, 131–50. New York: Routledge, 1996.

Haraway, Donna. *Primate Visions: Gender, Race, and Nature in the World of Modern Science.* New York: Routledge, 1989.

Harding, Sandra G. *Whose Science? Whose Knowledge?: Thinking from Women's Lives.* Ithaca, N.Y.: Cornell University Press, 1991.

Hardisty, Jean. *Mobilizing Resentment.* Boston: Beacon Press, 1999.

Hartocollis, Anemona. "Math Teachers Back Return of Education to Basic Skills." *New York Times,* April 15, 2000, A16.

Hatcher, Richard, and Ken Jones, eds. *Education After the Conservatives.* Stoke-on-Trent, England: Trentham Books, 1996.

Heineman, Kenneth J. *God Is a Conservative: Religion, Politics, and Morality in Contemporary America.* New York: New York University Press, 1998.

Henig, Jeffrey R. *Rethinking School Choice: Limits of a Market Metaphor.* Princeton, N.J.: Princeton University Press, 1994.

Herrnstein, Richard, and Charles Murray. *The Bell Curve: Intelligence and Class Structure in American Life.* New York: Free Press, 1994.

Hertzke, Allen D. *Echoes of Discontent: Jesse Jackson, Pat Robertson, and the Resurgence of Populism.* Washington, D.C.: Congressional Quarterly Press, 1992.

Heyrman, Christine L. *Southern Cross: The Beginnings of the Bible Belt.* New York: Knopf, 1997.

Hirsch, E. D. Jr. *The Schools We Need and Why We Don't Have Them.* New York: Doubleday, 1996.

Hobsbawm, Eric. *The Age of Extremes: A History of the World, 1914–1991.* New York: Pantheon, 1994.

Hogan, David. "Education and Class Formation." In *Cultural and Economic Reproduction in Education,* ed. Michael W. Apple, 32–78. Boston: Routledge, 1982.

Honderich, Ted. *Conservatism.* Boulder, Colo.: Westview Press, 1990.

House, Ernest. *Schools for Sale.* New York: Teachers College Press, 1998.

Howe, Irving. *World of Our Fathers.* New York: Harcourt Brace Javanovitch, 1976.

Huerta, Luis. "Losing Public Accountability: A Home Schooling Charter." In *Inside Charter Schools,* ed. Bruce Fuller, 177–202. Cambridge, Mass.: Harvard University Press, 2000.

Hunter, Allen. *Children in the Service of Conservatism: Parent–Child Relations in the New Right's Pro-Family Rhetoric.* Madison, Wisc.: University of Wisconsin, Institute for Legal Studies, 1988.

Jennings, Jack. "From the White House to the School House." In *American Educational Governance on Trial*, eds. William Lowe Boyd and Debra Miretzky, 291–309. Chicago: University of Chicago Press, 2003.

Jessop, Bob. *The Future of the Capitalist State.* Cambridge, Mass.: Polity Press, 2002.

Johnson, Dale, et al. *Trivializing Teacher Education.* New York: Rowman and Littlefield, 2005.

Jordan, Tim. *Cyberpower.* New York: Routledge, 1999.

Kao, Grace, Marta Tienda, and Barbara Schneider. "Racial and Ethnic Variation in Academic Performance." In *Research in Sociology of Education and Socialization, Volume 11*, ed. Aaron Pallas, 263–97. Greenwich, Conn.: JAI Press, 1996.

Katz, Michael B. *The Price of Citizenship.* New York: Metropolitan Books, 2001.

Katz, Michael B., Mark J. Stern, and Jamie J. Fader, "The New African American Inequality," *The Journal of American History* 92 (June 2005): 75–108.

Kearns, David T., and James Harvey. *A Legacy of Learning: Your Stake in Standards and New Kinds of Public Schools.* Washington, D.C.: The Brookings Institution, 2000.

Kelley, Dean M. *Why Conservative Churches Are Growing: A Study in Sociology of Religion.* New York: Harper & Row, 1972.

Kellner, Douglas. *Media Culture.* New York: Routledge, 1995.

Kelly, Robin D.G. "We Are Not What We Seem: Rethinking Black Working Class Opposition in the Jim Crow South," *The Journal of American History* 80 (June 1993): 75–112.

Kepel, Gilles. *Allah in the West: Islamic Movements in America and Europe.* Stanford, Calif.: Stanford University Press, 1997.

_____. *Jihad: The Trial of Political Islam.* Cambridge, Mass.: Belknap Press of Harvard University Press, 2002.

Kessler-Harris, Alice. *Out to Work: A History of Wage-Earning Women in the United States.* New York: Oxford University Press, 1982.

_____. *In Pursuit of Equity.* New York: Oxford University Press, 2001.

Kincheloe, Joe L., and Shirley R. Steinberg, eds. *White Reign: Deploying Whiteness in America.* New York: St. Martin's Press, 1998.

Kincheloe, Joe L., Shirley R. Steinberg, and Aaron D. Greeson, eds. *Measured Lies: The Bell Curve Examined.* New York: St. Martin's Press, 1996.

Kintz, Linda. *Between Jesus and the Market: The Emotions That Matter in Right-Wing America.* Durham, N.C.: Duke University Press, 1997.

Klatch, Rebecca E. *Women of the New Right.* Philadelphia: Temple University Press, 1987.

Klicka, Christopher. *The Right Choice: The Incredible Failure of Public Education and the Rising Hope of Home Schooling.* Gresham, Ore.: Noble Publishing Associates, 1992.

Kliebard, Herbert M. *The Struggle for the American Curriculum*, 2d ed. New York: Routledge, 1995.

_____. *Schooled to Work.* New York: Teachers College Press, 1999.

Koven, Seth, and Sonya Michel. "Introduction: 'Mother Worlds.'" In *Mothers of a New World,* eds. Seth Koven and Sonya Michel, 1–42. New York: Routledge, 1993.

_____, eds. *Mothers of a New World.* New York: Routledge, 1993.

Kristeva, Julie. "Women's Times." *Signs* 7 (Autumn 1981): 13–35.

Ladd-Taylor, Molly. *Mother-Work.* Urbana: University of Illinois Press, 1994.

Ladson-Billings, Gloria. *The Dreamkeepers: Successful Teachers of African American Children.* San Francisco: Jossey-Bass, 1994.

_____. "Just What is Critical Race Theory and What is it Doing in a Nice Field Like Education?" In *The RoutledgeFalmer Reader in Multicultural Education,* eds. Gloria Ladson-Billings and David Gillborn. New York: RoutledgeFalmer, 2004.

Ladson-Billings, Gloria, and David Gillborn, eds. *The RoutledgeFalmer Reader in Multicultural Education.* London: RoutlegeFalmer, 2004.

LaHaye, Beverly. "Women Restoring Righteousness." In *Judgement in the Gate: A Call to Awaken the Church,* ed. Richie Martin, 34–42. Westchester, Ill.: Crossway Books, 1986.

LaHaye, Tim, and Jerry B. Jenkins. *The Indwelling.* New York: Tyndale, 2000.

Larrain, Jorge. "Stuart Hall and the Marxist Concept of Ideology." In *Stuart Hall: Critical Dialogues in Cultural Studies,* ed. David Morley and Kuan-Hsing Chen, 47–70. New York: Routledge, 1996.

Larson, Edward. *Trial and Error: The American Controversy Over Creation and Evolution.* New York: Oxford University Press, 1989.

_____. *Summer of the Gods: The Scopes Trial and America's Continuing Debate Over Science and Religion.* New York: Basic Books, 1997.

Lauder, Hugh, and David Hughes. *Trading in Futures: Why Markets in Education Don't Work.* Philadelphia: Open University Press, 1999.

LeDoeuff, Michèle. *Hipparchia's Choice: An Essay Concerning Women, Philosophy, Etc.* Cambridge, Mass.: Basil Blackwell, 1991.

Lee, Stacy. *Unraveling the Model-Minority Stereotype.* New York: Teachers College Press, 1996.

Lesko, Nancy. *Act Your Age!* New York: Routledge, 2001.

Levine, David, Robert Lowe, Bob Peterson, and Rita Tenorio, eds. *Rethinking Schools: An Agenda for Change.* New York: New Press, 1995.

Levine, Lawrence W. *The Opening of the American Mind: Canon, Culture, and History.* Boston: Beacon Press, 1996.

Lewis, David Levering. *W.E.B. DuBois: Biography of a Race, 1868–1919.* New York: Henry Holt, 1993.

_____. *W.E.B. DuBois: The Fight for Equality and the American Century.* New York: Henry Holt, 2000.

Leys, Colin. *Market-Driven Politics: Neoliberal Democracy and the Public Interest.* New York: Verso, 2003.

Linn, Robert L. "Assessment and Accountability." *Educational Researcher* 29 (March 2000): 4–16.

Lipman, Pauline *High Stakes Education.* New York: Routledge, 2004.

Liston, Daniel. *Capitalist Schools.* New York: Routledge, 1988.

Liston, Daniel, and Kenneth Zeichner, *Teacher Education and the Social Conditions of Schooling.* New York: Routledge, 1991.

Loewen, James W. *Lies My Teacher Told Me: Everything Your American History Textbook Got Wrong.* New York: New Press, 1995.

Lowe, Robert, and Barbara Miner, eds. *False Choices: Why School Vouchers Threaten Our Children's Future.* Milwaukee, Wisc.: Rethinking Schools, 1992.

_____. *Selling Out Our Schools: Vouchers, Markets, and the Future of Public Education.* Milwaukee, Wisc.: Rethinking Schools, 1996.

Lukas, Gyorgy. *History and Class Consciousness.* Cambridge, Mass.: MIT Press, 1971.

Luke, Alan. "Series Editor's Introduction" to Jay Lemke, *Textual Politics.* Bristol, PA: Taylor & Francis, 1995.

Marquand, David. *The Progressive Dilemma.* London: Phoenix Books, 2000.

Marsden, George. *Understanding Fundamentalism and Evangelicalism.* Grand Rapids, Mich.: Eerdmans, 1991.

Marshner, Connie. *Can Motherhood Survive?* Brentwood, Ind.: Wolgemuth & Hyatt, 1990.

Marx, Karl, and Friedrich Engels. "Manifesto of the Communist Party." In *Marx and Engels: Basic Writings on Politics and Philosophy,* ed. Lewis S. Feuer, 1–41. New York: Anchor Books, 1959.

McAdam, Doug. "The Biographical Impact of Activism." In *How Social Movements Matter,* eds. Marco Giugni, Doug McAdam, and Charles Tilly, 119–146. Minneapolis: University of Minnesota Press, 1999.

McCalman, Janet. *Struggletown.* Melbourne: Hyland House, 1998.

McCarthy, Cameron. *The Uses of Culture.* New York: Routledge, 1998.

_____. Unpublished lecture at the International Sociology of Education Conference, University of Sheffield, Sheffield, England, January 2000.

McCarthy, Cameron, and Warren Crichlow, eds. *Race, Identity, and Representation in Education.* New York: Routledge, 1994.

McCarthy, Cameron, Warren Crichlow, Greg Dimitriadis, and Nadine Dolby, eds. *Race, Identity, and Representation in Education,* 2d ed. New York: Routledge, 2005.

McChesney, Robert. "Introduction" to Noam Chomsky, *Profit Over People: Neoliberalism and the Global Order,* 7–16. New York: Seven Stories Press, 1999.

McChesney, Robert, Ellen M. Wood, and John Bellamy Foster, eds. *Capitalism and the Information Age.* New York: Monthly Review Press, 1998.

McCulloch, Gary. "Privatizing the Past? History and Education Policy in the 1990s." *British Journal of Educational Studies* 45 (March 1997): 69–82.

McDonald, Morva. *Teacher Education for Social Justice.* New York: Routledge, in press.

McLaren, Peter. *Revolutionary Multiculturalism: Pedagogies of Dissent for the New Millennium.* Boulder, Colo.: Westview Press, 1997.

McNeil, Linda. *Contradictions of School Reform: Educational Costs of Standardization.* New York: Routledge, 2000.

_____. "Faking Equity: High-Stakes Testing and the Education of Latino Youth." In *Leaving Children Behind: How "Texas-style" Accountability Fails Latino Youth,* ed. Angela Valenzuela, 57–111. Albany: State University of New York Press, 2005.

McNeil, Linda, and Angela Valenzuela. "The Harmful Impact of the TASS System of Testing in Texas: Beneath the Accountability Rhetoric." In *Raising Standards or Raising Barriers: Inequality and High-Stakes Testing in Public Education,* eds. Gary Orfield and M. Kornhaber, 127–150. Cambridge, Mass.: Harvard Civil Rights Project, 2001.

Meier, Deborah. *The Power of Their Ideas.* Boston: Beacon Press, 1995.

_____. *In Schools We Trust: Creating Communities of Learning in an Era of Testing and Standardization.* Boston: Beacon Press, 2002.

Meier, Deborah, Theodore Sizer, Linda Nathan, and Abigail Thernstrom. *Will Standards Save Public Education?* Boston: Beacon Press, 2000.

Meier, Deborah, and George Wood, eds. *Many Children Left Behind: How No Child Left Behind is Damaging Our Children and Our Schools.* Boston: Beacon Press, 2004.

Menter, Ian, Yolanda Muschamp, Peter Nicholl, Jenny Ozga, and Andrew Pollard. *Work and Identity in the Primary School.* Philadelphia: Open University Press, 1997.

Meyer, David S. "How the Cold War Was Really Won: The Effects of the Antinuclear Movements of the 1980s." In *How Social Movements Matter,* eds. Marco Giugni, Doug McAdam, and Charles Tilly, 182–203. Minneapolis: University of Minnesota Press, 1999.

Middleton, Sue. *Disciplining Sexualities.* New York: Teachers College Press, 1998.

Mills, Charles W. *The Racial Contract.* Ithaca, N.Y.: Cornell University Press, 1997.

Moe, Terry. *Schools, Vouchers, and the American Public.* Washington, D.C.: Brookings Institution, 2001.

Molnar, Alex. *Giving Kids the Business: The Commercialization of America's Schools.* Boulder, Colo.: Westview Press, 1996.

_____. *Vouchers, Class Size Reduction, and Student Achievement.* Bloomington, Ind.: Phi Delta Kappan Education Foundation, 2000.

_____. *School Commercialism.* New York: Routledge, 2005.

Molnar, Alex, Philip Smith, John Zahorik, Amanda Palmer, Anke Halbach, and Karen Ehrle. "Evaluating the SAGE Program." *Educational Evaluation and Policy Analysis* 21 (Summer 1999): 165–177.

Moore, Kelly. "Political Protest and Institutional Change." In *How Social Movements Matter,* eds. Marco Giugni, Doug McAdam, and Charles Tilly, 97–115. Minneapolis: University of Minnesota Press, 1999.

Moses, Michele, S. "The Arizona Tax Credit and Hidden Considerations of Justice." Unpublished paper presented at the annual meeting of the American Educational Research Association, New Orleans, April 2000.

National Association of Evangelicals. "For the Health of the Nation: An Evangelical Call for Civic Resposibility." Available online at http://www.nae.net/images/civic_responsibility2.pdf.

Nord, Warren A. *Religion and American Education: Rethinking a National Dilemma.* Chapel Hill: University of North Carolina Press, 1995.

Novak, Michael. *Toward a Theology of the Corporation.* Washington, D.C.: American Enterprise Institute, 1990.

_____. *This Hemisphere of Liberty: A Philosophy of the Americas.* Washington, D.C.: American Enterprise Institute, 1992.

Numbers, Ronald L. *The Creationists.* New York: Alfred A Knopf, 1992.

_____. *Darwinism Comes to America.* Cambridge, Mass.: Harvard University Press, 1998.

_____. "Creationists and Their Critics in Australia." Unpublished paper, Department of the History of Medicine, University of Wisconsin, Madison.

Numbers, Ronald L., and John Stenhouse. "Antievolutionism in the Antipodes: From Protesting Evolution to Promoting Creationism in New Zealand." *British Journal for the History of Science,* in press.

Oakes, Jeannie. "Can Tracking Research Inform Practice?" *Educational Researcher* 21 (March 1992): 12–21.

Oakes, Jeannie, Karen H. Quartz, Steve Ryan, and Martin Lipton. *Becoming Good American Schools: The Struggle for Civic Virtue in Education Reform.* San Francisco: Jossey-Bass, 2000.

Oakes, Jeannie, Amy Stuart Wells, Makeba Jones, and Amanda Datnow. "Detracking: The Social Construction of Ability, Cultural Politics, and Resistence to Reform." *Teachers College Record* 98 (Spring 1997): 482–510.

O'Cadiz, Maria del Pilar, Pia L. Wong, and Carlos A. Torres. *Education and Democracy: Paulo Freire, Social Movements, and Educational Reform in Sao Paulo.* Boulder, Colo.: Westview Press, 1998.

Ohanian, Susan. *One Size Fits Few: The Folly of Educational Standards.* Portsmouth, N.H.: Heinemann, 1999.

O'Hear, Philip. "An Alternative National Curriculum." In *Educational Reform and Its Consequences,* ed. Sally Tomlinson, 55–72. London: IPPR/Rivers Oram Press, 1994.

O'Leary, Stephen D. *Arguing the Apocalypse: A Theory of Millennial Rhetoric.* New York: Oxford University Press, 1994.

Olssen, Mark. "In Defense of the Welfare State and of Publicly Provided Education." *Journal of Educational Policy* 11 (May 1996): 337–62.

Omi, Michael, and Howard Winant. *Racial Formation in the United States: From the 1960s to the 1990s,* 2d ed. New York: Routledge, 1994.

Opdycke, Sandra. *No One Was Turned Away.* New York: Oxford University Press, 1999.

Padilla, Raymond. "High-Stakes Testing and Educational Accountability as Social Construction Across Cultures." In *Leaving Children Behind: How "Texas-style" Accountability Fails Latino Youth,* ed. Angela Valenzuela, 249–262. Albany: State University of New York Press, 2005.

Pagels, Elaine. *The Origin of Satan.* New York: Random House, 1995.

Panitch, Leo, and Colin Leys. "Preface." In *Necessary and Unnecessary Utopias,* ed. Leo Panitch and Colin Leys, vii–xi. New York: Monthly Review Press, 1999.

Pedroni, Thomas. *Strange Bedfellows in the Milwaukee "Parental Choice" Debate,* unpublished Ph.D. dissertation, University of Wisconsin, Madison, 2003.

Penning, James, and Corwin Smidt. " Michigan 1998: The 'Right Stuff.'" In *Prayers in the Precincts,* eds. John Green, Mark Rozell, and Clyde Wilcox, 163–185. Washington, D.C.: Georgetown University Press, 2000.

Petrilli, Michael J. "School Reform Moves to the Suburbs." *New York Times,* July 11, 2005, A21.

Pink, William, and George Noblit, eds. *Continuity and Contradiction: The Futures of the Sociology of Education.* Cresskill, N.J.: Hampton Press, 1995.

Podheretz, Norman. *My Love Affair with America: The Cautionary Tale of a Cheerful Conservative.* New York: Free Press, 2000.

Porto Alegre City Secretariat of Education. "Cycles of Formation: Politic-Pedagogical Proposal for the Citizen's School." *Cadernos Pedagogicos* 9 (April 1999): 1–111.

Power, Sally, Tony Edwards, Geoff Whitty, and Valerie Wigfall. *Education and the Middle Class.* Buckingham: Open University Press, 2003.

Power, Sally, David Halpin, and John Fitz. "Underpinning Choice and Diversity." In *Educational Reform and Its Consequences,* ed. Sally Tomlinson, 26–40. London: IPPR/Rivers Oram Press, 1994.

Provenzo, Eugene F. Jr. *Religious Fundamentalism and American Education: The Battle for the Public Schools.* Albany: State University of New York Press, 1990.

Ranson, Stewart. "Theorizing Education Policy." *Journal of Education Policy* 10 (July 1995): 427–448.

_____. "Public Accountability in the Age of Neo-Liberal Governance." *Journal of Education Policy* 18 (September-October 2003): 459–480.

Ratner, Ellen. *101 Ways to Get Your Progressive Issues on Talk Radio.* Washington, D.C.: National Press Books, 1997.

Ravitch, Diane. *National Standards in American Education: A Citizen's Guide.* Washington, D.C.: The Brookings Institution, 1995.

_____. *Left Back.* New York: Simon and Schuster, 2000.

_____, ed. *Brookings Papers on Education Policy 2005.* Washington, D.C.: Brookings Institution, 2005.

Ray, Brian. *Home Schooling on the Threshold.* Salem, Ore.: National Home Education Research Institute, 1999.

Reed, Ralph. "Putting a Friendly Face on the Pro-Family Movement." *Christianity Today,* April 1993, 28.

_____. *Politically Incorrect.* Dallas: Word Publishing, 1994.

_____. *After the Revolution: How the Christian Coalition Is Impacting America.* Dallas: Word Publishing, 1996.

Re'em, Moshe. "Young Minds in Motion: Teaching and Learning About Difference in Formal and Non-formal Settings." Unpublished doctoral dissertation, University of Wisconsin, Madison, 1998.

Reese, William. *Power and the Promise of School Reform: Grassroots Movements During the Progressive Era.* Boston: Routledge and Kegan Paul, 1986.

Rhoads, Robert, and Carlos Alberto Torres, eds. *The Political Economy of Higher Education in America.* Stanford, Calif., Stanford University Press, in press.

Rich, Frank. "The God Racket, From DeMille to Delay." *New York Times,* March 27, 2005, AR1, AR30.

Robertson, Pat. *The Secret Kingdom.* Nashville, Tenn.: Thomas Nelson Publishers, 1982.

_____. *The New Millennium.* Dallas: Word Publishing, 1990.

_____. *The New World Order.* Dallas: Word Publishing, 1991.

_____. *The Turning Tide.* Dallas: Word Publishing, 1993.

_____. "Law Must Embrace Morality." *Christian American* 6 (April 1995): 16–17.

Robertson, Susan L. *A Class Act: Changing Teachers' Work, the State, and Globalization.* New York: Falmer Press, 2000.

Rorty, Richard. *Achieving Our Country: Leftist Thought in Twentieth-Century America.* Cambridge, Mass.: Harvard University Press, 1998.

Rosen, Gary. "Are School Vouchers Un-American?" *Commentary* 109 (February 2000): 26–31.

Rosenstock, Larry, and Adria Steinberg. "Beyond the Shop: Reinventing Vocational Education." In *Democratic Schools,* ed. Michael Apple and James Beane, 41–57. Alexandria, Va.: Association for Supervision and Curriculum Development, 1995.

Rosin, Hanna. "God and Country," *The New Yorker,* June 27, 2005, 44–49.

Roth, Wolff-Michael, and Angela Barton. *Rethinking Scientific Literacy.* New York: RoutledgeFalmer, 2004.

Rozell, Mark, and Clyde Wilcox. *Second Coming.* Baltimore: Johns Hopkins University Press, 1996.

Rudolph, John. *Scientists in the Classroom: The Cold War Reconstruction of American Science Education.* New York: Palgrave, 2002.

Ruiz de Velasco, Jorge. "Performance-Based School Reforms and the Federal Role in Helping Schools that Serve Language-Minority Students." In *Leaving Children Behind: How "Texas-style" Accountability Fails Latino Youth,* ed. Angela Valenzuela, 33–55. Albany: State University of New York Press, 2005.

Rury, John, and Jeffrey Mirel. "The Political Economy of Urban Education." In *Review of Research in Education, Volume 22,* ed. Michael W. Apple, 49–110. Washington, D.C.: American Educational Research Association, 1997.

Rushdoony, Rousas John. *The Institutes of Biblical Law.* Phillipsburgh, N.J.: Presbyterian and Reformed Publishing, 1973.

Schlafly, Phyllis. "Fact and Fiction About Censorship." Washington, D.C.: National Defense Committee, National Society, Daughters of the American Revolution, 1984.

Schorr, Jonathan. "Giving Charter Schools a Chance." *The Nation,* June 5, 2000, 19–23.

Schwartz Cowan, Ruth. *More Work for Mother.* New York: Basic Books, 1983.

Scott, Joan. "Multiculturalism and the Politics of Identity." In *The Identity in Question,* ed. John Rajchman, 3–12. New York: Routledge, 1995.

Seddon, Terri. "Markets and the English." *British Journal of Sociology of Education* 18 (June 1997): 165–85.

Segarra, Jose, and Ricardo Dobles, eds. *Learning as a Political Act: Struggles for Learning and Learning from Struggles.* Cambridge, Mass.: Harvard Educational Review Reprint Series No. 33, 1999.

Selden, Steven. *Inheriting Shame: The Story of Eugenics and Racism in America.* New York: Teachers College Press, 1999.

Sewell, Stacy Kinlock. "The 'Not-Buying' Power of the Black Community." *Journal of African American History* 89 (Spring 2004): 135–151.

Shapiro, Andrew L. "The Net That Binds." *The Nation,* June 21, 1999, 11–15.

Shipler, David. *The Working Poor.* New York: Knopf, 2004.

Skocpol, Theda. *Diminished Democracy.* Norman: University of Oklahoma Press, 2003.

Slack, Jennifer D. "The Theory and Method of Articulation in Cultural Studies." In *Stuart Hall: Critical Dialogues in Cultural Studies,* ed. David Morley and Kuan-Hsing Chen, 112–127. New York: Routledge, 1996.

Slaughter, Sheila, and Larry L. Leslie. *Academic Capitalism.* Baltimore: Johns Hopkins University Press, 1997.

Slaughter, Sheila, and Gary Rhoades. *Academic Capitalism and the New Economy.* Baltimore: Johns Hopkins University Press, 2004.

Slevin, James. *The Internet and Society.* Cambridge: Polity Press, 2000.

Smiley, Jane. "Stable Relationships," *The Guardian Review,* October 16: 4–6.

Smith, Adam. *The Wealth of Nations.* Oxford: Clarendon Press, 1976.

Smith, Christian. *American Evangelicalism: Embattled and Thriving.* Chicago: University of Chicago Press, 1998.

Smith, Gregory A. *Public Schools That Work: Creating Community.* New York: Routledge, 1993.

Smith, Kevin B., and Kenneth J. Meier, eds. *The Case Against School Choice: Politics, Markets, and Fools.* Armonk, NY: M. E. Sharpe, 1995.

Smith, Linda Tuhiwai, *Decolonizing Methodologies.* New York: Zed Books, 1999.

Smith, Mary Lee, Walter Heinecke, and Audrey Noble. "Assessment Policy and Political Spectacle." *Teachers College Record* 101 (Winter 1999): 157–91.

Smith, Mary Lee, with Linda Miller-Kahn, Walter Heinecke, and Patricia Jarvis. *Political Spectacle and the Fate of American Schools.* New York: RoutledgeFalmer, 2004.

Smith-Rosenberg, Carol. *Disorderly Conduct: Visions of Gender in Victorian America.* New York: Oxford University Press, 1985.

Stambach, Amy, and Miriam David. "Feminist Theory and Educational Policy: How Gender Has Been 'Involved' in Family School Choice Debates," *Signs* 30 (Winter 2005): 1633–1658.

Stearns, David, and James Harvey. *A Legacy of Learning: Your Stake in Standards and New Kinds of Public Schools.* Washington, D.C.: The Brookings Institution, 2000.

Steinberg, Jacques. "Blue Books Closed, Students Boycott Standardized Tests." *New York Times,* April 13, 2000, A1.

Stevens, Mitchell. *Kingdom of Children*. Princeton, N.J.: Princeton University Press, 2001.

Strasser, Susan. *Never Done*. New York: Pantheon, 1982.

Swartz, David. *Culture and Power: The Sociology of Pierre Bourdieu*. Chicago: University of Chicago Press, 1997.

Tate, William. "Critical Race Theory and Education." In *Review of Research in Education, Volume 22*, ed. Michael W. Apple, 195–247. Washington, D.C.: American Educational Research Association, 1997.

Teitelbaum, Kenneth. *Schooling for Good Rebels*. New York: Teachers College Press, 1996.

Therburn, Robert. *The Children Trap: Biblical Principles for Education*. Fort Worth, Texas: Dominion Press and Thomas Nelson, 1986.

Tomlinson, Sally, ed. *Educational Reform and Its Consequences*. London: IPPR/Rivers Oram Press, 1994.

_____. "New Inequalities: Educational Markets and Ethnic Minorities." Unpublished paper presented at the symposium on Racism and Reform in the United Kingdom at the annual meeting of the American Educational Research Association, San Diego, April 1998.

Valenzuela, Angela. "Accountability and the Privatization Agenda." In *Leaving Children Behind: How "Texas-style" Accountability Fails Latino Youth*, ed. Angela Valenzuela, 263–294. Albany: State University of New York Press, 2005.

_____. "Introduction: The Accountability Debate in Texas." In *Leaving Children Behind: How "Texas-style" Accountability Fails Latino Youth*, ed. Angela Valenzuela, 1–32. Albany: State University of New York Press, 2005.

_____, ed. *Leaving Children Behind: How "Texas-style" Accountability Fails Latino Youth*. Albany: State University of New York Press, 2005.

Van Dunk, Emily, and Anneliese Dickman. *School Choice and the Question of Accountability*. New Haven, Conn.: Yale University Press, 2003.

Van Vught, Johannes. *Democratic Organizations for Social Change: Latin American Christian Base Communities and Literacy Campaigns*. New York: Bergin & Garvey, 1991.

Vryhoff, Steven C. *Between Memory and Vision: The Case for Faith-Based Schooling*. Grand Rapids, Mich.: William Eerdmans Publishing Co., 2004.

Wacquant, Loic. "Foreword" to Pierre Bourdieu, *The State Nobility*, ix–xxii. Stanford, Calif.: Stanford University Press, 1996.

Watson, Justin. *The Christian Coalition: Dreams of Restoration, Demands for Recognition*. New York: St Martin's Press, 1997.

Wells, Amy S. *Time to Choose: America at the Crossroads of School Choice Policy*. New York: Hill & Wang, 1993.

_____. *Beyond the Rhetoric of Charter School Reform*. Los Angeles: University of California at Los Angeles, Graduate School of Education and Information Studies, 1999.

Wells, Amy S., Alejandra Lopez, Janelle Scott, and Jennifer Holme. "Charter Schools as Postmodern Paradox: Rethinking Social Stratification in an

Age of Deregulated School Choice." *Harvard Educational Review* 69 (Summer 1999): 172–204.

West, Cornel. *Prophesy Deliverance!: An Afro-American Revolutionary Christianity.* Philadelphia: Westminster Press, 1982.

_____. *Race Matters.* New York: Vintage Books, 1994.

Wheen, Francis. *Karl Marx: A Life.* New York: Norton, 1999.

White, Geoffrey, ed. *Campus, Inc.* New York: Prometheus Books, 2000.

Whitty, Geoff. "Sociology and the Problem of Radical Educational Change." In *Educability, Schools, and Ideology,* ed. Michael Flude and John Ahier, 112–137. London: Halstead Press, 1974.

_____. "Creating Quasi-Markets in Education." In *Review of Research in Education, Volume 22,* ed. Michael W. Apple, 3–47. Washington, D.C.: American Educational Research Association, 1997.

Whitty, Geoff, Tony Edwards, and Sharon Gewirtz. *Specialization and Choice in Urban Education.* London: Routledge, 1993.

Whitty, Geoff, Sally Power, and David Halpin. *Devolution and Choice in Education: The School, the State, and the Market.* Philadelphia: Open University Press, 1998.

Wilcox, Clyde, and Mark Rozell. "Conclusion: The Christian Right in Campaign '98.'" In *Prayers in the Precincts,* eds. John Green, Mark Rozell, and Clyde Wilcox, 287–297. Washington, D.C.: Georgetown University Press, 2000.

Williams, Raymond. *Marxism and Literature.* New York: Oxford University Press, 1977.

_____. *Keywords: A Vocabulary of Culture and Society.* New York: Oxford University Press, 1985.

_____. *Resources of Hope: Culture, Democracy, Socialism.* New York: Verso, 1989.

Willis, Paul. *Common Culture.* Boulder, Colo.: Westview Press, 1990.

Wilson, Glen Y. "Effects on Funding Equity of the Arizona Tax Credit Law." Paper presented at the annual meeting of the American Educational Research Association, New Orleans, April 2000.

Witte, John F. *The Market Approach to Education: An Analysis of America's First Voucher Program.* Princeton, N.J.: Princeton University Press, 2000.

Wong, Ting-Hong, and Michael W. Apple. "Rethinking the Education/State Formation Connection." Unpublished paper.

Wright, Erik O. *Classes.* New York: Verso, 1985.

_____. *Class Counts: Comparative Studies in Class Analysis.* New York: Cambridge University Press, 1997.

_____, ed. *The Debate on Classes.* New York: Verso, 1998.

Wyatt, Edward. "Investors See Room for Profit in the Demand for Education." *New York Times,* November 4, 1999, A1.

Zinn, Howard. *The Zinn Reader: Writings on Disobedience and Democracy.* New York: Seven Stories Press, 1997.

_____. *The Future of History: Interviews with David Barsamian.* Monroe, Maine: Common Courage Press, 1999.

Index

Notes are referred to by page number, the letter n for note, and the note number.

DATE DUE

Please remember that this is a library book,
and that it belongs only temporarily to each
person who uses it. Be considerate. Do
not write in this, or any, library book.